THE BROCKHAMPTON PRESS BOOK OF
VEGETARIAN COOKING

THE BROCKHAMPTON PRESS BOOK OF
VEGETARIAN COOKING

BROCKHAMPTON PRESS
LONDON

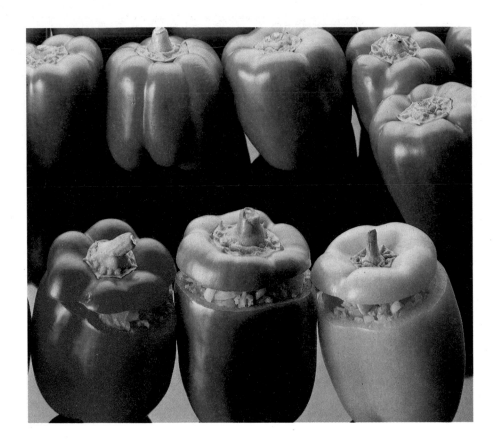

This edition published 1995 by Brockhampton Press,
a member of Hodder Headline PLC Group
20 Bloomsbury Street, London, WC1B 3QA

This arrangement © 1988 Marshall Cavendish Ltd

Prepared by Marshall Cavendish Books Ltd
58 Old Compton Street, London W1V 5PA

Printed in EC
ISBN 1-86019-192-4

CONTENTS

INTRODUCTION

Vegetarian cooking is becoming ever more popular. You may be vegetarian for health or for compassionate reasons or in order to stretch the family budget. One member of your family may suddenly decide to turn vegetarian overnight or you may have vegetarian guests to entertain. Whatever your reasons for deciding to cook vegetarian, a comprehensive, lively cookbook will always be useful. Even if you have been used to producing vegetarian meals for many years, looking at pages of appetizing recipes will give you new inspiration.

Vegetarian cooking has come a long way from the lentils and rice or vegetables in cheese sauce type of dishes. True, these can still be appetizing, but as more cooks have experimented, the combinations of ingredients and types of dish have become staggeringly varied. In the following pages you will find recipes for all occasions from family main meals to special dinner parties. There are snacks for light suppers or lunches and delicious breads, cakes and biscuits, suitable for family teas or lunchboxes.

Many of the recipes are based on fresh vegetables. They appear raw in salads, puréed to make soups or as part of a warming casserole. They are baked, simmered, stir-fried and braised and mixed with all manner of flavouring ingredients from curry to cheese. There are fritters and pâtés, stuffed vegetables and vegetables à la Grecque, besides the more exotic. Imagine the colour, for example, of a Beetroot Soufflé, or the light, fluffy texture of a Hot Carrot and Cheese Mousse.

Fruits also have their part to play in vegetarian cookery. Used fresh, they give extra flavour and texture to savoury salads; how about Cucumber and Strawberry or Watercress and Grapefruit? The best desserts are also fruit based and you'll find raw fruit salads, poached fruits, fruit fritters and fruit puddings, even a Rhubarb Roulade. Even savoury hot meals can be fruit based or fruit flavoured. Try an exotic Mixed Fruit Curry or Onion and Apple Fritters. Dried fruits are added to salads, curries and hot vegetables besides forming the base for some of the desserts.

In vegetarian cooking, protein is provided by eggs, cheese, pulses and nuts and the recipes in this book make use of these in many different ways. For instance, eggs are whisked into soufflés and roulades, while cheese is used to flavour sauces, dips, quiches and salads. Beans are rolled in cabbage leaves while lentils are turned into delicious curries or made into tasty patties. Nuts are added to salads, tossed into cooked vegetables, and also used to make nut roasts and cutlets, classic vegetarian fare.

All the recipes are healthy without being cranky. They contain only familiar ingredients that are easy to buy and none of the recipes work out to be expensive. All in all, this book will be an asset to any cook and will prove that vegetarian food is certainly never boring.

SOUPS
AND
STARTERS

The purpose of a starter is to stimulate the appetite and hint at the good things to come, so it should be both appealing and interesting. In this chapter you will find an inspiring selection of attractive and appetizing starters ranging from warming soups to tasty bean pâtés and individual salads – something for every occasion.

A delicious soup is a perfect opener to any meal. Easy to make, full of goodness and very economical, soups are particularly good for adding substance to family meals. The recipes in this chapter make excellent use of fresh, natural ingredients so you can choose the soup you want to serve according to what is freshest and best in the shops. Soup is a good freezer standby so when you've an abundance of seasonal vegetables, make an extra large batch of soup and freeze some for another time. It can be thawed and ready to serve very quickly.

When planning a meal, make sure that the soup you choose complements the main course so that you create a well-balanced meal. For instance, offer a thick, hearty soup as a substantial starter before a light main course, or serve a refreshing chilled soup as a delicious opener to a summer dinner party. Chunky vegetable soups also make nutritious and satisfying lunch or supper-time snacks, needing only the accompaniment of some bread and butter to make a complete meal. They can be made more filling by the addition of some grated cheese, or some garlic or herb bread 'floaters'.

As an alternative to soup, you can't go wrong with a traditional starter like pâté or corn on the cob. Salads make excellent starters too – choose from marinated vegetables, such as Leeks Vinaigrette, or try fresh ideas like Pear Salad Boats or Tarragon Cucumber Salad. New ways with hot vegetables include Mushrooms in Vine Leaves, Jerusalem Artichoke Fritters and Hot Beetroot Mousse.

Whether you are serving a starter or a soup, make it look good with attractive garnishes of chopped herbs, croûtons or decorative vegetables. A garnish is particularly important for a first course as it is the first thing your guests will see. You will find many original and exciting garnishing ideas featured throughout the recipes in this chapter.

Whether you are planning a family meal, an informal supper with friends or a lavish vegetarian feast, you are guaranteed to find the perfect starter here.

JAMES JACKSON

Broad bean and celery soup

SERVES 4-6

500 g/1 lb frozen broad beans (see Variation)
4 celery stalks, cleaned and chopped
1.25 L/2 pints vegetable stock
1 teaspoon chopped fresh thyme or ½ teaspoon dried thyme
salt and freshly ground black pepper
watercress sprigs, to garnish

1 Put the broad beans, celery, stock, thyme and salt and pepper to taste into a large saucepan and bring to the boil, stirring frequently. Skim off any scum with a slotted spoon, reduce the heat to low and simmer very gently for about 1-1½ hours or until both the vegetables are very soft and thoroughly cooked.

Cook's Notes

TIME
Preparation time is 20 minutes. Cooking time is 1¼-1¾ hours.

VARIATION
Fresh broad beans can be used instead of frozen, when in season. About 1 kg/2 lb broad beans in pods should give the correct weight for this recipe. Buy the beans when young and tender – once the pods have black patches they are past their best with tough, grey outer skins which are unpalatable – even in soup.

SPECIAL OCCASION
Swirl 1 tablespoon of double cream on the surface of each serving before adding the watercress.

FREEZING
Allow the soup to cool completely, then pour into rigid containers, leaving headspace. Seal, label and freeze for up to 6 months. To serve: reheat from frozen, stirring to prevent sticking. Add a little water if necessary.

● 60 calories/250 kj per serving

2 Allow the soup to cool a little, then pass it through a sieve or purée it in an electric blender. Put back in the rinsed-out pan and adjust seasoning if necessary.

3 Reheat the soup gently then pour into 4-6 warmed individual soup bowls. Garnish with a few small sprigs of watercress (see Special occasion). Serve at once, piping hot.

Bean and vegetable soup

SERVES 4

250 g/9 oz dried haricot beans,
   soaked overnight and
   drained
1 tablespoon vegetable oil
1 large onion, chopped
2 leeks, chopped
3 celery stalks, chopped
2 carrots, sliced
2 cloves garlic, crushed (optional)
700 ml/1¼ pints vegetable stock
225 g/8 oz can tomatoes
1 teaspoon dried oregano
salt and freshly ground black
   pepper
2 tablespoons chopped parsley, to
   garnish

1 Cover the beans with fresh hot
water and boil for 10 minutes, then
cover and simmer for about 2 hours
until they are tender. Drain.
2 Heat the oil in a large saucepan,
add the onion and fry gently for
2 minutes. Add the leeks, celery and
carrots to pan with garlic, if using,
and cook a further 2 minutes.

3 Add the stock and beans, together
with the tomatoes and their juice,
the oregano and plenty of salt and
pepper. Bring to the boil, then lower
the heat, cover and simmer for 30
minutes until the vegetables are
tender. ✳ Sprinkle with parsley.

Cook's Notes

TIME
Preparation takes 15
minutes, cooking time
is 2¾ hours.

SERVING IDEAS
Serve the soup with
plenty of hot, crusty
French bread.

VARIATIONS
Other varieties of dried
beans may be used,
such as red kidney, black-eye or
butter beans. The same cooking

instructions apply. Or use canned beans and start the recipe at
stage 2.

FREEZING
After stage 3, cool the
soup and pour into a
rigid container. Seal, label and
freeze for up to 3 months.
   To defrost: reheat slowly in a
pan, stirring from time to time
and add seasoning and stock if
required.

●285 calories/1200 kj per portion

Green pepper cream soup

SERVES 4

250 g/9 oz green peppers, deseeded (see Watchpoint)
25 g/1 oz margarine or butter
1 large onion, chopped
1 clove garlic, chopped (see Cook's tip)
15 g/½ oz plain flour
600 ml/1 pint vegetable stock
1 teaspoon chopped fresh herbs, or ½ teaspoon dried mixed herbs
salt and freshly ground black pepper
1 teaspoon lemon juice
150 ml/¼ pint single cream (see Economy)

1 Cut a few very thin rings from one of the peppers and set aside for garnish. Chop the remainder.

2 Melt the margarine in a heavy-based saucepan. Add the chopped peppers, onion and garlic and cook over very low heat for about 10 minutes, stirring frequently, until the vegetables are soft but not brown.

3 Sprinkle in the flour and cook for 1-2 minutes, stirring, then gradually stir in the stock. Add the herbs, and season to taste with salt and pepper. Cover and cook gently for 20-25 minutes until the vegetables are tender.

4 Leave to cool slightly, then transfer to a blender and blend for about 5 seconds until smooth. If you do not have a blender, work the vegetables through a sieve while still hot. Return the soup to the rinsed-out pan, add lemon juice and cream, then taste and adjust seasoning if necessary. Heat through thoroughly, but do not boil.

5 Serve hot, garnished with the reserved pepper rings.

FRED MANCINI

PAUL WEBSTER

Curried turnip soup

SERVES 4
500 g/1 lb small turnips, quartered
   (see Cook's tip)
salt
25 g/1 oz margarine or butter
1 small onion, finely chopped
2 teaspoons mild curry powder (see
   Variation)
600 ml/1 pint vegetable stock
1 teaspoon sugar
juice of ½ lemon
freshly ground black pepper
150 ml/¼ pint single cream
1 tablespoon finely chopped
   parsley, to garnish

1 Blanch the turnips by plunging them into a large pan of boiling salted water and simmering for 3 minutes. Drain at once.
2 Melt the margarine in a large saucepan and add the turnips with the onion. Cover the pan and cook for 5 minutes over very gentle heat, shaking the pan occasionally to prevent the vegetables from sticking.

Cook's Notes

 TIME
Preparation takes 10-15 minutes, cooking about 20 minutes.

 COOK'S TIP
Stage 1 can be omitted for new, summer turnips but winter turnips need to be peeled thickly to remove the fibrous matter, and the initial blanching is essential.

 FREEZING
Prepare the soup up to the end of stage 4 (never add the cream before freezing soup). Cool the soup and freeze in a rigid container for up to 1 month. To serve: reheat from frozen, gradually bring to the boil, reduce heat, then add the cream.
Freezing tends to affect the strength of the curry powder, so check the seasoning while you are reheating the soup.

 SERVING IDEAS
Serve with wholemeal bread and cheese for a warming, nourishing supper dish.

 VARIATION
This soup has a mild curry flavour acceptable to most tastes, but the amount of curry powder may be increased to 3 or even 4 teaspoons.

●140 calories/575 kj per portion

3 Stir in the curry powder, then pour in the stock. Add the sugar and lemon juice and season to taste with salt and pepper. Cover the pan and simmer over low heat for about 10 minutes or until the turnips are soft.
4 Press the turnips and liquid through a sieve, or leave to cool then purée in a blender. ✳
5 Return the turnip purée to the rinsed-out pan and heat through thoroughly. Taste and adjust seasoning then pour immediately into warmed individual soup bowls. Swirl cream into each portion and sprinkle with parsley.

13

Celery and Stilton soup

SERVES 4

1 head celery (see Cook's tip), finely chopped
100 g/4 oz Stilton cheese (see Variation), trimmed of rind
40 g/1½ oz butter
2 large leeks, thinly sliced
700 ml/1¼ pints vegetable stock
2 large egg yolks
50 ml/2 fl oz single cream
salt and freshly ground black pepper

1 Melt the butter in a large, heavy-based saucepan. Add the celery and leeks, cover and cook gently, stirring occasionally, for about 10 minutes, until the vegetables are softened but not coloured.
2 Add the stock and bring to the boil. Lower the heat and simmer, uncovered, for about 20 minutes, until vegetables are tender. Cool slightly, then work to a purée in a blender.
3 Return the soup to the rinsed-out pan and reheat gently, without bringing to the boil.
4 Meanwhile, beat the egg yolks and cream together until smoothly blended. In a separate bowl, mash the cheese to a coarse paste with a fork, then gradually work in the egg and cream mixture.
5 Stir a small ladleful of the hot soup into the cheese mixture, then pour the mixture back into the pan, stirring constantly until the soup has thickened slightly. ! Serve at once, in warmed individual bowls (see Serving ideas).

Cook's Notes

 TIME
Preparation time takes about 65 minutes.

 COOK'S TIP
Save the best leaves from the celery and add them to the pan with the chopped stalks—they give extra flavour. Reserve a few feathery ones from the inner stalks for a garnish, if wished.

 VARIATION
Use another type of blue cheese and adjust the quantity according to its strength or mildness of flavour.

 WATCHPOINT
Do not let the soup boil, or the egg and cream mixture will scramble.

SERVING IDEAS
Garnish each bowl with chopped fresh parsley, butter-fried croûtons or celery leaves. Serve with baps or granary rolls.

●285 calories/1200 kj per portion

MARTIN BRIGDALE

Thick country soup

SERVES 4
1 tablespoon vegetable oil
15 g/½ oz butter
1 onion, chopped
225 g/8 oz carrots, sliced
100 g/4 oz packet soup mix (see
  Buying guide)
850 ml/1½ pints vegetable stock
1 leek, white part only, chopped
1 stick of celery, chopped
1 teaspoon dried thyme
1 bay leaf
salt and freshly ground black pepper
1 tablespoon chopped fresh parsley

1 In a saucepan, heat the oil and
butter and gently cook the onion
and carrots for 10 minutes.
2 Add the soup mix together with
the stock, chopped leek, celery and
herbs. Bring to the boil, then lower
the heat, cover and simmer for
about 45 minutes.
3 Season the soup to taste with
salt [!] and pepper and stir in the
parsley. Serve at once.

MARTIN BRIGDALE

Cook's Notes

TIME
Preparation takes about
15 minutes, cooking
time is 45 minutes.

SERVING IDEAS
For lunch or supper,
serve some cheese and
biscuits and/or fruit after this
substantial soup.

WATCHPOINT
Do not add salt to
pulses until the end of
the cooking time as it toughens
the skins.

BUYING GUIDE
Packets of soup mix are
available in most health
food shops and some large
supermarkets. They usually
contain a mixture of lentils,
yellow and green split peas,
pearl barley and oatmeal.

VARIATION
For a sophisticated
flavour, try substituting
a bouquet garni for the thyme
and bay leaf.

●175 calories/750 kj per portion

PETER MYERS

Leekie oat broth

SERVES 4

100 g/4 oz leeks, thinly sliced
600 ml/1 pint vegetable stock
100 g/4 oz carrots, finely chopped
½ teaspoon dried mixed herbs
salt and freshly ground black pepper
25 g/1 oz porridge oats (see Cook's tip)
150 ml/¼ pint milk
2 tablespoons single cream or evaporated milk
100 g/4 oz Edam cheese, cubed, to serve

1 Pour the stock into a saucepan and bring to the boil. Add the leeks, carrots, herbs and salt and pepper to taste. Lower the heat, cover and simmer for 15 minutes or until the vegetables are tender.

2 Sprinkle the oats into the soup, stir in the milk and cook gently, uncovered, for 5 minutes, stirring occasionally, until thick. Stir in the cream or evaporated milk and heat through without allowing the soup to boil.

3 To serve: ladle into a warmed tureen or individual serving bowls and mix the cubes of Edam cheese into the soup. Serve at once, before the cheese has completely melted.

Cook's Notes

 TIME
This broth takes about 30 minutes to prepare and cook.

COOK'S TIP
The addition of porridge oats instead of flour as a thickener in this soup lends a pleasantly different flavour and texture to it.

VARIATION
Instead of leeks, use thinly sliced onions or dried onion flakes.

 WATCHPOINT
Do not add the cheese until the last minute—it should be soft not stringy.

● 160 calories/675 kj per portion

16

Creamy spinach and potato soup

SERVES 4

300 g/10 oz packet frozen spinach (see Cook's tips)
500 g/1 lb potatoes, cut into chunks
25 g/1 oz margarine or butter
1 onion, chopped
600 ml/1 pint vegetable stock (see Cook's tips)
few sprigs of parsley
pinch of freshly grated nutmeg
150 ml/¼ pint milk
150 ml/¼ pint single cream
2 teaspoons lemon juice
salt and freshly ground black pepper

CHEESE FLOATS

4 slices French bread, cut diagonally into 2 cm/¾ inch thick slices
75 g/3 oz Cheddar cheese, thinly sliced

1 Melt the margarine in a saucepan, add the onion and fry over moderate heat for 3 minutes, stirring. Add the frozen spinach, potatoes, vegetable stock, parsley and nutmeg.

Cook's Notes

 TIME
Preparation and cooking take 45 minutes.

 COOK'S TIPS
Use fresh spinach when available. Wash 500 g/1 lb spinach, remove central ribs and add with the potatoes.

Make the vegetable stock from a cube, available from most health food shops and delicatessens, or use the liquid saved after cooking vegetables.

 VARIATIONS
Any hard cheese can be used instead of Cheddar for the toasted cheese floats.

Alternatively, omit the cheese and spread the bread slices with herb or garlic butter. Toast the slices in the same way, spreading flavoured butter on the untoasted sides. Grill until the butter has melted.

 SERVING IDEAS
Serve as a light lunch or supper or serve as a starter for a dinner party, omitting the cheese floats: dilute the spinach and potato soup with extra milk or stock and serve it hot, garnished with a swirl of cream.

●395 calories/1650 kj per portion

2 Bring to the boil, then lower the heat, cover and simmer for about 20 minutes, until potatoes are tender.
3 Heat the grill to high.
4 Allow the mixture to cool slightly, then work in batches in a blender. Return to the rinsed-out pan, then stir in the milk, cream and lemon juice. Season with salt and pepper.

Reheat very gently without boiling.
5 Meanwhile, make the cheese floats: toast the slices of bread on one side, then lay the cheese slices on the untoasted sides and grill until the cheese has melted.
6 Pour the soup into 4 warmed individual bowls and top each with a cheese float. Serve at once.

Finnish vegetable soup

SERVES 4-6

500 g/1 lb potatoes (preferably new), diced
3 medium carrots, diced
100 g/4 oz cauliflower florets
50 g/2 oz frozen peas
100 g/4 oz frozen sliced green beans
850 ml/1½ pints vegetable stock
salt and freshly ground black pepper
25 g/1 oz margarine or butter
25 g/1 oz plain flour
1 large egg yolk
4 tablespoons double cream
¼ teaspoon sweet paprika
50 g/2 oz strong Cheddar or Cheshire cheese, grated, to serve

1 Put the potatoes, carrots, cauliflower, peas, beans and stock into a large saucepan. Season well with salt and pepper, bring to the boil and simmer uncovered for 10 minutes or until tender.

Cook's Notes

TIME
Preparation 10 minutes. Cooking the soup takes approximately 20 minutes.

COOK'S TIP
This hearty vegetable soup is a meal in itself, and is best eaten with a spoon and fork, not just a spoon.
It can be prepared up to the end of stage 3, cooled quickly, and stored in covered containers in the refrigerator for 24 hours.

VARIATION
Other vegetables such as tomatoes, mushrooms, courgettes and spinach may be used.

●350 calories/1450 kj per portion

2 Remove the pan from the heat and strain the stock into a bowl. Reserve the cooked vegetables.

3 Melt the margarine gently in the rinsed-out pan and sprinkle in the flour. Stir over low heat for 1-2 minutes until straw-coloured. Remove from the heat and gradually stir in the stock. Return to the heat and simmer, stirring, until thick and smooth.

4 In a small bowl, whisk the egg yolk into the cream with the paprika. Gradually whisk 4 tablespoons of the hot thickened stock into the egg and cream, then slowly stir the mixture back into the remaining thickened stock in the pan. Return the reserved vegetables to the pan, taste and adjust seasoning and heat through. Do not boil or it may curdle. Add a little extra vegetable stock or water if the soup is too thick.

5 Serve piping hot in warmed individual soup bowls, with the grated cheese handed separately in a bowl.

PAUL WILLIAMS

CHRIS KNAGGS

Watercress and kohl rabi soup

SERVES 4-6

1 bunch watercress, separated
  into sprigs
500 g/1 lb kohl rabi or turnips,
  diced (see Did you know)
25 g/1 oz margarine or butter
1 onion, chopped
1 L/1¾ pints vegetable stock
salt and freshly ground black
  pepper
150 ml/¼ pint single cream, to
  finish

1 Melt the margarine or butter in
a large saucepan, add the onion and
fry gently for 5 minutes until the
onion is soft and lightly coloured.
2 Add the diced kohl rabi and fry
gently, stirring, for 5 minutes.
3 Pour in the vegetable stock and
bring to the boil. Lower the heat

slightly, cover the pan and simmer
for about 45 minutes until the
kohl rabi are soft.
4 Reserve a few sprigs of watercress
for garnish and add the rest to the
soup. Bring back to the boil, then
lower the heat slightly and simmer
for 2 minutes.
5 Remove the pan from the heat and
press the soup through a sieve, or

leave to cool slightly, then purée in
a blender. Return the soup to the
rinsed-out pan and heat through
until bubbling.
6 Taste and adjust seasoning then
pour into warmed individual soup
bowls. Swirl cream into each
portion and garnish with the
reserved watercress sprigs. Serve
the soup at once.

Cook's Notes

 TIME
10 minutes preparation,
1 hour cooking.

 DID YOU KNOW
The purple-skinned
kohl rabi is believed
to have originated in the East.
It has a turnip-like flavour
and is prepared and worked in
the same way.

● 190 calories/800 kj per portion

 ECONOMY
Omit the cream, or sub-
stitute with creamy
milk or yoghurt (see Serving
ideas). This produces a less rich
but still creamy soup.

 SERVING IDEAS
This soup may be
served chilled, as well
as hot. When serving chilled,
allow it to cool then swirl
yoghurt into the soup.

ALAN DUNS

Bread and cheese soup

SERVES 4

12 × 1 cm/½ inch slices French
  bread
225 g/8 oz finely grated Cheddar
  cheese
40 g/1½ oz butter
175 g/6 oz onions, finely
  chopped
1 clove garlic, crushed (optional)
450 ml/16 fl oz vegetable stock
good pinch grated nutmeg
8 teaspoons finely grated Parmesan
  cheese

1 Melt the butter in a saucepan
then add the onions and garlic, if
using. Fry over gentle heat for 8-10
minutes until tender and lightly
browned. [!]
2 Stir in the vegetable stock and
season with grated nutmeg. Bring to
the boil then reduce heat, cover with
lid and simmer very gently for 10
minutes. [!]
3 Heat the oven to 200C/400F/Gas 6.

4 Fill four 300 ml/½ pint ovenproof
soup bowls (about 9 cm/3½ inches
in diameter) to within about 4 cm/
1½ inches of top with alternating
layers of French bread and finely
grated Cheddar cheese.
5 Gently pour in prepared onion
broth so that it only just covers the
bread and cheese. Allow to stand
for about 5-10 minutes. [!]

6 Place the bowls in a small roasting tin to catch any drips during
cooking. Sprinkle the top of each
bowl with 1 teaspoon Parmesan
cheese. Bake above centre of oven
for 15-20 minutes or until heated
through and golden brown on top.
Stand each bowl on an individual
serving plate, then sprinkle soup
with remaining Parmesan. Serve hot.

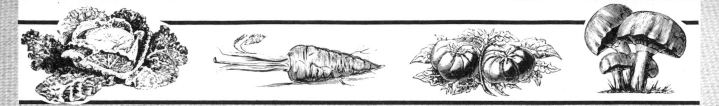

Cauliflower cheese soup

SERVES 4

250 g/9 oz cauliflower, broken into small florets
50 g/2 oz butter
1 onion, chopped
1 potato, thinly sliced
300 ml/½ pint vegetable stock
300 ml/½ pint milk
50 g/2 oz Cheddar cheese, grated
salt and freshly ground black pepper

GARNISH

4 tablespoons single cream
25 g/1 oz Cheddar cheese, grated
1 tablespoon chopped parsley

CHRIS KNAGGS

1 Melt the butter in a large saucepan, add the onion and fry gently for 5 minutes until soft and lightly coloured. Add the cauliflower florets and potato slices. Cover and cook the vegetables for 10 minutes.
2 Stir in the stock, bring to the boil, then cover and simmer for about 25-30 minutes, or until all the vegetables are very soft.
3 Transfer the vegetables and stock to the goblet of a blender and work until smooth. Return the purée to the rinsed-out pan and stir in the milk off the heat.
4 Heat the purée gently until simmering then remove from heat and stir in the grated cheese. Season to taste with salt and pepper.
5 Pour the soup into 4 warmed individual soup bowls and swirl 1 tablespoon cream into each (see Cook's tip). Place a quarter of the cheese on top of each serving and sprinkle over a little chopped parsley. Serve at once.

Cook's Notes

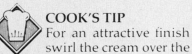

TIME
Preparation takes 5-10 minutes. Cooking time is 40-45 minutes.

COOK'S TIP
For an attractive finish swirl the cream over the entire surface of the soup in a light feathery pattern, rather than just in a single swirl.

SERVING IDEAS
Serve this very filling soup with Melba toast or crispbread.

● 300 calories/1250 kj per portion

Chilled cucumber soup

PAUL FORRESTER

SERVES 4

1 large cucumber, finely grated (see
  Preparation and Serving ideas)
450 ml/16 fl oz natural yoghurt
2 tablespoons wine vinegar
2 tablespoons chopped fresh dill, or
  2 teaspoons dried dillweed
2 tablespoons seedless raisins
2 hard-boiled eggs, finely chopped
1 large clove garlic, crushed
  (optional)
1 teaspoon caster sugar
1 large crisp dessert apple, cored
  and chopped
150 ml/¼ pint soured cream

1 In a large bowl combine all the
ingredients and stir well to mix
them thoroughly.
2 Cover the bowl and refrigerate for

at least 3 hours (see Cook's tip).
3 Pour the soup into a tureen or
spoon straight into individual
bowls and serve very cold.

Cook's Notes

 TIME
Total preparation time
is 40 minutes. Allow at
least 3 hours for chilling.

 PREPARATION
Do not remove the
cucumber peel unless it
is very tough.

 COOK'S TIP
If you are short of time,
chill the soup in the
freezer or refrigerator freezing
compartment for 30 minutes.

 VARIATIONS
Try mint or tarragon
instead of dill. Crisp
vegetables such as celery, fennel
and radishes may be used
instead of the apple.

 DID YOU KNOW
This is a Persian version
of an uncooked soup
that is enormously popular
throughout the Middle East.
Cucumber and yoghurt is a
favourite combination in
Middle Eastern countries

because its refreshing qualities
are particularly suited to the hot
climate.

 SERVING IDEAS
Reserve a little cucum-
ber, slice it very thinly
and float it on top of the soup
with a sprig of dill, mint or
tarragon, according to which
herb is used in the recipe. This
is a perfect soup to start off a
summer dinner party.

● 230 calories/950 kj per portion

DON LAST

Herby cream cheese salads

SERVES 4
200 g/7 oz cream cheese (see Buying guide)
5 tablespoons finely chopped fresh mixed herbs (see Preparation and Buying guide)
½ crisp lettuce (see Buying guide)
plain flour, for dusting

DRESSING
3 tablespoons olive oil
1 tablespoon white wine vinegar
½ teaspoon made English mustard
salt and freshly ground black pepper

1 Make the dressing: put the oil in a shallow bowl and mix in the vinegar and mustard with a fork. Season to taste with salt and freshly ground black pepper.
2 Spoon out the cream cheese into 20 small pieces and, with lightly floured hands, roll them into balls.

Spread the herbs out on a plate, then roll each ball in herbs to coat well. Refrigerate for 30 minutes.
3 Dip lettuce leaves in dressing to coat well. Divide the lettuce leaves

between 4 individual side plates, then place 5 herb-coated balls in the centre of the lettuce leaves. Sprinkle with salt and pepper to taste and serve (see Serving ideas).

23

DON LAST

Cucumber and yoghurt salad

SERVES 4

1 large cucumber, coarsely grated
(see Preparation)
1 teaspoon salt
2 × 150 g/5 oz cartons natural
yoghurt
1 large clove garlic, crushed
1-2 tablespoons chopped mint
freshly ground black pepper
fresh mint sprigs, to garnish
hot pitta bread, to serve

1 Put the grated cucumber into a large bowl, sprinkle with the salt and leave to stand for 30 minutes.
2 Turn the salted cucumber into a colander and then rinse under cold running water. Drain cucumber and return to rinsed-out bowl.
3 Stir in the yoghurt, together with the garlic, mint and pepper to taste.
4 Cover the salad and refrigerate for 2-3 hours until well chilled.
5 Serve the salad in a bowl on a large serving plate. Garnish with mint and serve at once with hot pitta bread (see Did you know).

PAUL WEBSTER

Crispy aubergine sticks with dip

SERVES 6
2 aubergines
vegetable oil, for frying

BATTER
225 g/8 oz plain flour
1 teaspoon baking powder
generous pinch of salt
**generous sprinkling of freshly
    ground black pepper**
200 ml/7 fl oz hot water
150 ml/¼ pint malt vinegar

DIP
150 ml/¼ pint soured cream
2 tablespoons snipped chives

1 Make the batter: sift the flour, baking powder, salt and pepper into a large bowl. Make a well in the centre and add the water. Using a whisk, gradually draw the flour into the liquid, then whisk in vinegar. Leave to stand for 30 minutes.
2 Meanwhile, halve the aubergines lengthways, then cut into long slices, about 1 cm/½ inch thick. Cut across the aubergine slices to make 5 cm/2 inch sticks.
3 Spread the sticks out on a large plate, sprinkle with salt and leave to stand for 30 minutes.
4 Meanwhile, make the dip: put the soured cream into a small serving bowl and mix in the chives. Season to taste with salt and pepper, cover and refrigerate until required.
5 Rinse the aubergines under cold running water, then pat them dry thoroughly with absorbent paper.
6 Heat the oven to 110C/225F/Gas ¼.
7 Heat the oil in a deep-fat frier to 180C/350F or until a stale bread cube browns in 60 seconds.
8 Piercing with a fork, dip each stick into the batter, one at a time, to coat well. Fry a batch of coated sticks in the oil for about 5 minutes until golden brown. Remove with a slotted spoon and drain on absorbent paper. Keep warm in the oven; cook remainder in same way.
9 Arrange the sticks on a warmed serving platter and serve them at once, with the chilled dip handed separately.

Cook's Notes

TIME
1 hour to make, including standing time.

SERVING IDEAS
These delicious sticks make an excellent start to an informal supper party and they are also ideal for serving with drinks.

● 320 calories/1325 kj per portion

JAMES JACKSON

Hummus with tahini

SERVES 4

100 g/4 oz dried chick-peas (see
    Buying guide)
4 tablespoons olive oil
1 large clove garlic, peeled and
    crushed (optional)
4 tablespoons lemon juice
4 tablespoons tahini paste (see
    Buying guide)
salt and freshly ground black pepper
¼ teaspoon paprika
few sprigs of fresh parsley and
    lemon wedges, to garnish

1 Put the chick-peas into a deep
bowl, cover with plenty of cold
water and leave to soak for several
hours or overnight.
2 Drain and rinse the chick-peas,
put them into a saucepan and cover
with fresh cold water. Bring to the
boil, then simmer for about 1 hour,
until tender, adding more water to
the pan during the cooking time if
the chick-peas become too dry.
3 Drain, reserving the liquid; cool.

Cook's Notes

TIME
Preparation time is 20
minutes, plus overnight
soaking, 1 hour cooking, then
cooling and 1 hour chilling.

BUYING GUIDE
Dried chick-peas are
available at health food
stores, but for a speedier, easier
method, use a 425 g/15 oz can
pre-soaked and pre-cooked
chick-peas and start from the
beginning of stage 3.
    Tahini is a thick paste made
from sesame seeds; it can be
bought from health food stores,
shops specializing in Middle
Eastern foods, and supermarkets.

PRESSURE COOKING
Chick-peas can be
cooked in a pressure
cooker. Soak and rinse as in
recipe, then cook for about 20
minutes at high (H) pressure.

SERVING IDEAS
For a delicious, unusual
first course serve chilled
hummus with warm pitta bread
or light wholewheat rolls, or as
a buffet-style dip with sticks of
carrot, celery, cucumber and
red and green peppers. It also
makes a good light lunch, with
a mixed salad.

●335 calories/1440 kj per portion

4 Reserve 12 chick-peas for garnish.
Put the remainder into a blender
with half the oil, the garlic, if using,
the lemon juice, tahini paste and
salt and pepper to taste. Blend to a
smooth purée, adding a little of the
reserved liquid if necessary to give a
consistency like thick mayonnaise.
Refrigerate for a minimum 1 hour.

5 To serve, spoon mixture into a
shallow dish, or 4 small individual
ones. Put the paprika into a small
bowl and gradually stir in the remaining olive oil to make a smooth
paste. Drizzle this over the top of
the hummus, garnish with the
whole chick-peas, lemon wedges,
and parsley sprigs. Serve chilled.

Lentil salad

SERVES 6
500 g/1 lb whole brown lentils,
    washed and drained
1 medium onion, halved
1 medium carrot, halved
2 celery stalks, halved
1 bay leaf
salt

DRESSING
3 tablespoons vegetable oil
1 tablespoon lemon juice
1/2 teaspoon dried mixed herbs
freshly ground black pepper
2-3 spring onions, finely chopped
2 celery stalks, thinly sliced
2 tablespoons chopped parsley
parsley sprigs and 1 lemon,
    quartered, to garnish

1 Put the lentils into a large saucepan with the onion, carrot, celery and bay leaf and cover with water. Bring to the boil, then lower the heat, cover and simmer gently for about 1 hour, or until the lentils are tender but not mushy. Check occasionally and add more boiling water if necessary. Add salt just before the end of cooking time.

2 Meanwhile, make the dressing: mix together the oil and lemon juice, stir in the mixed herbs and season well with salt and pepper.

3 Strain the lentils, discarding the liquid, vegetables and bay leaf, and turn the lentils into a bowl.

4 Immediately pour over the dressing and mix to blend thoroughly without breaking up the lentils (see Cook's tip). Stir in the spring onions and celery with the chopped parsley.

5 Allow to cool, cover the bowl, then chill in the refrigerator for about 2 hours.

6 Turn the lentil salad into a serving dish, and garnish with parsley sprigs and lemon or serve with a salad (see Serving ideas).

DON LAST

Asparagus pâté

SERVES 4

275 g/10 oz can asparagus tips
150 g/5 oz lemon mayonnaise (see
  Buying guide)
2 tablespoons double cream
salt and freshly ground black pepper
parsley sprigs, to garnish

1 Drain and discard liquid from can of asparagus and put all but 4 tips into a blender or food processor.
2 Add the mayonnaise, cream, salt (see Cook's tips) and pepper to taste and blend until purée is quite smooth (see Cook's tips).
3 Pour the purée into 4 individual ramekin dishes and put into refrigerator for 2-3 hours until firm.
4 Serve chilled, garnished with the parsley and reserved asparagus tips.

FRED MANCINI

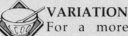

DON LAST

Cucumber scoops with dip

SERVES 4
1 large cucumber
1 teaspoon chopped fresh dill
salt and freshly ground black pepper
dill sprig, to garnish (optional)

DIP
500 g/1 lb carton natural yoghurt,
  chilled (see Buying guide)
100 g/4 oz walnut pieces, roughly
  chopped
1 clove garlic, crushed (optional)
1 teaspoon sweet paprika
¼-½ teaspoon chilli powder

1 Cut the cucumber into 5 cm/
2 inch chunks. Cut each cucumber
chunk into quarters, lengthways,
then sprinkle with the chopped dill
and salt and black pepper to taste.

2 Make the dip: put the yoghurt
into a bowl and stir lightly with a
fork. Add the walnuts, garlic, if
using, paprika and chilli. Season
generously with salt and pepper.
Mix with the fork until well
blended, then transfer to a small
serving bowl.

3 Put the bowl of dip in the centre
of a large serving plate, garnish
with a dill sprig and arrange the
cucumber around the edge. !

Cook's Notes

TIME
This unusual idea for a
light dip takes only
15 minutes to prepare.

WATCHPOINT
This dip should be
served at once; if left for
more than 30 minutes the walnuts lose their crispness and
may become a little bitter.

BUYING GUIDE
If possible, try to buy
thick or 'firm set'
yoghurt, so that the dip has

enough body to be scooped up
on to the cucumber wedges. If
only thin yoghurt is available,
replace a little of it with curd
cheese to add thickness.

SERVING IDEAS
Refreshing cucumber
wedges with a yoghurt-
based dip make a perfect summery first course. This dish is
also delicious served as a side
salad with curries and other
spicy dishes.

●210 calories/875 kj per portion

Tomato and basil mousse

SERVES 4
500 g/1 lb tomatoes, coarsely chopped (see Variations)
150 ml/¼ pint thick bottled mayonnaise
½ onion, grated
2 teaspoons chopped fresh basil (see Variations)
salt and freshly ground black pepper
3 teaspoons agar-agar
150 ml/¼ pint cold vegetable stock
150 ml/¼ pint double cream, lightly whipped

TO GARNISH
1 large tomato, skinned and coarsely chopped
pinch of chopped fresh basil (see Variations)

1 Pureé the tomatoes in a blender, then work them through a sieve to remove skins. Stir in the mayonnaise, onion, basil and salt and pepper to taste, then return to the blender and blend until smooth. Leave the mixture in the blender while preparing the agar-agar.

2 Sprinkle the agar-agar over 75 ml/ 3 fl oz of the stock in a small pan and stir to mix well. Boil gently and stir until the agar-agar has completely dissolved. Remove from the heat.

3 Add the agar-agar mixture to the tomato mixture in the blender, together with the remaining stock and the lightly whipped cream. Blend thoroughly.

4 Taste the mixture and adjust the seasoning if necessary. Pour the mixture into an 850 ml/1½ pint soufflé dish and refrigerate for 2-3 hours, until set.

5 Just before serving, prepare the garnish: mix the chopped tomato with the basil and a little salt and pepper to taste. Spoon the garnish in the centre of the mousse and serve at once with the accompaniment of your choice (see Serving ideas).

MARTIN BRIGDALE

Cook's Notes

TIME
Preparation takes about 30 minutes. Allow 2-3 hours setting time.

SERVING IDEAS
This summery mousse can be served as a starter, accompanied by thin triangles of toast, or as a light lunch dish with salad.

VARIATIONS
Use a 400 g/14 oz can tomatoes in place of the fresh tomatoes and omit the sieving in stage 1.

If you cannot find fresh basil, use fresh tarragon, mint or parsley instead. Do not use dried herbs in the recipe.

●440 calories/1850 kj per portion

Courgette and chive sticks

SERVES 4
500 g/1 lb courgettes
vegetable oil, for deep frying

BATTER
100 g/4 oz plain flour
salt and freshly ground black pepper
1 egg
150 ml/¼ pint milk
2 tablespoons snipped chives

1 Heat the oven to 110C/225F/Gas ¼.
2 To make the batter: sift the flour, a pinch of salt and a little freshly ground black pepper into a large bowl. Make a well in the centre of the flour mixture, break in the egg and add half the milk.
3 Beat with a wooden spoon, gradually drawing the flour into the liquid. Add the remaining milk and beat well until smooth. Stir in the chives, cover and set aside (see Cook's tip).
4 Cut the courgettes into sticks, about 4 cm/1½ inches long and 2 mm/⅛ inch wide. Pat courgette

sticks dry on absorbent paper.
5 Heat the oil in a deep-fat frier to 190C/375F or until a stale bread cube turns brown in 50 seconds.
6 Dip a small batch of the courgette slices into the batter one at a time, allowing any excess batter to run back into the bowl.

7 Deep fry the coated courgettes for 6-7 minutes until golden brown. Remove from the oil with a slotted spoon, drain on absorbent paper, then transfer to a warmed serving dish. Keep hot while frying the remaining courgette and chive sticks in the same way.

Cook's Notes

 TIME
Preparing courgettes and the batter takes about 10 minutes. Total cooking time is about 20 minutes.

 WATCHPOINT
The vegetable oil must be reheated between frying batches.

 SERVING IDEAS
To serve these courgette and chive fritter sticks as a starter, arrange on individual dishes and serve with a dressing such as blue cheese mixed with soured cream, or with thick bottled mayonnaise flavoured with tomato sauce. Alternatively, serve with drinks.

 COOK'S TIP
Although fritter batter does not need to stand before using, it can be made up to 1 day in advance, if covered and refrigerated.

VARIATIONS
For a crispy, fluffier batter: replace milk with 7 tablespoons water and 1 tablespoon of vegetable oil. Separate egg and add the yolk with the water and oil. Whisk the egg white separately and fold in just before using.

The chives may be replaced with snipped spring onion tops or a little crushed garlic.

●270 calories/1125 kj per portion

PETER MYERS

Mushroom loaf

SERVES 6-8
250 g/9 oz mushrooms
salt
3 carrots, cut into matchstick strips
100 g/4 oz French beans, cut in half
50 g/2 oz margarine or butter
1 onion, finely chopped
225 g/8 oz cottage cheese
5 eggs
1 teaspoon dried tarragon
¼ teaspoon curry powder
freshly ground black pepper
watercress, carrot sticks and French
    beans, to garnish
vegetable oil, for greasing

DRESSING
1 teaspoon French mustard
1 clove garlic, crushed (optional)
½ teaspoon curry powder
juice of ½ lemon
200 ml/7 fl oz olive oil

1 Heat the oven to 180C/350F/Gas 4. Grease a 1 kg/2 lb loaf tin, line the base with greaseproof paper and grease the paper.
2 Bring 2 pans of salted water to the boil. Cook the carrots in one pan for 10 minutes and the beans in the other pan for 6 minutes.
3 Meanwhile, melt the margarine in a frying-pan, add the onion and fry gently for 5 minutes until soft and lightly coloured. Set aside 3-4 mushrooms and finely chop the rest. Add the chopped mushrooms to the pan and cook for a further 5 minutes.
4 Drain the carrots and the beans.
5 Put the onion and mushroom mixture into a blender. Add the cheese, eggs, tarragon and curry powder and blend to a smooth, speckled mixture. Season to taste with salt and pepper.
6 Pour one-third of the mushroom mixture into the greased tin. Arrange the beans in a layer on top, then pour in another third of the mushroom mixture. Add a layer of carrots and pour in the remaining mushroom mixture.
7 Cover the loaf tightly with foil. Stand in a roasting tin, pour in boiling water to come halfway up the sides of the loaf tin. Bake in the oven for 1½ hours or until the mixture feels lightly set in the centre when pierced with a pointed knife.
8 Remove the loaf tin from the water, leave to cool, then refrigerate until completely cold.
9 Just before serving make the dressing: put all the ingredients in a screw-top jar with salt and pepper to taste. Shake well to mix, then pour into a jug.
10 To serve: turn the loaf out onto a serving plate, then slice the reserved mushrooms thinly and overlap them on top. Slice loaf and serve garnished with sprigs of watercress, carrot sticks and French beans. Hand the dressing separately.

Cook's Notes

TIME
25 minutes preparation and 1½ hours cooking, plus cooling time.

SERVING IDEAS
Serve as an unusual starter with wholemeal toast or as a light snack.

WATCHPOINT
Make sure that the carrots and beans are cooked until quite tender or the loaf will be difficult to slice.

VARIATIONS
If available, try using the Italian Ricotta cheese instead of cottage cheese.

● 450 calories/1875 kj per portion

FRED MANCINI

Spiced beetroot and apple

SERVES 6
500 g/1 lb cooked beetroot, skinned and diced
25 g/1 oz butter
1 large onion, finely chopped
500 g/1 lb cooking apples, peeled, cored and sliced
2 tablespoons water
25 g/1 oz light soft brown sugar
½ teaspoon freshly grated nutmeg
½ teaspoon ground cloves
salt and freshly ground black pepper

TO FINISH
150 ml/¼ pint soured cream
2 tablespoons snipped chives

1 Melt the butter in a large saucepan, add the onion and fry gently for about 5 minutes until soft.
2 Add the beetroot and apple and continue to fry gently for a further 10 minutes. Stir in the water, sugar, spices and salt and pepper to taste. Cover the pan and simmer gently for 40 minutes, stirring occasionally, until the apple is pulpy.
3 Press through a sieve, or leave to cool slightly, then work in a blender until smooth.
4 Transfer to a large bowl, leave to cool completely, ✳ then cover and refrigerate for at least 2 hours.
5 To serve: divide the purée between 6 ramekin dishes, smooth the surface, then top with soured cream and sprinkle with chives. Serve.

JAMES JACKSON

Cook's Notes

 TIME
15 minutes preparation; about 1 hour cooking and at least 2 hours chilling.

 SERVING IDEAS
Serve with hot garlic bread, toast or crispbreads as an unusual starter to a dinner party.

VARIATION
To serve as a hot vegetable accompaniment, ideal with a vegetable hotpot or warming winter casserole, do not purée the ingredients as in stage 3. Instead, transfer to a warmed serving dish, top with soured cream and chives and serve at once.

✳ **FREEZING**
Pour the cold purée into a rigid container, seal, label and freeze for up to 3 months. To serve: defrost in the covered container in the refrigerator for 6-8 hours. Whisk before putting into ramekins.

● 165 calories/700 kj per portion

PAUL WEBSTER

Iced tomato cocktail

SERVES 6
500 ml/17 fl oz carton tomato juice
1 tablespoon medium sherry
a few drops of Tabasco (optional)
celery salt
freshly ground black pepper
lemon and cucumber slices, to garnish

1 Put the tomato juice in the goblet of a blender, together with the sherry, Tabasco, if using, celery salt and freshly ground black pepper to taste. Blend until all the ingredients are well combined. Alternatively, mix well together with a balloon whisk.

2 Pour into a rigid container or freezer trays and freeze in the freezer compartment of a refrigerator or in the freezer for 2 hours until the mixture is firm around the sides (see Cook's tips).

3 Remove the container from the freezer and beat the icy mixture with a whisk or fork until evenly blended. Return to the freezer for a further 3-4 hours or until firmly frozen.

4 About 30 minutes before serving, transfer the frozen mixture to the main part of the refrigerator to allow it to soften slightly.

5 Spoon the mixture into individual glasses and garnish with a slice each of lemon and cucumber.

Cook's Notes

TIME
Preparation 5-10 minutes, freezing 5-6 hours.

COOK'S TIPS
If you are using the freezer compartment of the refrigerator, turn it to its coldest setting 1 hour before making the cocktail and remember to turn it back to its original setting when you have finished making the cocktails.

VARIATIONS
Add blanched and finely chopped green pepper or chopped mint or chives to the tomato mixture before freezing. Replace the sherry with vodka.

SERVING IDEAS
Serve as a refreshing starter before a meal, providing spoons for easy eating.

● 20 calories/85 kj per portion

34

MICHAEL KAY

Vegetable cocktail

SERVES 4-6

500 g/1 lb very ripe tomatoes, skinned, deseeded and chopped
finely grated zest and juice of ½ lemon
2 teaspoons caster sugar
1 tablespoon tomato purée
300 ml/½ pint vegetable stock
1 bunch watercress, stalks removed
1 large carrot, chopped
3 tablespoons chopped celery leaves
pinch of cayenne pepper
salt and freshly ground black pepper

1 Put the chopped tomatoes in a blender with the lemon zest and juice, sugar, tomato purée, and vegetable stock.

2 Reserve a few sprigs of watercress for the garnish and add the rest to the blender. Add the carrot, celery leaves and cayenne pepper and season to taste with salt and pepper.

3 Blend to a smooth purée (see Cook's tip). Taste and adjust seasonings, if necessary—the cocktail should taste slightly spicy. ✳

4 Pour the cocktail into a jug or container, cover and refrigerate for 2 hours. Pour into glasses and garnish with the reserved watercress sprigs. Serve chilled.

Cook's Notes

 TIME
10 minutes preparation, plus chilling for 2 hours.

 COOK'S TIP
If you do not have a blender, rub the tomatoes through a nylon sieve. Beat in the sugar, tomato purée, and vegetable stock. Finely chop the watercress sprigs and celery leaves and grate the carrot; stir them into the mixture and season to taste.

 ECONOMY
When tomatoes are out of season or too expensive, use 300 ml/½ pint tomato juice with an extra 1 tablespoon tomato purée.

 VARIATIONS
Instead of carrot, celery and watercress, use a combination of peeled and grated cucumber, chopped mint leaves, chopped spring onion or green or red pepper.

 FREEZING
To freeze the cocktail, pour into a rigid container, remembering to leave about 2.5 cm/1 inch headroom for the liquid to expand as it freezes. Seal, label and freeze for up to 2 months. To serve: defrost overnight in the refrigerator, then whisk and adjust seasoning.

●40 calories/150 kj per portion

Fruity mushroom cocktail

SERVES 4
250 g/9 oz small button mushrooms
1 tablespoon lemon juice
salt and freshly ground black pepper
½ small melon, deseeded
sweet paprika, to garnish

DRESSING
2 tablespoons double cream
4 level tablespoons thick bottled
   mayonnaise
1 tablespoon tomato purée
good pinch of curry powder
1 teaspoon brandy (optional)
8 crisp lettuce leaves, shredded

1 Put the mushrooms in a saucepan (see Cook's tip), sprinkle with the lemon juice and season to taste with salt and pepper. Cover the pan and cook gently for 5-7 minutes, shaking the pan from time to time, until the mushrooms are just tender. Cool.

2 Scoop the melon flesh into small balls, using a potato/melon baller. Mix the melon balls with the mushrooms.
3 To make the dressing: whip the cream until thick, then gently fold in the mayonnaise, tomato purée and curry powder. Add the brandy, if using, and blend together.
4 Arrange the shredded lettuce in the base of 4 individual dishes or ramekins. Divide the mushrooms and melon balls evenly between the glasses. Spoon over the dressing and sprinkle with a little sweet paprika.

Cook's Notes

 TIME
Cooking the mushrooms takes 5-7 minutes. Allow 30 minutes for cooling. Preparation then takes 10 minutes.

 SERVING IDEAS
The cocktail makes an unusual starter for a summer meal, served with triangles of lightly buttered wholemeal bread or chunks of hot French bread. Alternatively, try serving the cocktail as a refreshing side salad to a savoury pie or a cheese soufflé.

 COOK'S TIP
A saucepan with a non-stick surface, although not essential, is useful for recipes such as this where the mushrooms are cooked without fat and just a little liquid.

 VARIATIONS
Add some chopped celery and a few salted cashews to the melon and mushroom mixture. Or garnish with finely chopped walnuts instead of the sweet paprika.

●155 calories/650 kj per portion

ROGER PHILLIPS

Leeks vinaigrette

SERVES 4
1 kg/2 lb small leeks (see Buying guide and Preparation)

VINAIGRETTE DRESSING
4 tablespoons olive or sunflower seed oil
1½ tablespoons red wine vinegar
salt and freshly ground black pepper
pinch of chilli powder (optional)

TO GARNISH
1 teaspoon sweet paprika
1 tablespoon chopped fresh parsley
1 lemon, cut into wedges
sprigs of watercress

1 Make the dressing: put the oil and vinegar into a small bowl with salt and pepper to taste. Add the chilli powder, if using, then mix well with a fork until well blended.
2 Bring a pan of salted water to the boil and cook the leeks for 7-10 minutes until just tender. Drain thoroughly, then place in a shallow dish.
3 Pour the dressing over the leeks, while they are still hot, and turn them with a fork so that they are well coated with the dressing.
4 Leave for at least 2 hours to allow the leeks to cool and absorb the dressing, turning the leeks over once or twice more during this time.
5 Serve at room temperature, sprinkled with paprika and chopped parsley and garnished with lemon wedges and sprigs of watercress.

Cook's Notes

 TIME
Preparation takes 30 minutes, plus 2 hours for the leeks to cool in the dressing and 1 hour for cleaning, if necessary.

 BUYING GUIDE
Choose the thinnest, smallest leeks you can find for this recipe.

 PREPARATION
The leeks must be kept whole for this dish, but if they seem very dirty, a good way of cleaning them is to cut a cross in the leaf ends after trimming and stand them, leaf-end down, in a jug of cold water for at least an hour. This will draw out most of the dirt: any that remains will show up as dark patches under the skin and can be removed by making small slits and rinsing away.

 SERVING IDEAS
Serve on individual plates with warm bread or rolls as a first course. Alternatively, serve in a shallow serving dish as part of a salad selection for a lunch or buffet.

●195 calories/820 kj per portion

JAMES JACKSON

Pear salad boats

SERVES 4

4 large, firm ripe dessert pears (see Buying guide)
1 tablespoon lemon juice
1 small lettuce, leaves divided up
2 tablespoons mint leaves, chopped
1 head chicory, thinly sliced into rings (optional)

DRESSING
3 tablespoons clear honey
1 tablespoon lemon juice
1 tablespoon orange juice
3 tablespoons vegetable oil
salt and freshly ground black pepper
2 tablespoons chopped walnuts

1 Peel and halve the pears then, using a teaspoon, scoop out the core. Brush with lemon juice.
2 Reserve 8 small lettuce leaves for the garnish, and shred the rest.

3 Mix together the shredded lettuce, chopped mint leaves and chicory, if using, and spread over the base of a flat serving plate to cover it.
4 Make the dressing: put the honey into a small bowl and whisk in the lemon and orange juice with a balloon whisk. Gradually, but vigorously, beat in the vegetable oil and season to taste with salt and pepper. Stir in the walnuts.

5 Arrange the pear halves, cut side up, in a wheel pattern on the bed of salad leaves. To make salad boats: thread a cocktail stick through the top and bottom of each of the reserved lettuce leaves, to make 'sails'. Stick the cocktail sticks into the pears and moisten the pears with a little of the dressing (see Cook's tip), piling a few walnut pieces into the pear hollows. Serve the remaining dressing separately.

Cook's Notes

TIME
This decorative salad only takes about 15 minutes to prepare.

SERVING IDEAS
This fruit and nut salad makes a very light, appetizing first course. These boats would also look attractive as part of a cold buffet. Serve in avocado dishes.

BUYING GUIDE
Conference pears are a good choice.

COOK'S TIP
Do not moisten the pears with dressing until the last moment, and then only use a very little—otherwise the salad greens will wilt.

●220 calories/925 kj per portion

MARTIN BRIGDALE

Melon bowl salads

SERVES 4

2 ogen melons (see Buying guide)
175 g/6 oz Mozzarella cheese, cut
into 1 cm/½ inch cubes (see
Variation)
6 tomatoes, skinned and quartered
1 tablespoon snipped chives
1 tablespoon chopped basil or mint

DRESSING

2 tablespoons wine vinegar
6 tablespoons vegetable or olive oil
salt and freshly ground black pepper

1 Cut melons in half crossways or
vandyke them (see Serving ideas).
Discard the seeds and scoop out the
flesh with a melon baller or slice
into small cubes with a sharp knife.
Place the melon balls in a large bowl.

Wrap melon shells tightly in cling
film and refrigerate until required.
2 Add the cheese, tomatoes and
herbs to the melon balls.
3 Make the dressing: put dressing
ingredients into a screw-top jar with
salt and pepper to taste and shake

well to mix. Pour the dressing over
the salad and then toss thoroughly
(see Cook's tip).
4 Cut a thin slice from the base of
each melon shell so they stand
upright. Divide the salad between
the melon shells and serve at once.

Cook's Notes

TIME
This salad takes only
20 minutes to prepare.

COOK'S TIP
Chilling helps the fla-
vours to combine so, if
wished, cover the salad tightly
and refrigerate for 2 hours.

BUYING GUIDE
If ogen melons are not
available, use Gallia or
cantaloupe or 2 small honeydew melons.

SERVING IDEAS
Serve with hot garlic
bread as a starter.
To vandyke the melons: cut in a
zig-zag shape all round.

VARIATION
For a more piquant
salad, use 175 g/6 oz
Feta cheese in place of the Mozzarella cheese but crumble it
into the bowl instead of cutting
into cubes.

●370 calories/1550 kj per portion

39

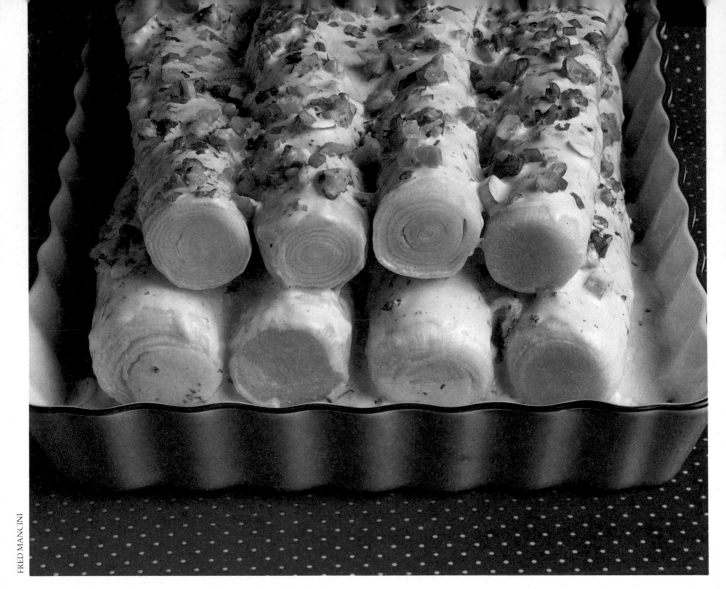

FRED MANCINI

Leeks in yoghurt sauce

SERVES 4
8 leeks (total weight about
   750 g/1½ lb)
salt

DRESSING
150 g/5 oz natural yoghurt
1 tablespoon thick mayonnaise
1 teaspoon French mustard
1 teaspoon white wine vinegar
2 spring onions, thinly sliced
2 tablespoons chopped parsley
freshly ground black pepper

TO GARNISH
25 g/1 oz walnuts, chopped
1 tablespoon snipped chives

1 Cook the leeks in boiling salted water for 8-10 minutes, or until they are just tender.

2 Meanwhile, beat together the yoghurt, mayonnaise, mustard and vinegar and stir in the onions and parsley. Season to taste with salt and pepper.
3 Drain the leeks, then pat them thoroughly dry with absorbent paper. Arrange them in two layers in a serving dish.
4 Pour the dressing evenly over the leeks while they are still hot (see Cook's tip), leave to cool, then cover the dish with a lid or cling film and refrigerate for at least 1 hour.
5 Just before serving, sprinkle with the walnuts and chives.

Cook's Notes

 TIME
Preparation takes 20 minutes. Allow a further hour for chilling.

 WATCHPOINT
The leeks must be thoroughly dry: any excess liquid would dilute and spoil the dressing.

COOK'S TIP
The leeks absorb the dressing better if it is added while they are still hot.

 SERVING IDEAS
This dish makes a good first course, served with crusty French bread or wholemeal or granary bread. It may also be served as a side salad: it would go particularly well with a cheesy dish.

 STORAGE
Leeks will keep in a cool place or salad drawer of the refrigerator for 4-5 days.

● 125 calories/525 kj per portion

Cardamom mushrooms

SERVES 4-6
500 g/1 lb button mushrooms,
   finely sliced
3 tablespoons olive oil
2 tablespoons water
juice of ½ lemon
6 cardamom seeds, crushed
salt and freshly ground black pepper
coriander sprigs and lemon twists,
   to garnish

1 Pour the oil into a frying-pan, then add the water and lemon juice and stir well to mix. Add the mushrooms and crushed cardamom seeds, then season to taste with salt and black pepper.
2 Bring to the boil, then lower the heat slightly and simmer gently for 10 minutes until the mushrooms are just tender.
3 Remove the pan from the heat, cover and leave the mushrooms to cool in the liquid for 2 hours.
4 Transfer all the mushrooms and liquid to a serving bowl. Garnish with sprigs of coriander and lemon twists and serve (see Cook's tip).

Cook's Notes

TIME
10 minutes preparation, then about 10 minutes cooking, plus 2 hours cooling.

SERVING IDEAS
These tasty, marinated mushrooms make a delicious starter, served in individual, shallow soup bowls and accompanied by chunks of French bread and butter, for mopping up the liquid. Alternatively, include them in a cold buffet, with other salads.

COOK'S TIP
Do not refrigerate salad before serving — the flavour of the mushrooms and cardamon will be much more pronounced if left to mellow at room temperature.

●105 calories/450 kj per portion

ALAN DUNS

FRED MANCINI

Tarragon cucumber salad

SERVES 6
2 cucumbers
150 ml/¼ pint double cream
1 teaspoon lemon juice
1 tablespoon finely chopped fresh
   tarragon (see Variation)

MARINADE
6 tablespoons olive oil
2 tablespoons tarragon vinegar
1 teaspoon finely chopped fresh
   tarragon (optional)
pinch of mustard powder
salt and freshly ground black pepper

1 Make the marinade: put all the ingredients in a screw-top jar, with salt and pepper to taste. Replace the lid firmly and shake well to mix the marinade thoroughly.
2 Peel and thinly slice cucumbers

Cook's Notes

TIME
This delicate-looking salad takes 45 minutes to make, including chilling and marinating time.

COOK'S TIP
For thin, even-sized slices, use a mandolin to cut up the cucumber. For a pretty effect, do not peel cucumbers completely; remove strips of peel with a cannelle knife before slicing.

SERVING IDEAS
Serve as an elegant first course to a dinner party, accompanied by Melba toast.

VARIATION
If fresh tarragon is unavailable, use parsley or chives instead, but bear in mind that the flavour will not be as delicate. Do not use dried tarragon as taste is too strong.

●185 calories/775 kj per portion

(see Cook's tip) and put in a bowl. Pour over the marinade and toss the slices to coat well. Cover the bowl and refrigerate for at least 30 minutes.
3 Just before serving, whip the cream until it stands in soft peaks, then stir in the lemon juice and salt to taste. Drain the cucumber slices

in a colander and discard the marinade and juices.
4 Arrange the cucumber slices on 6 small glass individual plates, piling them up attractively. Top each serving with the cream mixture and sprinkle with finely chopped fresh tarragon. Serve at once, while still well chilled (see Serving ideas).

Watercress mayonnaise salad

SERVES 4
6 hard-boiled eggs
8 medium-sized tomatoes,
   blanched and skinned
2 bunches watercress, stalks
   removed (see Buying guide)

DRESSING
1 bunch watercress, stalks removed
2 egg yolks
1 teaspoon Dijon mustard
juice of ½ lemon
300 ml/½ pint olive oil
salt and freshly ground black pepper

1 Make the dressing: purée the watercress in a food processor or blender. Add egg yolks, mustard and lemon juice and blend for a few minutes until well combined. Add the olive oil, drop by drop, very slowly and, as the mixture begins to thicken, gently trickle in remaining oil. Season to taste with salt and ground black pepper (see Cook's tip).

2 Cut 2 hard-boiled eggs in half widthways and place each half in the centre of a small plate. Cut the remaining 4 eggs lengthways into quarters and arrange them around the halved eggs.
3 Slice the tomatoes thinly and then arrange around the egg halves.
4 Chop the watercress very finely and divide it equally between the four plates, to form a border around the tomato slices.
5 Spoon the watercress dressing carefully over eggs and serve at once.

JAMES JACKSON

Tomatoes with soft cheese filling

SERVES 4

8 fairly large, firm ripe tomatoes (see Buying guide)
150 g/5 oz full-fat soft cheese
150 g/5 oz curd cheese
2 tablespoons top of the milk or single cream
2 tablespoons finely chopped parsley
2 teaspoons tomato purée
salt and freshly ground black pepper
8 sprigs of parsley, to garnish

DRESSING

6 tablespoons vegetable oil
2 tablespoons wine vinegar
½ teaspoon mustard powder
½ teaspoon dried basil
2 teaspoons caster sugar

1 Slice the tops off the tomatoes and reserve. Using a teaspoon, carefully scoop out the seeds and core (see Economy).
2 Put the cheeses in a bowl with the top of the milk or cream, parsley, tomato purée and salt and pepper to taste. Blend together smoothly. Spoon the mixture into tomatoes, piling it high, and replace the reserved tomato lids at an angle.
3 Place the stuffed tomatoes in a shallow dish. Beat together the dressing ingredients with a fork, adding salt and pepper to taste. Spoon the dressing over the tomatoes and chill in refrigerator for at least 30 minutes.
4 To serve: put 2 tomatoes on each of 4 plates. Beat the dressing remaining in the dish together again and sprinkle 1 teaspoon of the dressing over each tomato. Tuck a sprig of parsley beneath the lid of each tomato to garnish.

Melon and avocado salad

SERVES 6

1 large cantaloupe or charentais
   melon
2 large avocados
1 green pepper, deseeded and
   thinly sliced
6 lemon or lime slices, to garnish

DRESSING

6 tablespoons olive oil
1 tablespoon white or red wine
   vinegar
1 tablespoon lemon juice
1 tablespoon thick bottled
   mayonnaise
pinch of mustard powder
pinch of sugar
pinch of ground allspice
salt and freshly ground black pepper

1 Cut the melon in half and remove the seeds with a spoon. Using a melon baller, scoop out the flesh into a bowl. Alternatively, cut the melon into slices, remove the skin and cut the flesh into 2 cm/¾ inch cubes; transfer to a bowl. Tightly cover the bowl of melon balls or cubes with cling film and refrigerate until required.

2 Cut each avocado in half lengthways, twist the 2 halves apart and prise out the stone. Grip the skin at the pointed end, then peel back to remove. Cut the flesh into cubes, then add these to the bowl of melon (see Cook's tip).

3 Stir the pepper into the melon and avocado.

4 Make the dressing: put dressing ingredients in a screw-top jar with salt and pepper to taste. Shake well to mix.

5 Add the dressing to the melon mixture and mix together gently and evenly.

6 Spoon equally into 6 individual dishes. Cut into one side of each lemon slice, then arrange on the edge of each dish of salad. Serve at once (see Serving ideas).

ALAN DUNS

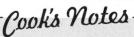

Cook's Notes

 TIME
20 minutes to prepare and assemble.

 SERVING IDEAS
This refreshing summer salad makes a very unusual first course – serve it with hot bread rolls.
  For a buffet party, serve the salad in a large bowl or in the 2 scooped-out melon halves.

 COOK'S TIP
Do not assemble more than 1 hour in advance, otherwise the avocado cubes may discolour.

 VARIATION
For extra colour, add 3 tomatoes, skinned, deseeded and thinly sliced.

●320 calories/1350 kj per portion

CHRIS KNAGGS

Cucumber boats

SERVES 4
1 large cucumber
150 ml/¼ pint water
2 tablespoons wine vinegar
salt and freshly ground black pepper
2 hard-boiled eggs
1 tablespoon olive oil
½ teaspoon mustard powder
1 small onion, finely chopped

TO GARNISH
watercress sprigs
radish waterlilies

1 Cut the ends off the cucumber, then cut the cucumber across into 4 equal-sized pieces. Remove the skin, then cut each piece in half lengthways and carefully scoop out the seeds in centre with a teaspoon.
2 Pour the water and vinegar into a saucepan and add a sprinkling of salt and pepper. Add the cucumber pieces and bring to the boil. Lower the heat slightly, cover the pan and simmer for 5-7 minutes, until the cucumber is tender. Drain in a colander and set aside to cool for about 1 hour.
3 Mash the eggs in a bowl with a fork. Add the olive oil, mustard, onion and salt and pepper to taste and mix well.
4 Arrange the cucumber pieces on a serving plate, hollowed-out sides upwards, and spoon the egg mixture into the cavities.
5 Arrange sprigs of watercress and radish waterlilies around the edge of the plate and between the pieces of cucumber. Serve at once.

Cook's Notes

TIME
40 minutes preparation, including cooking the cucumber; plus cooling time.

SERVING IDEAS
This makes an attractive and refreshing starter, served with thin slices of brown bread and butter. Or, it will make a lunch or supper snack for 2, with warm crusty bread.

WATCHPOINT
There will not be much liquid left towards end of cooking, so take care that the cucumber does not burn.

●90 calories/375 kj per portion

Fresh asparagus with egg dressing

SERVES 4
**500 g/1 lb fresh slender
   asparagus spears**
salt

CHOPPED EGG DRESSING
2 teaspoons lemon juice
1 tablespoon white wine vinegar
5 tablespoons olive oil
¼ teaspoon salt
freshly ground black pepper
¼ teaspoon mustard powder
1 teaspoon capers, chopped
1 teaspoon finely chopped parsley
1 teaspoon snipped chives
1 hard-boiled egg, finely chopped

1 Wash the asparagus stalks well in cold water, then trim the base of each spear, leaving 2 cm/¾ inch of the harder white stem.
Make sure the spears are trimmed to an even length, then divide into 4 separate bundles.
2 Tie each bundle securely with string in 2 places: just below the tips and towards the base.
3 Half-fill a deep narrow saucepan with lightly salted water and bring to the boil. Remove from the heat and stand the bundles of asparagus upright in the pan with the tips extending out of the water so that they cook in steam (see Cook's tip).
4 Cover the pan with foil to make a domed lid high enough to cover the asparagus without crushing the tips. Tuck the foil securely around the rim of the pan.
5 Return the pan to the heat, bring to the boil and boil gently for about 20 minutes, or until the thick part of the stem feels tender when pierced with a sharp knife.
6 Lift out the asparagus very carefully with kitchen tongs, then drain on absorbent paper. Lay on a clean, folded tea-towel and leave for at least 2 hours until cold.
7 Meanwhile, make the dressing: put all the ingredients in a screw-top jar and shake briskly.
8 Cut the strings around the asparagus with kitchen scissors, then arrange the cold spears on 4 individual plates. Pour dressing over each portion and serve at once.

MARTIN BRIGDALE

Cook's Notes

TIME
15 minutes preparation; about 20 minutes cooking the asparagus, plus at least 2 hours cooling time.

SERVING IDEAS
Serve as a starter for a special dinner, or as a light meal with crusty bread rolls and butter.

COOK'S TIP
If the pan is too wide to allow the asparagus to stand up firmly, place a jam jar filled with hot water in centre of pan and arrange asparagus around this. Add boiling water to half-fill pan, season with salt, continue as described.

● 190 calories/800 kj per portion

Broccoli butter toasts

SERVES 4

225 g/8 oz packet frozen broccoli
   spears (see Buying guide)
salt
4 large slices white or brown bread,
   crusts removed
65 g/2½ oz butter
½ teaspoon made English mustard
1½ tablespoons lemon juice
freshly ground black pepper
lemon twists, to garnish

1 Heat the grill to high.
2 Bring a saucepan of salted water
to the boil and add the broccoli.
Bring back to the boil, lower the heat
slightly, then cover and simmer
gently for 8-10 minutes or until just
tender.
3 Meanwhile, spread 1 side of each
slice of bread with some of the butter. Toast the slices on both sides,
buttered sides first. Remove from
the grill and spread the unbuttered
sides with the mustard. Cut each
slice in half diagonally and arrange,
mustard-side up, on a warmed
shallow serving dish.
4 Drain the broccoli and arrange the
spears on the toast, trimming the
stalks if necessary to make them fit.
Keep hot in a low oven.
5 Put the remaining butter in a
small saucepan, together with the
lemon juice and salt and pepper to
taste. Stir to blend, then heat gently
until the butter begins to froth.
Immediately pour the butter
mixture over the broccoli and serve,
garnished with lemon twists.

DON LAST

Sweet and sour mixed vegetables

SERVES 4

500 g/1 lb frozen mixed vegetables
salt
3 tablespoons clear honey
2 tablespoons sherry
1 tablespoon tomato ketchup
1-1½ tablespoons soy sauce
grated zest of 1 orange
1 teaspoon cornflour

1 Cook the vegetables in boiling salted water for 1-2 minutes less than packet instructions.
2 Meanwhile, make the sauce: combine the honey, sherry, tomato ketchup, soy sauce and orange zest in a saucepan and bring to the boil, stirring to mix well.

3 In a bowl, mix the cornflour to a paste with a little cold water. Stir a little of the hot sauce in the pan on to the cornflour paste, then pour this mixture back into the sauce in the pan. Bring to the boil, stirring all the time, then lower the heat and simmer for 1-2 minutes until the

sauce thickens.
4 Drain the vegetables thoroughly, then add them to the sauce. Turn gently until all the vegetables are well coated with the sauce, then transfer to a warmed serving dish. Serve at once, while the vegetables are piping hot.

Cook's Notes

TIME
Cooking, including making the sauce, takes 10-15 minutes.

VARIATIONS
The ingredients in a sweet and sour sauce can be varied greatly. Pineapple juice makes a good addition: substitute 3 tablespoons of this with 2 teaspoons brown sugar

instead of honey. Try adding a generous pinch of mustard powder or ground ginger for extra spiciness.

SERVING IDEAS
Serve the vegetables in this tangy sauce with wholemeal or French bread, making a quick and easy starter.

●155 calories/650 kj per portion

JAMES JACKSON

Sweet and sour corn on the cob

SERVES 4
4 corn on the cob
juice of 2 oranges
100 g/4 oz butter
50 g/2 oz light soft brown sugar
1 teaspoon wine vinegar
salt and freshly ground black pepper

1 Remove the husks and silky threads from the corn on the cob. Bring a large pan of water to the boil [!] add the corn, cover and boil for 6 minutes, until the corn is just tender.
2 Meanwhile, make the sauce: put the orange juice in a small pan with the butter and sugar. Using a wooden spoon, stir over low heat until the sugar has dissolved. Add the vinegar and salt and pepper to taste, then bring to the boil and boil quickly for 2-3 minutes, until the mixture becomes quite syrupy.

3 Drain the corn thoroughly, then transfer to 4 warmed individual dishes. Pour a little sauce over each cob and serve at once, with the remaining sauce served separately.

Cook's Notes

TIME
Preparation and cooking the sweet and sour corn take about 15 minutes.

SERVING IDEAS
Serve with brown bread to mop up the delicious sweet and sour sauce.
For easy serving and eating, there are specially designed corn on the cob holders. These are skewered into each end of the cob so that it can be gripped firmly.

WATCHPOINT
Never cook corn on the cob in salted water as this toughens the kernels.

COOK'S TIP
When corn on the cob is out of season, use frozen corn on the cob which is available in most large supermarkets. Cook it, too, in boiling unsalted water following packet instructions.

● 345 calories/1450 kj per portion

TIME
30 minutes preparation;
30 minutes cooking.

WATCHPOINT
The artichokes must not be overcooked or they will lose their nutty flavour.

BUYING GUIDE
Choose artichokes which are young and fresh: they quickly dry out once they have been cut and this toughens the leaves. The best artichokes will have about 15 cm/ 6 inches stalk left attached and the leaves will be stiff. Avoid any artichokes with brown outer leaves or with fully opened leaves as they will be past their prime.

SERVING IDEAS
Pull off each leaf with your fingers, dip in the melted butter and bite off the fleshy base of the leaf. Once all the leaves have been removed, cut up the remaining heart and dip in the butter before eating.
    Provide a dish or bowl for discarded leaves.

●335 calories/1400 kj per portion

Globe artichokes with butter

PAUL WEBSTER

SERVES 4
4 globe artichokes (see Buying guide)
1 L/2 pints cold water
juice of 1 lemon
salt
175 g/6 oz butter
1 clove garlic, crushed (optional)
freshly ground black pepper

1 Pour the measured cold water into a large bowl, then stir in half the lemon juice.
2 Bring a large pan of salted water to the boil.
3 Meanwhile, using a sharp knife, cut off the artichoke stalks, then slice off the top third of each

artichoke. Discard the trimmings.
4 Dip the cut leaves into the bowl of lemon water to prevent discoloration. Using scissors, trim any remaining sharp tips from the leaves, dip in lemon water, then open them to expose the central whiskery 'choke' surrounded by purple leaves. Pull out the purple leaves, then scoop out the hairy choke with a teaspoon and discard.
5 Add the artichokes to the boiling water and cook for 15-20 minutes or until an outer leaf of the artichoke

can be pulled out quite easily.
6 Just before the end of the cooking time, melt the butter in a small saucepan, add the garlic, if using, the remaining lemon juice and salt and pepper to taste. Heat through very gently; remove from heat.
7 Drain the artichokes well, then stand them upside down in a colander to extract all the water. Transfer to 4 warmed individual shallow bowls and serve a portion of the melted butter with each. Serve at once (see Serving ideas).

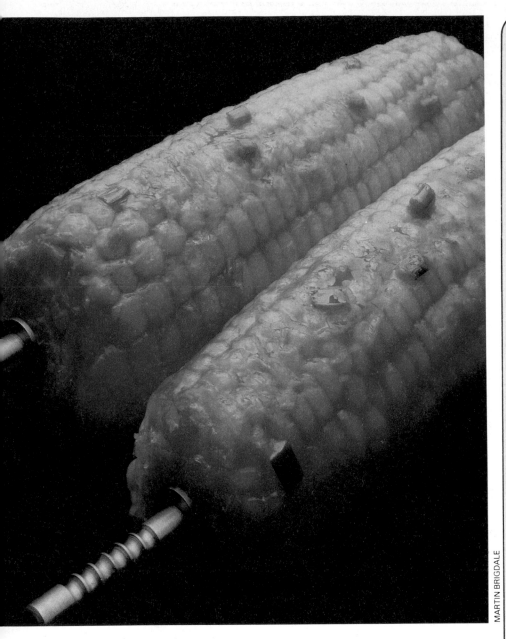

MARTIN BRIGDALE

 TIME
20 minutes preparation,
20 minutes cooking.

 COOK'S TIP
When corn on the cob is
out of season, you can
use frozen corn on the cob,
which is available in most large
supermarkets. Put the frozen
cobs in boiling water, bring
back to the boil, then drain at
once, place on the squares of foil
and spread with the butter
mixture.

 WATCHPOINT
Never cook corn on the
cob in salted water as
this toughens the kernels.

 VARIATION
Use finely chopped par-
sley instead of finely
snipped chives in the butter
mixture.

 SERVING IDEAS
Serve Devilled corn on
the cob on its own as a
vegetable starter, or to
accompany a main dish. Provide
plenty of paper napkins for
wiping buttery fingers.
For ease of serving, there are
specially-designed corn on the
cob holders available. These are
skewered into either end of the
cob, so that you can grip the cob
firmly without burning your
fingers.

 PREPARATION
To prepare the corn on
the cob:

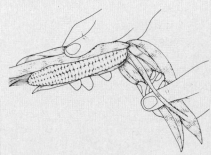

*Gently peel off the husk and pull
off the silk threads.*

Devilled corn on the cob

SERVES 4
**4 fresh or frozen corn on the cob
(see Cook's tip)**
75 g/3 oz butter, softened
4 tablespoons tomato ketchup
**1-2 tablespoons finely snipped
chives**

1 Heat the oven to 200C/400F/Gas 6.
2 Put the softened butter in a small
bowl and using a fork, blend in the
tomato ketchup and snipped chives.
Beat until the mixture is well combined and put aside.

3 Remove the husks and silky
threads from the corn on the cob (see
Preparation). Bring a large saucepan
of unsalted water to the boil. [!] Put
in the corn on the cob, bring back to
the boil and cook for 6 minutes.
Drain well.
4 Place each corn on the cob on a
piece of foil about 30 cm/12 inches
square, and spread with the butter
mixture. Bring the edges of the foil
together over each corn on the cob
and crimp them securely together,
to make a parcel.
5 Place the foil parcels on a baking
sheet or in a roasting tin and bake in
the oven for 20 minutes. Remove
from the foil and transfer to warmed
serving plates with the buttery
juices poured over.

●235 calories/1000 kj per portion

MARTIN BRIGDALE

Mushrooms in vine leaves

SERVES 4

8 large flat mushrooms (see Buying guide)
12-18 vine leaves (see Buying guide)
4 tablespoons olive oil
2 teaspoons finely chopped fresh marjoram, or 1 teaspoon dried marjoram
salt and freshly ground black pepper

1 Heat the oven to 180C/350F/Gas 4.
2 Rinse the vine leaves under cold running water, pat dry with absorbent paper, then use half to cover the bottom of an ovenproof dish or roasting tin. Sprinkle 1 tablespoon of the oil over the vine leaves.

3 Leaving the mushrooms whole, lay them on top of the vine leaves, stalk-side up. Sprinkle with the remaining oil and the marjoram, then season to taste with salt and pepper. Cover with the rest of the vine leaves.

4 Cook in the oven for 30-40 minutes.
5 Remove and discard the top layer of vine leaves, then divide the mushrooms and remaining leaves between 4 warmed individual plates. Serve at once.

Cook's Notes

TIME
15 minutes preparation and 40 minutes cooking.

BUYING GUIDE
Choose equal-sized mushrooms so that they cook evenly.
  Vine leaves are available from delicatessens in packets of brine. Any left-over vine leaves can be stored in the refrigerator for a few days.

SERVING IDEAS
These are delicious served as an appetizer with crunchy French bread. They are also good on toast as a simple supper dish.

VARIATION
If you like garlic, crush 2-3 cloves and use instead of the marjoram.

●130 calories/550 kj per portion

PAUL WEBSTER

Tomato and celery cases

SERVES 4

100 g/4 oz tomatoes, skinned,
   deseeded and chopped
2 celery stalks, chopped
65 g/2½ oz margarine or butter
1 small onion, chopped
75 ml/3 fl oz vegetable stock
¼ teaspoon dried thyme
salt and freshly ground black pepper
4 large slices white bread, crusts
   removed (see Cook's tip)
1 tablespoon finely chopped fresh
   parsley
4 teaspoons soured cream
celery leaves, to garnish

1 Heat the oven to 190C/375F/Gas 5.
2 Melt 15 g/½ oz margarine in a pan, add the onion and celery and cook gently for 5 minutes until the onion is soft and lightly coloured.
3 Add the tomatoes, stock, thyme and salt and pepper to taste. Bring to the boil, stirring, then lower the heat slightly. Cover and simmer for 30 minutes, stirring occasionally.

4 Meanwhile, melt the remaining margarine in a separate small pan. Cut each slice of bread into a 10 cm/4 inch square. Brush both sides with the melted margarine.
5 Press each slice of bread into an individual Yorkshire pudding tin (see Preparation).
6 Bake in the oven for 15-20 minutes until golden brown and crisp. Transfer the cooked cases to a serving platter and keep warm.
7 Stir the chopped parsley into the filling in the pan, taste and adjust the seasoning, then spoon into the cases. Top each case with a spoonful of soured cream, garnish with celery leaves and serve at once.

Cook's Notes

 TIME
Allow 1 hour to make these tomato and celery cases from start to finish.

 SERVING IDEAS
Serve these attractive cases as an unusual starter, as a side dish, or on their own for a light lunch or supper. The soured cream may be served separately if preferred.

 COOK'S TIP
It is important to use fresh bread for the cases—if it is a little dry, it will be difficult to press into the tins without cracking.

 PREPARATION
To shape the bread cases in the tins:

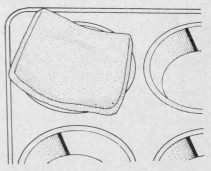

Press a slice of bread into the tin, leaving the corners protruding.

● 195 calories/800 kj per portion

54

Cauliflower in mushroom sauce

SERVES 4

1 cauliflower, broken into florets
salt
15 g/½ oz margarine or butter
175 g/6 oz button mushrooms,
   thinly sliced (see Buying guide)
15 g/½ oz plain flour
300 ml/½ pint single cream
pinch of freshly grated nutmeg
freshly ground black pepper

1 Bring a pan of salted water to the boil, add the cauliflower and bring back to the boil. Lower the heat slightly, cover and simmer for about 7 minutes, until the cauliflower is just tender.
2 Meanwhile, make the sauce: melt the margarine in a saucepan, add the mushrooms and fry gently for 5 minutes until softened. Sprinkle in the flour and stir over low heat for 1-2 minutes. Remove from heat then gradually stir in the cream. Return to heat and simmer, stirring, until the sauce thickens. Stir in the nutmeg and season to taste with salt and pepper.
3 Drain the cauliflower thoroughly in a colander, transfer to a warmed serving dish and pour the sauce over the top. Serve at once.

Cook's Notes

 TIME
This luxurious-tasting dish only takes 20 minutes to prepare and cook.

 BUYING GUIDE
Be sure to buy very small fresh white button mushrooms; darker ones would spoil the delicate colour of the sauce.

 ECONOMY
Replace half or all of the cream with the top of the milk.

 WATCHPOINT
Do not allow the cauliflower to become too soft; the stems should still feel slightly firm when tested with the point of a sharp knife.

SERVING IDEAS
Serve as a first course, arranged on individual plates and garnished with triangles of toast, spread with parsley butter. Alternatively, serve as a vegetable accompaniment.

●365 calories/1530 kj per portion

ROGER PHILLIPS

Baked tomatoes with avocado

SERVES 4

4 large tomatoes, each weighing
about 250 g/9 oz (see Buying
guide)
1 avocado
1 tablespoon lemon juice
1 teaspoon finely chopped fresh
basil
salt and freshly ground black pepper
250 g/9 oz Cheddar cheese,
grated
vegetable oil, for greasing
basil sprigs, to garnish

1 Heat the oven to 190C/375F/Gas 5 and grease an ovenproof dish.
2 Cut the tomatoes in half horizontally, then scoop out and reserve the flesh, taking care not to pierce the skins (see Cook's tip). Place the tomato cases in the prepared dish.
3 Cut the avocado in half lengthways, twist the 2 halves apart and prise out the stone. Grip the skin at the pointed end, then peel back to remove. Cut flesh into 1 cm/½ inch cubes and place in a large bowl.
4 Sprinkle the lemon juice over the avocado and then add the reserved tomato flesh and chopped basil. Season the avocado mixture to taste with salt and pepper, then carefully stir in half the grated cheese.
5 Divide the avocado mixture between tomato cases, piling it up neatly. Sprinkle over rest of cheese.
6 Bake in the oven for 15 minutes until heated through and beginning to bubble on the top. Garnish with basil sprigs and serve at once.

Cook's Notes

TIME
15 minutes preparation, 15 minutes cooking.

COOK'S TIP
Scoop out the flesh of the tomatoes with a grapefruit knife or a sharp-edged teaspoon.

SERVING IDEAS
Serve as an unusual starter on 4 individual plates lined with lettuce leaves. Alternatively, serve as a light snack or supper dish with hot garlic bread.

BUYING GUIDE
Buy large continental or 'beefsteak' tomatoes for this dish and select the ones which have flat bases so that they will stand upright.

●385 calories/1600 kj per portion

MICHAEL KAY

Aubergine and tomato bake

SERVES 6
2 large aubergines, cut into 1 cm/½
    inch slices
salt
2 tablespoons vegetable oil
1 onion, chopped
1-2 cloves garlic, crushed (optional)
625 g/22 oz can tomatoes, drained
    and roughly chopped
1 tablespoon tomato purée
freshly ground black pepper
1 teaspoon dried marjoram

TO GARNISH
2 tomatoes, sliced
chopped fresh parsley

1 Bring a large pan of salted water to the boil and add the aubergines (see Cook's tips). Simmer for 5 minutes then drain well in a colander.

2 Heat the oven to 180C/350F/Gas 4.
3 Heat the oil in a large frying-pan, add the onion and garlic, if using, and fry gently for 5 minutes until the onion is soft and lightly coloured.
4 Gently stir in the aubergines, tomatoes and tomato purée and cook over moderate heat for 2-3 minutes, stirring gently and occasionally. Season with salt and pepper to taste and stir in the marjoram.
5 Transfer to an ovenproof serving dish, cover and bake in the oven for 30 minutes.
6 Arrange the tomato slices across the top of the dish and sprinkle with parsley. Serve at once

Cook's Notes

 TIME
Preparation 15 minutes, cooking 30 minutes.

 COOK'S TIPS
Normally aubergines need to be salted and drained before cooking to remove the bitter juices. The simmering method used here means that this stage can be omitted. It also cuts down on the frying time needed which reduces the calorie content.

 SERVING IDEAS
Serve this easy vegetable bake as a light starter, accompanied with soured cream.

FREEZING
To freeze: cool at stage 5 and transfer to a rigid container. Seal, label and freeze. Store for up to 6 months. To serve: reheat from frozen at 180C/350F/Gas 4 for 1 hour.

●75 calories/325 kj per portion

Asparagus and tomato layer

SERVES 4
750 g/1½ lb asparagus spears (see Buying guide)
salt
500 g/1 lb tomatoes, skinned and sliced
1 tablespoon chopped fresh basil or parsley
freshly ground black pepper
40 g/1½ oz butter
50 g/2 oz Cheddar cheese, grated

1 Heat the oven to 190C/375F/Gas 5.
2 Wash the asparagus stalks well in cold water, then trim the base of each spear, leaving about 2 cm/¾ inch of harder white stem.

3 Put the asparagus in a pan large enough to hold them lying flat. Pour over enough boiling water just to cover the asparagus and add a good pinch of salt. Cover the pan and simmer very gently for 10 minutes until half cooked.
4 Lift out the asparagus very carefully with a fish slice and drain on absorbent paper.
5 Put half the asparagus in a shallow flameproof serving dish. Arrange half the sliced tomatoes over the asparagus, then sprinkle with half the basil and salt and pepper to taste. Dot with the butter. Layer the remaining asparagus and tomatoes on top and sprinkle with the remaining basil. Season to taste with salt and pepper.
6 Sprinkle the cheese over the top and cook in the oven for 30 minutes.

Cook's Notes

TIME
30 minutes preparation, 30 minutes cooking.

BUYING GUIDE
Frozen asparagus may be used if fresh is unavailable – defrost first.

SERVING IDEAS
This dish makes a luxurious starter or a rather special light lunch dish. Brown bread rolls are the only accompaniment needed.

●170 calories/700 kj per portion

Baked avocados

SERVES 4
2 avocados (see Buying guide)
50 g/2 oz cream cheese
25 g/1 oz shelled walnuts,
  roughly chopped
salt and freshly ground black pepper
walnut halves, shredded lettuce
  and chopped parsley, to garnish

1 Heat the oven to 190C/375F/Gas 5.
2 In a bowl, mix cream cheese and walnuts thoroughly. Season to taste with salt and pepper.
3 Cut the avocados in half [!] and remove the stones. Fill each cavity with the cream cheese mixture, then press the avocado halves together and wrap each one in foil. Bake in the oven for 30 minutes.
4 Unwrap the avocados, separate the halves and serve at once on beds of lettuce, garnished with the walnut halves and chopped parsley (see Serving ideas).

Cook's Notes

 TIME
Preparation takes about 10 minutes; cooking time is 30 minutes.

 SERVING IDEAS
Serve with hot garlic bread as a dinner party starter or as a light lunch or supper dish.

 BUYING GUIDE
The avocados should not be too ripe as they soften during cooking.

 VARIATIONS
1 tablespoon chopped chives or mint makes a delicious and colourful addition to the cream cheese filling.

[!] WATCHPOINT
Do not cut the avocados until just before filling and sealing, otherwise they will quickly discolour.

●330 calories/1375 kj per portion

MARTIN BRIGDALE

French beans Riviera

SERVES 4
500 g/1 lb whole French beans
salt
2 tablespoons tomato purée
1 tablespoon lemon juice
15 g/½ oz butter
50 g/2 oz pine nuts
freshly ground black pepper

1 Bring a pan of salted water to the boil and cook the beans for about 7 minutes or until just tender. ⚠ Drain thoroughly and return to pan.
2 Add the tomato purée, lemon juice, butter and pine nuts and toss over gentle heat for about 3 minutes.
3 Season with pepper, transfer to a warmed dish.

Cook's Notes

TIME
Preparation 5 minutes, cooking 10 minutes.

VARIATIONS
Omit the pine nuts and sprinkle with a few toasted breadcrumbs instead. Add a clove of crushed garlic with the lemon juice.

SERVING IDEAS
Serve cold as a starter or salad, or serve hot with rice or noodles.

WATCHPOINT
Do not overcook the beans: they should still retain a certain crispness.

DID YOU KNOW
Pine nuts, which are featured often in Mediterranean cookery, come from the seeds of the pine cone. Creamy white in colour and soft in texture, they have a distinctive taste that is very different from any other nut. They are sold ready-shelled from health food shops and good supermarkets.

●110 calories/450 kj per portion

PETER MYERS

Jerusalem artichoke fritters

SERVES 4
500 g/1 lb Jerusalem artichokes
salt
1 tablespoon lemon juice
vegetable oil, for deep-frying

BATTER
100 g/4 oz plain flour
½ teaspoon salt
1 large egg, separated
150 ml/¼ pint milk and water
    mixed (half and half)
1 tablespoon corn oil
1 teaspoon dried sage

1 Cook the Jerusalem artichokes for 25-30 minutes in boiling salted water until just tender.
2 Meanwhile, make the batter: sift the flour into a large bowl with the salt. Make a well in the centre. Beat the egg yolk into the milk and water mixture and pour it into the bowl, gradually drawing the flour into the liquid with a wooden spoon. When all the liquid is incorporated, beat well to make a smooth batter and stir in the corn oil and sage. Just before using, beat the egg white until stiff but not dry, then fold into the batter. [!]
3 When the artichokes are cooked, remove the skins and cut them into 1 cm/½ inch slices then drop the slices as you prepare them into cold water to which you have added the lemon juice. Drain the slices well on absorbent paper, then stir them carefully into the batter mixture, making sure that the slices do not break up and are thoroughly coated with batter.
4 In a deep-fat frier, heat oil to cover the artichoke slices, to a temperature of 190C/375F, or until a bread cube dropped into the hot oil will brown in 50 seconds.
5 Using a pair of kitchen tongs or a slotted spoon, remove the artichoke slices from the batter and drop them in batches into the hot oil. Deep-fry until the fritters are puffy and golden brown. Drain on absorbent paper and keep hot in a warmed serving dish while frying the remainder. Serve as soon as all the fritters are cooked.

PAUL WILLIAMS

Cook's Notes

TIME
Boiling the artichokes and preparing the batter takes 25-30 minutes. Peeling and slicing the cooked artichokes takes about 15 minutes: peeling can be fiddly but is easier once they are cooked. Frying takes 5-10 minutes.

●295 calories/1225 kj per portion

COOK'S TIP
Immerse the Jerusalem artichokes in water and lemon juice to prevent them discolouring.

[!] WATCHPOINT
Adding beaten egg white to batter makes it light and puffy. Use at once or the batter will flop.

61

Mushroom herb fritters

SERVES 4

250 g/9 oz mushrooms, about
   4-5 cm/1½-2 inches across
vegetable oil, for deep frying
chopped fresh parsley, to garnish

BATTER

100 g/4 oz plain flour
¼ teaspoon salt
freshly ground black pepper
1 tablespoon vegetable oil
150 ml/¼ pint cold water
½ teaspoon finely chopped fresh
   mint or ¼ teaspoon dried mint
1 teaspoon finely chopped fresh
   sage or ½ teaspoon dried sage
1 teaspoon finely chopped fresh
   thyme or ½ teaspoon dried thyme
1 egg white

1 Trim the mushroom stalks so that they are all of equal length.

2 To make the batter: sift the flour and salt into a bowl with a little pepper.

3 Make a well in the centre and pour in the oil and cold water. Using a wire whisk, gradually draw the flour into the liquid. When all the flour is incorporated, beat the mixture well to make a smooth batter and stir in the herbs.

4 In a deep pan heat the vegetable oil to 180C/350F or until a day-old 2.5 cm/1 inch bread cube browns in 60 seconds.

5 Meanwhile, when the oil is almost hot enough, whisk the egg white in a clean, dry bowl, until it forms stiff peaks. Fold into the batter with a metal tablespoon.

6 Divide the mushrooms into 3 batches. Using a slotted spoon, dip one batch into the batter to coat thoroughly. Lift out the mushrooms one by one, allowing excess batter to drip back into the bowl. Drop the coated mushrooms into the hot fat. Fry for about 5 minutes, turning the fritters once, until golden.

7 Remove with a slotted spoon and drain on absorbent paper. Keep warm while frying the remaining batches (see Cook's tip).

8 Place on a warmed serving platter, sprinkle with parsley and serve at once.

Cook's Notes

TIME
Preparation and cooking take 45 minutes.

COOK'S TIP
You will have to adjust the heat during cooking, to ensure that the oil stays at a constant temperature.

SERVING IDEAS
Arrange the fritters on individual plates and serve as a starter with tartare sauce, or serve as a hot snack.

●250 calories/1050 kj per portion

PETER MYERS

Cheesy cauliflower florets

SERVES 4
1 firm cauliflower
salt
vegetable oil, for deep frying

BATTER
50 g/2 oz plain flour
¼ teaspoon mustard powder
freshly ground black pepper
50 g/2 oz Parmesan cheese, grated
1 egg, separated
1 tablespoon vegetable oil
4 tablespoons water

1 Break the cauliflower into florets, about 4 cm/1½ inches at the widest point. Discard the thick main stem.
2 Bring a large saucepan of salted water to the boil, add cauliflower florets and bring back to the boil.

Lower the heat slightly, cover and simmer for about 5 minutes until the cauliflower is just tender.
3 Drain the cauliflower thoroughly in a colander and leave to cool.
4 Meanwhile, make the batter: sift the flour into a large bowl with the mustard, a pinch of salt and a sprinkling of pepper. Stir in the Parmesan. Make a well in centre. Beat the egg yolk with the oil and the water and pour into the well, gradually drawing the flour into the liquid with a wooden spoon. Beat well to form a coating batter.
5 Heat the oven to 110C/225F/Gas ¼.
6 Heat the oil in a deep-fat frier to 200C/400F or until a stale bread cube browns in 40 seconds.
7 In a clean dry bowl, whisk the egg white until standing in stiff peaks, then fold into the batter with a metal spoon.
8 Using a slotted spoon, dip a batch of cauliflower florets into the batter to coat well, then fry in

the oil for about 4 minutes, until golden brown. Remove with a slotted spoon and drain on absorbent paper. Keep warm in the oven while frying the remainder.
9 Serve at once, while still hot.

Celery in beer batter

SERVES 6-8
1 head celery
vegetable oil, for deep frying

BATTER
175 g/6 oz plain flour
¼ teaspoon salt
freshly ground black pepper
300 ml/½ pint beer (see Buying guide)

1 Cut off root ends of the celery and trim tops, reserving leaves for garnishing, if liked. Wash the celery stalks and remove any stringy bits. Cut into 2.5 cm/1 inch pieces.
2 Heat oven to 130C/250F/Gas ½. Heat the oil in a deep-fat frier to 190C/375F or until a cube of stale bread turns golden in 50 seconds.

3 Meanwhile, make the batter: sift the flour, salt and a generous sprinkling of pepper into a bowl. Make a well in the centre. Pour the beer into the well, gradually drawing the flour into the liquid with a wooden spoon to make a smooth thin batter.
4 Coat a few of the celery pieces in the batter, then transfer with a

slotted spoon to the hot oil and deep fry for 5 minutes until crisp and golden brown. Remove from pan and drain on absorbent paper. Transfer to a warmed serving dish and keep hot in the oven while frying the remaining celery pieces in the same way.
5 Garnish with the reserved celery leaves, if liked, and serve at once.

THEO BERGSTROM

Cheesy potato fritters

MAKES 20-24

1 kg/2 lb potatoes, grated (see Preparation)
100 g/4 oz full-fat soft cheese, flavoured with garlic and herbs
2 eggs
salt and freshly ground black pepper
vegetable oil, for frying
1 tablespoon snipped chives, to garnish (optional)

1 Heat the oven to 110C/225F/Gas ¼.
2 Put the cheese into a bowl and beat with a wooden spoon until soft. Beat in the eggs, then mix in the potatoes and season the fritter mixture with salt and freshly ground black pepper to taste.

3 Pour enough oil into a deep frying-pan to cover the base to a depth of 2.5 cm/1 inch. Heat the oil over moderate heat until sizzling hot, then fry the potato mixture in batches. Drop tablespoons of the mixture into the oil, spacing them well apart. Fry for about 3 minutes on each side until golden brown.
4 Remove from the pan with a slotted spoon, drain on absorbent paper, then transfer to a serving dish. Keep hot in the oven while frying the remaining mixture in the same way. Serve hot, garnished with the snipped chives, if liked.

Cook's Notes

 TIME
30 minutes preparation, about 20 minutes cooking time.

 SERVING IDEAS
Serve these cheesy potato fritters as a substantial starter or as a meal on their own with home-made tomato sauce. They may also be served as a vegetable accompaniment.

 PREPARATION
Grate the potatoes either by hand or in a food processor. To remove the excess liquid, drain them in a colander, preferably lined with a tea-towel. Gather the tea-towel up and squeeze out as much liquid from the potatoes as possible.

●70 calories/300 kj per fritter

CHRIS KNAGGS

Hot beetroot mousse

SERVES 4

750 g/1½ lb cooked beetroot, peeled
   and roughly chopped
1 vegetable stock cube, dissolved in
   125 ml/4 fl oz boiling water
50 g/2 oz margarine or butter
1 large onion, very finely chopped
50 g/2 oz plain flour
6 eggs, lightly beaten
good pinch of freshly grated
   nutmeg
salt and freshly ground black pepper
melted margarine, for greasing
watercress, to garnish

SAUCE

2 tablespoons snipped chives or
   spring onion tops
150 ml/¼ pint soured cream

1 Heat the oven to 190C/375F/Gas 5.
Brush a 1.1 L/2 pint ring mould
very generously with some melted
margarine.
2 Put the beetroot in a blender with
the stock and blend until thick and
smooth.
3 Melt the margarine in a saucepan,
add the onion and cook over
moderate heat for 5 minutes until
soft and lightly coloured. Sprinkle
in the flour and stir over low heat for
2 minutes. Gradually stir in the
beetroot mixture, then bring to the
boil and cook for 2 minutes, stirring
constantly.
4 Allow the mixture to cool slightly,
then add the beaten eggs, nutmeg
and salt and pepper to taste and mix
well. Pour the mixture into the
mould, stand it in a roasting tin and
pour in enough boiling water to
come two-thirds of the way up the
mould.
5 Bake in the oven for about 50
minutes, until a knife point inserted
in the mould comes out clean.
Meanwhile, stir the snipped chives
into the soured cream and season
with salt.
6 Remove the cooked mousse from
the water and leave to stand for 15
minutes (see Cook's tip). Very carefully, run a round-bladed knife
between the mousse and the sides of
the mould, then turn the mousse on
to a heated serving plate. Decorate
the top with sprigs of watercress
and serve at once, with the soured
cream sauce.

Cook's Notes

 TIME
35 minutes preparation,
about 50 minutes bak-
ing, then about 15 minutes
standing time.

 COOK'S TIP
The mousse is left to
stand after baking so
that the mixture 'settles' and
becomes slightly firmer. Do not
omit this standing time, or the
mousse may break.

 SERVING IDEAS
If wished, halve the
quantities of this recipe
and bake the mixture in four 150
ml/¼ pint ramekin dishes, to
serve individual portions of this
unusual and attractive starter.

●430 calories/1805 kj per portion

PETER MYERS

Stilton eggs

SERVES 4
100 g/4 oz Stilton cheese, rind
 removed
150 ml/¼ pint double cream
freshly ground black pepper
4 eggs
fresh tarragon leaves, to garnish
 (optional)

1 Heat the oven to 200C/400F/Gas 6.
2 Crumble the cheese into a bowl,
add the cream and beat until
smooth. Season the mixture to taste

with freshly ground black pepper.
3 Divide mixture between 4
individual ramekin dishes. Break
an egg into each. Place on a baking
sheet and bake eggs in the oven for

15-20 minutes until the mixture is
bubbling and eggs are just set.
4 Garnish with 2-3 tarragon leaves,
if using, and serve at once while still
piping hot (see Serving ideas).

Cook's Notes

TIME
Preparation and cook-
ing take 30 minutes.

VARIATION
Instead of cooking in
dishes, remove some
of flesh from jacket-baked potatoes, spoon the mixture into
them and bake as above.

SERVING IDEAS
Served with slices of
Melba toast, these eggs
make a delicious dinner party
starter. Alternatively, serve
them with bread and butter and
glasses of port as an unusual
light supper dish.

●360 calories/1500 kj per portion

67

Crunchy potato skins

SERVES 4

4 large potatoes, scrubbed
225 ml/8 fl oz soured cream
1 tablespoon snipped chives
salt and freshly ground black pepper
vegetable oil, for deep frying

1 Heat the oven to 200C/400F/Gas 6. Prick the potatoes all over with a fork, then bake in the oven for 1-1½ hours or until tender.

2 Meanwhile, mix the soured cream and chives together with salt and pepper to taste. Spoon into a serving bowl and refrigerate.

3 When the potatoes are tender, remove them from the oven and leave to cool slightly. Cut each one in half lengthways, scoop out the cooked potato and discard (see Economy). Cut skins in half again.

4 Heat the oil in a deep-fat frier with a basket to 190C/375F or until a day-old bread cube will brown in 50 seconds. Place the potato skins in the basket. Lower the basket into the oil and deep-fry for 2-3 minutes until they are brown and crispy.

5 Take the basket out of the oil, shake it, then lift the cooked potato skins on to absorbent paper. Drain, then put on to a serving plate.

6 Sprinkle with plenty of salt and serve at once, with the dip.

Cook's Notes

TIME
Preparation and cooking take about 2 hours.

SERVING IDEAS
These crispy cooked potato skins are an American idea – serve them before a main course of a vegetable pie and salad, or serve them as a snack on their own or with drinks.

ECONOMY
Mash all the left-over cooked potato flesh with plenty of butter and use as a topping for pies.

● 330 calories/1375 kj per portion

PAUL WEBSTER

Carrot and watercress castles

SERVES 4
500 g/1 lb carrots, sliced
1 bunch watercress
salt
175 g/6 oz potatoes, cut into large
   chunks
2 eggs, beaten
freshly grated nutmeg
freshly ground black pepper
margarine, for greasing
carrot curls, to garnish (see
   Preparation)

1 Heat the oven to 180C/350F/Gas 4 and then grease four 150 ml/¼ pint dariole moulds (see Cook's tip).
2 Bring a pan of salted water to the boil, add the carrots and potatoes and cook them for about 20 minutes until they are soft.
3 Meanwhile, chop the watercress finely, reserving a few sprigs for decoration.
4 Drain the carrots and potatoes, return to the pan and set over low heat for 1-2 minutes to dry off any excess moisture from vegetables.
5 Allow the vegetables to cool slightly, then purée in a blender or a food processor until smooth. Transfer purée to a bowl and add the watercress and eggs. Season to taste with freshly grated nutmeg, salt and freshly ground pepper, then stir to mix well.
6 Divide the carrot purée between the moulds and place them in a baking dish. Pour in enough boiling water to come halfway up the sides of the moulds, then bake castles in the oven for 30 minutes or until they are firm.
7 Run a round-bladed knife around the edge of each mould and turn out carefully. Garnish with the reserved watercress and carrot curls.

Cook's Notes

 TIME
These attractive moulds take 40 minutes to make and bake in total.

 COOK'S TIP
If dariole moulds are unavailable use tall cream caramel moulds or improvise with ovenproof china tea cups or ramekin dishes that hold at least 150 ml/¼ pint.

 VARIATION
As an alternative to watercress, chopped fresh tarragon combines well with carrot.

 PREPARATION
To make carrot curls for the garnish:

Using a potato peeler, pare strips off a carrot, then roll up and spear with cocktail sticks. Leave in iced water for 1 hour, then remove the sticks before use.

●105 calories/450 kj per castle

SNACKS

A vegetarian snack can be anything from a plate of bread and cheese or some sandwiches, to a hot savoury egg or vegetable dish. Above all, snacks should be simple to make, satisfying and nutritious – everything a hungry family needs to keep them going until the next main meal.

Most people manage on just one main meal a day with breakfast and a lighter meal making up the day's food. The 'snack' meal may be a quick bite in the middle of the day or something light and easily digested for supper in the evening. A good snack should also be versatile, to be eaten on the move, round the fire on a cold evening, or even to eat in the garden.

The supermarkets and shops are full of oven-ready snack meals to tempt us, but it is more economical, and far healthier, to prepare your own at home. It doesn't take long to prepare and cook any of the recipes in this chapter, and many of them can be cooked in advance and stored in the refrigerator ready to be served cold the moment they are required. Others can be prepared early in the day and simply cooked just before serving hot.

Meat eaters rely on meat as a valuable source of protein so, without it, vegetarians need to watch that their diet contains all that they need. It is likely that most of the day's protein will be provided by the main meal, but there are many high-protein foods that also make good snacks. Eggs and cheese have long been traditional alternatives for non-meat eaters, but it is worth remembering the high fat and cholesterol content of hard cheeses and eggs. Stick to low-fat hard cheeses, such as Edam, or cottage cheese, and restrict the number of eggs you eat.

Salads are an obvious choice for a snack as they can be prepared quickly from fresh ingredients and involve no cooking. On their own, though, salad ingredients contain no protein, so they are best served with some protein food. Add cheese or eggs, as in Lettuce with Cheese Sauce or Tangy Egg Salad, or nuts, grains or beans. Serve salads simply with bread and butter for a quick snack.

Freshly cooked vegetables also make a nutritious snack that can be ready very quickly. Again, most vegetables on their own do not provide protein, and even pulses need to be served with dairy produce, nuts, seeds or wholemeal bread to form balanced meals. However, vegetables can be the basis of many quick and easy snacks, and you will find some quite unusual and interesting new ways to cook them in the following recipes.

You will also find lots of old favourites in this chapter, including stuffed baked potatoes and pancakes, but with new ideas for fillings that will keep the family snacks interesting as well as satisfying and nutritious. You will no longer need to rely on convenience foods when it comes to preparing a quick snack for the family to enjoy.

Individual watercress pies

MAKES 4

RICH SHORTCRUST PASTRY
175 g/6 oz plain flour
pinch of salt
100 g/4 oz margarine
2 tablespoons chilled water
green food colouring
beaten egg or milk, to glaze

FILLING
2 bunches watercress, finely
  chopped
2 eggs, beaten
2 tablespoons melted butter
freshly grated nutmeg
salt and freshly ground black pepper

1 Heat the oven to 190C/375F/Gas 5.
2 Make the pastry: sift flour and salt into a bowl. Add margarine and rub into flour until mixture feels like fine breadcrumbs. Mix in just enough chilled water to draw the mixture together into a firm dough.
3 Divide pastry into 9 equal pieces. With lightly floured hands, roll 8 pieces into balls. On a lightly floured surface, roll into circles 12 cm/4½ inches in diameter.

Cook's Notes

 TIME
Preparation 25 minutes, cooking 35-40 minutes.

 SERVING IDEAS
Serve warm with a salad or cold for picnics.

 VARIATIONS
Add 25 g/1 oz finely grated cheese to filling. For a less substantial dish, use half the pastry and omit lids.

 WATCHPOINT
Work quickly at this stage as heat of filling will start to soften pastry.

 PREPARATION
To colour the decorative leaves:

Using a watercolour paintbrush, paint a little green food colouring on to the pastry leaves.

● 430 calories/1800 kj per pie

---

4 Line four individual Yorkshire pudding tins with rounds of pastry.
5 Mix filling ingredients in a bowl and season well with nutmeg, salt and freshly ground black pepper.
6 Spoon mixture into the pastry cases and bake, uncovered, for 15 minutes or until the pastry filling has completely set.
7 Remove from the oven, dampen edges of 4 remaining pastry rounds with water and place on top of the filling. Press edges together; seal with the prongs of a floured fork.
8 Roll out remaining pastry and use for leaves. Dampen undersides with water and press on top of pies. Make a small hole in centre of each pie, then colour the leaves (see Preparation) and brush rest of the pastry with beaten egg.
9 Return pies to oven and bake a further 20 minutes, or until pastry is cooked through and golden.
10 Cool for a few minutes, then transfer to a wire rack and serve.

Mushroom and cheese pirozhki

MAKES 24
25 g/1 oz butter
100 g/4 oz mushrooms, finely chopped
1 spring onion, finely chopped
75 g/3 oz full-fat soft cheese with herbs and garlic
½ teaspoon dillweed
salt and freshly ground black pepper
350 g/12 oz frozen shortcrust pastry, defrosted
1 egg yolk, lightly beaten, to glaze
vegetable oil, for greasing
parsley sprigs, to garnish (optional)

1 Heat the oven to 180C/350F/Gas 4 and grease a baking sheet with oil.
2 Melt the butter in a frying-pan and gently fry the mushrooms and spring onion for 3 minutes. Remove from heat and cool.
3 In a clean, dry bowl, mash the soft cheese with the dillweed. Stir in the mushrooms and spring onion, season to taste with salt and pepper, then refrigerate.
4 Meanwhile, roll out the pastry on a lightly floured work surface to a 5 mm/¼ inch thickness. Using a round pastry cutter or the rim of a glass, cut out circles approximately 7 cm/3½ inches in diameter.
5 Place 1 teaspoonful of the mushroom and cheese mixture on one half of each circle, taking care not to overfill the pastry circles or they will be very difficult to seal. Fold into a crescent shape and seal edges with water (see Preparation). Continue until all used.
6 Place crescents on prepared baking sheet and then brush each one with a little egg yolk to glaze. Bake in the oven for 30-40 minutes until the pastry is cooked and golden in colour. Transfer the mushroom and cheese pirozhkis to a warmed serving plate, garnish with the parsley sprigs, if using, and serve at once.

ALAN DUNS

Cook's Notes

TIME
Preparation takes about 35 minutes and cooking takes 30-40 minutes.

SERVING IDEAS
These pastries make a good lunch-time snack – serve with soup.

DID YOU KNOW
The name *pirozhki* is Russian for little pies that are small enough to be eaten out of the hand. They are the traditional accompaniment to borshch (beetroot soup).

PREPARATION
To make the pastry crescents:

Fold one half of pastry circle over half topped with mixture and press firmly along edges to seal.

●90 calories/375 kj per pie

Cheese crescents

MAKES 8

75 g/3 oz Leicester cheese, finely grated
400 g/13 oz frozen puff pastry, defrosted
15 g/½ oz butter, melted
1 teaspoon celery salt
1 teaspoon mustard powder
freshly ground black pepper
1 egg, beaten, to glaze

1 Roll out the pastry on a floured surface to a 40 × 20 cm/16 × 8 inch rectangle. Brush with melted butter and sprinkle over the celery salt, mustard powder and a little freshly ground black pepper.
2 Sprinkle two-thirds of the rectangle with 50 g/2 oz of the cheese. Fold the plain one-third of pastry over the cheese and then fold over again (see Preparation). Seal the edges by pressing down firmly with a rolling pin.
3 Roll out to a 30 cm/12 inch square and cut into four 15 cm/6 inch squares. Cut each one in half diagonally to give 8 triangles. Shape into crescents (see Preparation), then refrigerate for 15 minutes.
4 Heat the oven to 220C/425F/Gas 7.
5 Place crescents on a dampened baking sheet. Brush with the beaten egg and sprinkle a little of the remaining grated cheese over each.
6 Bake in the oven for 15-20 minutes until golden brown and well risen. Serve warm or cold.

JAMES JACKSON

Cook's Notes

TIME
These crescents are very easy to make, and they only take 10-15 minutes to prepare. Allow 15 minutes to chill the pastry, then baking time is 15-20 minutes.

SERVING IDEAS
These crescents can be served warm, or left to cool on a wire rack and eaten cold. Serve without butter as a snack or with cheese and celery for a light supper.

PREPARATION
To make and shape the cheese crescents:

1 *Fold the plain section of the pastry over the cheese, then fold over again. Seal edges by pressing down firmly with a rolling pin.*

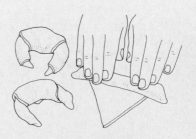

2 *Roll up the pastry triangles from the widest part, finishing with the tip underneath. Gently curve the ends to form a crescent shape.*

● 275 calories/1150 kj per crescent

ROGER TUFF

Cheese puffs

SERVES 4

75 g/3 oz Parmesan cheese, finely grated
1 whole egg
2 egg yolks
50 g/2 oz butter, melted
½ teaspoon mustard powder
good pinch of cayenne
salt
215 g/7½ oz frozen puff pastry, defrosted
1 egg white
extra grated Parmesan cheese, for sprinkling
300 ml/½ pint cheese sauce, to serve (see Cook's tips)

1 Heat the oven to 230C/450F/Gas 8.
2 Put the whole egg and egg yolks into a bowl. Beat together, then gradually blend in the melted butter and grated cheese. Add mustard and cayenne and season to taste with salt.
3 On a lightly floured surface roll out half the pastry to a 30 × 15 cm/ 12 × 6 inch rectangle. Spread the cheese mixture over the pastry leaving a 1 cm/½ inch border all around the rectangle.
4 Roll out the other half of the pastry to the same size and place it on top, pressing it down firmly and rolling it lightly to level the pastry.
5 Using a 6 cm/2½ inch round fluted (see Cook's tips) pastry cutter cut out 8 circles (see Cook's tips). Beat the egg white in a bowl and brush it over the top of the circles. Sprinkle over a little Parmesan cheese. Prick the tops.
6 Dampen a baking tray, place the rounds on it and bake in the oven for 15 minutes or until puffed up.
7 Meanwhile, make cheese sauce according to packet instructions. Serve the puffs with the cheese sauce handed separately.

Cook's Notes

TIME
Preparation takes 20 minutes and cooking the puffs in the oven takes about 15 minutes.

SERVING IDEAS
Serve these puffs with baked or grilled tomatoes and a green vegetable such as peas or beans.

COOK'S TIPS
A packet of cheese sauce mix is ideal.
Using a fluted pastry cutter will help to keep the pastry edges sealed and prevent the cheese mixture escaping.
Cut up trimmings and bake 5-10 minutes to make nibbles.

●325 calories/1375 kj per portion

Mixed vegetables à la grecque

SERVES 4

250 g/9 oz small button onions
350 g/12 oz frozen green beans,
  defrosted
175 g/6 oz button mushrooms,
  thickly sliced
salt
2 tablespoons chopped fresh
  parsley

SAUCE

6 tablespoons dry white wine or
  dry cider
4 tablespoons olive oil
4 tablespoons tomato purée
1 onion, thinly sliced
1 clove garlic, finely chopped
  (optional)
1 teaspoon mustard seed, or mixed
  pickling spice
freshly ground black pepper

PAUL WEBSTER

1 Bring a large pan of salted water to the boil and blanch the small onions for 3 minutes. Drain the onions thoroughly.

2 Make the sauce: put the wine, oil, tomato purée, sliced onion, garlic, if using, and mustard seed into a small pan. Stir well and bring to the boil, then lower the heat, cover the pan and simmer over very low heat for 25 minutes, stirring the sauce once or twice. Season the sauce to taste with salt and freshly ground black pepper.

3 Add the whole onions, beans and sliced mushrooms to the sauce and return to the boil. Cover the pan and simmer for 20 minutes. Taste and adjust seasoning, if necessary.

4 Remove from the heat and leave to cool, then transfer to a covered container. Stir in most of parsley and refrigerate for 30 minutes.

5 To serve: sprinkle with remaining parsley to garnish and serve for lunch or supper with wholewheat rolls to soak up the sauce. Or serve the mixed vegetables as a dinner party starter.

Cook's Notes

TIME
Preparing and cooking take about 1 hour. Allow time for cooling and chilling.

DID YOU KNOW
Vegetables cooked *à la grecque* are popular in France as well as their native Greece. For the authentic Greek flavour, use flat-leaved parsley.

VARIATIONS
Almost any vegetable can be cooked in this way, either singly or in any seasonal mixture. Blanch root vegetables and greens as the button onions. Add sliced courgettes or firm tomatoes to the sauce without precooking.

●180 calories/750 kj per portion

Blue cheese grapefruit

SERVES 4
2 large grapefruits
100 g/4 oz Mycella cheese (see Buying guide)
8 radishes, thinly sliced
salt and freshly ground black pepper
2 tablespoons clear honey
1 teaspoon made English mustard
watercress, to garnish

1 Halve the grapefruits and cut out the flesh with a curved grapefruit knife. Alternatively, run a small sharp knife between the flesh and rind, then remove all the flesh. Reserve the skins.

2 Holding the grapefruit over a large bowl to catch juices, separate into segments and discard all pith, membranes and pips.

3 Crumble the cheese into the bowl with the grapefruit and add the radishes. Season to taste.

4 Add the honey and mustard to the bowl and blend together.

5 Divide the mixture between the four reserved grapefruit skins. Garnish with watercress and serve at once (see Serving ideas).

Cook's Notes

 TIME
Preparation takes about 20 minutes.

 BUYING GUIDE
Mycella is a Danish blue cheese with a creamy texture and mild flavour that goes particularly well with the grapefruit. It is readily available in supermarkets. Alternatively, use 100 g/4 oz Stilton, Gorgonzola or Dolcelatte.

 SERVING IDEAS
For a refreshing slimmers' lunch, serve with a chicory or iceberg lettuce salad and crispbreads.

Alternatively, serve the blue cheese grapefruit filling in glass bowls as a first course for 6.

●140 calories/600 kj per portion

ALAN DUNS

Cheesy peas

SERVES 4
175 g/6 oz Cheddar cheese, grated
   (see Buying guide)
100 g/4 oz frozen peas
salt
4 tablespoons natural yoghurt
pinch of mustard powder
freshly ground black pepper
2 brown or white baps, sliced
watercress, to garnish (optional)

1 Bring a pan of salted water to the boil and cook the peas according to packet instructions. Drain the peas thoroughly.
2 Heat the grill to high.

3 In a bowl, mix together the cheese, yoghurt, mustard and peas. Season to taste with salt and freshly ground black pepper.
4 Toast the baps on one side.

Spread the cheese mixture on the untoasted side and grill until the cheese just melts.
5 Serve at once, garnished with watercress sprigs, if liked.

Cook's Notes

 TIME
Preparation and grilling time is 20 minutes.

 VARIATIONS
Substitute small cooked florets of cauliflower or broccoli, arranged around edge of the toast instead of peas.
   Place rings of red pepper on top of the cheese before grilling. Brown or white bread slices can be used instead of baps.

BUYING GUIDE
This dish tastes best if cooked with a mature or 'farmhouse' Cheddar cheese. Lancashire or Red Leicester can also be used successfully.

 WATCHPOINT
The cheese mixture will run if grilled too long – it does not need to be brown.

●265 calories/1100 kj per portion

Creamy mushrooms

MARTIN BRIGDALE

SERVES 4
350 g/12 oz button mushrooms (see Buying guide)
25 g/1 oz margarine or butter
1 onion, finely chopped
salt and freshly ground black pepper
freshly grated nutmeg
150 ml/¼ pint soured cream
½ teaspoon sweet paprika

1 Melt the margarine in a large frying-pan, add the onion and fry gently for 5 minutes until soft and lightly coloured.
2 Add the whole mushrooms, stir well and cook gently for 3 minutes, until they begin to soften
3 Season well with salt and pepper, and add grated nutmeg to taste.
4 Stir in the soured cream (see Cook's tip) and heat through for 1 minute over low heat.
5 Turn the mushroom mixture into a warmed serving dish, sprinkle with paprika and serve at once.

Cook's Notes

 TIME
5 minutes preparation, 10 minutes cooking.

 BUYING GUIDE
Buy small and even-sized mushrooms, since they are kept whole in this dish.

 VARIATION
Substitute snipped chives for the paprika.

 COOK'S TIP
Always stir soured cream before adding it to hot food—this helps to make a smooth sauce.

 SERVING IDEAS
Serve these deliciously creamy mushrooms on toast as a snack. Alternatively, they make an excellent accompaniment to plain boiled white or brown rice or ribbon noodles.

● 145 calories/605 kj per portion

Pulse-filled pittas

SERVES 4
250 g/9 oz split red lentils
40 g/1½ oz margarine or butter
1 onion, finely chopped
100 g/4 oz button mushrooms,
   thinly sliced
2 teaspoons ground cumin
450 ml/16 fl oz vegetable stock
2 tablespoons lemon juice
1 tablespoon finely chopped fresh
   parsley
salt and freshly ground black pepper
4 white or brown pitta breads
4 tomatoes, thinly sliced

1 Melt the margarine in a saucepan.
Add the onion and fry gently for 3-4
minutes until soft but not coloured.
Add the mushrooms and cumin and
fry for a further 2 minutes, stirring.
2 Add the lentils and stock to the
pan and bring to the boil, then turn
down the heat to very low. Cover

and simmer for 20-30 minutes,
stirring occasionally until the lentils
are soft and the liquid has been
absorbed.
3 Heat the grill to high.
4 Add the lemon juice and parsley
and season to taste with salt and
pepper. Keep warm over low heat,
stirring occasionally until the
mixture is really thick.

5 Dampen the pitta breads by
sprinkling them all over with cold
water, then toast them (see Cook's
tip) for 2-3 minutes on each side,
until just crisp. Cut them in half,
horizontally, and ease open with a
round-bladed knife. Divide the
lentil mixture between the pitta
'pockets' and slip a few tomato slices
into each one. Serve at once.

Cook's Notes

 TIME
Total preparation and
cooking time for this
wholefood snack is about 50
minutes.

 SERVING IDEAS
Fold a paper napkin
around each filled pitta,
so that it can be eaten in the
hand.
   Serve with a Greek-style salad
made with shredded lettuce or
white cabbage, sliced tomatoes,
cucumber and a few black
olives. Crumbled or cubed

Greek Feta cheese makes a tasty
topping to this salad; or
Caerphilly can be used as an
alternative if Feta is difficult to
obtain.

 COOK'S TIP
Dampening the pitta
breads keeps them soft
and prevents them becoming
dry and cracked when toasted. If
cut in half, they can be toasted
in an automatic 'pop-up'
toaster.

●495 calories/2075 kj per portion

MICHAEL KAY

Union snack

MAKES 4

4 large round soft rolls
75 g/3 oz margarine or butter, softened
75 g/3 oz Red Leicester cheese, grated
2 tablespoons thick bottled mayonnaise
1 teaspoon snipped chives
2 tomatoes, thinly sliced
salt and freshly ground black pepper
4 small lettuce leaves
50 g/2 oz Danish Blue cheese, thinly sliced
75 g/3 oz Edam cheese, thinly sliced
4 teaspoons sweet pickle

1 Cut 3 horizontal slits in each roll (see Preparation). Spread the layers with margarine.
2 Put the Leicester cheese in a bowl with the mayonnaise and chives. Beat well until thoroughly blended. Sprinkle the tomato slices with salt

Cook's Notes

 TIME
Preparation takes about 25 minutes.

 VARIATIONS
Ring the changes using other cheeses: mild-flavoured Cheddar, Stilton and Double Gloucester, or Caerphilly, Blue Cheshire and Gouda make good combinations for this snack.

 SERVING IDEAS
Wrapped individually in cling film, these cheesy-filled rolls make ideal picnic food.

●500 calories/2100 kj per roll

 PREPARATION
To cut slits in each roll ready for filling:

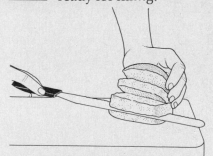

Slice through the roll horizontally, using a sharp knife and a sawing action. Do not cut right through the bread, the roll should be left 'hinged', to hold the filling and make the roll easier to eat.

and plenty of black pepper.
3 Place a lettuce leaf on the bottom layer of each roll and top with the blue cheese slices, dividing them equally between the rolls.
4 Spread the Leicester cheese

mixture on the middle layer of each roll. Arrange the Edam cheese and tomato slices on the final layer, topping the cheese and tomato with a teaspoonful of pickle. Press the top of each roll down lightly.

Nutty savoury scones

MAKES 6
275 g/10 oz self-raising flour
1 teaspoon baking powder
freshly ground black pepper
50 g/2 oz butter, diced
25 g/1 oz salted peanuts, chopped
1 egg, beaten
6-8 tablespoons milk
vegetable oil, for greasing

TOPPING
3 tablespoons smooth peanut butter
50 g/2 oz full-fat soft cheese
50 g/2 oz Danish Blue cheese,
  crumbled
1 tablespoon single cream
salt
mustard and cress, to garnish

1 Heat the oven to 220C/425F/Gas 7.
Lightly grease a baking sheet.

2 Sift the flour and baking powder into a bowl and season with pepper. Add the butter and rub it in with your fingertips until the mixture resembles fine breadcrumbs.
3 Stir in the chopped peanuts and beaten egg, and enough milk to mix to a soft dough.
4 Roll out the dough on a lightly floured surface until 2 cm/¾ inch thick and cut into rounds with a 7.5 cm/3 inch biscuit cutter. Roll out the trimmings and cut out more rounds until there are 6 of them altogether.
5 Place the scones on the baking sheet and bake for 15-20 minutes.
6 Meanwhile, make the topping: put the peanut butter and cheeses into a bowl. Add the cream and mix with a fork until evenly blended. Season lightly with salt and pepper.
7 Remove the cooked scones from oven, carefully cut in half, then spread with the topping. Serve hot, garnished with a few sprigs of mustard and cress.

MARTIN BRIGDALE

DON LAST

Courgette spread

SERVES 4

250 g/9 oz courgettes (see Buying guide)
100 g/4 oz curd cheese
100 g/4 oz mature Cheddar cheese, grated
50 g/2 oz chopped mixed nuts
2-3 tablespoons thick bottled mayonnaise
2 tablespoons lemon juice
1 tablespoon ground coriander
salt and freshly ground black pepper
stuffed green olives, sliced, to garnish

Cook's Notes

TIME
15 minutes preparation of the spread plus 1-2 hours chilling.

SERVING IDEAS
Spread on bread or crispbreads for a snack lunch or use as a sandwich filling. Alternatively, serve as a dip with sticks of raw vegetables (crudités) at the beginning of a meal, or with drinks at a party. Arrange the raw vegetables on a serving platter with the courgette spread in a bowl in the centre.

STORAGE
The spread can be kept in the refrigerator for up to 3-4 days but, because it will harden during this time, it needs to stand at room temperature for about 2 hours before it is served.

BUYING GUIDE
Choose firm, crisp courgettes. Soft ones have an unpleasantly bitter taste as well as being somewhat difficult to grate.

●280 calories/1175 kj per portion

1 Finely grate the courgettes into a large bowl.
2 Mix in all the other ingredients, except the olives, adding salt and pepper to taste. Stir until well mixed together.
3 Transfer the courgette mixture to a serving dish, level the surface, cover and refrigerate for 1-2 hours.
4 Garnish with the sliced stuffed green olives and serve at once as a spread or dip (see Serving ideas).

Apple and Stilton toasts

SERVES 4
5 small dessert apples
50 g/2 oz margarine or butter
50 g/2 oz blue or white Stilton cheese
50 g/2 oz cottage cheese
4 slices bread

1 Quarter, core and slice 4 apples. Melt the margarine in a frying-pan. Add the apple slices and fry over moderate heat for about 3 minutes until they are golden and puffy. Transfer to a plate with a fish slice.

2 Heat the grill to high.

3 Crumble the Stilton cheese into a bowl. Add the cottage cheese and mix thoroughly with a fork to blend.

4 Toast the bread on 1 side only. Place the cooked apple slices on the untoasted sides of the bread, then top with the Stilton and cottage cheese mixture.

5 Return to the grill and toast for 4-5 minutes until the cheese is bubbling and golden. Cut the crusts off the toast, if liked. Slice the remaining apple and place on top of the toasts to garnish. Serve at once.

Cook's Notes

TIME
This tasty snack takes only 10-15 minutes to prepare and cook.

ECONOMY
To cut down on the cost (and the calories) of this snack, use all cottage cheese.

SERVING IDEAS
As a snack, the toasts need no accompaniment. For a supper dish, double the quantities and serve with a chopped celery, cabbage and walnut salad.

VARIATION
Try using drained stewed or canned apricots instead of the cooked apple.

●270 calories/1125 kj per portion

THEO BERGSTROM

FRED MANCINI

Baked spinach omelette

SERVES 4
750 g/1½ lb fresh spinach, stalks and large midribs removed (see Cook's tip)
salt
50 g/2 oz margarine or butter
1 onion, finely chopped
4 large eggs, beaten
freshly ground black pepper

1 Heat the oven to 190C/375F/Gas 5.
2 Place the spinach in a large saucepan with only the water that clings to the leaves after washing. Sprinkle with salt, cover and cook over low heat for 5 minutes, shaking the pan constantly.
3 Meanwhile, melt half the margarine in a large frying-pan, add the onion and fry gently for 5 minutes until soft.
4 Drain the spinach very thoroughly and chop it roughly. Add the chopped spinach to the frying-pan and turn to coat in the margarine and onion mixture. Remove from the heat, add the remaining margarine and turn the spinach until the margarine is melted.
5 Season the eggs with salt and pepper, then pour half the eggs into a shallow ovenproof dish. Spread the chopped spinach evenly over the top, then cover with the remaining egg.
6 Bake in the oven for 15 minutes until the egg is set. Serve hot or cold, cut into wedges.

Cook's Notes

TIME
Preparation takes 25 minutes, including pre-cooking the spinach. Cooking in the oven takes 15 minutes.

 VARIATIONS
Add 25 g/1 oz finely grated Cheddar cheese to the eggs. The spinach may be seasoned with freshly grated nutmeg to taste.

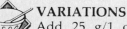 **SERVING IDEAS**
The spinach omelette may be eaten as a light meal in itself – serve it hot with jacket-baked potatoes, or cold with a salad of lentils.
Alternatively, serve it hot as a substantial accompaniment to a hot quiche or vegetable hotpot. It may also be served cold with homemade tomato sauce, cold ratatouille or a tomato salad.

 **COOK'S TIP**
Frozen chopped or cut leaf spinach is not really suitable for this recipe, as the spinach needs to be quite coarsely chopped.

WATCHPOINT
Turn the chopped spinach to coat thoroughly, but do not allow it to cook any further in the pan.

●325 calories/1365 kj per portion

ALAN DUNS

Pipérade

SERVES 4
250 g/9 oz red or green peppers,
deseeded and sliced
50 g/2 oz butter
1 onion, finely chopped
2 cloves garlic, crushed (optional)
225 g/8 oz can tomatoes, drained
and chopped
pinch of cayenne
salt and freshly ground black pepper
6 eggs
2 tablespoons milk

1 Melt the butter in a heavy-based frying-pan. Add the onion and the garlic, if using, and fry gently for 5 minutes until it is just soft and lightly coloured.
2 Add the peppers, tomatoes and cayenne and season with salt and pepper to taste. Simmer, stirring occasionally, for about 20 minutes, or until the pepper and tomato mixture is thick.
3 Lightly beat the eggs with the milk and a little salt and pepper.

Pour into the pan and cook for 2-3 minutes, stirring with a wooden spatula until the eggs are just set but not dry. Transfer the pipérade to a warmed serving dish and serve at once while piping hot.

Indian spiced omelette

SERVES 4
8 eggs
3 tablespoons cornflour
6 tablespoons natural yoghurt
1 onion, grated
4 teaspoons finely chopped fresh
  parsley
¾ teaspoon ground coriander
crushed seeds from 4 cardamom
  pods
½ teaspoon freshly ground black
  pepper
½ teaspoon salt
25 g/1 oz butter
parsley sprigs, to garnish

1 Put the cornflour in a bowl with 1 egg and beat with a fork until well blended. Add the remaining eggs and the other ingredients, except the butter and parsley, and then beat together until well combined.

2 Melt the butter in a large frying-pan with a lid over moderate heat. When just sizzling, pour in the egg mixture. Cover the pan, turn down the heat to very low and cook the omelette for about 30 minutes, until the egg is just set and the omelette is golden brown on the underside (see Cook's tip).

3 Invert a large plate over the frying-pan. Using one hand to hold the plate against the pan and the other to hold the handle of the pan, invert the 2 together, so that the omelette turns out on to the plate. Slide the omelette back into the pan, uncooked side downwards, and cook gently for a further 1-2 minutes, to brown the base of the omelette very lightly.

4 Turn the omelette out on to a serving plate (the browner side should be underneath) and leave to cool for about 5 minutes. Serve warm or cold, cut into quarters, garnished with sprigs of parsley.

Cook's Notes

TIME
Preparation takes about 30 minutes, cooking about 30 minutes.

COOK'S TIP
Oriental-type omelettes are quite solid and firm and require a longer cooking time than ordinary omelettes.

SERVING IDEAS
Serve the omelette with cucumber salad and poppadoms. For the salad, halve a cucumber lengthways and slice it very thinly. Mix in a serving dish with 1 tablespoon lemon juice, ½ teaspoon dried mint, ¼ teaspoon ground cumin, ½ teaspoon salt, and black pepper to taste.

●250 calories/1050 kj per portion

PAUL WEBSTER

PETER MYERS

Buck rarebit

SERVES 4
50 g/2 oz butter, softened
1 teaspoon mustard powder
pinch of sweet paprika
salt and freshly ground black
pepper
175 g/6 oz mature Cheddar cheese,
grated
1 tablespoon light ale
4 large rounds white or wholemeal
bread
few drops of vinegar
4 eggs
margarine or butter, for greasing

1 Heat the grill to high.
2 In a bowl, cream together the butter, mustard, paprika and salt and pepper to taste.
3 Stir in the grated cheese and ale, then stir again.

4 Grease a large frying-pan and half fill it with water. Grease 4 metal pastry cutters, put them in the pan, then bring the water to the boil.
5 Meanwhile, toast the bread, then spread thickly with the cheese topping. Place under the hot grill for 3-4 minutes or until topping

Cook's Notes

 TIME
Preparation and cooking take 15 minutes.

 DID YOU KNOW
Traditionally, a rarebit, or rabbit, is a tasty version of cheese on toast with either ale or wine added.

 WATCHPOINT
Do not spread cheese filling right to the edges.

●425 calories/1775 kj per portion

PREPARATION
To make attractively shaped poached eggs:

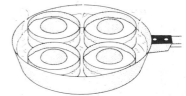

Break an egg into each cutter. Simmer until lightly set. Lift out carefully and then run a sharp knife round the inside of each cutter and lift off.

has melted and is golden brown.
6 Add a pinch of salt and a few drops of vinegar to the water in the frying-pan and poach the eggs for 3-4 minutes (see Preparation).
7 Arrange the prepared rarebits on warmed plates and top each with a poached egg. Serve at once.

Southern-style eggs

SERVES 4

2 tablespoons vegetable oil
2 medium onions, thinly sliced
400 g/14 oz can tomatoes
1 large red pepper, deseeded and
    chopped
1 clove garlic, crushed (optional)
½ teaspoon dried basil
salt and freshly ground black pepper
4 large eggs
4 slices white bread

1 Heat the oven to 180C/350F/Gas 4.
2 Heat the oil in a large frying-pan, or shallow flameproof dish, add the onions and fry gently for about 5 minutes until soft, but not coloured.
3 Add the tomatoes, with their juice, to the pan, breaking up the flesh with a spoon. Stir in the red pepper, garlic, if using, and the basil. Season to taste with salt and pepper. Simmer over low heat for 30 minutes until the liquid is reduced and thickened.
4 If using a frying-pan, transfer the tomato mixture to an ovenproof dish. Make 4 shallow hollows in the mixture with the back of a spoon and break an egg into each.

5 Cover the dish, using foil if it has no lid. [!] Cook in the oven for about 25 minutes until the whites of the eggs are just set.
6 Meanwhile, toast the bread, remove the crusts, and cut each slice in half diagonally. When the eggs are set, serve at once with the triangles of toast arranged round the edge of the dish.

CHRIS KNAGGS

Egg and avocado mayonnaise

SERVES 4

6 small eggs
2 small avocados
75 g/3 oz full-fat soft cheese
2 tablespoons thick bottled
mayonnaise
1 teaspoon lemon juice
salt and freshly ground black
pepper
bunch of watercress, washed
1 tablespoon chopped fresh parsley
thin slices of brown bread and
butter, to serve

1 Place the eggs in a small saucepan. Cover with cold water. Bring to the boil, then boil gently for 8 minutes. Drain and rinse under cold running water, until cool.
2 Meanwhile, cut the avocados in half lengthways, scoop out the flesh and put it into a bowl. Mash with a fork and then beat in the cheese followed by the mayonnaise. Stir in the lemon juice and season to taste with salt and pepper (see Cook's tip).
3 Shell the eggs then cut in half lengthways. Place 3 halves, cut side down, on beds of watercress on each of 4 small plates. Spoon the avocado mayonnaise over the eggs.
4 Sprinkle with parsley and serve with brown bread and butter.

Cook's Notes

TIME
Hard-boiling eggs and making mayonnaise will take 20 minutes.

COOK'S TIP
If a very smooth-textured mayonnaise is preferred, work the ingredients in a blender or food processor.

SERVING IDEAS
This is a surprisingly filling supper dish but for a more substantial meal, allow 2 eggs per person and serve with bowls of watercress, chopped chicory and celery.

! WATCHPOINTS
It is important not to overcook hard-boiled eggs, otherwise they develop an unpleasant rubbery texture and become indigestible. Eight to 11 minutes, depending on size, is the maximum suggested time. Rinsing in cold water is essential to ensure that the heat stored in the shell does not continue cooking the interior of the hard-boiled egg.

The mayonnaise should be used at once or the avocado flesh will discolour.

●390 calories/1625 kj per portion

FRED MANCINI

FRED MANCINI

Tangy egg salad

SERVES 4

4 large hard-boiled eggs
500 g/1 lb new potatoes, scrubbed or scraped
salt
250 g/9 oz shelled small fresh garden peas
3 tablespoons natural yoghurt
2 tablespoons thick bottled mayonnaise
1 tablespoon vegetable oil
75 g/3 oz Danish blue cheese, crumbled
radishes and cress sprigs, to garnish (optional)

1 Boil potatoes in salted water until tender. Drain, rinse under cold water, then drain again and halve.
2 Place the peas in a saucepan and sprinkle over ½ teaspoon salt. Pour over enough hot water to cover the peas, then simmer until nearly tender. Drain the peas, rinse under cold running water, then mix with the halved potatoes. Transfer carefully to a large serving plate.
3 Make the dressing: put the yoghurt, mayonnaise, oil and cheese in a blender or food processor and blend until smooth.
4 Cut the eggs in half and arrange them on top of the vegetables, then spoon over the dressing. Serve garnished with radishes and cress, if liked.

Cook's Notes

TIME
This salad takes 30 minutes to prepare.

SERVING IDEAS
Serve as a delicious lunch, perfect for hot summer days. This blue cheese dressing is very popular in the United States and can be used on all sorts of salads, or as a dip with crisp fresh vegetables.

●395 calories/1650 kj per portion

91

Spinach and carrot layer loaf

SERVES 4-6

750 g/1½ lb spinach, stalks and large midribs removed (see Buying guide)
750 g/1½ lb carrots, grated
salt
freshly grated nutmeg
1 teaspoon finely grated orange zest
freshly ground black pepper
50 g/2 oz margarine or butter
margarine, for greasing
orange slices and parsley sprigs, to garnish

1 Heat the oven to 180C/350F/Gas 4 and grease a 500 g/1 lb loaf tin.
2 Put the spinach into a large saucepan with only the water that clings to leaves after washing. Sprinkle with salt, cover and cook over low heat for 5 minutes, shaking the pan constantly until very soft.
3 Drain the spinach thoroughly and squeeze with your hand to remove as much water as possible. Chop finely, season to taste with salt and nutmeg, then set aside.
4 Mix carrots and orange zest together, then season with salt and pepper to taste. Put half in the tin, then cover with the spinach. Arrange the remaining carrots on top of the spinach. Set aside.
5 Heat the margarine in a small saucepan over low heat until melted then pour over carrots in the tin.
6 Bake in the oven for 1 hour. To serve: run a knife around sides of tin, invert a warmed serving plate on top and turn out loaf. Garnish with orange slices and parsley sprigs. Cut into slices and serve at once (see Serving ideas).

Cook's Notes

TIME
Preparation 20 minutes; cooking 1 hour.

VARIATION
Grated celeriac may be used instead of carrots.

BUYING GUIDE
When fresh spinach is unavailable, use 225g/8 oz frozen chopped spinach instead of fresh.

SERVING IDEAS
Serve as a light snack, accompanied by hot, wholemeal rolls and butter. Alternatively, serve loaf as a colourful vegetable accompaniment to either a cheesy quiche or hot soufflé.

For a more dramatic effect, try drizzling soured cream over the loaf before serving.

●180 calories/750 kj per portion

BOB KOMAR

Carrot ring

SERVES 4-6
1 kg/2 lb carrots, thinly sliced
salt
25 g/1 oz margarine or butter
150 ml/¼ pint vegetable stock
1 egg, beaten
50 g/2 oz Cheddar cheese, grated
freshly ground black pepper
generous pinch of nutmeg
generous squeeze of lemon juice
margarine, for greasing

1 Heat the oven to 180C/350F/Gas 4. Grease a 600 ml/1 pint ring mould thoroughly (see Cook's tips).
2 Bring a pan of salted water to the boil and cook the carrots in it for 10 minutes or until almost tender.
3 Drain well, then add the margarine and stock to the carrots in the pan and simmer, stirring occasionally, for about 10 minutes, until all the liquid has been absorbed.

4 Mash the carrots thoroughly with the beaten egg and the cheese and season well with pepper, nutmeg and lemon juice.
5 Transfer the carrot mixture to the ring mould. Press down well and smooth the top.

6 Bake in the oven for 30 minutes until set (it should be firm to the touch).
7 To unmould: run a knife round the edge, then invert a warmed serving plate on top and give a sharp jerk to unmould.

Cook's Notes

 TIME
Preparation and pre-cooking take 30 minutes; cooking time is 30 minutes.

 SERVING IDEAS
Pile freshly cooked green peas or sprigs of watercress into the centre of the ring and around the base, if wished. The ring would make a spectacularly different vegetable dish for a dinner party.

VARIATIONS
Use parsnips or swedes, cut into small dice, in place of the carrots, or try a mixture of the root vegetables.

 COOK'S TIPS
Be sure to use an ovenproof ring mould, not a mould suitable only for cold mixtures such as mousses.
Cooking time for carrots varies enormously depending on the season. Old carrots will take longer to cook than the time given in stage 2.

! WATCHPOINT
Be careful not to let the pan boil dry: you should watch it constantly, as the mixture does not contain much liquid, and may catch.

●180 calories/750 kj per portion

Hot stuffed tomatoes

SERVES 4

4 large tomatoes, each weighing about 250 g/9 oz (see Buying guide)
margarine, for greasing
salt
2 tablespoons vegetable oil
1 onion, finely chopped
100 g/4 oz chopped mixed nuts
100 g/4 oz soft wholewheat breadcrumbs
2 tablespoons chopped fresh parsley
1 teaspoon chopped fresh thyme
1 teaspoon chopped fresh marjoram
freshly ground black pepper

1 Heat the oven to 190C/375F/Gas 5. Lightly grease a shallow ovenproof dish with margarine.

2 Slice off the tops of the tomatoes and keep on one side for 'lids'. Scoop out the seeds with a teaspoon, taking care not to pierce the skins. Discard the seeds.

3 Sprinkle the insides of the tomatoes lightly with salt and place them upside down in a colander to drain.

4 Meanwhile, make the filling: heat the oil in a saucepan, add the onion and fry gently for 5 minutes until soft and lightly coloured. Remove from the heat and add the nuts, breadcrumbs, parsley, thyme and marjoram. Season with salt and pepper to taste.

5 Arrange the tomatoes in the prepared dish and spoon the filling into them, packing it in well. Replace the reserved 'lids', then bake in the oven, uncovered for 20-30 minutes until the tomatoes are tender. Serve at once while hot.

ALAN DUNS

Cook's Notes

TIME
Preparation 30 minutes, cooking 20-30 minutes.

SERVING IDEAS
Serve with cooked buttered noodles and a crisp green salad for a light supper; or as a starter, with triangles of hot buttered toast.

BUYING GUIDE
The very large continental tomatoes are best for this recipe. They can be obtained from many greengrocers and supermarkets; if they are not available, allow 2 medium-sized ones per person.

●290 calories/1225 kj per portion

Surprise potatoes

SERVES 4

4 large potatoes, unpeeled
150 g/5 oz cottage cheese
150 g/5 oz Cheddar cheese, grated
2 spring onions, finely chopped
2 gherkins, finely chopped
salt and freshly ground black pepper
50 g/2 oz butter
margarine, for greasing

1 Heat the oven to 180C/350F/Gas 4 and grease an ovenproof dish with margarine.

2 Bring the potatoes to the boil in salted water, lower the heat and cook for 20 minutes until tender.

3 Meanwhile, make the filling: put the cottage cheese in a bowl, together with the Cheddar cheese, onions, gherkins and salt and pepper to taste. Mix well.

4 Drain the cooked potatoes and, when cool enough to handle, cut them in half lengthways. Using a teaspoon carefully scrape out a hollow in each half (see Preparation).

5 Place 4 potato halves, hollow side upwards, in the ovenproof dish. Spoon the filling into the hollows, piling it up high. Place the other potato halves on top of the filled halves, to enclose the filling.

6 Top each potato with a knob of butter, cover the dish and bake in the oven for 1 hour until the potatoes are cooked through. Serve at once, straight from the dish.

TIME
45 minutes preparation, 1 hour cooking the assembled potatoes.

SERVING IDEAS
Served with a salad, these delicious stuffed potatoes make an excellent lunch or supper dish. Try serving them with hot ratatouille or a vegetable casserole for a more substantial meal.

VARIATION
Add 75 g/3 oz chopped fried mushrooms to the cheese filling.

PREPARATION
To hollow out the potato halves:

Scrape out the potato flesh to a depth of about 2.5 cm/1 inch, leaving a thick shell so that the potatoes will retain their shape.

●500 calories/2100 kj per portion

Thatched potatoes

SERVES 4

4 large potatoes, scrubbed (see
   Buying guide)
25 g/1 oz butter
1 onion, chopped
100 g/4 oz small button mushrooms,
   sliced
4-6 tablespoons milk
1 teaspoon made English mustard
2 teaspoons snipped chives (see
   Cook's tip)
salt and freshly ground black pepper
25 g/1 oz Cheddar cheese, finely
   grated

1 Heat the oven to 200C/400F/Gas 6.
2 Prick the potatoes all over with a
fork or fine skewer, place directly on
the oven shelf and bake in the oven
for 1½ hours or until tender when
squeezed in a cloth.
3 Melt the butter in a frying-pan,
add the onion and fry gently for 5
minutes until soft and lightly
coloured. Add the mushrooms and
continue cooking, stirring occasionally, for a further 5-6 minutes or

until the liquid has evaporated.
Transfer the onions and mushrooms
to a large bowl.
4 Cut the baked potatoes in half
lengthways and scoop out the
cooked potato from each half.
Add to the onion mixture in the
bowl, and beat together, adding
sufficient milk to give a smooth,
creamy consistency.

5 Beat in the mustard and chives
and season to taste with salt and
pepper.
6 Heat the grill to high. Pile the
mixture back into the potato skins
and fork over the tops to give a
thatched effect. Sprinkle with the
grated cheese.
7 Place under the grill for 10
minutes or until golden brown.

JAMES JACKSON

Cook's Notes

TIME
1½ hours baking the
potatoes, then 30
minutes preparation and final
cooking.

BUYING GUIDE
Choose potatoes suit-
able for baking. King
Edward or Desirée are good
choices and make sure they are
even-sized so that they will take
the same cooking time.

WATCHPOINT
Take care not to split the
potato skin when
removing the insides of the
potatoes.

COOK'S TIP
When fresh chives are
not available, use
freeze-dried chives or the green
tops of spring onions snipped
with scissors.

VARIATION
Add 2 chopped hard-
boiled eggs to the potato
before replacing in the skins.

SERVING IDEAS
Serve with soured cream,
fresh tomato sauce or
mayonnaise, accompanied by a
salad and wholemeal bread.

●270 calories/1135 kj per potato

James Jackson

Baked potatoes with spinach

SERVES 4

4 potatoes, each weighing about 250 g/9 oz, scrubbed (see Buying guide and Preparation)
250 g/9 oz spinach, stalks and midribs removed
salt
1 small clove garlic, crushed (optional)
pinch of freshly grated nutmeg
freshly ground black pepper
100 g/4 oz Cheddar cheese, grated

1 Heat the oven to 200C/400F/Gas 6.
2 Put the potatoes on a baking sheet and cook in the oven for 1½ hours until they are tender.
3 Put the spinach in a saucepan with only the water that clings to the leaves. Sprinkle with salt, cover the pan and cook over moderate heat for about 5 minutes until the spinach is soft and tender when it is tested.
4 Drain the spinach well, then chop roughly. Put in a bowl with the garlic, if using, grated nutmeg and salt and pepper to taste.
5 Hold the hot cooked potatoes with a cloth and cut in half lengthways, then scoop the potato flesh into the bowl of spinach, leaving the shells intact. Mix together with a wooden spoon, then spoon the mixture back into the potato shells, piling it up neatly in the centre.
6 Put the potatoes back on the baking sheet, and sprinkle them equally with the grated cheese. Return to the oven for 10-15 minutes until the cheese is melted and lightly browned. Serve at once.

Cook's Notes

 TIME
15 minutes preparation, 1¾ hours cooking.

 PREPARATION
Before baking, cut through the skins of the potatoes to mark where the potatoes will be cut in half lengthways after cooking. This will make the cooked potatoes easier to cut.

● 330 calories/1375 kj per portion

 BUYING GUIDE
King Edward or Désirée are the best potatoes to buy for baking whole and then stuffing.

 SERVING IDEAS
Served with salads, these filling potatoes make an excellent lunch or supper dish. Alternatively, serve as a two-in-one vegetable accompaniment to a warming winter soup.

Crispy courgettes

SERVES 4

500 g/1 lb small courgettes, cut into
   5 mm/¼ inch slices
4 tablespoons plain flour
salt and freshly ground black pepper
6 tablespoons olive oil
1 large clove garlic, crushed
   (optional)

1 Put the flour into a polythene bag
and season with salt and pepper.
Place the courgettes in the bag and
shake until they are lightly coated
with flour. [!]
2 Heat the oven to 110C/225F/Gas ¼.
3 Heat the oil in a large frying-pan
over high heat until the oil begins to
sizzle. Add the garlic, if using, stir
for a few seconds, then add half the
courgettes, a few at a time.
4 Fry for about 2 minutes until
golden brown on the underside,
then turn and fry until golden
brown on the other side.
5 Transfer the cooked slices with a
slotted spoon to a warmed serving
dish and keep hot in the oven while
frying the remaining courgettes. [!]
6 Sprinkle the courgettes with salt
and pepper and serve at once.

ROGER TUFF

JAMES JACKSON

Fennel and celery stir-fry

SERVES 4
1 large head fennel, sliced
1 head celery, sliced
3 tablespoons vegetable oil
2 tablespoons dry sherry
3 tablespoons soy sauce
salt
freshly ground black pepper
2 spring onions, finely sliced
celery leaves, to garnish

1 Heat the oil in a large frying-pan or wok, add the fennel and celery and fry over moderate heat for 2-3 minutes, stirring constantly

2 Add the sherry, soy sauce and salt and pepper to taste. Continue to stir over moderate heat for a further 2 minutes: the vegetables should be just crisp to the bite. Transfer to a warmed serving platter, sprinkle with the spring onions and garnish with the celery leaves. Serve at once.

Cook's Notes

 TIME
This Chinese-style dish takes 10 minutes.

DID YOU KNOW
Soy sauce is made from fermented soya beans. In China, where it originated, there are many different types, but the most commonly found soy sauce, available from larger supermarkets, comes in a light or rich variety. The light soy sauce has a more delicate flavour than the rich type and is the one most suitable for the unusual flavours combined in this dish.

 VARIATION
For a totally different flavour, try frying the vegetables in one of the bottled Chinese stir-fry sauces available from larger supermarkets.

● 130 calories/525 kj per portion

PETER MYERS

Nutty potato layer

SERVES 4

1 kg/2 lb potatoes, cut into 2 cm/
¾ inch cubes
salt
25 g/1 oz margarine or butter
2 onions, cut into 5 mm/¼ inch
   slices
3 tablespoons milk
pinch of grated nutmeg
freshly ground white pepper
75 g/3 oz Cheddar cheese, grated
   (see Cook's tip)
50 g/2 oz salted peanuts, roughly
   chopped
1 tablespoon chopped parsley

1 Heat the oven to 200C/400F/Gas 6.
2 Put the potatoes in a pan of salted water, bring to the boil, then lower the heat and simmer for about 10 minutes until tender.
3 Meanwhile, melt the margarine in a saucepan and fry the onions gently for 5 minutes until soft and lightly coloured. Drain on absorbent paper.
4 Drain the potatoes well and mash. Beat in the milk and nutmeg then season with salt and pepper to taste.
5 Spread one-third of the creamed potato over the base of a 1.25 L/2 pint ovenproof dish. Cover with half the onions and half the cheese. Repeat these layers once more and top with the remaining potato. Decorate the surface with a fork.
6 Sprinkle the peanuts over the

potato and bake in the oven for 30-35 minutes until golden.
7 Sprinkle the chopped parsley in the centre of the dish and serve at once.

Cook's Notes

TIME
35 minutes preparation, 30-35 minutes baking.

COOK'S TIP
This dish provides an ideal way of using any left-over cheese: any other hard cheese could be used instead of Cheddar.

● 405 calories/1700 kj per portion

Curried cauliflower

SERVES 4

1 large cauliflower, separated into
florets
2 tablespoons vegetable oil
1 large onion, chopped
1 clove garlic, crushed (optional)
1 tablespoon garam masala (see
Buying guide)
1 teaspoon ground ginger
½ teaspoon chilli powder
400 g/14 oz can tomatoes
salt

1 Heat the oil in a large heavy
saucepan, add the onion and garlic,
if using, and fry gently for 5 minutes
until soft and lightly coloured.
2 Add the spices and fry for a
further 1-2 minutes, stirring
constantly. Stir in the tomatoes,
increase the heat slightly and cook
for a further 10 minutes, breaking
up the tomatoes with a wooden
spoon.
3 Add the cauliflower to the pan
with salt to taste and stir well to coat
the florets in the tomato mixture.
Cover and cook for 15-20 minutes,
stirring occasionally to keep the
florets evenly coated in the sauce,
until the cauliflower is tender. !
4 Turn into a warmed serving dish
and serve at once.

Cook's Notes

TIME
Preparation takes 5
minutes; cooking, 30-35
minutes.

BUYING GUIDE
Garam masala is
available from Indian
food specialist shops, some
delicatessens and good
supermarkets which stock the
more unusual herbs and spices.
However, if you are unable to
obtain it, curry powder can be
used as a substitute.

● 105 calories/450 kj per portion

DID YOU KNOW
Garam masala is a
mixture of different
spices and is an important
flavouring agent for many
Indian dishes. The bought
variety will usually include a
blend of ground cardamom,
coriander, cumin, cloves and
peppercorns.

WATCHPOINT
Take care not to
overcook the cauli-
flower; if left in the pan too long
it will become soft and
disintegrate.

FRED MANCINI

101

Creamy parsnips with tomatoes

SERVES 4

**500 g/1 lb parsnips, cut into 5 mm/
¼ inch slices**
25 g/1 oz margarine or butter
salt
**250 g/9 oz tomatoes, skinned and
sliced**
freshly ground black pepper
½ teaspoon dried basil
4 tablespoons single cream
**2 tablespoons fresh white
breadcrumbs**
50 g/2 oz Cheddar cheese, grated

1 Heat the oven to 200C/400F/Gas 6.
Grease a fairly small shallow ovenproof dish with half the margarine.

2 Put the parsnips into a saucepan
of salted water and bring to the boil.
Lower the heat slightly and simmer
for 5 minutes, then drain the
blanched parsnips thoroughly in a
colander.
3 Lay one-third of the parsnips in
the base of the greased dish, and
cover with half the tomatoes.
Sprinkle with salt and pepper to
taste and half the dried basil, then
pour over 1 tablespoon of the
single cream.
4 Repeat the layers once, then top
with the remaining parsnips and
pour over the remaining cream.
Sprinkle with the crumbs and
grated cheese and dot with the
remaining margarine.
5 Bake in the oven for 30 minutes,
until the topping is golden brown.
Serve at once, straight from the
dish.

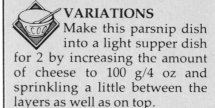

PETER MYERS

Tomatoes with onions and cream

SERVES 4-6

6 large ripe tomatoes (weighing about 500 g/1 lb), halved
3 tablespoons olive oil
500 g/1 lb onions, thinly sliced
salt and freshly ground black pepper
1 tablespoon chopped fresh basil, or 1 teaspoon dried basil
150 ml/¼ pint single or soured cream

1 Cut a cross on the cut sides of the tomato halves (see Cook's tip).
2 Heat the oil in a large frying-pan, add the onions and put the tomatoes, cut side uppermost, on top of the onions. Season well with salt and pepper and sprinkle over the basil.

3 Cook over gentle heat for 7-10 minutes until the tomatoes begin to soften.
4 Carefully turn the tomatoes over with a fish slice and cook for about 5 minutes on the cut side.

5 Pour the cream over the tomatoes and onions and warm through gently, but do not let the mixture boil. Taking care not to split the tomatoes, transfer to a warmed serving dish and serve at once.

Cook's Notes

 TIME
Preparation and cooking take about 20 minutes.

 COOK'S TIP
Cutting a cross in the tomatoes helps the heat penetrate evenly and prevents the tomatoes from splitting during cooking.

 WATCHPOINT
Do not let the tomatoes overcook or they will become mushy. They should just begin to soften, but still hold their shape. Cooking time will vary according to their ripeness and size.

 VARIATION
Try fresh or dried thyme instead of basil.

SERVING IDEAS
This makes a rather special snack if served on fried or hot French bread.

● 210 calories/875 kj per portion

PAUL WEBSTER

103

Potato and mushroom bake

SERVES 4

750 g/1½ lb potatoes, halved
salt
2 tablespoons vegetable oil
50 g/2 oz margarine or butter
100 g/4 oz button mushrooms,
   thinly sliced
1 teaspoon dried mixed herbs
freshly ground black pepper
2 large tomatoes, sliced

1 Heat the oven to 200C/400F/Gas 6.
2 Put the potatoes in a large saucepan with cold salted water to cover, bring to the boil and boil gently for 5 minutes. Drain the potatoes and allow to cool.
3 Meanwhile, heat the oil and half the margarine in a saucepan, add the mushrooms and toss them over moderate heat for about 3 minutes, until they have absorbed most of the fat. Remove the mushrooms with a slotted spoon.
4 Slice the potatoes thinly (see Preparation). Grease a shallow ovenproof dish with the fat remaining in the pan.
5 Arrange half the potatoes overlapping on the base of the dish. Cover with the mushrooms, sprinkle over half the herbs and season the vegetables well with salt and pepper.
6 Arrange the remaining potatoes in a layer to cover the mushrooms, then arrange the sliced tomatoes on top. Sprinkle them with the remaining herbs. Melt the remaining margarine and pour it over the dish.
7 Bake in the oven for 40-45 minutes, until the potatoes are tender when pierced with a fine skewer. Serve very hot, straight from the baking dish.

Cook's Notes

 TIME
Preparation, including parboiling the potatoes and cooking the mushrooms, takes 30 minutes. Cooking takes 40-45 minutes.

 PREPARATION
Slice the potatoes no thicker than 2 mm/⅛ inch, to make sure that they are really tender.

 SERVING IDEAS
This tasty potato dish is good with steamed broccoli or a fresh green salad. It also makes an excellent family dish when served with baked beans and buttered chunks of crusty French bread.

●225 calories/1050 kj per portion

MICHAEL KAY

FRED MANCINI

Fennel and apple gratin

SERVES 4

750 g/1½ lb fennel (see Buying guide)
300 ml/½ pint water
salt
about 150 ml/¼ pint milk
1 large cooking apple, weighing about 250 g/9 oz
50 g/2 oz margarine or butter
25 g/1 oz plain flour
freshly ground black pepper
1 tablespoon grated Parmesan cheese

1 Trim the fennel and reserve the feathery leaves for the garnish.
2 Cut the fennel into wedges lengthways and put in a saucepan.
3 Pour over the water, add a little salt and bring to the boil. Lower the heat, cover the pan and simmer for about 10 minutes until just tender.

4 Drain, reserving the cooking water. Make it up to 300 ml/½ pint with milk and set aside. Transfer the fennel to a warm serving dish and keep hot.
5 Peel and core the apple and cut into thin slices. Melt the margarine in a saucepan, add the apple slices and fry gently for 5 minutes until softened and beginning to brown. Remove the apple with a slotted spoon, drain well and arrange over the top of the fennel.
6 Heat the grill to high.
7 Sprinkle the flour into the melted margarine left in the pan and stir over low heat for 1-2 minutes. Remove from the heat and gradually stir in the milk mixture. Return to the heat and simmer, stirring, until thick and smooth. Season with salt and pepper to taste and pour over the fennel and apple.
8 Sprinkle the top with Parmesan cheese and place under the grill for a few minutes until lightly browned. Serve hot, garnished with the reserved fennel leaves.

Leeks in Caerphilly sauce

SERVES 4
500 g/1 lb young leeks (see Buying guide)
salt
margarine, for greasing
parsley sprigs or watercress sprigs, to garnish (optional)

SAUCE
25 g/1 oz butter
25 g/1 oz plain flour
425 ml/¾ pint milk
100 g/4 oz Caerphilly cheese, grated
½ teaspoon mustard powder
freshly ground black pepper

1 Heat the oven to 180C/350F/Gas 4 and generously grease a shallow ovenproof dish.
2 Trim the leeks, then cut a slit lengthways from the top almost to the base. Fan out and hold under cold running water to rinse off all the dirt.
3 Bring a large pan of salted water to the boil, add the leeks and simmer for about 8 minutes, until just tender. Drain well, pat dry on absorbent paper and arrange in a single layer in the bottom of the prepared dish.
4 To make the sauce: melt butter in a saucepan, sprinkle in plain flour and stir over low heat for 1-2 minutes until straw-coloured. Remove from the heat and gradually stir in the milk. Return to the heat and simmer, stirring, until thick and smooth.
5 Stir in 50 g/2 oz of the grated Caerphilly cheese, until melted. Add the mustard powder. Season to taste with salt and freshly ground black pepper.
6 Pour the sauce over the leeks and sprinkle with the remaining cheese. Bake in the oven for 35-40 minutes until the leeks are cooked through and the cheesy sauce is hot and bubbling.
7 Allow to cool for 5 minutes before serving straight from the dish. Garnish, if wished, with parsley or watercress sprigs.

JAMES JACKSON

Cook's Notes

TIME
20 minutes preparation, 35-40 minutes baking.

BUYING GUIDE
Always choose straight, slender leeks with green tops; avoid overlarge leeks or those with yellow discoloured or damaged leaves.

DID YOU KNOW
Caerphilly cheese was first made in a small Glamorgan village, where it was very popular with the Welsh miners, who loved its salty taste and moist texture – perfect with local beer.

● 275 calories/1150 kj per portion

Tomato layer bake

SERVES 4-6

750 g/1½ lb tomatoes, sliced and
   cores removed
2 tablespoons vegetable oil
2 onions, finely chopped
150 ml/¼ pint double cream
1 tablespoon dried basil
100 g/4 oz fresh white breadcrumbs
25 g/1 oz butter, diced
extra butter, for greasing

1 Heat the oven to 200C/400F/Gas 6
and grease a 1.25 L/2 pint ovenproof
dish with butter.
2 Heat the oil in a small frying-pan,
add the onions and fry gently for 5
minutes until soft and lightly
coloured. Remove the frying-pan
from the heat.
3 Arrange one-third of the sliced
tomatoes in the bottom of the
prepared dish, then sprinkle over
one-third of the onions, cream and
basil. Cover with one-third of the
fresh breadcrumbs
4 Repeat these layers twice more,
ending with a covering of fresh
breadcrumbs.
5 Dot with the butter and cook in
the oven for 30-40 minutes or until
the topping is golden brown. Serve
at once, straight from the dish.

Cook's Notes

TIME
Preparation and cook-
ing take about 1 hour
from start to finish.

VARIATION
You can substitute 2
tablespoons finely chop-
ped fresh basil for the dried,
when available.

SERVING IDEAS
This baked tomato dish
is delicious accompanied
by a crisp, fresh green salad.
To serve on its own as a tasty
supper dish, mix grated
Cheddar cheese with the
breadcrumbs before baking.

●365 calories/1525 kj per portion

TIME
Preparation and cooking take about 20 minutes.

SERVING IDEAS
Serve this Indian-style dish with chutney and poppadoms or chapatis as an interesting light snack. Alternatively, serve as an accompaniment to a meat curry.

● 130 calories/550 kj per portion

WATCHPOINT
The yoghurt will separate if added all at once to the hot sauce. Therefore, add it gradually, stirring quickly after each addition.

DID YOU KNOW
Frying spices gently in oil or fat releases their natural flavouring oils; these are then readily absorbed into other ingredients added to the pan.

VARIATIONS
Use 175 g/6 oz dried kidney beans instead of the canned variety. Before using, soak overnight, then fast boil in fresh water for 10 minutes, lower the heat and simmer for 1½ hours. Other beans such as haricots, butter beans, adzuki or black-eyed beans can be used instead of the kidney beans, either in canned or dried form.

Mahal kidney beans

SERVES 4
425 g/15 oz can red kidney beans, drained
25 g/1 oz margarine or butter
1 onion, finely chopped
1 clove garlic, crushed
1 teaspoon ground cumin
225 g/8 oz can tomatoes, drained and chopped
salt
freshly ground black pepper
3 tablespoons natural yoghurt
2 tablespoons fresh chopped parsley
coriander leaves, to garnish

1 Melt the margarine in a large wide pan, add the onion and garlic and fry gently for 5 minutes until the onion is soft and lightly coloured. Add the ground cumin to the pan and stir over low heat for a further 2 minutes (see Did you know).
2 Stir the tomatoes into the pan together with the beans and salt and pepper to taste. Continue to cook the mixture over moderate heat for 5 minutes, stirring occasionally, until the beans are heated through.
3 Remove the pan from the heat and add the yoghurt, 1 tablespoon at a time, mixing thoroughly after each addition. ❗ Heat through gently without allowing the mixture to come to the boil.
4 Transfer the beans to a warmed serving dish, sprinkle with chopped parsley and garnish the centre of the dish with coriander leaves. Serve at once (see Serving ideas).

THEO BERGSTROM

Haricot beans with apples

SERVES 4
100 g/4 oz dried haricot beans (see Cook's tips)
500 g/1 lb cooking apples
50 g/2 oz margarine or butter
2 tablespoons caster sugar
salt and freshly ground black pepper

1 Put the haricot beans in a deep bowl, cover with plenty of cold water and leave to soak overnight.
2 Drain and rinse the haricot beans, put them into a large saucepan and cover with fresh cold water. Bring to the boil, then reduce the heat and simmer for about 1 hour or until the beans are tender. Add more water to the pan during the cooking time if necessary. Drain and discard the cooking water.

3 Peel, quarter and core the apples, then slice thinly. Melt the margarine in a large saucepan, add the apples and cook gently for 10 minutes or until tender. Do not overcook or the apple slices will break up and become browned—they should be a very light golden in colour.
4 Add the haricot beans, sugar, and salt and pepper to taste. Cook over very gentle heat for 5 minutes until the beans are heated through. Turn into a warmed serving dish and serve at once.

Brussels sprouts purée

SERVES 4-6
750 g/1½ lb Brussels sprouts, fresh
   or frozen
salt
250 g/9 oz cooked potatoes, mashed
150 ml/¼ pint single cream
50 g/2 oz margarine or butter,
   melted
freshly ground black pepper
freshly grated nutmeg
40 g/1½ oz shelled walnuts,
   chopped, to garnish

1 If using fresh sprouts, trim them, discarding any tough outer leaves. Cut crosses in the stalk ends (see Cook's tips), then wash thoroughly under cold running water.

2 Cook the sprouts in boiling salted water for 8-10 minutes until just tender. Drain. Cook frozen sprouts according to packet instructions.

3 Purée the sprouts in a blender with the potatoes, cream and melted margarine (see Cook's tips).

4 Put the purée in a small saucepan, season well with salt, pepper and nutmeg and heat through over very low heat until completely warmed through.

5 Turn the purée into a heated serving dish and sprinkle with the walnuts to garnish. Serve at once.

Cook's Notes

TIME
Preparation 10 minutes, cooking and making the purée 20 minutes.

VARIATION
Bake the purée in moulds and serve turned out. Grease 4-6 individual moulds or a 600 ml/1 pint pudding basin and line the base of the moulds or basin with circles of greased greaseproof paper. Beat a large egg yolk into the purée, whisk the egg white until stiff and fold it in. Pour mixture into the moulds or basin, then set in a roasting tin and pour in boiling water to come halfway up the sides. Bake in an oven heated to 180C/350F/Gas 4 for about 15 minutes or until firm. Allow to cool slightly, then turn out and garnish with chopped walnuts.

COOK'S TIPS
Cutting a cross in the stalk ends of Brussels sprouts ensures they cook through quickly. If you use frozen sprouts, you do not need to cut a cross.

If you do not have a blender, beat the cream and melted margarine into the mashed potato. Chop the sprouts very finely and stir them in.

● 220 calories/900 kj per portion

THEO BERGSTROM

Baked parsnips with soured cream

SERVES 4
500 g/1 lb parsnips, sliced
2 tablespoons vegetable oil
1 large onion, sliced
300 ml/½ pint vegetable stock
½ teaspoon made English mustard
¼ teaspoon sweet paprika
150 ml/¼ pint soured cream
50 g/2 oz brown breadcrumbs (see Buying guide)
25 g/1 oz Cheddar cheese, grated

1 Heat the oven to 200C/400F/Gas 6.
2 Heat the oil in a large frying-pan, add the onion and fry gently for 5 minutes until soft and lightly coloured. Add the parsnips and continue frying gently for 3-4 minutes until the parsnips are beginning to soften.

3 Stir in the stock, mustard and paprika. Bring to the boil, then lower the heat slightly and simmer for 15 minutes. Remove from the heat and stir in the soured cream with a wooden spoon until it is thoroughly combined.

4 Spoon the mixture into an ovenproof dish. Mix the brown breadcrumbs with the cheese and sprinkle over the top. Bake in the oven for 1 hour until crisp and golden on top. Serve at once, straight from the dish.

Vegetable medley

SERVES 4
500 g/1 lb spring greens (see
  Preparation)
salt
25 g/1 oz butter
250 g/9 oz mushrooms, sliced
1 tablespoon lemon juice
6 tablespoons double cream
freshly ground black pepper
350 g/12 oz tomatoes, skinned and
  sliced
1 teaspoon dried basil
butter, for greasing

1 Heat the oven to 180C/350F/Gas 4
and grease an ovenproof dish with
butter.
2 Cook the greens gently for 5
minutes in a small amount of boiling salted water (see Cook's tip).
3 Meanwhile, melt the butter in a
saucepan, add the mushrooms and
cook over gentle heat until beginning to soften. Add the lemon juice
and cook for a further 1-2 minutes.
Remove with a slotted spoon.
4 Drain the greens thoroughly in a

colander, squeezing out all the
excess moisture by pressing down
on the greens with a plate. Transfer
to a bowl, stir in the mushrooms and
double cream and season to taste
with salt and pepper.
5 Put half the greens and mushroom mixture into the greased dish.
Cover with half the tomato slices
and season with salt and pepper.
Sprinkle over half the basil. Turn the

remainder of the greens and mushroom mixture into the dish, smooth
the surface and top with the
remaining tomato slices. Season
again with salt and pepper and
sprinkle with the remaining dried
basil.
6 Cover the dish with a lid or foil
and bake in the oven for 15-20
minutes. Serve at once, straight
from the dish.

Lettuce in cheese sauce

SERVES 4

1 large crisp-hearted lettuce (see
  Buying guide)
salt
25 g/1 oz butter
4 tablespoons vegetable stock

CHEESE SAUCE
25 g/1 oz margarine or butter
25 g/1 oz plain flour
300 ml/½ pint milk
50 g/2 oz Cheddar cheese, grated
¼ teaspoon made English mustard
freshly ground black pepper
1 tablespoon grated Parmesan
  cheese

1 Heat the oven to 180C/350F/Gas 4.
2 Discard the outer lettuce leaves if
coarse or damaged, but leave the
lettuce whole. Bring a saucepan of
salted water to the boil and put the
lettuce in it to blanch for 5 minutes.
Drain well.
3 Cut the blanched lettuce into
quarters and place in a shallow
flameproof dish. Dot with the butter
and pour the stock around the
lettuce in the dish. Cook in the oven
for 30 minutes or until the lettuce is
tender.
4 Meanwhile, make the sauce: melt
the margarine in a small saucepan,
sprinkle in the flour and stir over
low heat for 1-2 minutes until straw-
coloured. Remove from the heat and
gradually stir in the milk. Return to
the heat and simmer, stirring, until
the sauce is thick and smooth in
texture.
5 Remove from the heat and stir in
the Cheddar cheese until melted.
Stir in the mustard and season to
taste with salt and pepper. Heat the
grill to high.
6 When the lettuce is cooked, drain
well, reserving 2 tablespoons of the
cooking liquid. Return the cooked
lettuce to the dish.
7 Stir the reserved cooking liquid
into the cheese sauce.
8 Pour the cheese sauce evenly over
the lettuce in the dish. Sprinkle the
Parmesan cheese over the top and
set under the grill for a few minutes
until the cheese has melted and the
top is lightly browned. Serve hot.

PAUL WEBSTER

Cook's Notes

 TIME
Preparation takes about
15 minutes. Cooking
the lettuce and making the sauce
takes about 40 minutes.

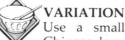 **VARIATION**
Use a small head of
Chinese leaves instead
of lettuce and extend the
cooking time if necessary.

 SERVING IDEAS
Serve with French bread
for lunch or supper.

 BUYING GUIDE
You need a really crisp,
firm lettuce for this dish:
Iceberg would be best, with its
firm, compact leaves.

●210 calories/875 kj per portion

Rösti

SERVES 4

500 g/1 lb potatoes, parboiled whole, cooled and skinned
1 large onion
salt and freshly ground black pepper
50 g/2 oz butter

1 Grate the potatoes and onion and mix together with lots of salt and pepper.
2 Melt half the butter in a shallow frying-pan and add the potato mixture. Flatten it down with a wooden spoon or spatula and cook over moderate heat for about 5 minutes.
3 Put a plate on top of the pan and turn the pan over so that the potato mixture falls on to the plate. Scrape out any bits left in the pan, then melt the remaining butter.

4 Slide the potato back into the pan so that the underside cooks. Cook for another 5 minutes or so. Slide or turn on to a warmed serving plate.

Cook's Notes

TIME
Preparation 60 minutes, allowing time for the potatoes to cook and cool. Cooking takes 10 minutes.

COOK'S TIP
The best way to cook potatoes for this dish is to parboil them in their skins. Test with the point of a sharp knife, and stop the cooking when there is still resistance to the knife (otherwise the potatoes will not grate). Leave them to cool, then peel off the skins and grate the potatoes.

SERVING IDEAS
For a complete meal, serve Rösti with fried eggs on top and accompanied by fresh homemade tomato sauce.

VARIATION
For a different flavour add a little grated mature Cheddar or Cheshire cheese to the grated potato and onion before cooking.

● 205 calories/875 kj per portion

PETER MYERS

Herby potato cake

SERVES 6
750 g/1½ lb potatoes
50 g/2 oz margarine or butter
1 large onion, thinly sliced
1 clove garlic, finely chopped
   (optional)
100 g/4 oz plain white or wholemeal
   flour
1 teaspoon bicarbonate of soda
salt and freshly ground black pepper
2 tablespoons chopped parsley
1 teaspoon dried thyme
1 large egg, beaten
margarine or butter, for greasing

1 Grate the potatoes into a large bowl of water and leave them to soak for 1 hour. !
2 Heat the oven to 180C/350F/Gas 4.
3 Melt half the margarine in a frying-pan. Add the onion and garlic, if using, and fry gently until soft but not coloured (about 10 minutes). Stir the remaining margarine into the pan until melted, then remove from the heat.
4 Sift the flour with the bicarbonate of soda on to a plate and season well with salt and pepper.
5 Drain the soaked potatoes in a colander, pressing down hard to remove as much water as possible.
6 Put the potatoes into a bowl. Mix in the flour and herbs, then the onion mixture, and finally the egg.
7 Press the mixture into a greased 25 cm/10 inch flan tin and bake in the oven for 1 hour, until the top is brown. ! Serve at once.

GRAHAM YOUNG

FRED MANCINI

Onion and apple fritters

SERVES 4-6
1 onion, finely chopped
2 dessert apples
freshly ground black pepper
3-4 tablespoons vegetable oil, for frying
parsley sprigs, to garnish

BATTER
100 g/4 oz plain flour
½ teaspoon salt
1 tablespoon finely chopped fresh sage (see Buying guide)
1 large egg, separated
1 tablespoon vegetable oil
150 ml/¼ pint water

1 Heat the oven to 110C/225F/Gas ¼.
2 Make the batter: sift the flour with the salt into a large bowl, then stir in the sage. Make a well in the centre and add the egg yolk, oil and half the water. Using a wire whisk, gradually draw the flour into the liquid.

When the flour is completely incorporated, gradually whisk in the remaining water to form a smooth batter. Cover the batter and leave to stand for 30 minutes.
3 Peel, core and finely chop the apples, then stir into the batter. Add the onion and season to taste with salt and black pepper.
4 Whisk the egg white in a clean, dry bowl until stiff, then lightly fold into the batter. ⚠
5 Heat 3 tablespoons vegetable oil in a large, heavy-based frying-pan. When the oil is sizzling, drop tablespoons of the mixture into the pan, shaping them into neat, even rounds with a fish slice. Fry over moderate heat for about 3 minutes until golden brown, then turn carefully and fry for a further 3 minutes on the other side.
6 Drain the fritters on absorbent paper, transfer to a serving platter and keep hot in the oven. Continue frying batches of fritters in the same way, adding more oil to the frying-pan as necessary.
7 Garnish the fritters with parsley sprigs and serve at once.

116

Parsnip and nutmeg croquettes

SERVES 4-6
750 g/1½ lb parsnips, cut into
    2.5 cm/1 inch chunks
salt
50 g/2 oz butter, diced
1 tablespoon milk
¼ teaspoon freshly grated nutmeg
1 tablespoon chopped fresh parsley
1 small egg, lightly beaten
freshly ground black pepper
75 g/3 oz dried white breadcrumbs
plain flour, for rolling
vegetable oil, for deep frying
parsley sprigs, to garnish

1 Bring the parsnips to the boil in salted water, lower the heat and cook for 20 minutes or until they are very tender.

2 Drain parsnips well and then return to the pan (see Cook's tip). Add the butter and milk and mash until smooth. Stir in the nutmeg, parsley and egg, then season to taste with pepper. Turn the mixture into a bowl, cover and allow to cool completely for about 1 hour.

3 Heat the oven to 110C/225F/Gas ¼.

4 Spread the breadcrumbs out on a plate. With floured hands, divide the parsnip mixture into about 20 equal-sized pieces; roll each piece into a ball. Roll the balls in the plate of breadcrumbs to coat each one thoroughly.

5 Heat the oil in a deep-fat frier to 190C/375F or until a stale bread cube browns in 50 seconds.

DON LAST

6 Fry a few of the croquettes for 4-5 minutes until golden brown. Drain on absorbent paper and keep hot in the oven while frying the remaining batches of parsnip croquettes. !

7 Garnish the parsnip and nutmeg croquettes with parsley sprigs and serve (see Serving ideas).

Cook's Notes

TIME
30 minutes preparation, plus 1 hour cooling. Frying takes about 20 minutes.

SERVING IDEAS
Parsnip and nutmeg croquettes are rather sweet and nutty tasting. Serve them as an accompaniment to plain dishes or include as part of a hot buffet with rice and pasta salads.

If preferred, try serving them as a tasty hot supper dish, topped with grated Cheddar cheese or a homemade tomato sauce – accompany with small bowls of watercress sprigs and cucumber wedges, garnished with chopped hard-boiled egg.

COOK'S TIP
Stir the parsnips over low heat for 1 minute to make sure that they are completely dry, otherwise the mix will be too mushy to shape.

●395 calories/1650 kj per portion

DID YOU KNOW
Nutmeg was a very popular spice in 17th century England, so much so that travellers often carried a small pocket grater around so they could have freshly grated nutmeg on their food and their drinks.

WATCHPOINT
Remember to reheat the vegetable oil between frying the separate batches of croquettes.

117

Potato and pepper pancakes

SERVES 4

500 g/1 lb potatoes (see Preparation)
50 g/2 oz green pepper, deseeded
   and finely chopped
1 onion, finely chopped
4 tablespoons plain flour
1 large egg
4 tablespoons milk
salt and freshly ground black pepper
25 g/1 oz margarine
5 tablespoons vegetable oil

1 Heat the oven to 110C/225F/Gas ¼.
2 Coarsely grate the potatoes into a colander and press down with a plate to squeeze out all the surplus liquid. Pat dry with absorbent paper and turn into a bowl. Stir in the green pepper, onion and flour (see Cook's tip).
3 Beat the egg with the milk, season to taste with salt and pepper, then add to the potato mixture. Mix well.
4 Heat the margarine and half the oil over moderate heat in a large heavy-based frying-pan. When sizzling, drop in tablespoonfuls of the potato mixture, flattening each mound into a pancake shape with a fish slice.
5 Fry the pancakes for about 4 minutes on each side until golden brown. Remove from the pan with a slotted spoon and drain on absorbent paper. Keep hot in the oven while frying the remaining mixture in the same way, adding more oil with each batch.
6 Arrange pancakes on a warmed serving dish and serve at once.

THEO BERGSTROM

Courgette fritters

SERVES 4
250 g/9 oz courgettes
50 g/2 oz Edam cheese, grated
3-4 tablespoons vegetable oil, for frying

BATTER
75 g/3 oz plain flour
salt and freshly ground black pepper
1 large egg, separated
2 teaspoons vegetable oil
150 ml/¼ pint water

1 Coarsely grate the courgettes into a colander and leave to stand for 35-40 minutes. Heat the oven to 110C/225F/Gas ¼.

2 Meanwhile, prepare the batter: sift the flour with a pinch of salt and a light sprinkling of pepper into a bowl. Make a well in the centre and add the egg yolk, oil and half the water. Mix together with a wooden spoon, gradually drawing in the flour from the sides of the bowl. When the flour is completely incorporated, slowly pour in the remaining water and beat well until smooth. Cover and leave to stand for 30 minutes.

3 Whisk the egg white in a clean dry bowl until stiff, then lightly fold into batter with a large metal spoon. ❗

4 Pat the courgettes dry with absorbent paper, then gently mix into the batter together with the grated cheese. Season if necessary.

5 Heat the oil in a large, heavy frying-pan and drop in tablespoons of the prepared mixture, allowing room for the fritters to spread. Fry over moderate heat for about 3-4 minutes, or until golden brown and beginning to set on top. Turn carefully and fry for a further 3-4 minutes until browned on the other side (see Cook's tip).

6 Drain well on absorbent paper and keep hot in the oven while frying the remaining fritters.

Cook's Notes

TIME
10 minutes preparation, plus 30 minutes standing, then 20 minutes cooking.

SERVING IDEAS
Serve as a hot supper dish with fresh tomato sauce and rice or potatoes. Alternatively, serve with salad and French bread and butter.

! **WATCHPOINT**
Fold the egg white into the batter at the last minute to produce the lightest, crispest result.

COOK'S TIP
Cooking time can be reduced by using 2 frying-pans at once instead of cooking in batches.

● 210 calories/875 kj per portion

GRAHAM YOUNG

ALAN DUNS

Watercress and potato croquettes

SERVES 4-6
750 g/1½ lb potatoes
salt
25 g/1 oz margarine or butter
2 tablespoons milk
freshly grated nutmeg
freshly ground black pepper
1 bunch watercress, finely chopped
2 eggs, beaten
flour, for dusting
50 g/2 oz blanched almonds, finely
    chopped
4 tablespoons fresh white
    breadcrumbs
150 ml/¼ pint vegetable oil

TO GARNISH
watercress sprigs
lime twists (optional)

1 Bring the potatoes to the boil in salted water, lower the heat and cook for 20 minutes.
2 Drain the potatoes and mash with the margarine and milk until smooth. Season to taste with nutmeg, salt and pepper, then beat in the watercress and about one-quarter of beaten eggs. Leave the mixture for about 30 minutes to cool.
3 Lightly dust a work surface with flour. Divide the mixture into 12 portions then, with floured hands, roll into cork shapes.
4 Mix the almonds with the breadcrumbs and spread out on a large flat plate. Dip the croquettes first in the remaining beaten egg, then roll in the almond and breadcrumb mixture. Refrigerate for at least 30 minutes (see Cook's tip).
5 Heat the oven to 110C/225F/Gas ¼.

6 Heat the oil in a large heavy-based frying-pan to 190C/375F or until a stale bread cube browns in 50 seconds.
7 Fry a batch of the croquettes in the hot oil for about 5 minutes, until golden brown and crisp, then remove with a slotted spoon and drain on absorbent paper. Keep warm in the oven while frying the rest of the croquettes. ✳
8 Garnish with watercress and lime twists, if liked, and serve.

Cook's Notes

TIME
40 minutes preparation; 30 minutes each cooling and chilling and about 15 minutes cooking.

FREEZING
Drain and cool the fried croquettes. Open freeze until solid, then pack in rigid containers, separating layers with foil. Seal, label and return to freezer for up to 3 months. To serve: defrost in a single layer on a baking sheet at room temperature for 2 hours, then cover and reheat in a 180C/350F/Gas 4 oven for 20 minutes.

SERVING IDEAS
Serve as a light snack with a salad, or these unusual croquettes would make an interesting accompaniment to a hot savoury dish.

COOK'S TIP
Chilling firms up the mixture, which helps to prevent the croquettes from breaking up during frying. However, chilling is not absolutely necessary if you are short of time – just take extra care when frying.

●410 calories/1725 kj per portion

Spinach pancakes

MAKES 8 PANCAKES
175 g/6 oz spinach, stalks and large midribs removed
vegetable oil, for greasing

BATTER
100 g/4 oz plain flour
½ teaspoon freshly grated nutmeg
salt
1 egg
125 ml/4 fl oz milk
125 ml/4 fl oz water

1 Put the spinach in a pan with only the water that clings to the leaves after washing and cook over moderate heat for 5 minutes until completely tender.
2 Drain the spinach well in a colander, pressing with a large spoon to extract as much moisture as possible, then chop it as finely as you can with a sharp pointed knife.
3 Make the batter: sift flour, nutmeg and salt into a bowl, make a well in the centre and add the egg, milk and water. Using a wire whisk, gradually draw the flour into the liquid and when the flour is completely incorporated, stir in the chopped spinach.
4 Heat a little oil in an 18 cm/7 inch frying-pan. Remove from the heat, pour in 2 tablespoons of the batter and tilt the pan until the batter evenly covers the base.
5 Return to the heat and cook until the top looks dry and the underside is golden brown. Loosen the edge with a palette knife and shake the pan, then toss the pancake over and cook on the other side for a further 20-30 seconds until golden. Lift the pancake on to a sheet of greaseproof paper.
6 Continue making pancakes in the same way, interleaving them with greaseproof paper. Stir the batter frequently and grease the pan with more oil as necessary.

Cook's Notes

TIME
40 minutes preparation and cooking in total.

SERVING IDEAS
If wished the pancakes can be filled: season 2 tablespoons cream cheese well with salt and pepper and spread on one end of each pancake. Fold the sides over the filling, then roll up.
Alternatively, for a more substantial dish, fill the pancakes with about 300 ml/½ pint well-flavoured cheese sauce mixed with 100 g/4 oz fried chopped mushrooms.

FREEZING
Cool completely, then wrap interleaved pancakes in foil, keeping them flat. Seal, label and freeze for up to 4 months. To serve: defrost in wrappings, then unwrap and put on an ovenproof plate over a pan of simmering water. Cover and reheat for 5-10 minutes.

●90 calories/375 kj per pancake

PAUL WEBSTER

MAIN DISHES

The main dish is the focal point of any meal, and the one that provides most in the way of satisfaction and nourishment. Whether you are planning a dinner party or a family meal, the choice of main dish will determine what will be served to start the meal and what will follow, as well as what accompanying dishes will be served.

For vegetarians, the main dish is less likely to be the major source of protein, as it is when serving a meat dish, and side dishes will usually be more substantial. Vegetables often replace meat in similar types of dish, such as in a vegetable pie or curry. This is very helpful if you are trying to encourage your family to adopt a vegetarian diet. The side dishes may also be the same as if the main dish was meat based. For example, a vegetable curry may be served with rice and all the other usual timbales traditionally served with curry.

Cheese and eggs are also important when it comes to cooking main dishes. Cheese features strongly in sauces, toppings and stuffings, and eggs can be used to make a host of delicious and unusual vegetable soufflés, quiches and flans. When making pastry use wholemeal flour whenever possible.

Pasta is a firm family favourite, and you will find several recipes in this chapter that combine pasta with vegetables and herbs in delicious main dishes. Try Herby Spaghetti or Wholewheat Pasta with Tomatoes to give the family an Italian treat. The sauces are altogether lighter and more wholesome than a traditional bolognese sauce. You will only need a green salad and perhaps some crusty French bread and butter for a complete meal.

There are also recipes in this chapter which will make ideal dishes to serve when you are entertaining. Don't worry if your guests are not vegetarians; they will enjoy sampling a different approach to eating, and will probably feel better for a meal of perfectly cooked vegetarian food. For an informal occasion, a pasta dish would be ideal, served with salads. For a more formal meal, choose something your guests will find interesting and impressive, such as Hot Carrot and Cheese Mousse or Carrot and Nut Roast, or stick to something homely and warming, such as Golden Vegetable Stew or Mixed Bean Casserole. Either way, your guests will probably find themselves enjoying new taste experiences.

One of the bonuses of a vegetarian diet is that you can enjoy the season's best fresh vegetables in a multitude of different ways, your diet changing with the seasons. So, for example, in the summer months when courgettes are abundant and cheap, you can offer your family Courgette Crumble or Stuffed Courgette Bake, with fresh green salads to accompany your choice. During the winter months, try Parsnip Soufflé or Bean-Stuffed Cabbage Leaves, or any of the many dishes containing dried pulses. Whatever you choose and whatever the occasion, you and your family can be sure of enjoying satisfying and nutritious vegetarian meals.

Courgette crumble

SERVES 4

750 g/1½ lb courgettes, trimmed
   and sliced
25 g/1 oz butter
salt and freshly ground black pepper
225 g/8 oz Cheddar or Cheshire
   cheese, grated
250 g/9 oz tomatoes, skinned and
   thinly sliced
1 teaspoon dried marjoram or mixed
   herbs
1 egg
150 ml/¼ pint milk
50 g/2 oz fresh white breadcrumbs
50 g/2 oz walnuts, roughly chopped

1 Melt the butter in a frying-pan
and fry the courgettes over moderate
heat, turning them once, for about
10 minutes, or until they are nearly
tender. Remove the pan from the
heat. Season the courgettes well
with salt and pepper.
2 Heat the oven to 190C/375F/Gas 5.
3 Arrange half the courgette slices
in a layer in the base of an 850 ml/1½
pint ovenproof dish. Sprinkle with
one quarter of the cheese, cover
with half the tomatoes and half the
dried herbs. Sprinkle on another
quarter of the cheese, then the
remaining courgettes, tomatoes and
herbs. Sprinkle on another quarter
of the cheese.
4 Beat together the egg and milk,
stir in the breadcrumbs and walnuts
and the remaining quarter of the
cheese. Spread the mixture over the
vegetables in the dish and smooth
the top. ✳
5 Stand the dish on a baking sheet
and bake for 25-30 minutes, until
the topping is crisp and firm. Serve
hot, straight from the dish.

ROGER PHILLIPS

Vegetable cobbler

SERVES 4-6
500 g/1 lb Jerusalem artichokes, peeled and cut into 2.5 cm/1 inch chunks (see Preparation)
salt
50 g/2 oz margarine or butter
1 onion, finely sliced
100 g/4 oz mushrooms, sliced
40 g/1½ oz plain flour
300 ml/½ pint milk
100 g/4 oz Cheddar cheese, grated
freshly ground black pepper
250 g/9 oz tomatoes, skinned and quartered

TOPPING
175 g/6 oz wholewheat flour
1 tablespoon baking powder
½ teaspoon salt
40 g/1½ oz butter, diced
25 g/1 oz shelled walnuts, finely chopped
¾ teaspoon dried mixed herbs
about 150 ml/¼ pint milk

1 Put the artichokes in a saucepan, cover with water and add a good pinch of salt. Bring to the boil, lower the heat slightly and simmer for 5-10 minutes until just tender. Drain, reserving the liquid.

2 Melt the margarine in a saucepan, add the onion and fry gently for 5 minutes until soft and lightly coloured. Add the mushrooms and continue cooking for 5 minutes. Transfer the vegetables to a plate with a slotted spoon.

3 Sprinkle the flour into the pan and stir over low heat for 1-2 minutes. Remove from the heat and gradually stir in 150 ml/¼ pint of the reserved artichoke liquid and the milk. Return to the heat and simmer, stirring, until the sauce is thick and smooth. Reserve 1 tablespoon of the cheese and stir the rest into the sauce. Season to taste with salt and freshly ground black pepper.

4 Stir in the artichokes, onion and mushrooms and tomatoes. Taste and adjust the seasoning, then turn the vegetable mixture into a 1.5 L/ 2½ pint casserole.

5 Heat the oven to 220C/425F/Gas 7.

6 Make the scone topping: sift the flour, baking powder and salt into a

large bowl. Tip the bran left in the sieve into the bowl and stir well to mix. Add the butter and rub it in with the fingertips until the mixture resembles fine breadcrumbs. Add the walnuts and herbs and gradually mix in enough milk to form a soft dough.

7 Turn the dough on to a lightly floured surface and roll out thinly. Cut into about 15 rounds using a 5 cm/2 inch cutter and arrange these on top of the casserole. Sprinkle with the reserved cheese.

8 Bake the casserole in the oven for about 30 minutes or until the scone topping has risen and is golden brown. Serve at once.

ROGER PHILLIPS

Cook's Notes

TIME
50 minutes preparation, 30 minutes baking.

SERVING IDEAS
This substantial vegetable casserole makes a complete meal in itself, and is ideal for a nutritious main supper dish.

VARIATION
Replace half the artichokes with potato and add cooked peas at stage 4 for extra colour.

PREPARATION
Peel the artichokes like potatoes, discarding the small knobs as you work. If the artichokes are to be left standing, cover with water to which a little vinegar or lemon juice has been added to prevent discoloration.

If the artichokes are very knobbly, boil in salted water until tender, then rub off the skins when cool enough to handle them.

● 540 calories/2275 kj per portion

PAUL WEBSTER

Mushroom and potato pie

SERVES 4-6
350 g/12 oz button mushrooms, halved or quartered if large
50 g/2 oz margarine or butter
3 celery stalks, finely chopped
1 onion, finely chopped
40 g/1½ oz plain flour
2 teaspoons sweet paprika
1 teaspoon dried thyme
¼ teaspoon cayenne
300 ml/½ pint milk
2-3 teaspoons lemon juice

TOPPING
750 g/1½ lb potatoes
salt
6 tablespoons milk
50 g/2 oz margarine or butter
freshly ground black pepper
sweet paprika, for sprinkling

1 Heat the oven to 190C/375F/Gas 5.
2 Cook the potatoes for the topping: bring them to the boil in salted water, lower the heat and cook for 20 minutes or until tender.
3 Meanwhile, melt the margarine in a saucepan, add the celery and onion and fry gently for 5 minutes until the onion is soft and lightly coloured. Add the mushrooms and cook for a further 2 minutes.
4 Sprinkle the flour over the mushroom mixture, stir until well incorporated, then add the paprika, thyme and cayenne. Remove from the heat and gradually stir in the milk. Return to the heat and simmer, stirring constantly, until

the sauce is thickened and smooth.
5 Remove from the heat and stir in the lemon juice. Season to taste with salt and set aside.
6 Drain the potatoes well, then mash them with the milk and margarine. Season with salt and pepper to taste.
7 Pour the mushroom mixture into an ovenproof dish. Spoon over the mashed potatoes, spreading evenly. Mark with a fork. Sprinkle with paprika (see Did you know), then bake for 20 minutes until heated through. Serve at once.

126

Steamed vegetable pudding

SERVES 4
PASTRY
250 g/9 oz self-raising flour
salt
125 g/4 oz shredded vegetable suet
½ teaspoon dried mixed herbs
freshly ground black pepper
butter, for greasing

FILLING
350 g/12 oz carrots, sliced
350 g/12 oz swede, diced
2 celery stalks, chopped
1 medium onion, roughly chopped
1 tablespoon plain flour
4 tablespoons vegetable stock
25 g/1 oz butter

1 Grease a 1.1 L/2 pint pudding basin with butter.
2 Make the pastry: sift flour and a pinch of salt into a bowl, add the suet, herbs and black pepper to taste and just enough cold water to bind the ingredients together in a soft dough. Roll out the dough on a floured surface and line prepared pudding basin (see Preparation).
3 Plunge the carrots, swede and celery into a pan of boiling salted water for 1 minute only. Drain and refresh under cold running water. Drain well, and mix with the onion.
4 Blend the flour and stock together to form a smooth paste and add to the vegetable mixture with salt and pepper to taste. Transfer to pastry-lined basin and dot with butter.
5 Cover top with dough lid, dampening the edges to seal. Trim the edges. Cover the pudding with greased and pleated greaseproof paper and secure in place with fine string, making a handle. Place basin in a large heavy-based saucepan and pour in enough hot water to come halfway up sides of basin. Cover pan with a well-fitting lid and steam pudding over low heat for 3 hours. Check the water level during cooking and top up with boiling water, as necessary.
6 Protecting hands with oven gloves, lift basin out of pan. Let the pudding stand for 5 minutes, then remove covering. Turn out on to a warmed serving dish. Serve at once.

DON LAST

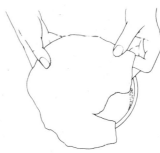

Crispy cauliflower bake

SERVES 4

1 small cauliflower, broken into
   florets
salt
1 bunch watercress, stalks removed
   (see Economy)
75 g/3 oz margarine
40 g/1½ oz plain flour
425 ml/¾ pint milk
pinch of freshly grated nutmeg
freshly ground black pepper
1 small egg
4 tablespoons double cream
65 g/2½ oz Cheddar cheese, grated
2 tablespoons crushed bran flakes
4 small slices white bread
margarine, for greasing

1 Heat the oven to 190C/375F/Gas 5
and grease a baking dish.
2 Bring a large pan of salted water
to the boil and cook the cauliflower
florets for 5 minutes.
3 Reserve a few watercress leaves
for the garnish, then add the
remainder to pan. Return to the boil
and then cook for a further 3
minutes. Drain cauliflower and
watercress thoroughly.

4 Put the cauliflower and watercress, a little at a time, into the
goblet of a blender and work to a
purée.
5 Melt 50 g/2 oz of the margarine in
a small pan, sprinkle in flour and
stir over low heat for 1-2 minutes
until it is straw-coloured. Remove
from the heat and gradually stir in
the milk. Return to the heat and
simmer, stirring, until thick and
smooth. Season with the nutmeg
and salt and pepper to taste and
simmer for 3 minutes. Remove from
the heat and beat in the egg.
6 Stir the vegetable purée into the
sauce. Stir in cream and 50 g/2 oz of
the cheese, then taste and adjust

the seasoning (see Cook's tip).
7 Pour vegetable mixture into the
prepared dish and level the top.
8 Mix together the bran flakes and
remaining cheese and scatter over
the top, then melt the remaining
margarine in a small pan and let it
drizzle over the topping.
9 Cook the dish in the oven for
30 minutes, or until the topping
is crisp and golden.
10 Make toast: about 10 minutes
before the end of the cooking
time, cut the slices of bread into
shapes with a cutter and toast them.
11 Serve the dish hot, garnished
with the reserved watercress leaves
and the toast.

MARTIN BRIGDALE

Potato and carrot layer

SERVES 6

1.5 kg/3 lb potatoes
750 g/1½ lb carrots, diced (see Buying guide)
salt
25 g/1 oz margarine or butter
1 onion, chopped
50 g/2 oz shelled walnuts, chopped
1 tablespoon lemon juice
1 tablespoon water
50 g/2 oz sultanas
1 small piece of stem ginger, with 1 tablespoon syrup reserved
freshly ground black pepper
a little milk

1 Heat the oven to 190C/375F/Gas 5. Grease an ovenproof dish, about 20 cm/8 inches in diameter and 13 cm/5 inches deep.

Cook's Notes

TIME
20 minutes preparation; 45 minutes cooking.

BUYING GUIDE
Avoid buying old, woody carrots as they take longer to cook and have very little flavour.

VARIATION
Slice the boiled potatoes instead of mashing them, and pour a little stock or milk over the dish after layering so that it does not become too dry during cooking.

● 350 calories/1475 kj per portion

2 Bring a pan of salted water to the boil and cook the potatoes for about 20 minutes or until tender.

3 Meanwhile, melt half the margarine in a large frying-pan, add the onion and fry gently for 5 minutes until soft and lightly coloured.

4 Stir in the carrots, walnuts, lemon juice, water and sultanas, cover and simmer gently for about 10 minutes until the carrots are barely tender.

5 Add the stem ginger and syrup, season to taste with salt and pepper, then remove from the heat.

6 Drain the cooked potatoes and mash them with a little milk and the remaining margarine. Beat until smooth then season to taste with salt and pepper.

7 Spread one-third of the potatoes in the dish and top with half the carrots. Repeat these layers again and finish with remaining potato.

8 Bake in the oven for 15-20 minutes. Serve at once.

Root vegetables braised in beer

SERVES 4

3 medium parsnips (total weight about 350 g/12 oz)

1 medium swede (weighing about 350 g/12 oz)

3 medium carrots (total weight about 250 g/9 oz)

25 g/1 oz margarine or butter

1 medium onion, finely chopped

300 ml/½ pint bitter beer (see Variations)

1 tablespoon tomato purée

1 teaspoon dried marjoram

1 teaspoon dried thyme

½ teaspoon dried sage

salt and freshly ground black pepper

1 Heat the oven to 180C/350F/Gas 4.

2 Cut the parsnips in half lengthways and remove the tough, fibrous cores with a small sharp knife. Chop the parsnips, swede and carrots into 1 cm/½ inch dice.

3 Melt the margarine in a flame-proof casserole. Add the onion and fry gently until soft but not coloured.

4 Add the diced vegetables to the casserole. Pour in the beer and bring to the boil. Remove from the heat, stir in the tomato purée and herbs and season with salt and pepper.

5 Cover the casserole and cook in the oven for 1 hour, until the vegetables are tender and nearly all the liquid has been absorbed.

DON LAST

Savoury celery supper

SERVES 4

1 head celery, cut into 2.5 cm/1 inch lengths
salt
2 tablespoons capers
2 tablespoons finely chopped fresh parsley
1 large gherkin, finely chopped
2 large potatoes, cooked and sliced
3 hard-boiled eggs, sliced
150 g/5 oz mature Cheddar cheese, grated
25 g/1 oz plain flour
2 × 150 g/5 oz cartons natural yoghurt
2 eggs, beaten
freshly ground black pepper
1 packet potato crisps, crushed
margarine, for greasing

1 Heat the oven to 190C/375F/Gas 5. Grease a 2 L/3½ pint ovenproof dish.

2 Bring a pan of salted water to the boil and cook the celery for 5-10 minutes until just tender.

3 Meanwhile, mix the capers, parsley and gherkin in a small bowl.

4 Drain the celery thoroughly and arrange half in the prepared dish. Cover with layers of half the potato slices, half the egg slices and 100 g/4 oz cheese, sprinkling half the caper, parsley and gherkin mixture between the layers. Repeat with the remaining ingredients, but reverse the order of the layers: egg, potato and celery sprinkling them with the remaining caper mixture.

5 In a bowl, blend the flour with a little of the yoghurt, then gradually whisk in the remainder. Mix in the beaten eggs, then season with salt and pepper to taste and pour into the dish.

6 Mix the reserved cheese with the crushed crisps and sprinkle over the surface. Bake in the oven for about 30 minutes.

7 Just before the end of the cooking time, heat the grill to high. When the mixture is cooked and the custard set, place the dish under the grill for about 5 minutes, or until the top is brown and crisp. Serve hot, straight from the dish.

PAUL WEBSTER

Cook's Notes

TIME
This supper dish takes 40 minutes to prepare, including hard-boiling the eggs and boiling the potatoes, and a further 35 minutes to cook.

VARIATIONS
Instead of the grated Cheddar cheese, pare off the rind from the same weight of ripe Camembert and cut it into thin slices before using in the dish and mixing with the crisps.

SERVING IDEAS
Serve with an apple, walnut, and shredded cabbage salad.

● 460 calories/1925 kj per portion

Aubergine supper

SERVES 4

750 g/1½ lb aubergines, skinned
    and cut into 1 cm/½ inch cubes
    (see Buying guide)
1 tablespoon salt
40 g/1½ oz margarine or butter
2 onions, chopped
40 g/1½ oz plain flour
3 large eggs, beaten
1 tablespoon lemon juice
freshly ground black pepper
2 large tomatoes, thinly sliced
4 black olives, halved and stoned
50 g/2 oz Cheddar cheese, grated
margarine, for greasing

1 Put the cubed aubergines in a colander and sprinkle them with the salt, tossing to coat evenly. Set the colander on a plate and leave to drain for 30 minutes.

2 Heat the oven to 200C/400F/Gas 6. Lightly grease a 1 L/2 pint shallow ovenproof dish. Rinse the drained aubergines thoroughly under cold running water, then drain well again and dry on absorbent paper.

3 Melt the margarine in a large saucepan. Add the cubed aubergines and chopped onions and cook over high heat for 5 minutes, stirring all the time. Reduce heat to moderate and cook, stirring all the time, for a further 5 minutes, or until the aubergine is soft and mushy.

4 Remove the pan from the heat and mash the aubergine with a fork. Leave to cool slightly, then sprinkle over the flour and stir it in well. Mix in the beaten eggs and lemon juice, then season with plenty of black pepper (do not add any salt as the mixture will be quite salty already).

5 Arrange half the tomato slices over the base of the prepared dish. Pour in the aubergine mixture and spread out evenly, then arrange the remaining tomato slices on top. Put halved olives on the tomato slices and sprinkle over the grated cheese.

6 Bake in the oven for about 40 minutes, until the aubergine mixture is set in the middle when tested with a knife. Serve hot or warm.

Cook's Notes

TIME
While the aubergines drain for 30 minutes, prepare the rest of the ingredients. Assembling the dish then takes 20 minutes. Baking takes 40 minutes.

SERVING IDEAS
This makes an excellent satisfying main course. Serve hot or warm, with a mixed salad and wholemeal bread and butter. Use a pie server or a fish slice for neat portions.

VARIATIONS
Lancashire, Gruyère or any good melting cheese could replace the Cheddar.

BUYING GUIDE
The aubergines should be a deep purplish-black and firm and shiny.

●270 calories/1125 kj per portion

132

DON LAST

Savoury potato roll

SERVES 4
750 g/1½ lb potatoes
15 g/½ oz margarine or butter
**100 g/4 oz mature Cheddar cheese,
   grated**
salt and freshly ground black pepper
**1-2 tablespoons grated Parmesan
   cheese**
vegetable oil, for greasing

FILLING
**750 g/1½ lb fresh spinach or 500 g/
   1 lb packet frozen leaf spinach**
100 g/4 oz curd cheese
freshly grated nutmeg

1 Bring the potatoes to the boil in water, lower the heat and then simmer for 20 minutes until tender.
2 Drain the potatoes well and mash with the margarine. ⚠ Add 75 g/ 3 oz of the grated Cheddar cheese and beat until smooth. Season to taste and set aside to cool.
3 Put spinach into a saucepan with

only the water that clings to the leaves after washing. Sprinkle with salt, cover and cook over low heat for 5 minutes, shaking the saucepan constantly. Or, cook frozen spinach according to packet instructions.
4 Drain the spinach thoroughly and chop finely. Add the curd cheese, nutmeg, salt and pepper, mix well.
5 Heat the oven to 200C/400F/Gas 6 and grease a baking tray.
6 Lightly oil a large piece of greaseproof paper and sprinkle with the Parmesan cheese. Spoon the cooled potato mixture into the

centre. With floured hands, pat out potato to a 30 × 25 cm/12 × 10 inch rectangle. Smooth the surface.
7 Spread spinach mixture evenly over potato to within 2.5 cm/1 inch of the edges, then, starting from 1 short end, lift paper to roll up the mixture like a Swiss roll.
8 Using 2 fish slices, transfer the roll to prepared tray, seam side down. Sprinkle with the remaining grated Cheddar cheese and bake above centre in the oven for 25-30 minutes, until golden. Transfer to a warmed serving plate and serve.

Cook's Notes

TIME
40 minutes preparation, 25-30 minutes cooking.

SERVING IDEAS
This potato roll makes a delicious lunch dish served with a fresh tomato sauce. Alternatively, serve as an unusual first course, or as a sophisticated vegetable accompaniment.

! WATCHPOINT
Make sure that the potatoes are very well drained; if necessary, return them to the saucepan after draining, and place over low heat for a few minutes to dry. Do not use a food processor to mash the potatoes; this makes the texture too liquid.

● 350 calories/1450 kj per portion

FRED MANCINI

Fennel with cheese

SERVES 4
2 fennel bulbs (total weight 750 g/
  1½ lb), thinly sliced (see
  Preparation)
salt
25 g/1 oz butter
25 g/1 oz plain flour
225 ml/8 fl oz milk
175 g/6 oz Gruyère or Cheddar
  cheese, finely grated
¼ teaspoon freshly grated nutmeg
freshly ground black pepper
50 g/2 oz Parmesan cheese, grated
margarine, for greasing

1 Heat the oven to 180C/350F/Gas 4.
Grease an ovenproof dish.
2 Bring a saucepan of salted water
to the boil, add the fennel, bring
back to the boil and cook for 6
minutes or until just tender.
3 Meanwhile, melt the butter in a
saucepan, sprinkle in the flour and
stir over low heat for 1-2 minutes
until straw-coloured. Remove from

the heat and gradually stir in the
milk. Return to the heat and
simmer, stirring, until thick and
smooth. Add grated Gruyère and
nutmeg and season to taste with salt
and pepper. Stir well until the
cheese is melted.

4 Drain the cooked fennel well,
then stir into the cheese sauce.
Transfer the fennel to the prepared
dish and sprinkle with Parmesan
cheese.
5 Bake in the oven for 15 minutes
until the topping is golden. Serve.

Cook's Notes

 TIME
Preparation 10 minutes;
cooking 30 minutes.

 SERVING IDEAS
Serve as a satisfying
main dish accompanied
by fried potatoes and a mixed
salad. Alternatively, serve with
crusty wholemeal bread.

FREEZING
This dish can be frozen
before baking: make in
a foil container, cover with the
lid, then seal, label and freeze
for up to 3 months. To serve:
bake from frozen in uncovered
foil container in a 190C/375F/
Gas 5 oven for 30 minutes.

 PREPARATION
To slice a bulb of
fennel thinly:

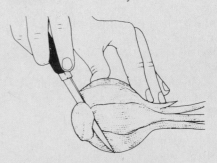

*Trim away bulb base and all wispy
leaves. Using a long, sharp knife,
cut through the fennel bulb
vertically.*

●375 calories/1575 kj per portion

Vegetables in curry sauce

SERVES 4
1 small cauliflower, divided into florets
250 g/9 oz small carrots, scraped and thickly sliced
250 g/9 oz French beans, trimmed and cut into chunks
250 g/9 oz shelled broad beans
salt

SAUCE
25 g/1 oz butter
25 g/1 oz plain flour
1 tablespoon mild curry powder
large pinch of ground ginger
300 ml/½ pint milk
2 tablespoons fresh orange juice
freshly ground black pepper
2 tablespoons single cream or top of the milk
1 tablespoon blanched almonds, halved
1 tablespoon chopped mint or parsley

1 Cook all the prepared vegetables together in boiling salted water until they are just tender — no more than 10 minutes. Do not allow them to become soft. Drain the vegetables, reserving the stock, and put them on a warmed serving dish. Keep hot.
2 To make the sauce: melt the butter in a saucepan, add the flour and stir to form a smooth paste, or roux. Stir in the curry powder and ginger and stir over moderate heat for 3 minutes.
3 Gradually pour on the milk, orange juice and 300 ml/½ pint of the reserved stock, still stirring. Bring to the boil and simmer for 3 minutes. Taste the sauce and season with pepper, and salt if necessary. Remove the pan from the heat and stir in the cream.
4 Pour the sauce over the vegetables, lightly tossing them with a fork to coat them. Scatter with the almonds and chopped mint or parsley and serve at once.

PETER MYERS

Cook's Notes

TIME
The preparation of the vegetables will take about 10 minutes, and the cooking of the vegetables and sauce about 25 minutes altogether.

 FREEZING
Use 1 tablespoon cornflour in place of flour if you wish to freeze the sauce. It is best to freeze the vegetables and sauce separately.

COOK'S TIP
To blanch almonds: boil for 30 seconds, then pinch off the skins.

● 240 calories/1000 kj per portion

ROGER PHILLIPS

Caponata

SERVES 4
3 aubergines, diced
salt
1 large head celery
100 g/4 oz black olives, stoned and
    sliced (see Buying guide)
2 tablespoons drained capers
6 tablespoons vegetable oil
1 onion, thinly sliced
25 g/1 oz sugar
75 g/3 oz tomato purée
100 ml/3½ fl oz white wine vinegar
2 tablespoons finely chopped fresh
    parsley
freshly ground black pepper

1 Put the diced aubergines in a colander in layers, sprinkling salt between each layer. Cover with a plate and place a heavy weight on top. Leave for about 1 hour to draw out the bitter juices.
2 Cut off root ends of the celery and

trim tops. Wash and remove any stringy bits. Cut each stalk in half.
3 Bring a large pan of water to the boil, add the celery and boil for 3 minutes. Drain and when cool enough to handle, slice thinly. Put in a large serving dish together with the olives and capers.
4 Rinse the salted aubergines under cold running water and pat dry with absorbent paper.
5 Heat 4 tablespoons oil in a large frying-pan, add the diced aubergines and fry over moderate heat for 3-4 minutes — they should still be quite firm. Transfer with a slotted spoon to the serving dish.
6 Heat the remaining oil in the pan, add the onion and fry gently for 5 minutes until soft and lightly coloured. Add sugar and tomato purée and cook for 3 minutes, stirring.
7 Add the vinegar and simmer for a further 4 minutes, stirring constantly. Stir in the parsley and season to taste with salt and pepper.
8 Pour the sauce over the vegetables, stir well, cool, then cover and refrigerate overnight.

Mixed fruit curry

SERVES 2

1 banana
½ honeydew melon, cut into
  2.5 cm/1 inch cubes (see
  Buying guide)
100 g/4 oz each green and black
  grapes, halved and deseeded
1 orange, divided into segments
1 red dessert apple, cored (see
  Cook's tips)
50 g/2 oz creamed coconut, broken
  into pieces (see Buying guide)
2 tablespoons curry paste (see
  Cook's tips)
150 ml/¼ pint soured cream

1 Put the coconut, curry paste and soured cream into a large saucepan. Stir over low heat until the mixture is well blended.

2 Peel the banana, cut into 1 cm/½ inch slices and add to pan with the melon, grapes and orange. Cook gently, stirring, for 3-4 minutes until the fruit is warm. Cut the apple into wedges, stir in and warm through. Spoon into a serving dish and serve at once.

Cook's Notes

TIME
20 minutes preparation,
5-6 minutes cooking.

SERVING IDEAS
Serve hot with plain boiled rice. Alternatively, serve for a snack or as part of a buffet party accompanied by salads.

BUYING GUIDE
Blocks of creamed coconut are available in packets from supermarkets and Indian food shops.
  Choose a melon that is not too ripe or it will break up.

VARIATIONS
Add 100 g/4 oz walnut pieces or salted roast peanuts to the fruit mixture for a more crunchy effect.

COOK'S TIPS
Use an apple corer to remove the core and leave the skin on to add colour.
  Use curry paste for this dish rather than curry powder. As the dish is only cooked for a few minutes, curry powder will give an uncooked flavour to the sauce.

● 280 calories/1150 kj per portion

ALAN DUNS

Split pea and carrot loaf

SERVES 4

250 g/9 oz green split peas (see Buying guide)
25 g/1 oz margarine or butter
1 onion, chopped
1 carrot, weighing about 75 g/3 oz, finely chopped
1 tablespoon chopped fresh mint, or 1 teaspoon concentrated mint sauce
1 egg, beaten
salt and freshly ground black pepper
melted margarine, for greasing
25 g/1 oz butter, melted
75 g/3 oz toasted breadcrumbs
sprig of fresh mint, to garnish

MARTIN BRIGDALE

1 Line the base and sides of a 500 g/1 lb loaf tin with non-stick parchment paper and grease the paper well with the melted margarine.
2 Put the split peas into a saucepan with enough cold water to cover generously. Bring to the boil, then lower the heat slightly and simmer gently, uncovered, for about 45 minutes, until the peas are tender. Top up with water as necessary. Drain the cooked peas thoroughly (see Cook's tip), then mash and put in a large bowl.
3 Heat the oven to 190C/375F/Gas 5.
4 Melt the margarine in a saucepan, add the onion and carrot and fry gently for 5 minutes until onion is soft and lightly coloured.
5 Mix the onion and carrot into the split peas, together with the mint and egg. Season to taste with salt and pepper and spoon the mixture into the prepared loaf tin.
6 Bake, uncovered, in the oven for 1 hour. ✳
7 To serve: turn the loaf out on to a board and peel off the lining paper. Brush liberally with the melted butter and press the breadcrumbs on to the top and sides, to coat well. Lift the loaf on to a serving plate, garnish with fresh mint and serve sliced.

Cook's Notes

 TIME
65 minutes preparation including 45 minutes simmering the peas. Baking in the oven then takes 1 hour.

 SERVING IDEAS
This economical yet nourishing loaf is excellent with roast potatoes and gravy as a family meal.

 BUYING GUIDE
Split green peas are available from good supermarkets.

 COOK'S TIP
Save the cooking water from the split peas; it makes nutritious stock.

 VARIATION
Split yellow peas may be used instead of split green peas—they are very similar in taste.

 FREEZING
This loaf freezes well. Bake for just 30 minutes, then cool completely. Open freeze until solid, then remove from the tin. Leave the paper lining on the loaf, then wrap in a polythene bag. Seal, label and return to the freezer for up to 2 months. To serve: remove bag, then replace loaf in tin and defrost for about 4 hours at room temperature. Bake in a 190C/ 375F/Gas 5 oven for 30-40 minutes and coat with breadcrumbs.

● 310 calories/1300 kj per portion

Nutty rissoles

MAKES 12

225 g/8 oz mixed nuts, finely
  chopped (see Buying guide)
25 g/1 oz butter
175 g/6 oz onions, finely chopped
1 large clove garlic, crushed
  (optional)
175 g/6 oz mushrooms, finely
  chopped
100 g/4 oz fresh wholemeal
  breadcrumbs
1 tablespoon finely chopped fresh
  parsley
2 teaspoons dried mixed herbs
2 tablespoons tomato purée
1 teaspoon soy sauce
1 egg, beaten
salt and freshly ground black pepper
3-4 tablespoons plain flour, for
  coating
a little vegetable oil, for frying
mushroom slices and walnut
  halves, to garnish

1 Melt the butter in a saucepan
then add the onions and garlic, if
using, and fry over gentle heat for
4-5 minutes until soft.
2 Remove the pan from the heat
and stir in the nuts, mushrooms,
breadcrumbs, parsley and mixed
herbs until well blended. Add the
tomato purée and soy sauce and
sufficient beaten egg to bind the
mixture together. Season to taste
with salt and pepper.
3 Roll heaped tablespoons of the
mixture in flour to form 12 balls
then flatten them into rissoles about
7.5 cm/3 inches in diameter.
4 Arrange the prepared rissoles on
a floured baking sheet and leave in
the refrigerator or in a cold place for
about 1 hour.
5 Heat the oven to 110C/225F/Gas ¼.
6 Heat a little vegetable oil in a
large frying-pan and fry the rissoles
in 2 batches, cooking them for 3-5
minutes on each side or until crisp
and golden brown. Remove with
slotted spoon; drain on absorbent
paper. Put them in the oven to keep
warm while cooking the remaining
rissoles. When all the rissoles are
cooked, garnish with mushroom
slices and walnut halves and serve
them at once, while still piping hot.

JAMES JACKSON

Lentil patties

SERVES 4
100 g/4 oz split red lentils
3 tablespoons vegetable oil
1 onion, finely chopped
75 ml/3 fl oz water
225 g/8 oz can tomatoes
salt and freshly ground black pepper
2 eggs, beaten
25 g/1 oz cornflakes, crushed

1 Heat 1 tablespoon oil in a saucepan, add the onion and fry gently for 5 minutes until soft and lightly coloured. Stir in the lentils, water and tomatoes with their juices. Season to taste with salt and black pepper.
2 Bring to the boil, then lower the heat slightly, cover and simmer for 40-45 minutes until the mixture is soft and thick. Stir the mixture from time to time.
3 Remove the pan from the heat and stir in 2 tablespoons beaten egg, reserving the remainder in a shallow bowl. Leave the lentil mixture to cool and then refrigerate for at least 2 hours.
4 Divide the lentil mixture into 8 pieces, then shape each piece into a small flat cake.
5 Spread the crushed cornflakes out on a large flat plate. Dip the patties first in the reserved beaten egg, then in the crushed cornflakes, to coat the patties evenly.
6 Heat the remaining oil in a frying-pan, add the patties and fry over moderate heat for 2 minutes on each side until browned and crisp.
7 Remove from the pan with a slotted spoon, drain on absorbent paper and serve at once.

Cook's Notes

TIME
Allow 1 hour to prepare and cook the patties, and at least 2 hours to chill them.

 WATCHPOINT
Stir the mixture more frequently towards the end of the cooking time—it has a greater tendency to stick to the pan as it thickens.

FREEZING
Drain and cool the patties. Open freeze until solid, then pack in rigid containers, separating layers with foil. Freeze for up to 3 months. To serve: defrost in a single layer on a baking sheet at room temperature for 2 hours, then reheat, covered with foil, in a 180C/350F/Gas 4 oven for 20 minutes.

SERVING IDEAS
Serve with a fresh green or tomato salad.

● 230 calories/950 kj per portion

Carrot and nut roast

SERVES 4
250 g/9 oz carrots, coarsely grated
100 g/4 oz cashew nuts or pieces (see Economy)
100 g/4 oz walnut pieces
100 g/4 oz granary or wholewheat bread
50 g/2 oz margarine or butter
1 onion, finely chopped
6 tablespoons hot vegetable stock
2 teaspoons yeast extract
1 teaspoon honey
1 teaspoon dried mixed herbs
2 teaspoons lemon juice
salt and freshly ground black pepper
margarine or butter, for greasing

1 Heat the oven to 180C/350F/Gas 4. Grease an 850 ml/1½ pint shallow ovenproof dish. Grind the cashews, walnuts and bread together in batches in a blender until they are fairly fine. Tip them into a bowl.

2 Melt the margarine in a saucepan, add the onion and fry gently for 5 minutes until soft and lightly coloured. Add the carrots and cook, stirring, for a further 5 minutes. Remove from the pan with a slotted spoon and add to the nuts and bread in the bowl.

3 Put the hot stock in a bowl, add the yeast extract and honey and stir until dissolved. Stir into the nut mixture with the herbs and lemon juice. Taste the mixture and season with salt and pepper. ⚠

4 Spoon mixture into prepared dish and bake in the oven for 45 minutes. Serve hot or cold (see Serving ideas).

PAUL WEBSTER

Cook's Notes

 TIME
35 minutes preparation and 45 minutes baking.

 SERVING IDEAS
Serve hot with baked potatoes, sliced tomatoes and a green vegetable or salad or serve cold with mixed salads. This carrot and nut roast is best served straight from the dish. It can be cut into thick slices or wedges depending on the shape of the dish that is being used.

 ECONOMY
Some health food shops and supermarkets sell broken nuts which are less expensive than whole nuts.

 WATCHPOINT
Taste the mixture before adding any salt, particularly if using salted nuts.

 COOK'S TIP
This dish can be made ahead and then reheated in a 180C/350F/Gas 4 oven for about 30 minutes.

VARIATION
Use any combination of nuts in this dish, as long as their total weight is the same as the nuts used here.

●450 calories/1875 kj per portion

141

Golden vegetable stew

SERVES 4

500 g/1 lb pumpkin, peeled,
   deseeded and cut into
   2 cm/¾ inch cubes
3 tablespoons vegetable oil
1 onion, chopped
250 g/9 oz carrots, thinly sliced
100 g/4 oz red lentils
400 g/14 oz can tomatoes
300 ml/½ pint vegetable stock
½ teaspoon ground mace
salt and freshly ground black pepper

SERVING IDEAS
This vegetarian stew is a warming and nourishing supper dish. Top each serving with a dollop of soured cream, if wished, and accompany with warmed crusty brown bread rolls.

● 215 calories/900 kj per portion

VARIATIONS
A 200 g/7 oz can sweet-corn, drained, is a tasty addition to this stew. Or, for a lighter dish, omit the soured cream and add the juice of ½ lemon and some chopped fresh parsley.

? DID YOU KNOW
Pumpkins, believed to be one of the oldest of cultivated vegetables, provide the mineral calcium as well as vitamins A and C.

1 Heat the oil in a saucepan and fry onion and carrots over moderate heat for 5 minutes.

2 Add the lentils, tomatoes with their juice, stock and mace, and season with salt and pepper to taste. Bring to the boil, lower the heat, cover the pan and simmer gently for 15 minutes.

3 Add the pumpkin to the pan, cover and then simmer gently for a further 15 minutes.

4 Taste and adjust the seasoning if necessary. Serve the stew piping hot, in warmed individual bowls.

MARTIN BRIGDALE

ROGER PHILLIPS

Lentil curry

SERVES 4

250 g/9 oz split red lentils (see
   Buying guide)
600 ml/1 pint water
1 bay leaf
salt
freshly ground black pepper
25 g/1 oz margarine
1 tablespoon vegetable oil
1 onion, finely chopped
1 clove garlic, crushed (optional)
1 teaspoon ground coriander
1 teaspoon ground cumin
½ teaspoon ground ginger
¼ teaspoon chilli powder
1 tablespoon wine vinegar
fresh coriander or continental
   parsley, to garnish

Cook's Notes

 TIME
10 minutes preparation,
30 minutes cooking.

 SERVING IDEAS
Serve this nutritious
lentil curry as a main
meal with plain boiled white
or brown rice and poppadums.

 BUYING GUIDE
Split red lentils are
readily available from
supermarkets; they take a
shorter time to cook than other
types of lentils which is a bonus
for the busy cook.

● 185 calories/775 kj per portion

1 Place the lentils in a saucepan
with the water, bay leaf and salt and
pepper to taste. Cover the pan,
bring to the boil and simmer for
about 20 minutes until the lentils are
swollen and the water has been
absorbed to give a thick consistency
like porridge.
2 Meanwhile, heat the margarine
and oil in a separate saucepan, add
the onion and garlic, if using, and

fry gently for 5 minutes until soft
and lightly coloured.
3 Combine all the ground spices
and mix to a paste with the vinegar.
Add the paste to the onion, and cook
gently for 3 minutes, stirring.
4 Add the cooked lentils and stir
well to mix. Cover the pan and cook
gently for 5 minutes. Transfer to a
warmed serving dish, garnish with
coriander and serve.

143

MARTIN BRIGDALE

Mixed bean casserole

SERVES 4-6

100 g/4 oz haricot beans
100 g/4 oz brown beans (see
  Buying guide)
100 g/4 oz black-eyed beans (see
  Did you know)
1 green pepper, deseeded
2 tablespoons vegetable oil
1 large onion, chopped
1 small head of celery, chopped
2 cloves garlic, crushed (optional)
793 g/1 lb 12 oz can tomatoes
425 ml/¾ pint water
1 vegetable stock cube (see
  Variation)
2 teaspoons dried oregano
salt and freshly ground black pepper

1 Put the haricot beans into 1 bowl and the brown and black-eyed beans together in another. Cover both of them with cold water and leave to soak overnight.
2 Drain the brown and black-eyed beans, rinse under cold running water, then put into a medium-sized saucepan and cover with fresh cold water. Bring to the boil and then boil for 15 minutes. ⚠ Drain and rinse the haricot beans, then add to the pan and bring back to the

boil, lower the heat, cover and continue cooking for a further 30 minutes.
3 Meanwhile, cut a few slices from the green pepper and reserve for the garnish. Chop the remaining pepper. Heat the oil ·in a large heavy-based pan and gently fry the onion, celery, the chopped green pepper and garlic, if using, for 10 minutes. Add the tomatoes and water, then crumble in stock cube

and add the oregano and salt and freshly ground black pepper to taste. Bring to the boil.
4 Drain the beans, add to the pan of vegetables, cover and cook gently for 1 hour or until the beans are very tender. Taste and adjust the seasoning, if necessary. Transfer to a warmed serving dish and serve at once (see Cook's tip), garnished with the reserved green pepper rings linked together, if liked.

144

FRED MANCINI

Egg and mixed bean curry

SERVES 4
4 eggs
250 g/9 oz dried mixed beans, soaked overnight (see Buying guide)
chopped parsley, to garnish

CURRY SAUCE
2 tablespoons vegetable oil
1 onion, finely chopped
1 clove garlic, crushed (optional)
1 tablespoon curry powder
1 teaspoon mild curry paste
25 g/1 oz cornflour
600 ml/1 pint vegetable stock
1 cooking apple, peeled, cored and grated
2 teaspoons redcurrant jelly
1 tablespoon ginger marmalade
juice of ½ lemon
2 tablespoons sultanas

1 Drain the beans, transfer to a saucepan, cover with fresh cold water [!] and bring to the boil. Boil vigorously for 10 minutes, then lower the heat, half cover the pan with a lid and simmer for 1 hour or until all the beans are just tender.
2 Meanwhile, make the sauce: heat the oil in a heavy-based pan, add the onion and garlic, if using, and fry gently for 2 minutes. Stir in the curry powder, curry paste and cornflour and stir over low heat for 1-2 minutes. Gradually stir in the stock and add the apple, redcurrant jelly, ginger marmalade, lemon juice and sultanas. Bring to the boil, stirring, then lower the heat and simmer for 45 minutes, stirring occasionally to prevent sticking.
3 Drain beans and add to sauce, then cook gently for 10 minutes.
4 Meanwhile, hard-boil the eggs for 10 minutes then, holding the eggs in a tea-cloth, remove their shells, and halve eggs lengthways.
5 Arrange the egg halves on a warmed serving dish. Pour the sauce over the eggs, garnish with parsley and serve at once.

Cook's Notes

 TIME
Preparation takes 20 minutes and cooking 1 hour 10 minutes.

 COOK'S TIP
Vegetable stock may be made from stock cubes, available from most supermarkets, or you can use water in which you have previously boiled fresh vegetables.

 BUYING GUIDE
Use a mixture of beans that take a similar time to cook, such as red kidney, pinto and black beans.

 SERVING IDEAS
Serve with a border of freshly cooked brown rice sprinkled with a mixture of finely chopped parsley and snipped chives. Accompany with side dishes of mango chutney, thinly sliced banana sprinkled with lemon juice, sliced cucumber in natural yoghurt and chopped peppers.

 WATCHPOINT
Do not add salt during the cooking as this makes the skins tough.

● 425 calories/1775 kj per portion

145

MARTIN BRIGDALE

Curried broad beans

SERVES 6

2 × 225 g/8 oz packets frozen broad
   beans
15 g/½ oz margarine
1 onion, finely chopped
1 clove garlic, finely chopped
   (optional)
1 tablespoon curry powder
400 g/14 oz canned chopped
   tomatoes
1 green pepper, deseeded and
   chopped
2 teaspoons lemon juice
salt and freshly ground black pepper
coriander leaves, to garnish
   (optional)

1 Melt the margarine in a large
saucepan, add the onion and garlic,
if using, and fry gently for 5 minutes.
2 Add the curry powder to the pan
and cook, stirring, for 1 minute. Stir
in the tomatoes, then add the green
pepper, lemon juice and beans,
lower heat, cover and simmer for
7 minutes, stirring occasionally.
3 Season to taste with salt and
pepper and cook, covered, for a
further 5 minutes. Transfer to a
warmed dish, garnish with
coriander, if liked, and serve at once.

Cook's Notes

TIME
5 minutes preparation,
20 minutes cooking for
this dish.

SERVING IDEAS
Serve this interesting
broad bean dish as an
unusual hot main course. Serve
with a tomato and onion salad
and hot pitta bread.

Alternatively, serve as an accompaniment to baked potatoes
or stuffed tomatoes.

VARIATION
Frozen peas or French
beans can be cooked in
exactly the same way as the
broad beans.

● 75 calories/310 kj per portion

Spicy red beans

SERVES 4

225 g/8 oz red kidney beans, soaked
  overnight
2 tablespoons vegetable oil
2 onions, thinly sliced
1 clove garlic, chopped (optional)
½ teaspoon ground mixed spice
¼ teaspoon cayenne pepper
600 ml/1 pint vegetable stock
2 tablespoons tomato purée
2 tablespoons white wine vinegar
1 bay leaf
salt

1 Drain the soaked beans, rinse under cold running water, then place in a large saucepan and cover with fresh cold water. Bring to the boil, boil for 15 minutes, then drain thoroughly.

2 Heat the oven to 180C/350F/Gas 4.

3 Heat the oil in a flameproof casserole, add the onions, garlic, if using, mixed spice and cayenne and fry over low heat for about 10 minutes until the onions are soft but not coloured.

4 Stir the beans into the casserole. Pour in the stock, increase the heat and bring to the boil. Stir in the tomato purée, vinegar, bay leaf and a pinch of salt.

5 Cover the casserole and transfer to the oven. Cook for about 2 hours until the beans are soft and most of the stock is absorbed.

6 Discard the bay leaf, then taste and adjust seasoning. Serve the Spicy red beans hot, straight from the casserole.

MARTIN BRIGDALE

Cheesy stuffed peppers

SERVES 4

4 red peppers, each weighing about 175 g/6 oz, tops sliced off and deseeded (see Variations)
3 tablespoons vegetable oil
1 onion, chopped
75 g/3 oz fresh brown breadcrumbs
75 g/3 oz Cheddar cheese, grated
75 g/3 oz almonds (see Buying guide)
2 tomatoes, skinned and chopped
1 tablespoon tomato purée
1 teaspoon dried thyme
salt and freshly ground black pepper
vegetable oil, for greasing

1 Bring a large saucepan of water to the boil, add the pepper cases and tops and blanch by boiling for 3 minutes. Drain thoroughly.
2 Heat the oven to 190C/375F/Gas 5.

3 Grease a shallow ovenproof dish generously with oil and arrange the pepper cases in the dish, side by side.
4 Heat the oil in a saucepan, add the onion and fry gently for 10 minutes until lightly browned. Remove the pan from the heat and stir in the remaining ingredients with salt and pepper to taste.
5 Divide the mixture between the pepper cases and replace tops.
6 Bake the peppers, uncovered, in the oven for about 40 minutes, until the filling is lightly browned. Serve hot, straight from the dish.

Cook's Notes

TIME
15-20 minutes preparation, and 40 minutes cooking.

SERVING IDEAS
These peppers make a delicious light supper or lunch dish; serve them with buttered noodles and a green salad.

BUYING GUIDE
Flaked or nibbed almonds can be used straight from the packet; whole or blanched almonds will need chopping first.

VARIATIONS
Use green, yellow or black peppers instead of red; add 100 g/4 oz finely chopped mushrooms with the tomatoes. Other nuts could be used instead of almonds: walnuts are particularly good, or mixed chopped nuts

●390 calories/1630 kj per portion

Sunflower seed peppers

SERVES 2

2 green peppers, halved lengthways and deseeded (see Buying guide)

2 tablespoons sunflower or vegetable oil

1 large onion, chopped

1 red pepper, deseeded and cut into 1 cm/½ inch squares

500 g/1 lb tomatoes, skinned and chopped

100 g/4 oz button mushrooms, quartered

50 g/2 oz sunflower seeds, toasted (see Buying guide and Preparation)

½ teaspoon dried thyme

¼ teaspoon sweet paprika

salt and freshly ground black pepper

40 g/1½ oz Edam or Gouda cheese, roughly grated

4 black olives (optional)

1 Heat the oil in a medium saucepan, add the onion and fry gently for 5 minutes until soft and lightly coloured. Add the red pepper and fry for a further 2 minutes, stirring. Add the tomatoes, mushrooms, toasted sunflower seeds, thyme, paprika and salt and pepper to taste, then cook over a moderate heat for 10 minutes, stirring constantly until the mixture is thick.

2 Meanwhile, bring a saucepan of salted water to the boil. Put in the green pepper halves, bring back to the boil and simmer for 6 minutes, until just tender. Drain thoroughly.

3 Heat the grill to high. Put the green pepper halves on the grill rack and season them inside with salt and pepper. Pile the sunflower seed mixture into the pepper halves, pressing it down with a spoon. Sprinkle the grated cheese lightly on top; garnish with olives, if liked.

4 Grill for a few minutes, until the cheese is melted but not brown. Serve at once.

FRED MANCINI

Vegetable stuffed marrow

SERVES 6

1 marrow
250 g/9 oz carrots or swede
2 potatoes
salt
3 tablespoons vegetable oil
15 g/½ oz margarine or butter
1 onion, chopped
4 celery stalks, thinly sliced
50 g/2 oz mushrooms, thinly sliced
1 tablespoon chopped fresh parsley,
    or 1 teaspoon dried parsley
1 egg
150 ml/¼ pint milk
50 g/2 oz fresh white breadcrumbs
50 g/2 oz Cheddar cheese, grated
freshly ground black pepper

1 Cut the ends from the marrow and completely remove the skin if wished. Cut the marrow in half lengthways and, with a tablespoon scoop out and discard the seeds and fibrous tissue (see Cook's tips).
2 Cook the carrots and potatoes together in salted boiling water for 10-15 minutes, until they are almost tender. Drain and leave to cool.

3 Heat the oven to 180C/350F/Gas 4.
4 Heat the oil and margarine in a large frying-pan and fry the onion and celery over moderate heat for 5 minutes, stirring occasionally, until the onion is soft and lightly coloured. Add the mushrooms, stir and cook for 1 minute. Set aside.
5 Cut the carrots and potatoes into 5 mm/¼ inch cubes. Stir them into the frying-pan with the parsley.
6 In a bowl, beat together the egg and milk. Stir in the breadcrumbs and cheese. Pour into the pan, mix and season with salt and pepper.

7 Place the marrow, cut sides up, on a working surface and pack the filling into the cavities of each half. Sandwich the halves of the marrow together again and wrap the marrow closely in foil, sealing the joins tightly.
8 Place the marrow on a baking tray and bake in the oven for 1½-1¾ hours, or until it is tender.
9 Carefully unwrap the foil and, with 2 fish slices, transfer the marrow to a warmed serving dish. Drain off the juices left in the foil into a small sauceboat.

Cook's Notes

 TIME
Preparation and cooking time is 2-2¼ hours.

COOK'S TIPS
Another way to scoop out the seeds from the marrow is to cut off a slice from each end. Then, using a melon baller or a strong teaspoon, and working from each end, scoop out the seeds and fibres until you have a clear tunnel right through. A tunnelled marrow is easy to slice.

 FREEZING
You can freeze the marrow, ready filled and wrapped in foil, for up to 3 months. To serve: stand the frozen parcel on a baking tray and cook at 190C/375F/Gas 5 for 1¾-2 hours.

SERVING IDEAS
As the marrow is crammed with vegetables, it makes an ideal main course.

●240 calories/1000 kj per portion

Stuffed courgette bake

SERVES 4

4 courgettes, total weight about 750 g/1½ lb (see Buying guide)
salt
25 g/1 oz margarine or butter
2 large onions, finely chopped
500 g/1 lb tomatoes, skinned and chopped
1 clove garlic, crushed (optional)
freshly ground black pepper

SAUCE

50 g/2 oz margarine or butter
50 g/2 oz plain flour
600 ml/1 pint milk
100 g/4 oz Cheddar cheese, grated

1 Heat the oven to 190C/375F/Gas 5.
2 Cut courgettes in half lengthways and scoop out the seeds with a teaspoon. Discard the seeds.
3 Bring a pan of salted water to the boil and cook the courgettes for 5-10 minutes, until just tender. ! Drain well, then carefully pat dry with absorbent paper and then set aside.
4 Make the filling: melt the margarine in a frying-pan, add onions and fry gently for 5 minutes until soft and lightly coloured. Add the tomatoes and garlic, if using, and cook for about 10 minutes, stirring occasionally until fairly thick.
5 Meanwhile make the sauce: melt the margarine in a saucepan, sprinkle in the flour and stir over low heat for 1-2 minutes until straw-coloured. Remove from heat and gradually stir in the milk. Return to heat and simmer, stirring, until thick and smooth. Remove from heat, stir in half the cheese until melted, then season with salt and pepper, to taste.
6 Pour half the sauce into a shallow ovenproof dish and place the courgette halves on top, hollowed-side up. Fill the cavities with the tomato mixture, piling it up well. Carefully spoon remaining sauce over top of courgettes and sprinkle with remaining grated cheese.
7 Bake in the oven for 40-45 minutes, until the top is golden. Serve at once, straight from the dish (see Serving ideas).

Cook's Notes

 TIME
50 minutes preparation; 40-45 minutes cooking.

 BUYING GUIDE
Buy large courgettes that will hold filling.

 SERVING IDEAS
Serve as a nutritious main course with rice. The rice can be cooked in the oven at the same time as the courgettes: put 1 part rice to 2 of water in a flameproof casserole. Add salt, bring to boil, cover and place below centre of oven.
Alternatively, serve as a light lunch or supper dish, with bread and butter.

! **WATCHPOINT**
Do not allow the courgettes to become too soft, otherwise they will collapse during baking.

●435 calories/1825 kj per portion

Bean-stuffed cabbage leaves

SERVES 4
12 white cabbage leaves
1 tablespoon vegetable oil
1 onion, finely chopped
100 g/4 oz haricot beans, soaked
**   overnight (see Buying guide)**
600 ml/1 pint vegetable stock
salt
1 tablespoon tomato purée
juice of 1 lemon
freshly ground black pepper

1 Heat the oil in a large saucepan, add the onion and fry gently for 5 minutes until soft and lightly coloured. Drain the beans and add them to the pan with the stock. Bring to the boil, then lower the heat slightly and simmer for about 1 hour or until the beans are tender.
2 Meanwhile, bring a pan of salted water to the boil. Remove the tough rib at the base of the cabbage leaves and blanch the leaves, 2 at a time, in the boiling water until pliable. Drain carefully, refresh under cold running water, then lay flat and pat dry with absorbent paper.
3 Drain the beans, then mash them roughly with a wooden spoon. Stir in the tomato purée, half the lemon juice and salt and pepper to taste.
4 Place 1 tablespoon of the bean mixture at the stalk end of 8 cabbage leaves. Fold the 2 sides over the filling, then roll up each cabbage leaf to form a neat parcel.
5 Line a large saucepan with the remaining cabbage leaves and tightly pack the cabbage rolls into the pan, join side down. Pour over the remaining lemon juice and enough cold water to cover. Sprinkle with salt, then place a small plate on top of leaves to keep them in place.
6 Bring to the boil, cover the pan, then lower the heat slightly and simmer gently for 1 hour.
7 Remove the plate and transfer the rolls to a warmed serving platter with a slotted spoon. Serve at once.

JAMES JACKSON

152

Braised stuffed artichokes

SERVES 4

4 globe artichokes
salt
½ lemon
1 tablespoon lemon juice
25 g/1 oz butter
300 ml/½ pint dry white wine
1 onion, finely chopped
2 carrots, quartered

STUFFING

50 g/2 oz butter
50 g/2 oz mushrooms, finely
   chopped
50 g/2 oz fresh white breadcrumbs
2 tablespoons chopped fresh
   parsley
2 teaspoons dried mixed herbs
2 cloves garlic, crushed
finely grated zest of 1 lemon
freshly ground black pepper

1 Bring a large pan of salted water to the boil.
2 Meanwhile, prepare the artichokes: using a sharp knife, cut off the artichoke stalks, then slice off the top third of each artichoke. Discard the trimmings. Rub the cut surfaces with the lemon to prevent discoloration.
3 Using scissors, trim any remaining sharp tips from the leaves, rub with lemon, then open them to expose the central whiskery 'choke', surrounded by purple leaves. Pull out the purple leaves, then scoop out the hairy chokes with a teaspoon and discard.
4 Add the lemon juice to the boiling water and then add the artichokes and cook for 15-20 minutes or until an outer leaf of the artichokes can be pulled out quite easily.
5 Meanwhile, make the stuffing: melt the butter in a saucepan, add the mushrooms and fry gently for 5 minutes until soft and lightly coloured. Transfer to a bowl and stir in remaining stuffing ingredients. Season to taste with salt and pepper and mix well.
6 Drain the artichokes, then stand upside down in a colander to extract all the water.
7 Heat the oven to 180C/350F/Gas 4.
8 Stand the artichokes upright and

spoon the stuffing into the centres. Place in an ovenproof dish, then put a knob of butter on top of each.
9 Pour the wine around the artichokes, then add the onion and carrots to the wine. Season lightly with salt and pepper, cover the dish with foil and cook in the oven for about 40 minutes. Serve hot, straight from dish.

Cook's Notes

TIME
About 1 hour preparation time, then 40 minutes for cooking.

SERVING IDEAS
These stuffed artichokes make a substantial and unusual main dish to serve with bread and butter. They would also make a rather special starter.
Serve each artichoke with a little wine sauce and provide teaspoons with which to eat the stuffing. To eat the leaves: pull off each leaf with your fingers and bite off the fleshy base of the leaf. Once all the leaves and stuffing have been eaten, cut up and eat the remaining heart.

Remember to provide a bowl for discarded leaves.

●245 calories/1025 kj per portion

ROGER PHILLIPS

Potato gnocchi and tomato sauce

SERVES 4
750 g/1½ lb potatoes
100 g/4 oz plain flour
25 g/1 oz butter, softened
pinch of freshly grated nutmeg
1 egg yolk, beaten
50 g/2 oz Parmesan cheese, grated
margarine or butter, for greasing

TOMATO SAUCE
1 small onion, finely chopped
1 clove garlic, crushed (optional)
150 g/5 oz can tomato purée
300 ml/½ pint water
1 teaspoon sugar
1 bay leaf
pinch of dried basil
salt and freshly ground black pepper

1 Make the sauce first: place all the ingredients in a pan with salt and pepper to taste. Bring to the boil, then lower the heat, cover and simmer gently for 30 minutes.
2 Meanwhile, bring the potatoes to the boil in salted water, lower the heat and cook for 20 minutes until

tender. Drain, then pass through a sieve into a bowl.
3 Work the sauce through a sieve, then return to the rinsed-out pan. Set aside. Grease an ovenproof dish and heat oven to 110C/225F/Gas ¼.
4 Beat the flour into the potatoes with the butter, nutmeg and salt and pepper to taste. Add just enough of the beaten egg yolk to bind the mixture. [!] Work in 40 g/1½ oz of the grated Parmesan.
5 Bring a large pan of lightly salted water to a simmer.
6 Meanwhile, turn the potato mixture on to a floured surface, divide into 3 and form each piece into a roll about 2.5 cm/1 inch in diameter. Cut each roll into 2.5 cm/1 inch slices.
7 Drop slices from 1 roll into the simmering water. Cook for about 5 minutes, or until they rise to the surface and look puffy. Remove with a slotted spoon, place in the prepared dish and keep hot in the oven while you cook the remaining pieces in the same way.
8 Reheat the tomato sauce. Heat the grill to high.
9 Pour a little of the warmed tomato sauce over the gnocchi and top with the remaining Parmesan. Place

under the grill for about 5 minutes until the top is golden and bubbling. Serve at once, with the remaining sauce handed separately in a warmed jug.

Cook's Notes

TIME
The cooking and preparation should take about 1¼ hours, plus 30 minutes for chilling.

SERVING IDEAS
Serve for supper followed by a green salad.

WATCHPOINT
Be careful not to make the mixture too wet. Then, to help shape it easily, refrigerate for 30 minutes.

DID YOU KNOW
Gnocchi is the Italian word for dumplings. They are most commonly made using semolina.

●380 calories/1600 kj per portion

154

Marrow kofta

SERVES 4

750 g/1½ lb marrow, skinned deseeded and diced
1 large onion, finely chopped
1 tablespoon chopped fresh coriander leaves
salt and freshly ground black pepper
2 tablespoons plain flour
vegetable oil, for shallow frying
coriander sprigs and onion rings, to garnish

SAUCE

2 tablespoons vegetable oil
1 medium onion, finely chopped
1 clove garlic, crushed
1 green chilli, chopped
1 tablespoon garam masala
225 g/8 oz can tomatoes
275 g/10 oz can mild curry sauce

1 Bring a pan of salted water to the boil and cook the marrow for 5 minutes until soft. Drain marrow and then pat dry on absorbent paper. Mash with a fork and drain again to remove excess liquid. Add the onion, coriander, salt and pepper to taste and the flour. Mix well and refrigerate for about 1 hour.
2 With lightly floured hands, roll the chilled marrow mixture into balls, 1 tablespoon at a time. Arrange in a dish on absorbent paper and refrigerate for 1 hour.
3 Meanwhile, make the sauce: heat the oil in a pan and fry the onion, garlic and chilli gently for 5 minutes.
4 Add the garam masala and salt and pepper to taste and fry for a further 2 minutes, stirring all the time. Stir in the tomatoes with their juice, breaking the tomatoes up with a wooden spoon. Add the curry sauce, stir it in, then increase the heat slightly and cook for 15 minutes, stirring occasionally.
5 Heat the oven to 110C/225F/Gas ¼.
6 Heat the oil in a pan and fry the marrow balls in batches for about 8-10 minutes, turning frequently. Remove from pan with a slotted spoon, drain on absorbent paper and keep warm while cooking the remainder of the marrow balls.
7 Arrange the cooked marrow balls in a warmed shallow serving dish, drizzle a little of the curry sauce over the top and garnish with coriander sprigs and onion rings. Hand remaining sauce separately.

Cook's Notes

TIME
The preparation and cooking time for the balls is about 50 minutes, plus 2 hours chilling time. Allow 30 minutes to prepare and cook the sauce during chilling time.

SERVING IDEAS
Serve as an unusual lunch or supper dish. Kofta are delicious served on a bed of plain boiled brown or white rice and accompanied by a fresh green salad.

WATCHPOINT
Make sure that all the excess liquid is drained away from the marrow mixture after mashing, otherwise it will be too mushy to hold a good shape when rolled.

DID YOU KNOW
Kofta is an Indian term for vegetables, or meat, or a mixture of the two made into small balls and fried.

●290 calories/1200 kj per portion

Brown rice ring

SERVES 4

150 g/5 oz brown rice
salt
1 red pepper, deseeded and diced
(see Preparation)
1 green pepper, deseeded and
diced
25 g/1 oz margarine or butter
1 Spanish onion, chopped
250 g/9 oz tomatoes, skinned,
deseeded and chopped
½ small cucumber, diced (see
Cook's tip)

DRESSING

3 tablespoons vegetable oil
1 teaspoon wine vinegar or lemon
juice
pinch of mustard powder
pinch of caster sugar
salt and freshly ground black pepper

1 Rinse the rice and put it into a
large saucepan of boiling salted
water. Bring to the boil again,
reduce heat and simmer, very
gently, for about 40 minutes, until
the rice is cooked and has absorbed
all the water. ! If necessary, add
more boiling water during cooking.
Rinse under cold running water and
leave in a sieve to drain thoroughly.
2 Meanwhile, soften the diced
peppers slightly by plunging them
into boiling water for 30 seconds.
Drain and refresh immediately
under cold running water.
3 Melt the margarine in a frying-
pan, add the onion and cook over
gentle heat for 5 minutes until it is
soft and translucent. Remove from
the heat and stir in the peppers,
tomatoes and cucumber.
4 Put the ingredients for the
dressing in a large bowl and whisk
with a fork to blend thoroughly.
5 Add the drained rice to the
dressing with the vegetables and
gently mix all the ingredients
together, using 2 forks. Pack into a
850 ml/1½ pint plain ring mould
and refrigerate for at least 1 hour.
6 To unmould: run a knife around
the ring mould. Invert a serving
plate on top and give the mould a
sharp tap. Serve chilled.

JAMES JACKSON

Curried rice

SERVES 6
100 g/4 oz medium-grain or Italian rice
salt
175 g/6 oz can pimientos, drained
1 green pepper, deseeded and chopped
2 tomatoes, skinned, deseeded and chopped
2 spring onions, thinly sliced
2 tablespoons blanched almonds, roughly chopped
4 tablespoons canned sweetcorn, drained
1 tablespoon seedless raisins
1 tablespoon sultanas
margarine or butter, for greasing
watercress sprigs, to garnish

DRESSING
5 tablespoons olive oil
1 tablespoon red wine vinegar
2 teaspoons lemon juice
1 clove garlic, crushed (optional)
1 teaspoon caster sugar
1 teaspoon mild curry powder

1 Cook the rice in a large pan of boiling salted water for 10-12 minutes, until it is just tender. Drain the rice in a colander, rinse under cold running water, drain again and turn into a large bowl.

2 Chop one of the canned pimientos. Cut the remaining ones into long strips about 1 cm/½ inch thick and reserve for the garnish.

3 Stir the chopped pimiento into the rice, together with the green pepper, tomatoes, spring onions, almonds, sweetcorn, raisins and sultanas. Mix well together so that the vegetables and fruit are distributed evenly.

4 Make the dressing: put all the dressing ingredients into a screw-top jar, add salt to taste and shake well. Mix the dressing into the rice mixture.

5 Pack the rice mixture into a 600 ml/1 pint bowl, pushing it firmly down with the back of a large spoon. Cover the bowl with cling film and set aside to cool.

6 Unmould the rice salad on to a plate (see Cook's tip). Arrange pimiento on the top in a wheel pattern and garnish with watercress. Serve at once.

Cook's Notes

TIME
Total preparation and cooking time is 30 minutes.

COOK'S TIP
To unmould the rice salad, run a thin-bladed knife around the inside of the bowl to loosen it. Put a flat serving plate over the bowl and, holding the two firmly together, invert the bowl. Give a sharp shake to release the rice mould. Stand the plate on a surface and gently lift off the bowl, taking care not to damage the mould.

PREPARATION
To skin the tomatoes, cover them with boiling water and leave for 1 minute; then plunge into cold water. Stab a tomato with a fork, remove from the water and peel away the skin with a sharp knife. Repeat with the others.

●215 calories/900 kj per portion

Hot beans and rice

SERVES 4-6

425 g/15 oz can red kidney beans, drained

250 g/9 oz long-grain rice

2 tablespoons vegetable oil

1 onion, finely chopped

1 clove garlic, crushed (optional)

1 red pepper, deseeded and thinly sliced

1 green pepper, deseeded and thinly sliced

2 celery stalks, finely chopped

2 large tomatoes, skinned, deseeded and chopped

1 tablespoon sweet paprika

1 teaspoon cayenne pepper

freshly ground black pepper

600 ml/1 pint water

salt

celery leaves, to garnish

PAUL WEBSTER

1 Heat the oil in a heavy-based saucepan, add the onion and garlic, if using, and fry gently for 5 minutes until soft and lightly coloured.

2 Add the sliced red and green peppers and celery and fry for a further 3 minutes. Add the tomatoes, drained beans, rice, paprika, cayenne and black pepper. Stir and cook for a further minute.

Pour in the water, stir the mixture well and bring to the boil.

3 Cover and simmer gently for 25 minutes until the rice is tender and all the liquid has been absorbed. Season with salt and pepper to taste.

4 Spoon the mixture into a warmed serving dish, garnish with the celery leaves and serve the bean and rice salad at once.

Cook's Notes

TIME
Preparation takes about 20 minutes, final cooking takes 25 minutes.

SERVING IDEAS
This substantial dish goes particularly well with plainly cooked vegetables. To serve cold as a salad, allow to cool, then toss in an oil and vinegar dressing.

VARIATIONS
Use 250 g/9 oz dried kidney beans instead of the canned type. Soak the beans overnight, then put them in a pan and cover with fresh water. Boil briskly for at least 10 minutes then simmer gently for 1½-2 hours. Drain and proceed with the recipe.

● 395 calories/1650 kj per portion

Stuffed cabbage pie

SERVES 4-6

1 green cabbage, weighing about
    1 kg/2 lb
175 g/6 oz long-grain rice
salt
15 g/½ oz margarine or butter
1 onion, chopped
1 cooking apple, weighing about
    150 g/5 oz
50 g/2 oz stoned dates, chopped
1 orange (see Preparation)
75 g/3 oz Cheddar cheese, grated
1 egg, beaten
freshly ground black
    pepper
margarine, for greasing

1 Heat the oven to 180C/350F/Gas 4 and grease an ovenproof dish 20 cm/ 8 inches in diameter and 7.5 cm/3 inches deep.

2 Bring a pan of salted water to the boil and cook the rice for about 10 minutes until just tender.

3 Meanwhile, remove about 8 outer leaves of the cabbage and cut off any thick hard midribs. Bring another pan of salted water to the boil and blanch the cabbage leaves for 4 minutes. Drain and set aside. Chop the remaining cabbage and reserve.

4 Melt the margarine in a large saucepan, add the onion and fry gently for 5 minutes until soft.

5 Add the chopped cabbage to the pan and cook over moderate heat, stirring, for 5 minutes. Peel, core and chop the apple and add to the pan. Cook for a further minute.

6 Drain the rice thoroughly and add to the pan with the dates, orange zest and juice. Remove from heat.

7 Line the base and sides of the dish with half the blanched cabbage leaves, arranging them so that they overlap and allowing them to overhang the dish. Stir the cheese and egg into the rice mixture, season to taste with salt and pepper, then spoon into the lined dish. Level the surface of the mixture and cover with the remaining leaves. Fold over overhanging leaves.

8 Cover the dish tightly with foil and cook for 45 minutes.

9 Loosen the sides with a knife and turn out on to a warmed plate.

JAMES JACKSON

Cook's Notes

 TIME
45 minutes preparation, including boiling the rice and blanching the leaves, then 45 minutes in the oven.

 PREPARATION
Grate the zest of half the orange and squeeze the juice from the whole orange.

● 370 calories/1560 kj per portion

 SERVING IDEAS
Serve as a complete meal with a home-made tomato sauce poured over the top. Cut the pie into wedges, to serve, and accompany with brown bread and butter.

 VARIATION
Use soaked dried apricots or drained canned apricots instead of the dates.

159

PETER MYERS

Herby spaghetti

SERVES 4
500 g/1 lb spaghetti
2 tablespoons olive oil
1 medium onion, chopped
1 clove garlic, crushed (optional)
1 green pepper, deseeded and chopped
100 g/4 oz mushrooms, sliced
2 × 400 g/14 oz cans tomatoes
salt and freshly ground black pepper
25 g/1 oz margarine or butter
50 g/2 oz Parmesan cheese, grated
2 teaspoons Italian seasoning (see Did you know)

1 Heat the oil in a saucepan, add the onion, garlic, if using, green pepper and mushrooms and fry over moderate heat for about 10 minutes until softened, stirring occasionally.

2 Stir the tomatoes with their juice into the softened vegetables, breaking them up with a wooden spoon, and bring to the boil. Lower the heat, add salt and pepper to taste, then simmer for 20 minutes, stirring occasionally.

3 Meanwhile, cook the spaghetti in a large pan of boiling salted water for 10-12 minutes or until *al dente* (tender, yet firm to the bite).

4 Drain the spaghetti thoroughly, then return to the rinsed-out pan. Add the margarine, half the Parmesan, the Italian seasoning and salt and pepper to taste. Toss quickly until all the strands of spaghetti are coated, then transfer to a warmed serving dish.

5 Taste and adjust the seasoning of the tomato sauce, then immediately pour over the spaghetti and mix well. Sprinkle with the remaining Parmesan and serve at once. Or if you prefer, hand the sauce separately.

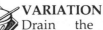

Tagliatelle with sorrel sauce

SERVES 4

100 g/4 oz sorrel (see Buying guide)
25 g/1 oz butter
150 ml/¼ pint vegetable stock
15 g/½ oz plain flour
150 ml/¼ pint double cream
freshly ground black pepper
little freshly grated nutmeg
salt
500 g/1 lb fresh tagliatelle
(see Buying guide)
finely snipped chives, to garnish

1 Wash the sorrel well and remove any thick stalks. Dry the sorrel in a salad spinner, or leave to drain in a colander until dry.
2 Melt half the butter in a saucepan, add the sorrel leaves and stir over moderate heat for 4-5 minutes, until the sorrel is completely soft and reduced to a small mass.
3 Put the sorrel in a blender with the stock and blend until smooth.

4 Melt the remaining butter in the rinsed-out saucepan, sprinkle in the flour and stir over low heat for 1-2 minutes until straw-coloured. Gradually stir in sorrel and stock mixture and simmer, stirring, until smooth and well combined.
5 Remove from the heat, then stir in the cream and season to taste with pepper and nutmeg. Heat through without boiling.

6 Meanwhile, bring a large pan of salted water to the boil and cook the fresh tagliatelle for 5 minutes or until it is just tender but still firm to the bite *(al dente)*.
7 Drain the pasta well, then return to the pan, pour the sauce over and toss until the pasta is evenly coated. Transfer to a warmed serving dish, sprinkle with snipped chives and serve at once.

Cook's Notes

 TIME
Only about 20 minutes to prepare the sauce and cook the fresh pasta.

BUYING GUIDE
Sorrel is not often available in shops, but it is easy to grow from seed in the garden for harvesting in summer. If unobtainable, fresh spinach or watercress may be used as a substitute.

Fresh pasta is far superior in taste and texture to dried and can now be bought from some large supermarkets, as well as from delicatessens and from speciality Italian food shops.

SERVING IDEAS
Sorrel sauce has a very subtle flavour which enhances mild-flavoured foods. Try it poured over vegetable kebabs, soya burgers, baked potatoes, boiled eggs or a simple French omelette.

● 660 calories/2750 kj per portion

Quick and easy homemade pasta

SERVES 2

225 g/8 oz plain flour
salt
75-100 ml/3-3½ fl oz cold water

1 Sift the flour and ¼ teaspoon salt into the goblet of a blender or food processor. Work for a few seconds, gradually adding the water ! until a dough is formed which has the consistency of fine breadcrumbs, but forms into a ball when it is pressed together (see Variations).

2 Remove the dough, press it into a ball, then place on a lightly floured surface and cut the dough into two equal halves.

3 Roll out 1 piece of dough very thinly so that the board can just be seen through the dough – it should measure 30 × 25 cm/12 × 10 inches. Trim off any dry edges of the dough with a sharp knife.

4 Fold and cut the dough to make long narrow ribbons (see Variations). Let pasta dry for 2-3 minutes while rolling, folding and cutting second piece of dough. Allow this batch of the pasta to dry for 2-3 minutes before cooking.

5 Bring a large pan of well salted water to boil and plunge all the pasta into it. Bring back to the boil and cook for 30 seconds. Drain and serve at once. Serve with your favourite pasta sauce, or buttered and then sprinkled with freshly grated Parmesan cheese and freshly ground black pepper.

Cook's Notes

TIME
The pasta takes only 15 minutes to make; cooking it takes about 1 minute.

! WATCHPOINT
Add the water slowly when making the pasta, as it is important not to get the dough too wet.

✳ FREEZING
Fresh pasta freezes well: do not pull the ribbons apart after cutting dough. Wrap cut 'sausage' in foil, seal, label and freeze for 2-3 months. To serve: thaw overnight in refrigerator or cook straight from frozen for an additional 2 minutes, stirring constantly to pull the dough ribbons apart as they soften.

COOK'S TIP
If you wish to make pasta for 4, double the quantities here, then cut dough into 4 pieces, as large quantities of pasta dry out and become difficult to handle.

VARIATIONS
When making dough, add an egg for a tastier pasta. Or, to make pretty green pasta, add a drop of green food colouring to the water.
Cut the dough into very thin ribbons. These are ideal for serving in soup and are a great favourite with children.

●400 calories/1675 kj per portion

Spinach and mushroom lasagne

SERVES 4

200 g/7 oz green lasagne (see Buying guide)
2 tablespoons vegetable oil
1 onion, finely chopped
125 g/4 oz button mushrooms, sliced
500 g/1 lb frozen spinach, defrosted and well drained
1-2 tablespoons lemon juice
¼ teaspoon freshly grated nutmeg
salt and freshly ground black pepper
225 g/8 oz cottage cheese
100 g/4 oz Cheddar cheese, grated
margarine, for greasing

SAUCE
25 g/1 oz margarine or butter
15 g/½ oz plain flour
225 ml/8 fl oz milk
4-5 tablespoons grated Parmesan cheese

1 Heat the oil in a heavy-based pan and fry the onion for 3-4 minutes, until soft but not coloured. Add the mushrooms and cook, stirring, for 5 minutes. Add the spinach, lemon juice and nutmeg and season with salt and pepper. Simmer for 5-6 minutes, stirring occasionally.

2 Meanwhile, mix the cottage cheese with the grated Cheddar in a bowl; season to taste with pepper.

3 Heat the oven to 190C/375F/Gas 5. Grease a 19-20 cm/7½-8 inch square, shallow ovenproof dish.

4 Make the sauce: melt margarine in a small pan, sprinkle in the flour and stir over a low heat for 1-2 minutes, until straw-coloured. Remove from heat and gradually stir in the milk. Return to the heat and simmer, stirring, until thick and smooth. Add the Parmesan cheese and salt and pepper to taste.

5 Put one-third of the lasagne in the prepared dish, spread with half the cottage cheese mixture, then half the spinach mixture. Repeat the layers. Cover with the remaining lasagne and spread sauce on top.

6 Bake in oven for 30-35 minutes, until the top is bubbling and golden. Leave to cool slightly before serving (see Cook's tip) and serve straight from the dish.

PETER MYERS

 Cook's Notes

 TIME
20 minutes preparation and 30-35 minutes to bake the dish.

 VARIATION
Substitute a 275 g/10 oz can artichoke hearts for half the spinach and put these in the second layer. Drain the artichoke hearts thoroughly before arranging over the cottage cheese mixture.

 BUYING GUIDE
Buy precooked lasagne for this dish.

 COOK'S TIP
Leaving the lasagne to cool slightly after baking gives the layers a chance to firm up slightly so that they will be easier to cut into neat portions when serving.

SERVING IDEAS
A simple tomato or grated carrot salad, garnished with chopped parsley, is all that is needed with this delicious lasagne for a nutritious lunch or supper dish.

● 585 calories/2450 kj per portion

163

Tagliatelle in parsley sauce

SERVES 4

350 g/12 oz fresh tagliatelle (see Buying guide)
1 tablespoon vegetable oil
grated Parmesan cheese, to serve

SAUCE

100 g/4 oz fresh parsley sprigs
2 large cloves garlic, chopped
25 g/1 oz pine kernels (see Buying guide)
150 ml/¼ pint olive oil (see Economy)
salt
50 g/2 oz Parmesan cheese, grated
freshly ground black pepper

1 First make the sauce: put the parsley, garlic, pine kernels and oil into a blender (see Cook's tips). Add pinch of salt and puree for 1 minute. Add all of the grated Parmesan cheese and puree for 1 minute more,
then season with pepper to taste.
2 Bring a large pan of salted water to the boil. Add the oil and tagliatelle and stir once. Bring back to the boil and cook for 2-3 minutes until *al dente* (tender, yet firm to the bite).
3 Drain the tagliatelle well, then
turn into a warmed serving dish. Stir the sauce and add to the dish. Quickly toss the tagliatelle with 2 forks to mix it with the sauce. Serve at once while still hot, with a bowl filled with grated Parmesan cheese handed separately.

PAUL WEBSTER

Wholewheat pasta with tomatoes

SERVES 4

275-350 g/10-12 oz wholewheat spaghetti (see Cook's tips)
50 g/2 oz grated Parmesan cheese, to serve

TOMATO SAUCE

750 g/1½ lb tomatoes, skinned and roughly chopped
25 g/1 oz butter
2 tablespoons olive or vegetable oil
2 onions, roughly chopped
1 clove garlic, crushed (optional)
225 ml/8 fl oz vegetable stock (see Buying guide)
65 g/2½ oz currants
2 teaspoons wine vinegar
1 teaspoon sugar
1 bay leaf
½ teaspoon dried basil
½ teaspoon dried thyme
¼ teaspoon ground cinnamon
salt and freshly ground black pepper

Cook's Notes

TIME
Preparation and cooking take 1¼ hours.

COOK'S TIPS
Wholewheat spaghetti has a mild, nutty flavour and, because of its high-fibre content, may take longer to cook than ordinary spaghetti.

The tomato sauce can be made in advance and reheated just before serving.

BUYING GUIDE
Vegetable stock cubes are available from health food shops and delicatessens. However, if they are difficult to obtain, use the liquid saved from cooking vegetables or, if you prefer, use red wine instead of vegetable stock in this recipe and omit the sugar from the tomato sauce.

● 505 calories/2125 kj per portion

1 Make the sauce: heat the butter and oil in a large saucepan, add the onions and fry gently for 5 minutes until soft and lightly coloured.

2 Add the remaining sauce ingredients with salt and pepper to taste. Bring to the boil then lower the heat and simmer, uncovered, for 40-50 minutes, until thick, stirring occasionally and breaking up the tomato pieces with a wooden spoon (see Cook's tips).

3 Bring a large pan of salted water to the boil and cook the spaghetti for 15-20 minutes or until tender, yet firm to the bite. Drain the spaghetti thoroughly in a colander.

4 Divide the spaghetti between 4 warmed individual serving plates or shallow soup bowls and top each with a ladleful of the hot sauce. Serve at once, with the grated Parmesan cheese handed separately in a small bowl.

CHRIS KNAGGS

Spaghetti supreme

SERVES 4

250 g/9 oz wholewheat spaghetti
salt
1 teaspoon vegetable oil
50 g/2 oz butter
200 g/7 oz blue Stilton cheese, cut
   into small cubes
25 g/1 oz walnut pieces, roughly
   chopped
150 ml/¼ pint single cream
freshly ground black pepper
65 g/2½ oz watercress, trimmed of
   thick stalks, finely chopped

1 Bring a large saucepan of salted water to the boil. Swirl in the oil, then add the spaghetti. Bring back to the boil and simmer for about 20 minutes, until the spaghetti is tender but still firm to the bite.

2 Meanwhile, melt the butter in a small saucepan. Add the Stilton and cook over very low heat, mashing with a wooden spoon, until the cheese has melted. Remove the pan from the heat and then stir in the chopped walnuts. Gradually add the cream, stirring vigorously. Season with a little salt and plenty of pepper. Set aside until just before the spaghetti is ready to serve.

3 Return the sauce to low heat, add the watercress and warm through. ⚠

4 Drain the spaghetti and rinse with boiling water. Drain again and transfer to a warmed serving dish. Pour over the sauce and then toss gently until the spaghetti is evenly coated with sauce. Serve the dish at once (see Serving ideas).

Cook's Notes

 TIME
Preparation takes about 30 minutes.

⚠ **WATCHPOINT**
Warm the cheese sauce through gently – it will separate if it becomes too hot. If this does happen, remove pan from heat and beat the sauce with a wooden spoon until it is thick and creamy.

 VARIATION
Try other shapes of wholewheat pasta, such as macaroni or shells or tagliatelle.

SERVING IDEAS
Serve with a crisp green or mixed salad, and a bottle of red wine.

● 625 calories/2600 kj per portion

MARTIN BRIGDALE

166

Brie quiche

SERVES 4
215 g/7½ oz shortcrust pastry,
    defrosted if frozen
lightly beaten egg white, to seal
    (optional)
sliced tomato, to garnish (optional)

FILLING
250 g/9 oz Brie cheese, rind
    removed and reserved, cut into
    2.5 cm/1 inch squares
150 ml/¼ pint single cream
3 eggs
½ teaspoon light soft brown sugar
pinch of ground ginger
pinch of ground turmeric
pinch of salt

1 Heat the oven to 200C/400F/Gas 6.
2 On a lightly floured surface, roll
out the pastry to line a 20 cm/8 inch
loose-based flan tin or flan ring set
on a baking sheet. Prick the base
lightly with a fork. Place a large

Cook's Notes

TIME
Preparing and cooking
take about 1½ hours.
Allow 15 minutes to cool.

COOK'S TIP
The squares of rind rise
to the top of the filling
and melt to form a golden crust
over the top of the quiche.

SERVING IDEAS
This quiche makes a
filling lunch or supper

dish served with a tomato or
fresh green salad.
    As the cooked quiche looks
like a whole small Brie cheese –
particularly if a plain flan ring
is used for baking – this dish
would make an unusual substitute for a cheese course at a
dinner party.
    Brie quiche can also be
served cold, but the flavour is
best when it is warm.

●555 calories/2325 kj per portion

circle of greaseproof paper or foil in
the pastry case and weight it down
with baking beans. Bake in the oven
for 10 minutes.
3 Remove the beans and paper or
foil, brush the inside of the pastry
case with beaten egg white, if
using, and return the pastry case to
the oven for a further 5 minutes.
4 Meanwhile, put the cheese in a
blender with the remaining filling
ingredients and blend until smooth.

5 Lower the oven temperature to
180C/350F/Gas 4. Arrange the
squares of Brie rind over the base of
the pastry case and pour over the
filling (see Cook's tip). Bake in the
oven for 30-40 minutes, until the
filling is set and brown.
6 To serve: leave the quiche for
about 15 minutes to cool. Remove
from the tin and transfer to a warm
serving plate. Garnish with tomato,
if liked, and serve warm or cold.

DON LAST

167

PETER MYERS

Watercress quiche

SERVES 4-6
2 bunches watercress, finely
   chopped
225 g/8-9 oz shortcrust pastry,
   defrosted if frozen
350 g/12 oz cottage cheese,
   sieved
3 eggs, beaten
3 tablespoons milk
pinch of cayenne
salt and freshly ground black pepper
lightly beaten egg white, to seal
sprigs of watercress, to garnish

1 Heat the oven to 200C/400F/Gas 6.
2 Roll out the pastry on a lightly
floured surface and use to line a
23 cm/9 inch flan tin. Prick base
with a fork. Place a large circle of
greaseproof paper or foil in the
pastry case and weight it down with
baking beans. Bake in the oven for
10 minutes.
3 Remove the paper or foil lining
and beans, brush the inside of the
pastry case with beaten egg white,
then return the pastry to the oven for
a further 5 minutes.
4 Meanwhile, make the filling: put
the sieved cottage cheese into a large
bowl, add the chopped watercress,
beaten eggs and milk and mix well
with a fork. Add the cayenne and
season to taste with salt and
pepper. ⚠
5 Spoon the filling into the cooked
pastry case and spread evenly.
6 Return to the oven for about 45
minutes, or until the filling has set
and is golden brown on top. Serve
hot, warm or cold, garnished with
the watercress sprigs.

168

Cheese and beetroot slice

SERVES 4-6
100 g/4 oz plain flour
100 g/4 oz wholemeal flour
¼ teaspoon salt
50 g/2 oz butter, diced
50 g/2 oz solid vegetable oil, diced
4-6 teaspoons iced water

FILLING
175 g/6 oz Lancashire cheese, grated
(see Variations)
175 g/6 oz cooked beetroot, skinned
and coarsely grated (see Buying
guide)
1 small onion, finely grated
1 teaspoon French mustard
2 tablespoons thick bottled
mayonnaise
1 tablespoon sweet pickle
salt and freshly ground black pepper

1 Make the pastry: sift both flours into a bowl with the salt. Add the butter and solid oil and rub into the flours with your fingertips until the mixture resembles fine crumbs. Add the water gradually and mix well to make a fairly firm dough that is not too dry and crumbly. Wrap in cling film and refrigerate for 30 minutes.
2 Heat the oven to 200C/400F/Gas 6.
3 Meanwhile, make the filling: in a bowl mix together the cheese, beetroot, onion, French mustard, mayonnaise, pickle and salt and pepper to taste.
4 Roll out half the pastry on a lightly floured surface and use to line a shallow 18 cm/7 inch square tin. Roll out the remaining pastry into a square slightly larger than the top of the tin and set aside.
5 Spread the filling over the pastry in the tin. Dampen the edges of the pastry with water, then lay the reserved pastry square over the top. Press it on to the side of the pastry lining above the level of the filling, then trim level with the top of the tin.
6 Brush with cold water, sprinkle lightly with salt, then make a hole in the top for the steam to escape. Bake just above the centre of the oven for 30-35 minutes, or until crisp.
7 Serve hot, warm or cold, cut into slices or squares.

MARTIN BRIGDALE

Cook's Notes

 TIME
This unusual pastry dish takes about 45 minutes to prepare and 30-35 minutes to bake.

 BUYING GUIDE
Bottled pickled beetroot can be used instead of the fresh cooked beetroot. Drain it well and omit the pickle.

●605 calories/2550 kj per portion

 VARIATIONS
Make the pastry and filling into 4-6 pasties. Use any well-flavoured cheese.

FREEZING
When cold, cut into slices and wrap individually in cling film, then in foil. Freeze for up to 6 weeks. To serve: defrost at room temperature for 2-3 hours. If liked, heat through in a 190C/375F/Gas 5 oven for 15 minutes.

DON LAST

Cauliflower cheese flan

SERVES 4-6
225 g/8 oz cauliflower florets
175 g/6 oz frozen shortcrust pastry, defrosted
225 ml/8 fl oz milk
3 eggs
100 g/4 oz Cheddar cheese, finely grated
salt and freshly ground black pepper
watercress sprigs, to garnish

1 Heat the oven to 200C/400F/Gas 6.
2 Place cauliflower florets in a large saucepan and just cover with cold water. Bring to the boil and boil for about 5 minutes. Drain, rinse well under cold water, then drain again very thoroughly and pat quite dry.

3 On a lightly floured surface, roll out the pastry to line a 20 cm/8 inch plain flan ring on a baking sheet.
4 Arrange the cauliflower in the pastry-lined flan ring (see Cook's tip). In a bowl, whisk together the milk, eggs and 75 g/3 oz of the cheese, season to taste with salt and pepper and pour over cauliflower.

Sprinkle evenly with the remaining grated Cheddar cheese.
5 Cook in oven for 40-45 minutes until the filling has only just set. Remove from the oven, leave to cool slightly, then carefully remove the flan ring and slide the flan on to a plate. Serve at once, garnished with the watercress (see Serving ideas).

170

Marrow and walnut flan

SERVES 4
1 kg/2 lb marrow, skinned,
  deseeded and roughly chopped
25 g/1 oz shelled walnuts, chopped
215 g/7½ oz frozen shortcrust
  pastry, defrosted
25 g/1 oz margarine or butter
1 large onion, chopped
salt and freshly ground black pepper
50 g/2 oz Cheddar cheese, grated
plain flour, for dusting
walnut halves and tomato slices,
  to garnish

1 Heat the oven to 200C/400F/Gas 6.
2 Roll out the pastry on a lightly floured surface and line a 20 cm/ 8 inch fluted flan dish. Sprinkle half the walnuts over the base of the pastry case and press lightly into the pastry.
3 Prick the base with a fork. Place a large circle of greaseproof paper or foil in the pastry case, weight it down with baking beans and bake blind in the oven for 15 minutes.
4 Meanwhile, melt the margarine in a large frying-pan, add marrow and the chopped onion and fry gently for about 15 minutes until the vegetables are soft. Season to taste with salt and black pepper.
5 Remove the baking beans and greaseproof paper or foil from the flan case and return to the oven for a further 10-15 minutes, until the case is crisp and the sides are beginning to brown. !
6 Spoon the vegetables into the cooked flan case and sprinkle the remaining walnuts and the cheese on top. Return to the oven for 5 minutes until the cheese has melted completely.
7 Remove the flan from the oven and allow to cool for 5 minutes. Garnish the flan with walnut halves and tomato slices and serve while warm (see Serving ideas).

Cook's Notes

 TIME
The flan takes about 1 hour to prepare and bake in total.

 SERVING IDEAS
Serve as a nutritious main meal with baked potatoes and a green vegetable. Alternatively, allow to cool completely and serve cold with a mixed salad.

 VARIATION
Courgettes make a very good alternative to marrow; do not peel them.

! **WATCHPOINT**
Make sure that the base of the flan case has dried out properly or the flan will be soggy.

● 410 calories/1725 kj per portion

DON LAST

ALAN DUNS

French onion flan

SERVES 4-6
750 g/1½ lb onions, finely sliced
225 g/8 oz shortcrust pastry,
    defrosted if frozen
40 g/1½ oz butter
2 tablespoons vegetable oil
egg white, for glazing (optional)
225 ml/8 fl oz single cream
3 egg yolks
½ teaspoon freshly grated nutmeg
salt and freshly ground black pepper

1 Heat the oven to 200C/400F/Gas 6.
2 Roll out the pastry on a floured surface and use to line a 23 cm/9 inch loose-bottomed flan tin or flan ring standing on a baking sheet. Prick the pastry base all over with a fork, then refrigerate for about 30 minutes.

3 Meanwhile, heat the butter with the oil in a large frying-pan and add the onions. Stir them round well, then cover the pan and leave to fry gently for about 30 minutes on a very low heat, stirring from time to time until they are soft and golden.
4 Line the pastry case with greaseproof paper or foil and weight it down with baking beans or rice. Bake in the oven for 10 minutes.
5 Remove the greaseproof paper and the beans, and brush the inside of the pastry with beaten egg white, if wished. Return the flan tin to the oven and bake for a further 5 minutes. Remove from the oven and set aside. Reduce the oven temperature to 180C/350F/Gas 4.
6 Mix the cream and egg yolks together in a bowl, stir in the nutmeg and season to taste with salt and pepper.
7 Spoon the cooked onions into the prepared pastry case and pour over the egg and cream mixture.

8 Bake in the oven for 35 minutes until the filling is set, then remove from the oven and leave to stand for at least 5-10 minutes. Remove the tin and place the flan on a serving plate. Serve warm or cold.

172

Mushroom and pimiento roll

SERVES 4

350 g/12 oz button mushrooms, chopped
185 g/6½ oz can pimientos, drained and chopped
50 g/2 oz margarine or butter
175 g/6 oz onion, finely chopped
salt and freshly ground black pepper
400 g/13 oz frozen puff pastry, defrosted
beaten egg, to glaze
flour, for dusting
150 ml/¼ pint soured cream, to serve

1 Heat the oven to 190C/375F/Gas 5.
2 Melt the margarine in a large frying-pan, add the onion and fry gently for about 5 minutes, until soft and lightly coloured.
3 Add the mushrooms, stir well and cook gently for about 5 minutes, stirring occasionally, until all the liquid has evaporated.
4 Transfer the fried mixture to a large bowl, add the chopped pimientos and mix well. Season generously with salt and pepper, then leave until cool.
5 Meanwhile, roll out the pastry thinly on a lightly floured surface to a neat rectangle about 45 × 35 cm/ 18 × 14 inches.
6 Drain the cooled mushroom mixture [!] and spread over the pastry, leaving a pastry border all round of about 1 cm/½ inch. Starting at 1 long edge, roll up the pastry. Gently press the roll to flatten the shape slightly, then tuck the ends in and brush with water so that they stick.
7 Dampen a large baking sheet and using 2 fish slices, carefully transfer the pastry roll to the sheet, join side down. Brush all over with the beaten egg (see Cook's tip).
8 Bake for 25 minutes. Serve hot, cut into slices with soured cream.

JAMES JACKSON

Cook's Notes

TIME
Preparation 30 minutes, cooking 25 minutes.

WATCHPOINT
The cooled mushroom mixture must be completely dry before spreading on to the pastry. Drain it through a colander (reserve the liquid for use in a soup).

COOK'S TIP
For an interesting presentation, the roll may be curved slightly into a U-shape before baking.

SERVING IDEAS
For a lunch or supper dish, serve with a mixed salad, or serve as a first course.

● 480 calories/2025 kj per portion

Egg and vegetable flan

SERVES 4

150-175 g/5-6 oz shortcrust pastry,
  defrosted if frozen

FILLING

40 g/1½ oz margarine or butter
100 g/4 oz button mushrooms (see
  Cook's tips), sliced
25 g/1 oz plain flour
½ teaspoon curry powder
300 ml/½ pint milk
4 hard-boiled eggs, shelled and
  neatly chopped
100 g/4 oz frozen peas, cooked
salt and freshly ground black pepper

1 Heat the oven to 200C/400F/Gas 6.
2 Roll out the pastry on a lightly floured surface and use it to line an 18 cm/7 inch flan tin. Trim the edges and prick the base in several places with a fork. Place a circle of greaseproof paper or foil in the pastry case and weight it down with a thick even layer of baking beans. Bake for 10 minutes.
3 Remove the greaseproof paper and beans, then return the pastry case to the oven. Bake for a further 10-15 minutes, or until the pastry is crisp and lightly golden.
4 Meanwhile, make the filling: melt the margarine in a saucepan and cook the mushrooms for 2-3 minutes, stirring occasionally. Remove from the pan with a slotted spoon, draining all the margarine back into the pan.
5 Sprinkle the flour and curry powder into pan. Stir over low heat for 1-2 minutes. Remove from the heat and gradually stir in the milk. Return to the heat and simmer, stirring, until thick and smooth.
6 Gently fold the chopped eggs and peas into the sauce. Season to taste with salt and pepper, then return to very low heat and warm through gently. Lastly, fold in the mushrooms (see Cook's tips). Pour the mixture into the cooked pastry case. Serve hot or cold.

PAUL WEBSTER

Cornmeal pie

SERVES 4

175 g/6 oz cornmeal (see Did you know)
salt
3 tablespoons vegetable oil
150 ml/¼ pint hot water
1 large onion, chopped
3 celery stalks, chopped
1 tablespoon tomato purée
freshly ground black pepper
100 g/4 oz Cheddar cheese, grated
4 tomatoes, skinned and sliced
6-8 stuffed olives, sliced
melted margarine, for greasing

1 Heat the oven to 180C/350F/Gas 4. Grease the base and sides of a 22-23 cm/8½-9 inch loose-based flan tin.
2 Place the cornmeal, pinch of salt and 2 tablespoons vegetable oil in a bowl and pour on the hot water. Stir well, then mix with your fingers to form a smooth, soft dough.

3 Line the prepared flan tin with the warm dough, gently kneading it into place with your fingers. Set aside to cool.
4 Heat the remaining oil in a frying-pan. Add the onion and fry gently for 5 minutes until soft and lightly coloured. Add the celery and cook gently for another 10 minutes, stirring occasionally. Stir in the tomato purée and season to taste with salt and pepper.
5 Sprinkle about one-third of the cheese evenly over the cornmeal base, then add the onion and celery mixture. Top with another third of the cheese. Arrange the sliced tomatoes on top, then sprinkle over the remaining cheese. Bake in the oven for about 35 minutes until the topping is golden.
6 Remove the flan from the oven, arrange the sliced olives decoratively on top, then return to the oven for a further 5 minutes. Remove from tin and serve hot.

DON LAST

175

Cabbage koulibiaka

SERVES 4

500 g/1 lb crisp cabbage (see Buying
  guide), coarse leaves and stalks
  removed, sliced
50 g/2 oz butter
1 onion, chopped
3 hard-boiled eggs, chopped
1 teaspoon dillweed
1 tablespoon chopped fresh parsley
2 good pinches sugar
salt and freshly ground black pepper
400 g/14 oz frozen puff pastry,
  defrosted
1 egg, beaten, to seal and glaze

1 Heat the oven to 220C/425F/Gas 7.
Line a baking sheet with foil.
2 Put the cabbage in a colander and
slowly pour over a kettle of boiling
water. Leave to stand for 2 minutes,
until the cabbage is just cool enough
to handle, then press the cabbage
down with the back of a spoon in
the colander to extract all the
excess moisture.
3 Melt half the butter in a medium-
sized saucepan and cook the onion
over moderate heat for 3 minutes,

until soft. Add the cabbage, stir
well, then cook over moderate heat
for 5-6 minutes, stirring frequently,
until the cabbage is cooked but still
crisp. Remove from the heat and
add the eggs, dillweed, parsley and
sugar. Season well with salt and
freshly ground black pepper.
4 Cut off about 175 g/6 oz of the
pastry, roll it out on a lightly floured
surface and trim to a 30 × 15 cm/
12 × 6 inch rectangle. Lay it on
prepared baking sheet. Pile cabbage
filling on to the pastry, leaving a
2.5 cm/1 inch border. Brush the
border with beaten egg.
5 Roll out the remaining pastry and
trim to a 33 × 20 cm/13 × 8 inch
rectangle. Lay the pastry over the
filling, press the edges together to
seal and flute decoratively. Make
3 holes in the top of the pie and
decorate with 'leaves' made from
pastry trimmings. Brush over
with beaten egg, to glaze.
6 Bake in the oven for 25 minutes,
until well risen and golden brown,
then reduce the oven temperature
to 190C/375F/Gas 5 and bake for a
further 15 minutes.
7 Remove pie from oven. Melt
remaining butter and pour it into
pie by inserting a funnel into each
hole. Serve at once, piping hot.

Cook's Notes

TIME
50 minutes preparation,
and 40 minutes baking.

BUYING GUIDE
Buy a crisp cabbage for
this recipe, such as a
Savoy or a Primo.

WATCHPOINT
The holes you make in
the top of the pie
should be large enough to take
a funnel after baking, so that
you can pour in melted butter.

SERVING IDEA
Serve the pie hot, with
chilled soured cream.

DID YOU KNOW
This dish is a version of
the Russian Koulibiaka
(also known as Coulibiac) – a
very grand fish pie which at
one time was served at great
occasions of state. For everyday
use, the dish was made from
humbler ingredients.

●610 calories/2550 kj per portion

Spinach and cheese pie

SERVES 4-6

2 × 400 g/12 oz cans leaf spinach,
 well drained (see Cook's tips)
215 g/7½ oz frozen puff pastry,
 defrosted
600 ml/1 pint milk
2 × 25 g/1 oz packets cheese
 sauce mix
freshly ground black pepper
3 hard-boiled eggs, sliced
100 g/4 oz mushrooms, sliced
50 g/2 oz Cheddar cheese, grated

Cook's Notes

 TIME
Preparation takes about 35 minutes and cooking time is 35-45 minutes.

 SERVING IDEAS
Serve as a lunch or supper dish with green beans or cauliflower.

 VARIATION
Line the pie dish with pastry and add chopped cooked potatoes to filling for a more substantial dish.

COOK'S TIPS
Drain the spinach in a colander and press it well with the back of a spoon to remove as much liquid as you can, otherwise the finished pie filling will be too watery and the pastry will become soggy.

As both the canned spinach and the packet sauce are already salted, do not add any more salt when seasoning the spinach pie.

●535 calories/2225 kj per portion

1 Heat the oven to 220C/425F/Gas 7.
2 Use almost all the milk to make the cheese sauce, according to the packet instructions, reserving 4 tablespoons to glaze pie top. Season to taste with black pepper (see Cook's tips).
3 Arrange half of the eggs over the base of a 23 cm/9 inch shallow pie dish or flan tin, then top with a layer each of half the mushrooms and half the spinach. Pour over half the sauce. Repeat the layers with the remaining eggs, mushrooms, spinach and sauce and sprinkle with grated cheese over the top.
4 On a lightly floured surface, roll out the pastry and use to make a lid. Reserve the pastry trimmings.
5 Place pastry lid on top, pressing down the edges well to seal. Knock up and flute. Roll cut pastry trimmings and make decorations. Brush with a little milk and place on top. Brush the pastry lid with the milk and then make a hole in the centre of the pie lid.
6 Cook in oven for 35-45 minutes, until the pie is golden brown. Serve the pie at once, while piping hot.

French bread pizza

SERVES 6

1 large French loaf, cut in half
  horizontally (see Buying guide)
25 g/1 oz butter
100 g/4 oz button mushrooms,
  thinly sliced
25 g/1 oz capers, drained
175 g/6 oz Mozzarella cheese,
  grated
black olives and spring onions, to
  garnish (optional)

TOMATO SAUCE

1 tablespoon vegetable oil
1 onion, thinly sliced
1 clove garlic, crushed (optional)
1 small green pepper, deseeded
  and thinly sliced
400 g/14 oz can tomatoes
100 g/4 oz tomato purée
1 teaspoon dried mixed herbs
1 bay leaf
1 teaspoon sugar
pinch of celery salt
salt and freshly ground black pepper

1 Make the tomato sauce: heat the oil in a heavy-based saucepan, add the onion, garlic, if using, and green pepper and fry gently for 5 minutes until the onion is soft.

2 Add the tomatoes with their juice, the tomato purée, herbs and bay leaf, sugar, celery salt, and a generous sprinkling of salt and black pepper. Stir well, bring to the boil, then lower the heat slightly and simmer gently for 20 minutes, stirring occasionally, until tomato sauce is fairly thick.
3 Meanwhile, heat the grill to moderate (see Cook's tip).
4 Melt the butter in a small pan, add the mushrooms and fry gently for 2-3 minutes until tender. Set aside in a warm place.
5 Cut each half of the bread across into 3 even-sized pieces. Place under the grill, cut-side up, for about 2 minutes until the surface is lightly crisp and evenly coloured.
6 Divide the tomato sauce between the 6 bread pieces, spreading the sauce over the toasted surface to cover it completely.
7 Spoon the mushrooms on to the tomato sauce, dividing equally between the slices of bread, then sprinkle each with the capers. Top with the grated cheese and grill for 10 minutes until cheese bubbles. Garnish with black olives and spring onions, if using, and serve.

MARTIN BRIGDALE

Golden savoury pancakes

MAKES 8

1 small green pepper, deseeded
   and finely chopped
15 g/½ oz butter
salt
250 g/9 oz carrots
vegetable oil, for frying
2 lemons cut in wedges and
   chopped fresh parsley,
   to garnish

BATTER

100 g/4 oz plain flour
2 eggs
300 ml/½ pint milk
2 teaspoons snipped chives
freshly ground black pepper

1 Melt the butter in a small pan, add the green pepper and fry over low heat for 3 minutes, stirring occasionally. Remove from the heat and set aside.

2 Bring a pan of salted water to the boil and cook carrots for 8 minutes, or until just tender.

3 Meanwhile, make the batter: sift the flour and ½ teaspoon salt into a bowl. Make a well in the centre and add the eggs and milk. Using a whisk, gradually draw the flour into the liquid. When all the flour is completely incorporated, stir in snipped chives and season with pepper. Cover and set aside.

4 Drain the carrots, chop finely and set them aside.

5 Uncover the batter, stir in the green pepper and chopped carrots and beat well.

6 To make the pancakes: heat a little oil in an 18 cm/7 inch frying-pan. Remove from heat, pour in 2 tablespoons of batter and tilt pan until batter evenly covers base.

7 Return to heat and cook until top looks dry and underside is golden. Loosen edge with a palette knife and shake pan, then toss pancake over and cook on other side for a further 20-30 seconds until golden. Lift pancake on to a sheet of greaseproof paper.

8 Continue making pancakes in the same way, interleaving them with greaseproof paper. Grease the pan with more oil as necessary. ✳

9 Fold the pancakes neatly in half, then fold these in half again. Arrange 2 on each of 4 plates. Serve with the lemon wedges dipped into the chopped fresh parsley.

MARTIN BRIGDALE

Cook's Notes

 TIME
Preparing the batter and making pancakes takes about 40 minutes.

 VARIATIONS
Use small amounts of other cooked, chopped vegetables to flavour the pancake batter and to add texture and colour. Try courgettes, mushrooms, broccoli spears or cauliflower florets.

 SERVING IDEAS
Serve with a lemon sauce: boil about 6 tablespoons lemon juice until reduced to 2 tablespoons; lower heat and beat in 100 g/4 oz butter, cut into small pieces; add salt, pepper and snipped chives to taste.

✳ **FREEZING**
Allow the pancakes to cool thoroughly, then wrap in foil. Seal, label and freeze for up to 4 months. To serve: reheat the foil parcel in a 190C/375F/Gas 5 oven for 20-30 minutes.

● 125 calories/525 kj per pancake

JAMES JACKSON

Beetroot soufflé

SERVES 4
**500 g/1 lb cooked beetroot, skinned
    and diced**
175 ml/6 fl oz orange juice
40 g/1½ oz margarine or butter
40 g/1½ oz plain flour
4 eggs, separated
salt and freshly ground black pepper
margarine, for greasing

1 Heat the oven to 200C/400F/Gas 6.
Lightly grease a 1.7 L/3 pint soufflé
dish with margarine.
2 Put diced beetroot in a blender
with the orange juice and blend
until thick and smooth.
3 Melt the margarine in a medium-
sized saucepan, sprinkle in the flour
and stir over a low heat for
2 minutes, until straw-coloured. Remove the pan from the heat and
gradually stir in the beetroot mixture. Bring slowly to boil, then
cook gently for 2-3 minutes, stirring
continuously (see Cook's tips).

Leave to cool until lukewarm (about
15 minutes), stirring occasionally.
4 Beat egg yolks into mixture,
1 at a time, then season well with
salt and pepper. In a clean dry
bowl, whisk the egg whites until
they stand in stiff peaks. Using a
metal spoon, fold 2 tablespoons of
the whisked egg whites into the

beetroot mixture (see Cook's tips)
and then lightly fold in the rest. ⚠
5 Pour the mixture into the
prepared soufflé dish. Bake in oven
for about 30 minutes, until the
soufflé trembles lightly when dish is
tapped. If the soufflé wobbles, it
needs cooking just a little longer.
Serve at once, from the dish.

Cook's Notes

TIME
40 minutes preparation;
about 30 minutes cook-
ing in the oven.

COOK'S TIPS
Wear an apron when
preparing this dish as
the thickened beetroot mixture
spatters while cooking and
stirring in stage 3.

A small proportion of the
whisked whites are added to
'loosen' the basic soufflé
mixture; this makes it easier to
incorporate the rest of the egg
whites without too much loss
of whisked-in air.

SERVING IDEAS
This tasty and attractive
soufflé makes a very
appealing light supper served
with a green vegetable. It is also
a good accompaniment to main-
dish salads.

WATCHPOINT
Stop folding as soon as
the egg whites are
all incorporated. Overmixing
at this stage will drive out air
that has been beaten into the
egg whites: this will result in a
heavy-textured soufflé.

●250 calories/1025 kj per portion

Surprise soufflé Saint Germain

SERVES 4

750 g/1½ lb peas, unshelled
   weight, shelled (see Buying
   guide)
salt
1 tablespoon vegetable oil
100 g/4 oz button mushrooms,
   finely chopped
4 teaspoons finely chopped onion
25 g/1 oz butter
25 g/1 oz plain flour
150 ml/¼ pint milk
4 large eggs, separated
pinch of freshly grated nutmeg
freshly ground black pepper
margarine, for greasing

1 Bring a pan of salted water to the boil, add the peas and simmer for about 20 minutes until quite tender. Drain well, then press through a sieve or purée in a blender.
2 Heat the oven to 200C/400F/Gas 6 (see Cook's tip). Grease a 1L/2 pint soufflé dish.
3 Heat the oil in a frying-pan, add the mushrooms and onion and fry gently for 5 minutes until soft and lightly coloured. Set aside.
4 Melt the butter in a saucepan, sprinkle in the flour and stir over low heat for 1-2 minutes until straw-coloured. Remove from the heat and gradually stir in the milk. Return to heat and simmer, stirring, until thick and smooth. Stir in the pea purée and remove the pan from the heat.
5 Add the egg yolks, one at a time, beating well after each addition. Season with nutmeg and salt and pepper to taste.
6 In a clean, dry bowl, whisk the egg whites until they stand in stiff peaks. Fold into pea mixture.
7 Add 2 tablespoons of pea mixture to mushrooms and fold in lightly.
8 Spoon half the pea mixture (without mushrooms) into the soufflé dish. Spoon the mushroom mixture into a mound in the centre. !
Cover with remaining pea mixture.
9 Bake in the oven for about 40 minutes or until the soufflé is well risen and golden. Serve the soufflé at once, straight from the soufflé dish.

Cook's Notes

TIME
50 minutes preparation; 40 minutes cooking.

BUYING GUIDE
This amount of fresh peas in their pods will yield about 250 g/9 oz shelled peas. Alternatively, use 250 g/9 oz frozen peas, but boil for only 8 minutes in stage 1.

COOK'S TIP
For the best results, preheat a baking sheet on shelf on which the soufflé is to be cooked. The extra heat from the sheet, at the base of the soufflé, helps the cooking and rising.

WATCHPOINT
Add the mushroom mixture gently – the mushrooms will sink but will keep together to form a surprise centre in the soufflé.

SERVING IDEAS
This soufflé is ideal as a light lunch dish, served with a salad of cress, chicory and orange in a sharp oil and vinegar dressing.

DID YOU KNOW
In French cooking, the name *Saint Germain* implies that peas are included.

●260 calories/1075 kj per portion

Savoury bread and butter pudding

SERVES 4

6 thin slices white bread, crusts
   removed (see Economy)
40 g/1½ oz butter, softened
1 onion, finely chopped
50 g/2 oz Cheddar cheese, grated
2 eggs
1 egg yolk
300 ml/½ pint milk
salt and freshly ground black pepper
parsley sprigs, to garnish

1 Melt 15 g/½ oz of the butter in a small saucepan. Add the onion and fry gently for 5 minutes. Set aside.
2 With remaining butter grease an ovenproof dish and spread the bread. Cut each slice into 2 triangles and arrange half, butter side up, in the dish. Sprinkle over half the cheese and half the onion.
3 Arrange the remaining bread slices on top, butter side down. Sprinkle over the remaining cheese and onion. Beat eggs, egg yolk and milk together, then season to taste.
4 Slowly pour the egg mixture over the bread and butter. Cover and set aside for 30 minutes to let the bread soak (see Cook's tips).
5 Meanwhile, heat the oven to 180C/350F/Gas 4.
6 Uncover the pudding and bake just above the centre of the oven for 40-45 minutes until the top has browned and the custard has set. Garnish with parsley and serve.

PAUL WEBSTER

Parsnip soufflé

SERVES 4
500 g/1 lb parsnips, cut into chunks
   (see Preparation)
salt
40 g/1½ oz margarine or butter
40 g/1½ oz plain flour
300 ml/½ pint milk
4 large eggs, separated
freshly grated nutmeg
freshly ground black pepper
butter, for greasing

Cook's Notes

TIME
Preparation takes about 1 hour, cooking 50 minutes.

WATCHPOINTS
The parsnips should be very tender before they are mashed, for smooth results.

The egg whites must be folded in gently so that you do not beat out any of the air. Always use a large metal spoon for folding in egg whites.

PREPARATION
If the parsnips are very woody, remove the centre cores, but remember to make up the lost weight with extra parsnip chunks.

SERVING IDEAS
Serve with a salad selection or with a green vegetable to make a complete vegetarian meal.

●300 calories/1250 kj per portion

1 Heat the oven to 190C/375F/Gas 5. Lightly grease the inside of a 1.5 L/2½ pint soufflé dish.
2 Place the parsnips in a saucepan, cover with cold salted water and bring to the boil. Cover, then simmer for 20-30 minutes, or until tender.
3 Drain the parsnips well and mash them thoroughly with a fork or potato masher while still hot.

4 Put the margarine, flour and milk into a pan. Bring to the boil slowly, whisking constantly with a balloon whisk. Lower the heat and simmer for 2-3 minutes until thick and smooth, whisking from time to time.
5 Beat the sauce into the mashed parsnips until well mixed, then beat in the egg yolks 1 at a time. Add nutmeg and salt and pepper to taste.

6 Whisk the egg whites until they are just standing in soft peaks, then fold gently into the parsnip mixture with a metal spoon until thoroughly incorporated.
7 Pour the soufflé mixture into the prepared dish and smooth the surface, then immediately bake in the oven for 50 minutes until golden, puffed up and springy to touch. Serve at once.

Hot carrot and cheese mousse

SERVES 4
600 g/1¼ lb carrots, sliced
salt
3 eggs, beaten
50 g/2 oz Cheddar cheese, grated
50 g/2 oz fresh white breadcrumbs
150 ml/5 fl oz soured cream
¼ teaspoon dried tarragon
   (optional)
freshly ground black pepper
margarine, for greasing
sprigs of tarragon or parsley,
   to garnish

1 Heat the oven to 190C/375F/Gas 5. Grease a 1.25 L/2 pint soufflé dish.
2 Bring the carrots to the boil in a little salted water, lower the heat and cook for 20 minutes or until very tender. Drain the carrots and place in the goblet of a blender. Add the beaten eggs and blend to a purée. Alternatively, work the cooked carrots through a sieve, then mix in the beaten eggs.
3 Place the carrot and egg purée in a bowl. Mix in the cheese, breadcrumbs and soured cream.

Add the tarragon, if using, and season to taste with the salt and pepper.
4 Pour the mixture into the prepared soufflé dish. Bake for 50 minutes or until the mousse is lightly browned on top and set in the centre. Garnish with sprigs of tarragon and serve at once.

MARTIN BRIGDALE

184

DON LAST

Cauliflower soufflé

SERVES 4

350 g/12 oz cauliflower florets, cut
   into 2 cm/¾ inch pieces
salt
40 g/1½ oz margarine or butter
40 g/1½ oz plain flour
300 ml/½ pint milk
4 eggs, separated, plus 1 egg
   white
1 teaspoon made English mustard
175 g/6 oz Cheddar cheese or Red
   Leicester, grated
freshly ground black pepper
margarine, for greasing

1 Heat the oven to 180C/350F/Gas 4
and grease a 2 L/3½ pint soufflé
dish.
2 Bring a pan of salted water to the
boil and cook the cauliflower for
about 2 minutes until just tender.
Drain well and pat dry with

absorbent paper. Put in a bowl.
3 Melt the margarine in a saucepan,
sprinkle in the flour and stir over
low heat for 1-2 minutes until straw-
coloured. Remove from the heat and
gradually stir in the milk. Return to
the heat and simmer, stirring, until
thick and smooth.
4 Remove the pan from the heat.
Beat the egg yolks and quickly stir
into the sauce. Stir in the mustard
and cheese and season to taste with
salt and pepper. Fold the sauce into
the cauliflower florets.
5 In a clean, dry bowl whisk the egg
whites until they stand in stiff peaks
then, using a metal spoon, gradually
fold into the cauliflower mixture in a
figure-of-eight motion. Use the
edges of the spoon to cut through
the mixture.
6 Turn the mixture into the
prepared soufflé dish (see Cook's
tip) and bake for 55 minutes, until
well risen and golden. When lightly
shaken, it should only wobble
slightly. Serve at once, straight from
the dish.

Cook's Notes

TIME
25 minutes preparation,
55 minutes cooking.

 WATCHPOINT
Do not overcook the
cauliflower. Also make
sure it is thoroughly drained—
any water clinging to it will
make the souffle mixture too
runny.

COOK'S TIP
You can prepare a
soufflé in advance, re-
frigerating it for up to 4 hours
before cooking. Cook for an
extra 10 minutes in this case.

SERVING IDEAS
Serve with a colourful
salad such as tomato or
red cabbage, or with ratatouille.

●445 calories/1880 kj per portion

Savoury scramble

SERVES 4

750 g/1½ lb small potatoes, cut into
   5 mm/¼ inch thick slices
salt
50 g/2 oz margarine or butter
1 tablespoon olive oil
25 g/1 oz whole blanched almonds
6 spring onions, cut into 5 mm/
   ¼ inch slices
6 eggs
freshly ground white pepper
2 tablespoons single cream
1 teaspoon chopped fresh thyme
   (see Cook's tip)
½ teaspoon chopped fresh
   rosemary (see Cook's tip)

Cook's Notes

TIME
15 minutes preparation,
30 minutes cooking.

VARIATIONS
Use sage, chives and
tarragon instead of
thyme and rosemary.

Unpeeled new potatoes can
be used: scrub well before slicing and cooking in the same way.
Fry 50 g/2 oz sliced mushrooms
with the onions.

! **WATCHPOINT**
Do not overcook the
potatoes when boiling
them or they will not keep their
shape when frying.

SERVING IDEAS
Serve scramble with
tomato halves and
sliced cucumber to add colour
and flavour to the dish. The
potatoes can be sprinkled with 1
tablespoon chopped fresh parsley or a little sweet paprika
before the scrambled eggs are
spooned on top.

COOK'S TIP
Make sure that the
herbs are chopped fine-
ly before adding them to the
scrambled eggs or the flavour
will be too strong.

●435 calories/1825 kj per portion

1 Bring the potatoes to the boil in salted water, lower the heat and cook for 4 minutes until just tender when pierced with a knife. **!** Drain the potatoes well.
2 Melt half the margarine in a frying-pan with the oil. Add the almonds and potatoes and cook gently, turning, for about 10 minutes until the potatoes are golden. Add the spring onions and cook for a further 3-4 minutes. Keep warm.
3 Meanwhile beat the eggs with a little salt and pepper.
4 Melt the remaining margarine in a saucepan and add the eggs. Cook over low heat, stirring, until the eggs are just set but not dry.
5 Remove from the heat and beat in the cream, thyme and rosemary.
6 Arrange the potato slices on a large warmed serving plate. Spoon the scrambled eggs into the centre and serve at once.

ALAN DUNS

THEO BERGSTROM

Carrot and potato soufflé

SERVES 4

500 g/1 lb carrots, cut into 2.5 cm/
   1 inch pieces
350 g/12 oz potatoes, cut into
   2.5 cm/1 inch pieces
salt
25 g/1 oz margarine or butter
2 tablespoons milk
4-5 teaspoons French mustard
100 g/4 oz mature Cheddar cheese,
   finely grated
5 eggs, separated
freshly ground black pepper
margarine, for greasing

1 Bring the carrots to the boil in a large saucepan of salted water, lower the heat and cook for about 15 minutes or until tender.

2 Meanwhile, in a separate saucepan, cook the potatoes in the same way for about 10 minutes or until tender.
3 Heat the oven to 200C/400F/Gas 6. Grease a 1.5 L/2½ pint soufflé dish.
4 Drain the cooked vegetables and transfer to a clean saucepan. Mash with the margarine and milk until smooth. Transfer to a large bowl (see Cook's tip) and mix in the mustard, cheese, egg yolks and salt and pepper to taste. Beat with a wooden spoon until smooth.
5 In a clean, dry bowl, whisk the egg whites until stiff but not dry. Using a large metal spoon, fold them lightly into the carrot and potato mixture. Pour into the prepared dish and bake in the oven for 35 minutes, or until the soufflé is well-risen and golden. When lightly shaken, it should only wobble very slightly. Serve at once, straight from the soufflé dish.

Cook's Notes

TIME
Preparation takes about 40 minutes, cooking in the oven about 35 minutes.

SERVING IDEAS
The soufflé makes a perfect main course, accompanied by a lightly tossed green salad.

COOK'S TIP
The reason for mashing the carrots and potatoes in the pan, then transferring the mixture to a bowl, is to cool the mixture sufficiently for the egg yolks to be stirred in. If the mixture is too hot the yolks will scramble when they are added.

●380 calories/1575 kj per portion

GRAHAM YOUNG

Curried eggs

SERVES 4

8 hard-boiled eggs
25 g/1 oz margarine or butter
1 onion, chopped
2 teaspoons curry powder
1 tablespoon plain flour
600 ml/1 pint vegetable stock
1½ tablespoons apricot jam
2 teaspoons lemon juice
1 teaspoon tomato purée
1 apple, peeled, cored and chopped
4 tablespoons sultanas
1 large banana
¼ teaspoon salt, or to taste
extra banana slices, to garnish

1 Melt the margarine in a saucepan, add the onion and fry over gentle heat for about 5 minutes, until soft and translucent. Sprinkle in the curry powder and stir over low heat for 2 minutes. Sprinkle in the flour and stir over low heat for a further 2 minutes, until straw-coloured.
2 Remove the pan from the heat and gradually stir in the stock, until smooth. Then stir in the apricot jam, lemon juice and tomato purée. Return to heat and bring to boil.

3 Add the apple and sultanas, then cover the pan, reduce the heat and simmer the mixture very gently for about 30 minutes.
4 Slice the eggs in half lengthways, and slice the banana. Add the eggs

and banana to the sauce, taking care not to break up the eggs. Simmer for a further 5 minutes, then add salt to taste. Transfer carefully to a warmed serving dish and serve at once, garnished with extra banana slices.

Broccoli and eggs au gratin

SERVES 4

500 g/1 lb frozen broccoli spears
salt
25 g/1 oz margarine or butter
25 g/1 oz plain flour
300 ml/½ pint milk
75 g/3 oz Cheddar cheese, grated
freshly ground black pepper
6 eggs, hard-boiled and halved
  lengthways
margarine, for greasing

1 Cook the broccoli in boiling salted water according to packet instructions, until just tender.
2 While the broccoli is cooking, make the sauce; melt the margarine in a saucepan, sprinkle in the flour and stir over low heat for 2 minutes until straw-coloured. Remove from the heat and gradually stir in the milk. Return to the heat and simmer, stirring, until thick and smooth. Add 50 g/2 oz of the cheese and stir until melted then add salt and pepper to taste. Remove from the heat.
3 Heat the grill to moderate and grease a shallow flameproof dish with margarine. Drain the broccoli spears and arrange them in a single layer in the dish.
4 Arrange the eggs, cut side down (see Variation), on top of the broccoli. Pour the cheese sauce evenly over the top [!] and sprinkle with the remaining cheese.
5 Set the dish under the grill for a few minutes until the top is bubbling and golden brown. Serve the eggs and broccoli at once, straight from the dish.

CHRIS KNAGGS

Egg and onion bake

SERVES 4

4 eggs
2 large onions, finely chopped
salt and freshly ground black pepper
600 ml/1 pint hot milk (see
Cook's tip)
75 g/3 oz Cheddar cheese, grated
15 g/½ oz margarine or butter
1 tablespoon vegetable oil
2 tablespoons chopped fresh chervil
(see Variation)
margarine, for greasing

SAUCE
25 g/1 oz margarine or butter
25 g/1 oz plain flour
300 ml/½ pint milk
100 g/4 oz Cheddar cheese, grated

1 Heat the oven to 150C/300F/Gas 2 and grease a 1.25 L/2 pint ovenproof dish with margarine.

2 Put the eggs in a bowl and season with salt and pepper. Whisk the eggs, then whisk in the milk and cheese and pour into the prepared dish. Half-fill a roasting tin with boiling water and place the dish in the tin. Bake in the oven for 1½ hours or until the mixture is firm.

3 About 15 minutes before the end of the cooking time, heat the margarine and oil in a frying-pan. Add the onions and fry gently for 5 minutes until soft and lightly coloured. Stir in the chervil and remove from the heat.

4 Heat the grill to high.

5 Meanwhile, make the sauce: melt the margarine in a small saucepan, sprinkle in the flour and stir over low heat for 1-2 minutes until straw-coloured. Remove from the heat and gradually stir in the milk. Return to the heat and simmer, stirring, until thick and smooth. Stir in half the grated cheese and season to taste with salt and pepper.

6 When the egg mixture is cooked, spoon the onion mixture over top.

7 Spoon the sauce over onions and sprinkle with the remaining cheese.

8 Place the dish under the grill until the cheese has melted and is golden brown and bubbling. Serve at once.

Cook's Notes

 TIME
Preparing and cooking this dish take about 1 hour 35 minutes.

 SERVING IDEAS
Serve with chips and a tossed green salad.

 VARIATION
If chervil is unavailable, use parsley instead.

 COOK'S TIP
The hot milk speeds up the cooking process as it starts to set the egg yolks.

●540 calories/2275 kj per portion

Supper eggs

SERVES 4

750 g/1½ lb potatoes, cut into large
   chunks (see Buying guide)
4 eggs (see Buying guide)
25 g/1 oz butter
1 Spanish onion, chopped
1 tablespoon milk
75 g/3 oz Cheddar cheese, grated
salt and freshly ground black pepper
50 g/2 oz Double Gloucester
   cheese, grated

1 Put potatoes in a large saucepan, cover them with cold water and bring to the boil. Simmer gently for about 20 minutes until tender.
2 Meanwhile, melt the butter in a frying-pan, add the onion and fry for 5 minutes until the onion is soft and lightly browned.
3 Drain the potatoes well, then return to the saucepan and mash with the milk until smooth. Stir in the onion and butter mixture and the Cheddar cheese. Season this mixture to taste with salt and freshly ground black pepper.
4 Heat the grill to medium.
5 Spoon the potato mixture into a shallow flameproof dish. Fluff up the surface of the potato with a fork. Using the back of a spoon, make 4 shallow depressions in potato, about 7.5 cm/3 inches wide and no more than 1 cm/½ inch deep.
6 Break an egg into each hollow and place the dish under the grill for 7-10 minutes, until the eggs are just barely set.
7 Remove dish and allow eggs to cool for 2 minutes (see Cook's tip). Sprinkle with Double Gloucester cheese and serve at once.

ALAN DUNS

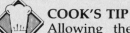

TIME
Preparation takes about 30 minutes. Cooking the eggs takes 9-12 minutes.

VARIATION
Put a layer of sliced skinned tomatoes in the base of the dish before putting the mashed potato on top.

COOK'S TIP
Allowing the eggs to stand before serving helps the egg white to firm and set completely (it continues to cook by retained heat) without the yolks becoming overcooked and tough.

●405 calories/1700 kj per portion

BUYING GUIDE
Use old floury, potatoes like King Edwards or Desirées for the best results.
  For this dish, try to make sure the eggs are as fresh as possible. They will taste much better and the egg white will be thicker and less inclined to run out of the potato hollows.

Tasty cheese cakes

MAKES 8
100 g/4 oz Red Leicester or Cheshire cheese, coarsely grated
100 g/4 oz mature Cheddar cheese, finely grated
25 g/1 oz margarine or butter
1 small onion, very finely chopped
150 g/5 oz fresh white breadcrumbs
½ teaspoon dried thyme
100 g/4 oz cottage cheese
salt and freshly ground black pepper
2 eggs, beaten
2 tablespoons chopped fresh parsley
vegetable oil, for frying

GARNISH
8 small gherkins, halved
8 stuffed olives, halved

1 Melt the margarine in a frying-pan. Add the onion and fry gently for 5 minutes until soft and lightly coloured. Remove from the pan with a slotted spoon and cool on absorbent paper.

Cook's Notes

TIME
These cakes take about 1 hour to prepare, chill and cook.

WATCHPOINT
Do not fry the cheese cakes longer than it takes to brown the outside or the cheese will melt too much.

VARIATIONS
Use different cheeses such as Derby or Double Gloucester.

FREEZING
Open freeze until solid, pack in rigid container, separating layers with foil. Seal, label and return to freezer for up to 1 month. To serve: defrost then shallow fry for 4-6 minutes.

COOK'S TIP
Refrigerating the cheese cakes helps them hold their shape better while they are cooking.

●250 calories/1060 kj per portion

2 In a bowl, mix the grated cheeses with 75 g/3 oz of the breadcrumbs, the thyme, cottage cheese, and salt and pepper to taste. Add two-thirds of the egg and mix thoroughly.

3 Divide the mixture into 8 and shape each portion into a flat round cake. Refrigerate for 30 minutes (see Cook's tip).

4 Mix the remaining egg with 1 teaspoon of cold water in a shallow bowl. Mix the remaining bread-crumbs with the parsley, salt and pepper and spread out on a flat plate.

5 Coat the cakes in the egg, then in the breadcrumb mixture. ✳

6 Heat about 1 cm/½ inch of oil in a frying-pan until it is hot enough to turn a stale bread cube golden in 50 seconds. Add the cakes to the pan and fry for 2-3 minutes on each side until browned. [!] Drain well on absorbent paper.

7 Serve at once, garnished with gherkin and olive halves.

DON LAST

Swiss cheese pudding

SERVES 4

175 g/6 oz Gruyère cheese, grated
butter or margarine
8 slices medium thick white sliced
   bread
2 eggs
300 ml/½ pint vegetable stock
75 ml/3 fl oz double cream
salt and freshly ground black pepper

1 Heat the oven to 180C/350F/Gas 4.
2 Generously butter the bread on 1 side and grease a deep ovenproof dish (see Cook's tips).
3 Place half the bread, buttered side up, in the dish and sprinkle the cheese on top.
4 Cover with the remaining bread slices.
5 In a bowl, mix the stock, eggs and cream and season to taste with salt and pepper. Pour over the bread.
6 Leave to stand for 30 minutes for the bread to soak up the egg mixture (see Cook's tips).
7 Bake in the oven for 45 minutes until golden and slightly crispy. Serve hot straight from the dish.

Cook's Notes

TIME
Preparation takes 10 minutes and cooking 45 minutes, but allow another 30 minutes for soaking.

COOK'S TIPS
If you prefer a crisper pudding, cook in a shallower dish for 30 minutes only. The pudding will be drier because the heat will be dispersed over a wider area.

While the bread is soaking, press it down several times to make sure the top layer is moistened by the egg and cream mixture.

SERVING IDEAS
Serve with a homemade tomato sauce and a crisp mixed salad tossed in dressing.

●625 calories/2650 kj per portion

LAURIE EVANS

SIDE DISHES

The purpose of a side dish is not only to accompany and supplement a main dish, but also to complement it in terms of flavour, colour and texture. Plainly-cooked hot vegetables are the traditional accompaniment, both to main meat and main vegetable dishes, but they can be made much more exciting and interesting than that, as the following recipes will show.

A side dish will normally be less substantial than a main dish and more than one may be served at a time. 'Meat and two veg.' is the classic example! The recipes in this chapter include a mixture of simple vegetable dishes to serve with filling and rich main dishes, as well as more substantial dishes to serve with light main dishes. For example, a dish like Cauliflower with Cider Cream is quite rich and filling in itself and is best served with a light vegetable soufflé, but Mange-Tout in Butter, or Steamed Courgettes are lightly cooked vegetables that could be served with almost any hot main dish. The recipes make good use of the full range of vegetables available to us, including some of the less familiar such as celeriac and artichokes, and combines them with other vegetables, fruit or herbs and spices to delicious effect. Small salads also make ideal accompanying dishes; they are dealt with in the next chapter.

If your main dish is low in protein, you will need to rely on your side dishes to increase the total protein in the meal. Any dish containing grains, nuts, seeds or pulses (beans, peas or lentils) will contain protein along with other valuable nutrients. It is important to cook vegetables in ways that do not remove all their natural goodness. For example, try not to overcook vegetables, especially if boiling them, or most of the vitamins and minerals will end up in the water. Steaming is a better method to use. When cooked, vegetables should be tender but still slightly crisp. As with many root vegetables, most of the goodness in potatoes lies just beneath the skin, so cook and eat them without peeling whenever possible. Plain potatoes baked in their jackets make an excellent accompaniment to many dishes, and you will find lots of new and unusual ways to cook and serve potatoes in this chapter.

An accompaniment need not only be a vegetable dish or salad. To complete a main course, you could serve plain boiled brown or white rice or wholewheat pasta, or try one of the less familiar grains such as bulgur wheat or couscous. Alternatively, some bread and butter might be the only extra 'side dish' you need. Sauces, chutneys and pickles also make flavoursome accompaniments to many vegetarian main dishes.

Side dishes may not be the most important part of a meal but they do add different and complementary colours, textures and flavours, as well as contributing to the overall nutritional content of the meal. You will find plenty to choose from here, no matter what main dish you are planning to serve, and the Serving Ideas will help you make the choice.

CHRIS KNAGGS

Steamed courgettes

SERVES 4

500 g/1 lb courgettes (see Buying guide), cut into 1 cm/½ inch slices
1-2 tablespoons chopped parsley
1 teaspoon dried dillweed
100 g/4 oz butter, softened
salt and freshly ground black pepper

1 In a bowl, beat the herbs into the butter and season with salt and pepper. Transfer the butter to a sheet of greaseproof paper, shape it into a roll, wrap in foil and place in the freezer or freezing compartment of the refrigerator until required.
2 Put the sliced courgettes into a steamer (see Cook's tips). Stand the steamer in a saucepan and pour in boiling water to come just to the base of the steamer. !
3 Set the pan over moderate heat so that the water is gently boiling. Cover and cook for 10 minutes until tender but still firm.

4 Remove the steamer from the pan and transfer the courgettes to a warmed serving dish.
5 Cut the butter into neat, thin slices and arrange on top of the courgettes. Serve at once.

Cook's Notes

 TIME
Preparation takes about 10 minutes, cooking about 10 minutes.

 WATCHPOINT
No water must be allowed to get into the steamer.

 COOK'S TIPS
Steaming is an excellent way of cooking vegetables as it retains so much of their goodness. A collapsible steamer is a particularly useful investment, as it takes up so little storage space.

If you do not have a steamer, put the courgettes into a colander over boiling water. Cover and cook as described.

 BUYING GUIDE
Buy small courgettes as they are usually firmer and sweeter than the larger ones, which tend to be bitter.

● 200 calories/850 kj per portion

Courgettes with onion and nuts

SERVES 4
500 g/1 lb courgettes
50 g/2 oz butter
2 tablespoons water
salt
1 onion, sliced into rings
25 g/1 oz pine nuts
freshly ground black pepper

1 Cut the courgettes into quarters lengthways, then cut across to make even-sized sticks.

2 Melt half the butter in a saucepan with the water and a pinch of salt. Add the courgettes, cover the pan and cook gently for 10 minutes until the courgettes are just tender. Shake the pan occasionally during this time to ensure that they cook evenly.

3 Meanwhile, melt the remaining butter in a frying-pan, add the onion rings and fry briskly for 3 minutes until lightly browned. Transfer with a slotted spoon to a plate and set aside.

4 Add the pine nuts to the pan and fry for 2 minutes, stirring, until golden brown.

5 Drain the courgettes, season to taste with salt and pepper, and transfer them to a warmed shallow serving dish. Arrange the onion rings down the centre of the courgettes and sprinkle the pine nuts over the top.

DON LAST

Marrow in onion sauce

SERVES 4
about 500 g/1 lb marrow, deseeded and cubed (see Cook's tips)
4-6 celery stalks, chopped
salt and freshly ground black pepper
butter, for greasing
chopped fresh parsley, to garnish

SAUCE
50 g/2 oz margarine or butter
2 onions, finely chopped
25 g/1 oz plain flour
300 ml/½ pint milk

1 Heat the oven to 180C/350F/Gas 4 and grease a 1.5 L/2½ pint heatproof glass dish.
2 Arrange the marrow and celery in the dish in alternate layers, starting and finishing with a layer of marrow

and sprinkling each layer with salt and pepper to taste.
3 Make the sauce: melt the margarine in a saucepan, add the onions and fry gently for 5 minutes until soft and lightly coloured.
4 Sprinkle the flour into the pan and stir over low heat for 1-2 minutes. Remove from the heat and gradually stir in the milk. Return to the heat

and simmer, stirring, until thick. Add salt and pepper to taste and simmer gently for 2-3 minutes (see Cook's tips).
5 Pour the sauce over the vegetables in the casserole, cover and cook in the oven for 40-45 minutes, until the vegetables are tender.
6 Sprinkle the dish with chopped parsley and serve at once.

Cook's Notes

TIME
15 minutes preparation, 50-55 minutes cooking, including making the sauce.

VARIATION
The marrow can be replaced by the same weight of courgettes, cut into 5 mm/¼ inch slices. Arrange in layers as above and cook for 40-45 minutes.

COOK'S TIPS
If the marrow is young it can be cooked with the skin on, otherwise it should be peeled as the skin can be tough and unpalatable.
For a smooth-textured finish, pass the cooked sauce through a sieve at this stage, or purée in a blender.

●190 calories/800 kj per portion

DON LAST

Nutty courgettes

SERVES 4

750 g/1½ lb courgettes, cut into
   5 mm/¼ inch slices
25 g/1 oz margarine or butter
2 cloves garlic, crushed (optional)
75 g/3 oz shelled walnuts, roughly
   chopped
generous pinch of salt
freshly ground black pepper

1 Melt the margarine in a frying-pan, add the crushed garlic, if using, and fry gently for 1-2 minutes, until soft and lightly coloured.

2 Add the sliced courgettes, stir well to coat thoroughly in the margarine, then fry over low heat for 10 minutes, turning occasionally.

3 Add the chopped walnuts, the salt and a generous sprinkling of black pepper. Cook for a further 5 minutes until the courgettes are tender, stirring occasionally. Transfer to a warmed serving dish and serve at once.

Cook's Notes

TIME
5 minutes preparation;
15 minutes cooking.

VARIATIONS
For extra flavour, trim and chop a bunch of spring onions, then fry with the garlic before adding the courgettes. Or add 2 tablespoons chopped fresh parsley and 1 tablespoon snipped chives to the courgettes, about 5 minutes before the end of cooking time.

COOK'S TIP
You can use frozen courgettes for this dish. For best results, drop the frozen courgettes into boiling salted water, bring back to the boil and boil for 1 minute. Drain, then add to the melted margarine together with the chopped walnuts. Fry for 5 minutes.

●170 calories/725 kj per portion

MICHAEL KAY

DON LAST

Buttered peas and cucumber

SERVES 4
350 g/12 oz frozen peas (see Buying guide)
1 cucumber, peeled
salt
50 g/2 oz butter
sprig of fresh mint, or ¼ teaspoon dried mint
½ teaspoon sugar
freshly ground black pepper

1 Cut the cucumber into pieces about 2.5 cm/1 inch long, then cut each piece again into 2 cm/¾ inch thick slices.
2 Place cucumber in a colander and sprinkle with 1 teaspoon salt. Weight down with a plate and drain for 15 minutes (see Cook's tip).

3 Melt the butter in a pan, add the cucumber, cover and cook gently for 5 minutes, stirring occasionally.
4 Add the frozen peas, mint, sugar and pepper to taste. Mix well, then simmer gently for about 10 minutes until the peas are quite tender.
5 Remove the mint sprig, if using, then taste and adjust seasoning. Transfer to a warmed serving bowl.

Cook's Notes

 TIME
Preparation takes 25 minutes, including salting the cucumber. Cooking takes about 15 minutes.

 BUYING GUIDE
This is a particularly good way of cooking the larger, less expensive varieties of frozen peas.

 VARIATION
Fry 2 finely chopped shallots or 3-4 spring onions for 2-3 minutes and add to the cucumber together with the other ingredients.

 COOK'S TIP
If you are short of time, the salting may be omitted, but the dish will have more liquid. Salting drains out some of the excess moisture.

 SERVING IDEAS
This fresh-tasting vegetable dish is especially good with spicy dishes.

● 150 calories/625 kj per portion

Mange-tout in basil butter

SERVES 4

500 g/1 lb mange-tout, topped and
    tailed (see Buying guide)
salt
50 g/2 oz butter, softened
1 teaspoon dried basil (see
    Buying guide)
½ teaspoon grated orange zest
freshly ground black pepper
2 orange twists, to garnish

1 Bring a pan of salted water to the
boil, add the peas and bring back to
the boil. Lower the heat, cover and
simmer for 5 minutes until just
tender, but still crisp.

2 Meanwhile, beat the butter in a
small bowl with the basil, orange
zest and a little pepper. Mix until
well blended.

3 Drain the pods thoroughly in a
colander, then return to the pan.
Add the butter mixture and toss
gently over low heat until the pods
are thoroughly coated.

4 Turn the peas into a warmed
serving dish, garnish with orange
twists and serve at once.

Cook's Notes

TIME
Preparation and cooking
of the mange-tout take
about 15 minutes.

BUYING GUIDE
Choose bright, crisp
pods that have no yel-
low markings. Avoid very large
pods, they will be past their
best and rather tough.
    If fresh basil is available, use 2
teaspoons in place of the dried
basil.

 WATCHPOINTS
Take care not to over-
cook the peas or they
will lose some of their texture
and colour.
    Make sure that the peas are
very well drained before tossing
them in butter.

● 105 calories/450 kj per portion

THEO BERGSTFOM

MICHAEL KAY

Peas 'n' sweetcorn

SERVES 4

150 ml/¼ pint vegetable stock (see Buying guide)
3 small onions, each cut lengthways into 6 sections
1.5 kg/3 lb peas (unshelled weight, see Buying guide)
300 g/10 oz frozen sweetcorn or 300g/11½ oz can, drained
3 tablespoons chopped fresh parsley
salt and freshly ground black pepper
knob of butter, to serve

1 Bring the stock to the boil in a saucepan and add the onions. Cover the pan, lower the heat and simmer for 10 minutes.

2 Add the peas and sweetcorn to the stock, then stir in the parsley and salt and pepper to taste (see Cook's tips). Bring to the boil. Cover the pan, lower the heat and simmer for about 10 minutes, or until the peas are tender (see Cook's tips).

3 Drain the peas and sweetcorn and transfer to a warmed serving dish. Top with a knob of butter and serve.

Cook's Notes

TIME
Preparation takes about 10 minutes, cooking takes about 20 minutes.

BUYING GUIDE
Vegetable stock cubes are readily available in supermarkets, but you could use vegetable cooking water instead.
1.5 kg/3 lb peas in the pod will yield approximately 500 g/1 lb shelled peas, and this is the quantity you will need if you are using frozen peas.

SERVING IDEAS
This versatile accompaniment goes well with many main course dishes.

COOK'S TIPS
If the vegetable stock seems quite salty, only pepper is needed for seasoning.
Fresh peas take about 10 minutes to cook, depending on how young they are. Frozen peas cook in half the time.

● 170 calories/700 kj per portion

202

Green pease pudding with mint

SERVES 4

250 g/9 oz green split peas (see Variation)

15 g/½ oz margarine or butter

2 tablespoons chopped fresh mint, or 2-3 teaspoons mint sauce concentrate

salt and freshly ground black pepper

1 tablespoon vegetable oil

1 large onion, sliced into rings

1 Put the split peas in a saucepan and cover with cold water. Bring to the boil, then cook, uncovered, for about 40 minutes, until very tender (see Cook's tip).

2 Drain the cooked split peas, reserving some of the liquid, and mash the peas lightly with a spoon.

Add the margarine, mint and salt and pepper to taste, then stir in some of the reserved liquid, if needed, to make a soft consistency.

3 Spoon the mixture into a warmed serving dish and keep warm.

4 Heat the oil in a frying-pan, add the sliced onion and fry until evenly browned.

5 Garnish the pease pudding with the fried onion rings and serve at once.

ROGER PHILLIPS

Broad beans in their pods

SERVES 4-6
500 g/1 lb young broad beans in pods (see Buying guide)
pinch of salt
25 g/1 oz butter
juice of ½ lemon
2 tablespoons chopped fresh parsley
freshly ground black pepper

1 Top and tail the beans, then remove any strings. Put the beans in a saucepan and pour over enough water to just cover them. Add the salt, cover the pan and bring to the boil, then lower the heat slightly and simmer for about 5 minutes until just tender.
2 Meanwhile, melt the butter in a separate pan, add the lemon juice, parsley and pepper to taste. Stir together and remove from the heat.
3 Drain the beans and place in a warmed serving dish. Pour over the melted butter mixture and serve at once (see Serving ideas).

Cook's Notes

 TIME
10 minutes preparation, 5 minutes cooking.

 SERVING IDEAS
Serve hot as a vegetable accompaniment to any savoury dish. Alternatively, leave until cold and serve as an unusual salad.

 BUYING GUIDE
Broad beans used in this dish must be very young — the beans should scarcely have formed in their pods and the complete pod should only be about 10 cm/ 4 inches long.

 VARIATION
Fry some chopped onion in the butter before adding to the beans: omit the lemon juice.

●175 calories/300 kj per portion

ROGER PHILLIPS

Broad beans and peaches

SERVES 4

1 kg/2 lb broad beans (unshelled weight) or 500 g/1 lb frozen
salt
large sprig fresh mint
3 fresh peaches, skinned (see Preparation)
mint sprigs, to garnish

DRESSING

2 tablespoons olive or sunflower oil
1 tablespoon white wine vinegar
2 tablespoons finely chopped fresh parsley or coriander
freshly ground black pepper

1 Bring a large pan of salted water to the boil, add the beans and mint and bring back to the boil. Lower the heat slightly and simmer for about 6 minutes until just tender.
2 Meanwhile, make the dressing:
pour the oil into a large bowl, add the vinegar, parsley and salt and pepper to taste, then mix well together with a fork.
3 Drain the beans thoroughly, then immediately put them into the bowl of dressing. ⚠ Toss well to combine, then cover and leave for at least 1 hour until completely cold.
4 Just before serving, slice the peaches very thinly, then gently stir them into the cold beans. Taste and adjust seasoning, if necessary. Transfer salad to a serving bowl, garnish with mint and serve at once, while peaches are still firm.

Broad beans in green sauce

SERVES 4

500 g/1 lb shelled broad beans
sprig of fresh rosemary or pinch of
   dried rosemary
salt

SAUCE

25 g/1 oz margarine or butter
20 g/¾ oz plain flour
150 ml/¼ pint milk
4 tablespoons finely chopped fresh
   parsley
freshly ground black pepper
sprigs of parsley, to garnish

1 Heat the oven to 110C/225F/Gas
¼. Put the beans into a large
saucepan and add the rosemary
with a pinch of salt. Pour over
boiling water to just cover.

2 Cover the pan, bring to the boil,
reduce heat and simmer gently for
5-10 minutes until tender (see
Cook's tips).
3 Drain the beans, reserving 150 ml/
¼ pint of the cooking water and
discarding the sprig of rosemary, if
used. Put the beans in a warmed
serving dish and keep warm in the
oven.
4 Make the sauce: melt the
margarine in a small saucepan,
sprinkle in the flour and stir over
low heat for 1-2 minutes until straw-
coloured. Remove from the heat and
gradually stir in the milk and
reserved cooking water. Return to
the heat and simmer, stirring, until
thick and smooth.
5 Stir the chopped parsley into the
sauce and season to taste with salt
and pepper. Simmer gently, stirring
for 2 minutes (see Cook's tips).
6 Pour the green sauce over the
broad beans in the dish and serve
hot, garnished with parsley sprigs.

PAUL WEBSTER

LAURIE EVANS

Cheesy runner beans

SERVES 4

700 g/1¼ lb fresh runner beans,
    thinly sliced into 2.5 cm/1 inch
    lengths, or 500 g/1 lb frozen beans
salt
40 g/1½ oz butter
1 bunch spring onions, cut into 5
    cm/2 inch lengths
100 g/4 oz Double Gloucester
    cheese with chives, cut into
    1 cm/½ inch cubes
½ teaspoon dried tarragon
freshly ground black pepper

1 Bring a pan of salted water to the boil and cook the fresh beans for 5-7 minutes. If using frozen beans, cook according to packet instructions. Drain the beans well in a colander.
2 Melt the butter in a pan, add the onions and fry gently for 3 minutes.

3 Add the beans and cheese to the pan, then stir in the tarragon and season to taste with salt and pepper. Cook for a further 2 minutes over low heat, stirring constantly, until the cheese is beginning to melt. Serve at once.

THEO BERGSTROM

French beans with sunflower seeds

SERVES 4

500 g/1 lb French beans, topped and
    tailed
salt
2 tablespoons vegetable oil
2 small onions, thinly sliced
1 tablespoon chopped fresh mixed
    herbs (see Buying guide)
4 tablespoons sunflower seeds (see
    Buying guide)
freshly ground black pepper

1 Bring a pan of salted water to the
boil and cook the French beans for
10-15 minutes until just tender. !
Drain thoroughly.
2 Heat the oil in a frying-pan, add

the onions and then fry gently for
5 minutes until soft and lightly
coloured. Sprinkle in herbs and
sunflower seeds and continue to fry
for a further 5 minutes until the
sunflower seeds are light brown.

3 Add the beans, season to taste
with salt and pepper and stir over
high heat for 1-2 minutes until
heated through.
4 Transfer to a warmed serving
dish and serve at once.

Cook's Notes

 TIME
Quick to prepare, this
dish takes about 25
minutes from start to finish.

 SERVING IDEAS
Serve with a cheese dish
and tomato sauce.

 WATCHPOINT
Do not overcook the
beans – they need to be
kept whole during frying.

 BUYING GUIDE
During the summer
months, take advantage
of the abundance of fresh herbs.
To enhance the beans in this
recipe, choose from marjoram,
parsley, rosemary and basil.
    Sunflower seeds are available
at health food stores. They are
rich in vitamin B and a good
source of minerals.

● 145 calories/625 kj per portion

PETER MYERS

French bean special

SERVES 4
500 g/1 lb frozen French beans
salt
1 teaspoon chopped fresh parsley

SAUCE
3 egg yolks
1 tablespoon white wine vinegar
a small pinch of freshly grated
   nutmeg
1 teaspoon sugar (optional)
2 tablespoons double cream
1 hard-boiled egg, finely chopped
freshly ground black pepper

1 Bring a large pan of salted water to
the boil, add the beans and cook for
8 minutes or until the beans are just
tender.

2 Meanwhile, make the sauce: put
the egg yolks, vinegar, nutmeg and
sugar, if using, into a heatproof
bowl then stand the bowl over a pan
of gently simmering water.
Whisk over very low heat for about 6
minutes, or until the mixture
thickens enough to coat the back of a
spoon.

3 Remove the pan from the heat and
immediately beat in the cream and
chopped hard-boiled egg. Season
the mixture to taste with salt and
pepper.
4 Drain the beans and turn them
onto a warmed serving plate. Pour
over the sauce and garnish with
chopped parsley. Serve at once.

FRED MANCINI

Crunchy Brussels sprouts

SERVES 4-6
750 g/1½ lb fresh Brussels sprouts
salt
25 g/1 oz margarine or butter
2 tablespoons vegetable oil
25 g/1 oz fresh white breadcrumbs
25 g/1 oz Parmesan cheese, finely
grated

1 Cut a cross in bottom of sprouts. Bring a pan of salted water to the boil, add the sprouts and bring to the boil. Lower the heat, cover and simmer gently for 10 minutes or until barely tender. Remove the sprouts from the heat and drain thoroughly in a colander.

2 Heat the margarine and 1 table-

Cook's Notes

 TIME
The preparation and cooking of the dish take a total of 30 minutes.

 VARIATION
Layer the cooked sprouts with fresh breadcrumbs and Parmesan cheese. Sprinkle the top with 50 g/2 oz grated Emmental cheese and dot with butter. Bake in a 200C/400F/Gas 6 oven for 10 minutes or until cheese has melted.

 WATCHPOINT
Take care not to break up the sprouts at this stage—they look much more attractive if kept whole.

 SERVING IDEAS
These sprouts make a delicious accompaniment to vegetable casseroles or stews. Serve with grilled tomatoes and fluffy creamed potatoes.

● 185 calories/775 kj per portion

spoon of the oil together in a large frying-pan. Add the sprouts and fry over moderate heat, stirring constantly, for 2-3 minutes until coated in the margarine and oil. ⚠

3 Add the remaining oil to the pan,

then sprinkle in the breadcrumbs and Parmesan cheese. Mix carefully to combine, then fry over low heat for 2 minutes or until the breadcrumbs are lightly browned. Serve at once in a warmed serving dish.

Sesame sprouts

SERVES 4
750 g/1½ lb Brussels sprouts

SAUCE
50 g/2 oz margarine or butter
1 onion, finely chopped
1 clove garlic, crushed (optional)
25 g/1 oz plain flour
4 tablespoons tahini paste (see Buying guide)
½ vegetable stock cube, crumbled
350 ml/12 fl oz orange juice
150 ml/¼ pint water
1 teaspoon clear honey
salt and freshly ground black pepper
2 teaspoons sesame seeds and orange twists, to garnish

1 Wash and trim the Brussels sprouts, discarding any tough or discoloured outer leaves. Cut a cross in stem end of each sprout.

PAUL WEBSTER

TIME
Preparing and cooking the sprouts take about 30 minutes.

SERVING IDEAS
Serve this unusual sprout dish as an accompaniment to a vegetable pie or casserole, lentil patties or a nut roast. The tangy sauce is also excellent with steamed broccoli, green beans or other green vegetables which are in season.

BUYING GUIDE
Tahini paste is made from sesame seeds and is available from health food shops, Greek delicatessens and some large supermarkets. Sesame spread, which is made with roasted sesame seeds, can also be used. If unavailable, crush 3 tablespoons sesame seeds with 1 tablespoon oil in a pestle and mortar.

●315 calories/1325 kj per portion

2 Bring a pan of salted water to the boil and cook the Brussels sprouts for 8-10 minutes, until tender but still firm to the bite.

3 Meanwhile, make the sauce: melt the margarine in a small saucepan, add the onion and the garlic, if using, and fry gently for 5 minutes until the onion is soft and lightly coloured. Sprinkle in the flour and stir over low heat for 3 minutes.

Add the tahini paste and crumbled stock cube and stir until smooth. Gradually stir in the orange juice and water then simmer, stirring until thick and smooth. Stir in the honey and season to taste.

4 Drain Brussels sprouts, transfer to a warmed serving dish and pour over the sauce. Sprinkle with sesame seeds, garnish with orange twists and serve at once.

FRED MANCINI

Cauliflower with cider cream

SERVES 4
1 cauliflower (see Buying guide)
salt

SAUCE
25 g/1 oz butter
1 tablespoon plain flour
150 ml/¼ pint dry strong cider
**good pinch of freshly grated
    nutmeg**
4 tablespoons double cream
freshly ground black pepper
sweet paprika, to finish

1 Bring a large pan of salted water to the boil, add the cauliflower, bring back to the boil and cook for about 15-20 minutes.
2 Meanwhile, make the sauce: melt the butter in a small saucepan, sprinkle in the flour and stir over low heat for 1-2 minutes until straw-coloured. Gradually stir in the cider, then add the nutmeg and bring to the boil. Simmer for 1 minute, stirring, until thick and smooth.
3 Remove from the heat and beat in the double cream. Season with salt and a generous sprinkling of black pepper, then reheat the sauce gently if necessary. !
4 Drain the cauliflower, transfer to a warmed serving dish ! and pour over the sauce. Sprinkle the top with paprika and serve at once.

Cook's Notes

 TIME
Total preparation and cooking time is only about 25-30 minutes.

 BUYING GUIDE
Choose a firm, white cauliflower with as much fresh, tender green around it as possible. The inner green leaves can be left on during cooking as they help to keep the cauliflower firmly together and add flavour.

●140 calories/600 kj per portion

 WATCHPOINTS
Do not allow to boil after adding the cream.
The finished dish looks best if the cauliflower is kept whole, so transfer it carefully.

 SERVING IDEAS
The cider cream sauce is very rich, so this dish should be served only with other plainly-cooked fresh vegetables. Served simply with crusty bread and butter, it could be a meal in itself for a light lunch or supper.

CHRIS KNAGGS

Cauliflower with asparagus sauce

SERVES 4

500 g/1 lb cauliflower, broken into florets
salt
hard-boiled egg, chopped to garnish

SAUCE

15 g/½ oz margarine
15 g/½ oz plain flour
275 g/10 oz can asparagus spears, drained and liquid reserved
2 tablespoons cold water
3 tablespoons single cream
freshly ground black pepper

1 Bring a pan of salted water to the boil, add the cauliflower florets and simmer for about 15 minutes until just tender.

2 Meanwhile, make the sauce: melt the margarine in a saucepan, sprinkle in the flour and stir over low heat for 1-2 minutes until straw-coloured. Mix the asparagus liquid with the water then gradually add to the pan and simmer, stirring, until thick and smooth.

3 Remove from heat and stir in the cream, then add the asparagus spears. Crush the asparagus with a potato masher until well blended into the sauce, then season to taste with salt and pepper. ⚠ Return to heat and heat through gently, stirring with a wooden spoon.

4 Drain the cauliflower well and arrange in a warmed serving dish. Pour the sauce over the cauliflower, garnish with the chopped egg and serve at once.

Cook's Notes

TIME
This dish takes about 20 minutes to prepare.

SERVING IDEAS
Serve with vegetable lasagne.

WATCHPOINT
Season the asparagus sauce lightly.

● 110 calories/450 kj per portion

MARTIN BRIGDALE

Broccoli with egg topping

SERVES 4
500 g/1 lb broccoli (see Buying guide)
salt
50 g/2 oz butter
50 g/2 oz fresh white breadcrumbs
2 hard-boiled eggs, finely chopped (see Preparation)
finely grated zest and juice of ½ lemon
1 tablespoon chopped fresh parsley
freshly ground black pepper

1 Divide the broccoli into spears leaving small leaves attached.
2 Bring a pan of salted water to the boil, add the broccoli (see Cook's tip), cover and simmer for about 5 minutes until the broccoli is tender but not soft.
3 Meanwhile, make the topping: melt the butter in a frying-pan, add the breadcrumbs and fry over moderate heat, stirring, for about 5 minutes.
4 Add the finely chopped eggs to the fried crumbs together with the lemon zest and juice, parsley and salt and pepper to taste. Fry gently for 1-2 minutes until heated through.
5 Drain the broccoli thoroughly and transfer to a warmed serving dish. Sprinkle the topping over the broccoli and serve at once.

Cook's Notes

TIME
20 minutes preparation including hard-boiling the eggs; 10 minutes cooking.

SERVING IDEAS
The lemony flavour of this broccoli dish goes well with a vegetable soufflé. The colour provides a good contrast.

COOK'S TIP
Try and arrange the broccoli spears in the saucepan so that the stems are immersed in the water and the heads are just above the water, cooking in the steam.

BUYING GUIDE
You can use any of the broccoli family for this recipe: try calabrese or cauliflower.

PREPARATION
Boil the eggs for 10 minutes, then immediately hold under cold running water, and tap the shells against the side of the sink to crack them. This will stop further cooking and prevent a dark rim from forming around the egg yolks, which is caused by over-cooking.

●180 calories/750 kj per portion

Stir-fried broccoli and peppers

SERVES 4

500 g/1 lb frozen broccoli florets, defrosted and drained
1 red pepper, deseeded and cut into thin strips
2 tablespoons vegetable oil
1 clove garlic, crushed (optional)
salt and freshly ground black pepper
25 g/1 oz butter

1 Divide the broccoli into smaller florets, by slicing lengthways through the stalks.

2 Heat the oil in a large heavy-based frying-pan, add the red pepper and garlic, if using, and fry gently for 5-10 minutes.
3 Increase the heat to moderate, add the broccoli, season with salt and pepper to taste and fry, stirring constantly, for 5-6 minutes until just cooked through.
4 Transfer the vegetables to a warmed serving dish and dot with the butter. Serve at once.

CHRIS KNAGGS

DON LAST

Rumbledethumps

SERVES 4
500 g/1 lb potatoes, cut into chunks
   (see Economy)
500 g/1 lb green cabbage, finely
   shredded
salt
50 g/2 oz margarine or butter
2 tablespoons snipped chives
freshly ground black pepper

1 Bring the potatoes to the boil in salted water, lower the heat and cook for 15 minutes or until they are tender.

2 Meanwhile, put the shredded cabbage in a saucepan, add just enough cold water to cover and add a pinch of salt. Bring to the boil, then lower the heat and simmer for 3-5 minutes until tender. Drain well and set aside.

3 Drain the potatoes and mash with the margarine (see Cook's tip). Beat in the drained cabbage until well incorporated.

4 Stir in the chives, add salt and pepper to taste and mix well.

5 Pile into a warmed serving dish and serve at once.

Cook's Notes

TIME
15 minutes preparation; 15 minutes cooking.

ECONOMY
This is an excellent way of using up left-over potatoes and/or cabbage.

DID YOU KNOW
This unusually named dish hails originally from the Scottish borders.

VARIATIONS
Use spring onion tops instead of chives. Freshly grated nutmeg makes a good addition too.

SERVING IDEAS
The dish may be lightly browned before serving: pile the mixture into an ovenproof dish and bake in a 200C/400F/Gas 6 oven for 15-20 minutes. Alternatively, shape mixture into patties, dust with flour and fry in oil.

COOK'S TIP
To cut down on preparation time, use a hand-held electric beater to mash the potato. Mix in the remaining ingredients at slow speed.

●205 calories/875 kj per portion

Cabbage in creamy horseradish sauce

SERVES 4-6
750 g/1½ lb firm white cabbage
salt

SAUCE
25 g/1 oz butter
25 g/1 oz plain flour
300 ml/½ pint milk
2 tablespoons horseradish relish
pinch of freshly grated nutmeg
freshly ground black pepper
chopped parsley, to garnish

1 Cut the cabbage into quarters. Discard the tough or discoloured outer leaves and tough inner core. Chop or shred the cabbage finely.
2 Have ready a pan of boiling salted water, drop in the cabbage and quickly return to the boil. Continue to boil for 5-8 minutes. **!**
3 Meanwhile, make the sauce: melt the butter in a small saucepan, sprinkle in the flour and stir over low heat for 2 minutes until straw-coloured. Remove from the heat and gradually stir in the milk. Return to the heat and simmer, stirring until thick and smooth. Add the horse-radish relish and nutmeg, and salt and pepper to taste.
4 Drain the cabbage well, then combine with the sauce. Return to the rinsed-out cabbage pan, reheat gently and turn into a warmed serving dish. Serve at once.

Cook's Notes

 TIME
20 minutes to make the whole dish.

 VARIATION
Instead of horseradish, substitute 1 teaspoon caraway seeds. These combine especially well with cabbage of all kinds, and give the dish an Eastern European flavour.

! **WATCHPOINT**
It is very important not to overcook the cabbage —once it becomes limp, even a delicious sauce will not retrieve it from disaster!

 SPECIAL OCCASION
For a more sumptuous (and quicker) dish, sub-stitute 300 ml/½ pint single cream for the white sauce. Season the cream with the horseradish and nutmeg, and salt and pepper to taste, then pour it over the drained cabbage. Heat through very gently or the cream will separate.

 SERVING IDEAS
Serve with hot savoury quiches or pies.

●135 calories/575 kj per portion

PAUL WILLIAMS

FRED MANCINI

Tempting cabbage

SERVES 4

50 g/2 oz butter
1 onion, chopped
1 clove garlic, crushed (optional)
750 g/1½ lb green cabbage,
   shredded
6 tablespoons water
salt and freshly ground black pepper
2-3 tablespoons single cream or
   soured cream
1-2 teaspoons poppy seeds (see
   Buying guide)

1 Melt the butter in a saucepan, add the onion and garlic, if using, and fry gently for 5 minutes until the onion is soft and lightly coloured.
2 Stir in the shredded cabbage, then pour in the water. Season with salt and pepper to taste and stir well together.

3 Cover with a lid and cook briskly for 7-8 minutes, shaking the pan and stirring the cabbage from time to time to stop it from sticking to the base of the pan.
4 Remove the lid, drain off excess liquid and cook, uncovered, for 1 minute to evaporate any remaining liquid.
5 Add more salt and pepper if necessary, transfer to a warmed serving dish and spoon the cream over the top. Sprinkle with poppy seeds and serve at once.

Cook's Notes

TIME
Preparation 15 minutes, cooking and serving 10 minutes.

! WATCHPOINT
Take care not to over-cook at this stage; the cabbage should be barely tender.

? DID YOU KNOW
Cabbage is rich in vitamin C and other nutrients but they are lost with overcooking.

VARIATIONS
For slimmers, top the cooked cabbage with natural yoghurt instead of cream.
   Toasted sesame seeds can be used as a garnish instead of the poppy seeds.

 BUYING GUIDE
Poppy seeds are available from delicatessens, health food shops and good supermarkets.

●165 calories/695 kj per portion

218

Hot coleslaw

SERVES 4

750 g/1½ lb hard white cabbage, finely shredded
salt
1 tablespoon vegetable oil
1 small onion, finely chopped
2 carrots, grated
2 tablespoons soured cream
2 tablespoons thick bottled mayonnaise
1 teaspoon made English mustard
1 teaspoon lemon juice
freshly ground black pepper

1 Bring a pan of salted water to the boil and cook the cabbage for 3-5 minutes until lightly cooked. Drain well.

2 Meanwhile, heat the oil in a frying-pan over moderate heat. Add the onion, fry for 5 minutes until lightly coloured and remove with a slotted spoon.

3 Stir the grated carrots and fried onion into the drained cabbage. Mix in the soured cream, mayonnaise, mustard and lemon juice. Season well with salt and pepper and toss well until thoroughly coated.

4 Transfer to a frying-pan and stir over gentle heat for 2-3 minutes until the vegetables are heated through. Spoon on to a warmed serving dish and serve at once.

Cook's Notes

TIME
10 minutes preparation, 10 minutes cooking.

VARIATIONS
Use fresh cream instead of soured cream with a little extra lemon juice. Fry a little chopped green or red pepper with the onion before adding it to the cabbage.

●150 calories/625 kj per portion

JAMES JACKSON

PAUL WEBSTER

Creamy piquant cabbage

SERVES 4
1 Savoy cabbage, weighing about
   850 g/1¾ lb (see Buying guide)
salt

SAUCE
50 g/2 oz butter
50 g/2 oz plain flour
425 ml/¾ pint vegetable
   stock
150 ml/¼ pint single cream
3 tablespoons medium-dry sherry
2 teaspoons French mustard
2 tablespoons finely chopped
   parsley
2 teaspoons lemon juice
freshly ground black pepper

1 Remove the tough outer leaves
from the cabbage and trim the stalk.
Cut the cabbage into quarters.
2 Bring a pan of salted water to the
boil, add the cabbage and bring

Cook's Notes

TIME
Preparation and cook-
ing take 20 minutes.

WATCHPOINT
Make sure the sauce is
off the heat when the
lemon juice is added. If the
sauce is too hot it may separate.

SERVING IDEAS
This delicious dish is
a good accompaniment
for a hot vegetable pie.

BUYING GUIDE
Savoy cabbages have a
beautiful green colour
with just a touch of blue, and are
distinguished from other types
of cabbages by their crimp-
ed leaves.
   This recipe can be made with
other varieties of green cabbage, but the texture will be
slightly coarse and the flavour
less mild.

● 275 calories/1150 kj per portion

back to the boil. Lower the heat,
cover and simmer for about 10
minutes, until the cabbage is just
tender when pierced with a knife.
3 Meanwhile, make the sauce: melt
the butter in a saucepan, sprinkle in
the flour and stir over low heat for
1-2 minutes until straw-coloured.
Gradually stir in the stock, then
bring to the boil and simmer,
stirring until thick and smooth.

4 Gradually stir in the cream,
sherry, mustard and parsley and
heat through gently. Remove from
the heat and stir in the lemon
juice [!] and salt and pepper.
5 Remove the cabbage from the pan
with a slotted spoon and drain well
in a colander, rounded side up.
Transfer the drained cabbage to a
warmed serving dish, pour over the
sauce and serve at once.

Curried spinach

SERVES 4

1 kg/2 lb fresh spinach, stalks and
  coarse mid-ribs removed (see
  Buying guide)
2 tablespoons vegetable oil
1 onion, chopped
1 large clove garlic, crushed
  (optional)
1 teaspoon ground coriander
1 teaspoon ground cumin
½ teaspoon ground turmeric
¼ teaspoon ground ginger
¼ teaspoon chilli powder
½ teaspoon salt
1 tablespoon lemon juice

1 Heat the oil in a large frying-pan,
add the onion and garlic, if using,
and fry gently for 5 minutes until
soft and lightly coloured.

2 Add spices and salt and fry for 5
minutes, stirring constantly.
3 Shake the spinach well and add to
the pan with only the water that still
clings to the leaves. Add the lemon
juice and cook for 10 minutes over
moderate heat, turning the spinach
until it softens.
4 Transfer to a warmed serving dish
and serve at once.

CHRIS KNAGGS

Stir-fried spring greens

SERVES 4
1 kg/2 lb spring greens (see Cook's tip)
75 g/3 oz butter
1 teaspoon white wine vinegar
salt
3 tablespoons double cream
freshly ground black pepper
freshly grated nutmeg

1 Cut the greens into 2.5 cm/1 inch strips, discarding the central stem. Wash thoroughly under cold running water. Drain well.
2 Melt the butter in a wok or large pan, add the greens and stir them around until well coated with butter. Add the wine vinegar and a little salt. Cover the pan and cook over gentle heat for about 5 minutes. Shake the pan frequently during this time.

3 Stir in the cream, plenty of pepper and nutmeg to taste. Continue to cook for a further 3-4 minutes, stirring all the time. Turn into a warmed serving dish and serve at once, while the greens are still crisp.

Cook's Notes

TIME
Preparation takes 15 minutes, cooking about 10 minutes.

COOK'S TIP
If the greens are old and rather tough, it is best to blanch them first: plunge washed but unsliced greens in a saucepan of boiling water. Bring back to the boil, reduce the heat and simmer for 1 minute. Drain at once and refresh under cold running water. Shake dry in a colander.

SERVING IDEAS
The greens are particularly good with a nut or lentil roast. They could also be served with lasagne.

●220 calories/925 kj per portion

DON LAST

Curly kale with orange butter

SERVES 4
350 g/12 oz curly kale, shredded
50 g/2 oz butter, softened
finely grated zest of ½ orange
1 tablespoon orange juice
1 tablespoon fresh brown
   breadcrumbs
salt and freshly ground black pepper

1 Beat the butter in a bowl with the orange zest, orange juice and breadcrumbs. Season with salt and pepper to taste. Put on a piece of greaseproof paper and shape into a pat. Place in the freezer or freezing compartment of the refrigerator until required.
2 Bring a little salted water to the

boil in a pan, add kale and return to the boil. Lower the heat, cover and simmer gently for 6-8 minutes, or until the kale is tender but still firm (see Cook's tip).

3 Drain well, then transfer the kale to a warmed serving dish.
4 Cut the butter into small pieces, place on top of the kale and toss well. Serve at once.

Cook's Notes

 TIME
Preparation takes about 10 minutes and cooking about 10 minutes.

 COOK'S TIP
Use a steamer if you have one—steaming is an excellent way to cook kale because it prevents overcooking and soggy results. Put the shredded kale into the steamer and stand the steamer in a saucepan. Pour in boiling water to come just to the base of the steamer and set the pan over moderate heat so that the water is gently boiling. Cover and steam the kale for 10-12 minutes until tender.

DID YOU KNOW
Kale, or curly kale as it is sometimes called, is a member of the cabbage family. Its fibrous, tightly curled leaves can vary in colour from dark green to purple.

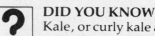 ●120 calories/500 kj per portion

223

Cucumber crisp

SERVES 4
**1 large cucumber
salt
50 g/2 oz Cheddar cheese, grated
25 g/1 oz fresh white breadcrumbs
freshly ground black pepper
25 g/1 oz butter
vegetable oil, for greasing**

1 Heat the oven to 200C/400F/Gas 6.
2 Cut the unpeeled cucumber into pieces about 5 cm/2 inches long. Cut each piece in half lengthways then cut each piece into 4 lengthways to make long finger shapes. Remove and discard the cucumber seeds if they are very large.
3 Bring a pan of salted water to the boil and cook the cucumber in it for 4 minutes, then drain well.
4 Grease a small ovenproof dish and arrange half the cucumber pieces over the base.
5 Mix together the cheese and breadcrumbs and sprinkle half the mixture over the cucumber. Season with black pepper and dot with half the butter.
6 Cover with the remaining cucumber pieces and scatter the rest of the breadcrumb mixture over the top. Dot with the remaining butter and season with more pepper.
7 Bake in the oven for 20-30 minutes or until the top is crisp and brown. Serve at once.

FRED MANCINI

224

Crispy salad skewers

SERVES 12

24 spring onions
½ cucumber
24 large radishes
1 small red pepper, deseeded and cut into squares
1 small green pepper, deseeded and cut into squares
4 celery stalks, thickly sliced
6 tomatoes, quartered
2 small lettuces, leaves separated
2 tablespoons finely chopped fresh parsley
1 clove garlic, crushed
2 tablespoons snipped chives, or spring onion tops
2 teaspoons dried mixed herbs
salt and freshly ground black pepper

Cook's Notes

TIME
2-3 hours soaking the spring onions, and then 45 minutes to make the salad.

SERVING IDEAS
These attractive salad skewers make perfect buffet accompaniments as they may be eaten with the fingers and have a dry dressing.

VARIATIONS
Add stoned black or green olives to give even more colour and variety to the salad skewers.

Use chopped fresh basil or tarragon in the garlic and herb dressing in place of the chopped parsley, if preferred.

● 25 calories/100 kj per portion

1 Trim each onion to a length of 10 cm/4 inches. Then make 2-3 cuts, 2.5 cm/1 inch long, at each end. Leave to soak in a bowl of iced water for 2-3 hours until the ends have curled to make tassels.
2 Cut the cucumber into halves lengthways, then cut each half across into fairly thick slices.

3 In a small bowl, thoroughly mix the parsley with the garlic, chives and dried mixed herbs.
4 About 30 minutes before serving, thread all the salad ingredients on long skewers. Arrange the skewers on a large flat plate, season well with salt and pepper, then sprinkle with the parsley mixture.

DON LAST

Glazed carrots and onions

SERVES 4

1 kg/2 lb old carrots (see Buying
 guide)
salt
4 teaspoons sugar
50 g/2 oz butter
1 small onion, finely chopped
4 tablespoons vegetable stock
freshly ground black pepper
chopped fresh parsley, to garnish

1 Cut each carrot into 4 lengthways,
then cut away the hard yellow core.
Cut each quarter into 2.5 cm/1 inch
pieces, then form the carrot pieces
into even-sized almond shapes (see
Preparation). ✳
2 Bring the carrots to the boil in
salted water. Add the sugar, bring
back to the boil, then lower the heat,
cover and simmer gently for 6
minutes until the carrots are almost
tender but not cooked through.
3 Meanwhile, melt the butter in a
heavy-based frying-pan (see Cook's
tip), add the onion and fry gently for
5 minutes until it is soft and lightly
coloured.
4 Drain the carrots well, then add to
the onion. Mix carefully to coat the
carrots in the butter. Add the stock,
increase the heat to moderate and
cook, uncovered, for 3 minutes until

the stock has almost all evaporated. Shake the pan frequently to
prevent the carrots and onions from
sticking to the pan.

5 Sprinkle with pepper to taste and
the parsley. Stir carefully, then
transfer to a warmed serving dish
and serve at once.

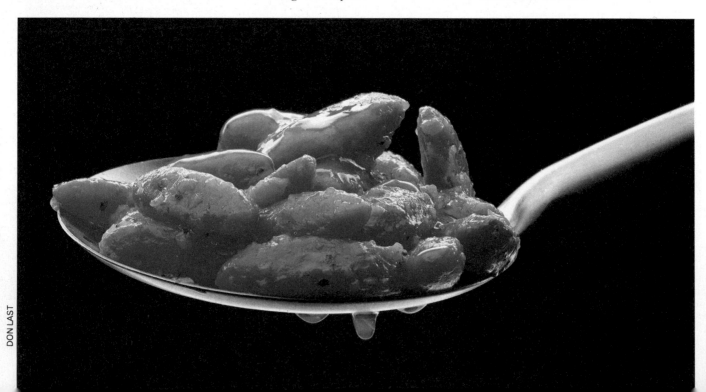

DON LAST

Zesty carrots

SERVES 4

750 g/1½ lb small carrots, sliced
   thickly
finely grated zest and juice of
   1 lemon
25 g/1 oz butter
1 teaspoon light soft brown sugar
salt and freshly ground black pepper
2 tablespoons cold water
lemon slices and finely snipped
   chives, to garnish

1 Put carrot slices into a saucepan
with the lemon zest and the juice,
the butter, sugar, salt and pepper to
taste, ⚠ and the water.
2 Place the pan over high heat and
bring to the boil, then cover with a
tight-fitting lid. Lower the heat and
simmer gently for 40 minutes, until
carrots are just tender and the liquid
has reduced to a glaze.
3 Turn the glazed carrots into a
warmed serving dish. Garnish with
lemon slices and snipped chives.

Cook's Notes

 TIME
20 minutes preparation
and 40 minutes cooking.

 SERVING IDEAS
This dish is delicious as
an accompaniment to
any hot dish.

 WATCHPOINT
Be very careful when
seasoning as the liquid
is going to be evaporated or
absorbed by the carrots and
none will be discarded.

 VARIATIONS
Use a lime or an orange
instead of lemon.

●90 calories/375 kj per portion

PETER MYERS

Sweet and sour carrots

SERVES 4-6

500 g/1 lb carrots, thickly sliced if
  large or old
salt
2 tablespoons vegetable oil
1 medium onion, sliced
3 celery stalks, sliced
25 g/1 oz blanched almonds,
  halved, to finish

SAUCE

2 teaspoons soy sauce
2 teaspoons cornflour
1 tablespoon brown sugar
1 tablespoon cider vinegar
2 teaspoons lemon juice

1 Cook the carrots in boiling salted
water for about 10-20 minutes until
barely tender. ! Drain and reserve
stock.

2 Heat the oil in a frying-pan, add
the onion and celery and fry over
moderate heat for about 5 minutes,
stirring constantly. Do not allow the
vegetables to brown.

3 Add the drained carrots to the pan
and stir to coat them in oil. Remove
the pan from the heat.

4 To make the sauce: mix together
in a saucepan the soy sauce and cornflour, then add the sugar, vinegar
and lemon juice and stir in 150 ml/¼
pint of the reserved carrot stock.

5 Pour the sauce over the vegetables
in the pan and bring to the boil,
stirring all the time. Boil briskly for 3
minutes, stirring occasionally.

6 Turn the vegetables into a warmed
serving dish and scatter with the
almonds. Serve immediately.

CHRIS KNAGGS

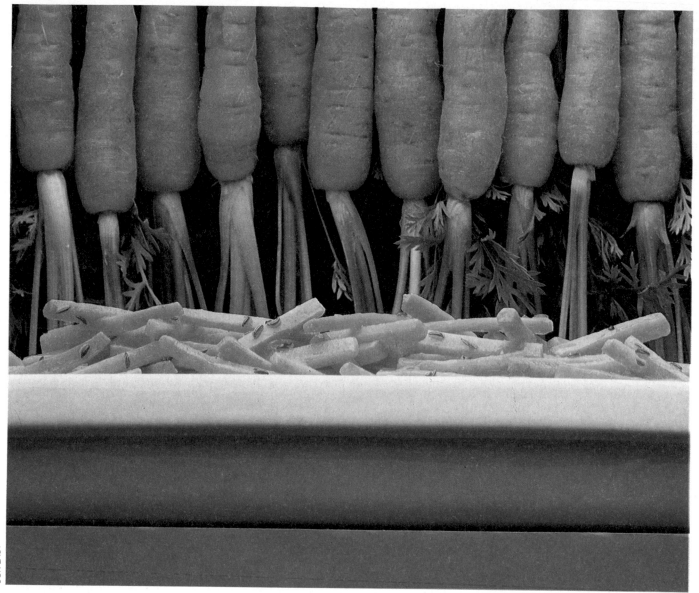

Carrots with caraway seeds

SERVES 4
500 g/1 lb carrots, cut into 5 cm/
** 2 inch matchstick strips**
40 g/1½ oz butter
1 teaspoon caraway seeds
salt and freshly ground black pepper

1 Bring a pan of water to the boil and plunge the carrots into it. Return to the boil and simmer for about 5 minutes, until the carrots are almost tender: they should still be quite crisp and firm. Drain them thoroughly.
2 Melt the butter in the saucepan and add the carrot sticks. Sprinkle

the caraway seeds into the pan and stir well over low heat until the sticks are evenly coated.

3 Season to taste with salt and pepper, tip into a warmed serving dish and serve at once.

Cook's Notes

 TIME
Preparation and cooking take 20-25 minutes.

 VARIATIONS
When in season, use new young baby carrots. In this case keep them whole, and cook for about 8 minutes. You can also substitute crushed coriander seeds for the caraway seeds, which will give the dish a sweet orangey flavour—coriander tastes faintly like orange peel.

 SERVING IDEAS
This dish is a good accompaniment to a spicy vegetable casserole, or a vegetable pie.

 DID YOU KNOW
Carrots are an important source of vitamin A—the theory that they help you to see in the dark stems from the fact that a deficiency of vitamin A leads to night blindness.

●105 calories/450 kj per portion

PAUL WEBSTER

Peppers in tomato juice

SERVES 4

250 g/9 oz green peppers, deseeded and sliced
250 g/9 oz red peppers, deseeded and sliced
1 tablespoon vegetable oil
25 g/1 oz butter or margarine
1 small onion, finely chopped
1 clove garlic, crushed (optional)
1 teaspoon dried rosemary
½ teaspoon sugar
300 ml/½ pint tomato juice
salt and freshly ground black pepper

1 Heat the oil and butter in a frying-pan, add the onion and fry gently for 5 minutes until soft and lightly coloured. Add the peppers and garlic, if using, and fry for a further 5 minutes, stirring occasionally.

2 Stir half the rosemary and the sugar into the tomato juice. Season with salt and pepper and pour over the ingredients in the pan.

3 Simmer, uncovered, for about 10 minutes, stirring occasionally, until the peppers are tender and the tomato juice has reduced to a sauce. Transfer to warmed dish, sprinkle with remaining rosemary.

Stir-fried carrots and peppers

SERVES 4

350 g/12 oz carrots, peeled and cut into 'shavings' (see Preparation)
2 tablespoons vegetable oil
½ onion, finely chopped
½ green pepper, finely chopped
½ red pepper, finely chopped
2 tablespoons soy sauce
2 tablespoons medium sherry
freshly ground black pepper

1 Heat the oil in a wide shallow frying-pan and stir-fry the onion over a moderate heat for 2 minutes. Add the carrots and peppers and stir-fry for about 3 minutes, until carrots are cooked but still crisp.

2 Add the soy sauce and sherry to the pan with pepper to taste. Stir-fry for a further 30 seconds. Turn into a warmed serving dish and serve at once while still piping hot.

Cook's Notes

 TIME
Preparing and cooking take 25-30 minutes.

 PREPARATION
To make the carrot 'shavings':

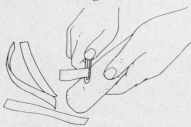

Hold the thin end of the carrot firmly with the fingers of one hand. Rest carrot on board and draw a vegetable peeler along the length of the carrot to make 'shavings'. Turn the carrot, as necessary, to make more shavings.

●100 calories/425 kj per portion

MARTIN BRIGDALE

231

THEO BERGSTROM

Spicy yellow potatoes

SERVES 4

1 kg/2 lb potatoes (see Buying guide)
salt
225 g/8 oz frozen peas
2 tablespoons vegetable oil
1 onion, finely chopped
1 clove garlic, crushed (optional)
2 teaspoons whole black mustard seeds, crushed
1 teaspoon ground turmeric
1 teaspoon very finely grated fresh root ginger
25 g/1 oz butter
2 tablespoons milk
coriander leaves, to garnish

1 Bring the potatoes to the boil in a large saucepan of salted water, lower the heat and simmer for 20 minutes until tender.

2 Meanwhile, cook the peas according to packet instructions.
3 Heat the oil in a frying-pan, add the onion and garlic, if using, and fry gently until the onion is soft and lightly coloured. Add the crushed mustard seeds, turmeric and ginger and cook for 1 minute, stirring.
4 Drain the potatoes thoroughly [!]

and mash with the butter and milk (see Cook's tip). Drain the peas.
5 Stir the onion mixture into the mashed potatoes and beat well to mix. Stir in the drained peas and season to taste with salt.
6 Turn the potatoes into a warmed serving dish, garnish with coriander leaves and serve at once.

Tipsy new potatoes

SERVES 4-6
1 kg/2 lb small even-sized new
  potatoes
4 tablespoons olive oil
1 teaspoon coriander seeds,
  crushed
150 ml/¼ pint dry white wine

1 Scrape the potatoes, then heat the
oil in a large frying-pan over moderate heat.
2 When the oil is sizzling, add the
potatoes, cover, and fry for about 10
minutes, shaking the pan occasionally, until the potatoes are
browned all over.
3 Sprinkle the coriander over the
potatoes, then pour the wine into
the pan.
4 Continue to cook potatoes for
5-10 minutes, shaking the pan until
the wine has been absorbed, and
the potatoes are crisp and tender.
Serve the potatoes at once, while
still hot (see Serving ideas).

Cook's Notes

TIME
5 minutes preparation,
then 15-20 minutes
cooking time.

ECONOMY
It makes sense to buy
an inexpensive bottle of
wine purely for cooking. Once
opened, keep it in a cool place,
ready for when a small quantity
of wine is needed.

SERVING IDEAS
Based on a dish from
Cyprus, these potatoes
go well with vegetable kebabs.

VARIATIONS
Large potatoes may also
be used – cut them into
cubes before frying.
  Add a clove of garlic to the
pan while frying, then discard
before adding the coriander to
the potatoes.

● 330 calories/1375 kj per portion

Potatoes gratin dauphinois

SERVES 8

1.8 kg/4 lb potatoes (see Buying guide)
65 g/2½ oz butter, softened
1 small clove garlic, crushed
salt
700 ml/1¼ pints milk
300 ml/½ pint double cream

1 Heat the oven to 220C/425F/Gas 7.
2 Cut the potatoes into very thin slices, about 2 mm/⅛ inch thick.
3 Put a small knob of the softened butter and the garlic into a large ovenproof dish measuring about 30 × 25 × 5 cm/12 × 10 × 2 inches. Brush the butter and garlic all over the inside of the dish.
4 Arrange a layer of the potatoes, overlapping, in the bottom of the dish, then sprinkle with salt. Continue layering the potatoes, seasoning each layer with salt, until all the potatoes are used up.
5 Pour the milk into the dish, then pour the cream over the top – the milk and cream should barely cover the potatoes. Dot the top with the remaining butter.

6 Bake the potatoes, uncovered, in the oven for 20 minutes, then lower the oven temperature to 180C/350F/ Gas 4 and continue cooking for a further 1-1¼ hours until the potatoes have absorbed the milk and cream and top is golden brown. Remove from the oven and serve at once while piping hot.

Cook's Notes

 TIME
About 1¾ hours to prepare and cook this dish.

 WATCHPOINT
Take care not to overcook and dry out the potatoes; they should be moist.

 BUYING GUIDE
Choose a firm potato, such as King Edward or Desirée, for this dish.

? DID YOU KNOW
This is a classic French potato dish, called *dauphinois* because it originated in the Dauphine district of the French Alps. In this part of France, it is often made sprinkled with about 100 g/4 oz grated Gruyère cheese before baking. For a less expensive version, use Cheddar instead.

●455 calories/1900 kj per portion

JAMES JACKSON

234

Pommes Anna

SERVES 4
750 g/1½ lb potatoes
50 g/2 oz butter, softened
salt and freshly ground black pepper
margarine, for greasing

1 Heat the oven to 200C/400F/Gas 6.
2 Rub half the butter around the inside of a deep 15 cm/6 inch sandwich cake tin.
3 Slice the potatoes thinly (see Preparation) and arrange in neat overlapping circles in cake tin, sprinkling each layer with salt and pepper and small dots of the remaining butter. Press down gently compressing the potato layers into the tin, then cover them with greased greaseproof paper or foil.
4 Bake in the top of the oven for about 1 hour until the potatoes are cooked through.
5 To serve: remove the greaseproof paper or foil, run a knife around the sides of the tin, then invert a plate on the top. Invert the cake tin on to the plate, remove the tin and serve at once (see Serving ideas).

Cook's Notes

TIME
15 minutes preparation;
1 hour cooking.

PREPARATION
Do not soak potatoes in water after peeling and slicing them as the starch helps to hold the potato cake together.
To make sure the potatoes are sliced thinly and evenly, use a mandolin slicer.

● 235 calories/975 kj per portion

DID YOU KNOW
This buttery potato cake is one version of the classic French potato dish that was created in the time of Napoleon III. It was probably named after a courtesan.

SERVING IDEAS
A delicious way of enhancing the natural flavour of potatoes, this dish makes an excellent accompaniment to any hot dish. It is also good cold with salads.

Noisette potatoes

SERVES 4
1.5 kg/3-3½ lb potatoes (see
   Buying guide)
salt
75 g/3 oz butter
rosemary sprigs or fresh mint
   leaves, to garnish (optional)

1 Peel the potatoes and put them
into a large pan of cold salted water.
Leave to soak for at least 2 hours
(see Cook's tips).
2 Drain the potatoes and, using a
melon baller, scoop out as many
balls of potato from each as possible
(see Economy).
3 Bring a pan of salted water to the
boil, add the potato balls and cover
the pan with a lid. Bring to the boil,
lower the heat and simmer gently
for 4 minutes until potatoes are
beginning to soften (see Cook's
tips). Drain the potatoes.
4 Melt the butter in a heavy-based
frying-pan. Add potato balls and fry

over moderate heat, shaking pan
frequently, for about 10 minutes or
until the potatoes are crisp and
golden on the outside but soft inside when they are pierced gently in
the centre with a fine skewer.

5 Remove the potatoes from the
pan with a slotted spoon and drain
on absorbent paper. Transfer to a
warmed dish, sprinkle with salt and
serve garnished with rosemary
sprigs or mint leaves, if using.

Cook's Notes

TIME
Preparation, including
soaking, parboiling and
cooling, is 3 hours; cooking is
then only about 10 minutes.

BUYING GUIDE
Old all-purpose pota-
toes such as red or
Desirée varieties are best for
this dish.

SERVING IDEAS
These potatoes make a
good accompaniment to
most savoury dishes.

ECONOMY
Use any left-over trim-
mings for soups, stews
and thickening sauces.

COOK'S TIPS
Soaking the potatoes
before cooking helps
remove excess starch which
would tend to make potatoes
stick together during frying.
   Parboiling potatoes shortens
the final cooking time and it
helps produce a tender centre
with a beautifully crisp shell.

? DID YOU KNOW
These noisette potatoes
(from the French for
'nut'), when dressed with some
concentrated meat gravy and
fresh parsley make the classic
French dish *pommes de terre à la
parisienne*.

●425 calories/1775 kj per portion

Two-way potatoes

SERVES 4

750 g/1½ lb potatoes, scrubbed but
   unpeeled and cut into 5 mm/¼
   inch slices (see Buying guide)
25 g/1 oz margarine or butter
3 tablespoons vegetable oil
225-300 ml/8-11 fl oz boiling water
8 spring onions, finely chopped
6 sage leaves, chopped, or
   ½ teaspoon dried sage
3 tablespoons freshly chopped
   parsley
salt and freshly ground black pepper

1 Heat the margarine and oil in a
large heavy frying-pan. Add the
sliced potatoes, turn them to coat
thoroughly in the margarine and oil,
then cook over moderate heat for 20
minutes. Turn the potatoes several
times with a fish slice, so that they
cook evenly and do not stick.

2 Add 225 ml/8 fl oz boiling water to
the pan.

3 Add the spring onions and herbs
and season well with salt and
pepper. Boil, uncovered, for about
10 minutes until all the water has
evaporated and the potatoes are
cooked through. If still not quite
done, add 75 ml/3 fl oz boiling water
and cook for 5 minutes, until the
liquid is absorbed. Serve at once.

PAUL WEBSTER

Oven-baked new potatoes

SERVES 4

750 g/1½ lb small new potatoes (see
  Buying guide and Preparation)
4 sprigs of mint
4 sprigs of parsley
salt and freshly ground black pepper
25 g/1 oz butter
1 tablespoon chopped fresh mint or
  1 teaspoon dried mint
1 tablespoon chopped fresh parsley

1 Heat the oven to 180C/350F/Gas 4.
Put the potatoes in a 1.5 L/2½ pint
casserole.
2 Tuck the mint and parsley sprigs
amongst the potatoes and season
with salt and pepper. Dot the butter
over the top.

3 Cover the casserole and bake in
the oven for 45-60 minutes until
tender when pierced with a fine
skewer. Using 2 spoons, turn the

potatoes until evenly coated with
the melted butter. Sprinkle with
the chopped mint and parsley and
serve at once.

Cook's Notes

 TIME
Preparation takes 5
minutes, cooking 45-60
minutes, depending on the size
of the potatoes.

 ECONOMY
Cook the potatoes when
you are using the oven
at the same temperature for
another dish.

 SERVING IDEAS
These easy-to-cook
potatoes are particularly
good with vegetable casseroles.

 PREPARATION
Peeling new potatoes is
very time-consuming
and not necessary: all they need
is a good scrub with a brush to
remove any earth.

BUYING GUIDE
Choose small, even-
sized potatoes that will
take the same amount of
cooking time. Maris Piper or
Cyprus new potatoes are best
choices for this recipe.

●205 calories/850 kj per portion

JAMES JACKSON

Curried potatoes

SERVES 4
500 g/1 lb potatoes, cut into
  even-sized chunks
2 tablespoons vegetable oil
15 g/½ oz butter
2 onions, chopped
1 clove garlic, crushed (optional)
2 teaspoons ground coriander (see
  Buying guide)
2 teaspoons ground cumin
pinch of chilli powder
225 g/8 oz can tomatoes
300 ml/½ pint water
salt and freshly ground black pepper
chopped fresh parsley or coriander,
  to garnish

1 Heat the oil and butter in a large saucepan, add the onions and garlic, if using, and fry gently for 5 minutes until the onions are soft and lightly coloured.
2 Add the coriander, cumin and chilli powder to the pan. Cook gently for 1 minute, stirring constantly, then add the tomatoes with their juice, the water and potatoes. Season to taste with salt and pepper.

3 Bring to the boil, then lower the heat slightly, cover and simmer gently for about 25 minutes, until the potatoes are tender. Taste and adjust seasoning if necessary. Transfer to a warmed serving dish, sprinkle with chopped parsley or coriander and serve at once.

DON LAST

Crunchy potato scallops

SERVES 4
500 g/1 lb potatoes, thinly sliced

BATTER
50 g/2 oz plain flour
2 teaspoons baking powder
1 teaspoon salt
about 150 ml/¼ pint water
vegetable oil, for deep frying

1 Put the potatoes in a bowl, cover with cold water and leave to soak.
2 Make the batter: sift the flour, baking powder and salt into a large bowl and make a well in the centre. Gradually pour the water into the well, drawing the flour into the liquid with a wooden spoon, until a smooth batter is formed.

3 Heat the oil in a deep-fat frier to 170C/325F or until a stale bread cube browns in 75 seconds. Heat the oven to 110C/225F/Gas ¼.
4 Drain the potato slices, then pat dry with a clean tea-towel. Add one-third of the potato slices to the batter and stir carefully until they are well coated. [!]

5 Using 2 forks, lift out the potato slices and carefully drop them into the oil. Fry for 3 minutes, turning occasionally, until golden.
6 Remove with a slotted spoon and drain on absorbent paper. Transfer to a warmed serving dish and keep warm in the oven while frying the remaining slices. Serve at once.

Cook's Notes

 TIME
20 minutes preparation; 12 minutes frying.

 WATCHPOINT
Take care not to break the potato slices when stirring in the batter.

 VARIATION
Try using sliced turnips instead of potatoes.

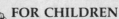 **FOR CHILDREN**
These fried potato slices will be a great hit with children – serve them with vegetable or cheese patties, plus grilled tomatoes and baked beans. They are also delicious served for breakfast with fried eggs and grilled tomatoes, as a substitute for fried bread.

●205 calories/850 kj per portion

240

Oaty fried potatoes

SERVES 4
500 g/1 lb small new potatoes
salt
1 large egg, beaten
3 tablespoons porridge oats
50 g/2 oz butter
1 bunch watercress, divided into
  sprigs, to garnish

1 Bring a large pan of salted water to the boil, add the potatoes and cook for about 15 minutes, until just tender. Drain well and leave to cool slightly.

2 Put the beaten egg on a plate and dip the potatoes in it, to coat thoroughly, shaking off any excess.

3 Put the porridge oats on a plate. Coat a few potatoes at a time in the oats so that they are well covered (see Cook's tip).

4 Melt the butter in a frying-pan until just beginning to sizzle, then add the oat-covered potatoes. Fry them over moderate heat, turning frequently, for about 5 minutes until an even golden brown.

5 Transfer the potatoes to a warmed serving dish and insert watercress sprigs at regular intervals between the potatoes. Serve at once.

Cook's Notes

TIME
Preparation takes about 5 minutes. Boiling and frying takes about 30 minutes.

SERVING IDEAS
This is a delicious way to serve potatoes with a main vegetarian dish. They would go well with quiches, patties, flans or soufflés, but try to avoid serving them with another crisp-coated fried food, such as fritters.

COOK'S TIP
Press the oats on with your fingers to make them adhere firmly.

●280 calories/1175 kj per portion

CHRIS KNAGGS

Potato cakes

SERVES 4
500 g/1 lb potatoes
250 g/9 oz large carrots (see Buying guide)
salt
1 tablespoon grated onion
2 tablespoons beaten egg
freshly ground black pepper
2 tablespoons vegetable oil

1 Put the potatoes in a saucepan together with the carrots and cover with salted water. Bring to the boil then lower the heat slightly. Cover and simmer for 5 minutes. Drain the vegetables and leave to cool.

2 Grate the cold potatoes and carrots on a coarse grater to give long, thin shreds. Place in a bowl, add onion and mix together.

3 Stir the beaten egg into the vegetable mixture and season to taste with salt and pepper.

4 Divide the mixture into 8 and shape each piece into a round about 7.5 cm/3 inches in diameter and 1 cm/½ inch deep (see Cook's tips).

5 Heat the oil in a frying-pan, add 4 of the cakes and fry over moderate heat for about 5 minutes, turning until browned and crisp.

6 Remove from the pan with a slotted spoon and drain on absorbent paper. Keep hot while frying the remaining cakes in the same way (see Cook's tips). Serve hot (see Serving ideas).

TONY ROBINS

PAUL WILLIAMS

Mashed medley

SERVES 4
350 g/12 oz parsnips
250 g/9 oz swede
250 g/9 oz carrots
salt
25 g/1 oz margarine or butter
2-3 tablespoons milk
freshly ground black pepper

1 Peel and quarter the parsnips. Remove the centre core if woody.
2 Peel the swede and cut it into 2.5 cm/1 inch chunks.
3 Scrape the carrots and cut thickly.

4 Cook all the vegetables together in boiling salted water until just soft. Drain.
5 Melt the margarine in a saucepan and add the milk. Add the cooked vegetables and mash together.
6 Stir in lots of freshly ground black pepper. Serve very hot.

Cook's Notes

TIME
Preparation about 15 minutes, cooking a further 15 minutes.

SERVING IDEAS
Grate 25-50 g/1-2 oz Cheddar cheese and sprinkle it over the cooked vegetables.

●120 calories/500 kj per portion

SPECIAL OCCASION
Cook and purée each vegetable separately, substitute single cream for milk and add 15 g/½ oz butter to each vegetable, then arrange in sections in a circular dish. Flavour the parsnips with grated nutmeg, the carrots with a pinch of ground coriander and 1 teaspoon of sugar, the swede with 1 tablespoon lemon juice.

Asparagus with new potatoes

SERVES 4
**500 g/1 lb fresh slender asparagus
spears**
1.75 L/3 pints water
salt
1 kg/2 lb small new potatoes

PARSLEY BUTTER SAUCE
50 g/2 oz butter
juice of ½ lemon
**4 tablespoons chopped fresh
parsley**
freshly ground black pepper

1 Divide the asparagus spears into 4 separate bundles and tie each bundle securely with string in 2 places: just below the tips and towards the base (see Preparation).
2 Bring the water with 1 teaspoon salt to the boil in a large deep saucepan (about 3 L/5¼ pints capacity).
3 Remove the pan from the heat and add the potatoes. Pack them round the pan and then stand the bundles of asparagus upright in the centre with their tips extending out of the water (they will cook in the steam).
4 Cover the saucepan with foil to make a domed lid high enough to cover the asparagus completely without crushing the tips. Crimp the foil well around the pan edge (it is important that none of the steam escapes during cooking).
5 Return the pan to the heat, bring back to the boil and boil gently for about 20 minutes, or until the asparagus stalks feel tender when pierced with a sharp knife.
6 Meanwhile, make the sauce: heat the butter very gently in a small saucepan until it is just melted. **!** Remove from the heat and stir in the lemon juice and parsley. Season to taste with salt and pepper.
7 Lift out the asparagus bundles with kitchen tongs. Drain them thoroughly **!** then cut the string with kitchen scissors and carefully untie the bundles. Drain the potatoes.
8 Arrange the potatoes around the outside of a warmed serving dish with the asparagus in the centre. Pour the sauce evenly over the vegetables and serve at once.

DON LAST

JOHN WOODCOCK

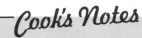
Cook's Notes

TIME
Preparation takes 30 minutes. Cooking takes about 20 minutes.

PREPARATION
To prepare asparagus spears for cooking:

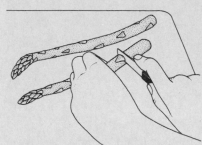

1 *Young asparagus spears may just need to be trimmed of any discoloured parts at the ends.*

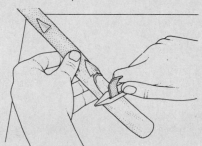

2 *With tougher stalks, shave off any stringy fibres with a sharp knife or vegetable peeler.*

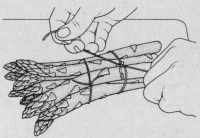

3 *Make sure spears are trimmed to an even length, then tie in 2 places with string.*

WATCHPOINTS
Remove the butter from the heat as soon as it has melted, or it will turn brown.
Asparagus needs to be drained thoroughly so that no liquid remains to dilute the sauce. After initial draining, lay on a clean, folded tea-towel to absorb any liquid remaining.

●325 calories/1350 kj per portion

French-style peas and potatoes

SERVES 4

100 g/4 oz shelled fresh peas

15 g/½ oz cornflour

300 ml/½ pint milk

salt and freshly ground black pepper

25 g/1 oz margarine or butter

500 g/1 lb small new potatoes, scrubbed

8 spring onions, chopped

8 large lettuce leaves, shredded

a little extra milk (optional)

1 In a bowl, mix the cornflour to a smooth cream with a little of the milk. Stir in the rest of the milk. Season with plenty of salt and pepper.

2 Melt the margarine in a large saucepan and pour in the cornflour and milk mixture. Bring to the boil, stirring all the time.

3 Lower the heat and add the potatoes and spring onions. Cover and simmer very gently for 30 minutes.

4 Add the peas and continue simmering for a further 10 minutes.

5 Add the lettuce and a little more milk if the sauce is getting too thick. Stir well, bring back to the boil and remove immediately from the heat. Taste and adjust seasoning if necessary. Transfer to a warmed serving dish and serve at once.

CHRIS KNAGGS

Cook's Notes

TIME
Preparation and cooking take about 50 minutes.

WATCHPOINT
Be sure to use a non-stick saucepan and keep the temperature low after the sauce has boiled or it may catch on the bottom of the pan.

SERVING IDEAS
Serve with a hot vegetable pie or a nut roast.

● 230 calories/975 kj per portion

PETER MYERS

Honey and mustard turnips

SERVES 4-6
750 g/1½ lb turnips, cut into 1 cm/
    ½ inch slices
salt
25 g/1 oz margarine or butter
2 tablespoons clear honey
2 teaspoons soft brown sugar
1 tablespoon French mustard
freshly ground black pepper

1 Heat the oven to 180C/350F/Gas 4.
2 Put the turnips into a saucepan of salted water and bring to the boil. Lower the heat and simmer for 5 minutes, then drain the turnips very thoroughly.

3 Meanwhile, melt the margarine in a small flameproof casserole over gentle heat. Stir in the honey, sugar, mustard, and pepper to taste and let the mixture bubble gently.

4 Tip the turnip slices into the honey mixture, turning them so they are well coated. Cover and cook gently for about 45 minutes until tender, stirring occasionally.

Cook's Notes

TIME
Preparation time is about 10 minutes, including parboiling the turnips. The dish then takes 45 minutes to cook.

SERVING IDEAS
These turnips are an ideal accompaniment to many main dishes, particularly vegetable casseroles and hot-pots and other warming winter dishes. The sweet-sour sauce has a strong taste, so avoid serving with delicate flavours.

VARIATION
Parsnips can also be cooked in this way. Cut them into quarters and remove the central woody core. Parboil for 5 -10 minutes, then cook for about 30 minutes until tender.

●115 calories/500 kj per portion

Turnips in onion sauce

SERVES 4-6
750 g/1½ lb large turnips, thinly
    sliced (see Cook's tip)
salt
25 g/1 oz margarine or butter
250 g/9 oz onions, very finely
    chopped
25 g/1 oz plain flour
350 ml/12 fl oz milk
4 teaspoons finely chopped
    fresh parsley
freshly ground black pepper
parsley sprigs, to garnish

1 Bring a pan of salted water to the
boil, add the turnips and bring to
the boil. Lower the heat, cover and
simmer gently for about 10 minutes
or until the turnip slices are just
tender when pierced with a knife.

2 Meanwhile, make the sauce: melt
the margarine in a saucepan, add
the onions and fry gently for 5
minutes until soft and lightly
coloured. Sprinkle in the flour and
stir over low heat for 1-2 minutes,
until straw-coloured. Remove from
the heat and gradually stir in the
milk. Return to the heat and
simmer, stirring, until thick and
smooth.

3 Stir the chopped parsley into the
sauce and season to taste with salt
and pepper. Drain the turnips
thoroughly and add to the sauce.
Stir for 2-3 minutes to heat through,
then transfer to a warmed serving
dish and serve at once, garnished
with parsley sprigs.

MARTIN BRIGDALE

Cook's Notes

 TIME
This dish takes about
30 minutes to prepare,
including the cooking time.

 COOK'S TIP
If only small turnips are
available, quarter them,
but do not slice thinly. Cook in
boiling salted water for 5
minutes until just tender, then
drain and add to the sauce.
Finish the dish in the same way
as described above.

 WATCHPOINT
Do not boil the turnips
for too long or they will
be too soft to hold their shape
when stirred into the onion
and parsley sauce.

 VARIATION
For a simple lunch or
supper dish, put the
turnips and sauce in a shallow,
heatproof dish and sprinkle the
top with grated Gruyère or
Cheddar cheese. Grill until

golden and serve with buttered
toast or French bread.
    The turnips may be replaced
with potatoes, swede or carrots:
boil until just tender, then add
to the sauce.

SERVING IDEAS
Serve this homely dish
with a cheesy main
course flan or soufflé and a
green vegetable.

● 160 calories/675 kj per portion

Parsnip special

SERVES 4-6

750 g/1½ lb parsnips, halved
   lengthways and cut into 1 cm/½
   inch slices (see Buying guide)
salt
50 g/2 oz margarine or butter
100 g/4 oz button mushrooms,
   sliced
50 g/2 oz broken walnut pieces
1 teaspoon sweet paprika
150 ml/¼ pint vegetable stock
freshly ground black pepper

1 Drop the sliced parsnips into
boiling salted water, bring back to
the boil and boil gently for about 5
minutes, until the parsnips are just
tender. Drain well.
2 Melt the margarine in a large
saucepan, add the sliced mushrooms and fry, stirring, for 1
minute. Add the drained parsnips,
walnut pieces, paprika, stock, a
little salt and plenty of pepper.
3 Boil the mixture rapidly for 2

minutes, stirring and turning the
parsnips so that they become
thoroughly coated in the sauce.
Taste and adjust seasoning, then
turn into a warmed serving dish.
Serve at once.

Cook's Notes

 TIME
Preparation and cook-
ing take 20 minutes.

 SERVING IDEAS
The unusual combina-
tion of parsnips, walnuts
and mushrooms is particularly
delicious. Serve with plain
vegetable dishes as a substantial
accompanying dish.

 BUYING GUIDE
Buy parsnips from the
greengrocer if possible,
rather than from the super-
market where they are sold in
polythene bags which make
them sweat and lose their
flavour.

! WATCHPOINT
Do not boil the sliced
parsnips for too long, or
they will become too soft to hold
their shape when they are
cooked again with the mushrooms and walnuts.

●245 calories/1025 kj per portion

MICHAEL KAY

CHRIS KNAGGS

Parsnip chips

SERVES 4
1 kg/2 lb large parsnips (see Buying guide)
salt
50 g/2 oz plain flour
vegetable oil, for deep-frying

TO SERVE
25 g/1 oz Parmesan cheese, finely grated
a little sweet paprika, to sprinkle

1 Cut the parsnips in half lengthways, cut away any hard central cores then cut into strips, about 5 cm/2 inches long and 1 cm/½ inch wide.
2 Place the parsnip strips in a bowl of iced water and leave to stand for 30 minutes.
3 Transfer the strips with a slotted spoon to a saucepan and cover with salted water.
4 Bring to the boil, then remove from the heat, drain thoroughly in a colander and pat dry on absorbent paper.
5 Place the flour in a polythene bag, add a pinch of salt, then toss the parsnip strips in the flour to coat them.
6 Heat the oil in a deep-fat frier with a basket to 190C/375F, or until a day-old bread cube browns in 50 seconds.
7 Lift the basket out of the oil and put in half the strips. Lower the basket into the frier and cook for 4-5 minutes or until the chips are crisp and golden brown. Lift out the basket, shake off excess fat and turn the chips on to a plate covered with absorbent paper. Drain well, then transfer to a serving dish and keep hot while frying the remaining strips in the same way.
8 To serve: sprinkle with the Parmesan cheese and a little paprika.

249

Swede and turnip parcels

SERVES 4
250 g/9 oz swede
250 g/9 oz turnips
about ¼ teaspoon freshly grated
   nutmeg
salt and freshly ground black pepper
butter, for greasing

TO GARNISH
1 tablespoon chopped fresh parsley
2 slices lemon, halved

MARTIN BRIGDALE

Cook's Notes

TIME
20 minutes preparation,
30-40 minutes cooking.

SERVING IDEAS
If wished, the individual parcels can be opened and garnished, then resealed and served to guests to open themselves.

VARIATIONS
Carrots and parsnips can also be cooked in this way so that you can swap the combinations. If using parsnips you will need to allow a little extra weight, since the hard central cores must be cut away.

● 40 calories/160 kj per portion

1 Heat the oven to 200C/400F/Gas 6. Thickly butter 4 pieces of foil, each about 23 cm/9 inches square.
2 Cut the swede and turnips into sticks about 5 cm/2 inches long and 5 mm/¼ inch wide. Mix them together with the nutmeg and salt and pepper to taste, then divide equally between the pieces of foil, placing the mixture in the centre of each. Bring the edges of the foil together and turn the edges over several times to seal the parcels completely.

3 Place the parcels on a baking sheet and cook in the oven for 30-40 minutes until the vegetables are tender when pierced with a knife.
4 Place the parcels on a warmed serving dish, turn back the foil, sprinkle the vegetables with parsley and top each portion with half a slice of lemon. Serve at once.

Swede and sprouts with thyme

SERVES 4
250 g/9 oz swede
500 g/1 lb Brussels sprouts
225 ml/8 fl oz vegetable stock
salt
25 g/1 oz margarine or butter
½ teaspoon dried thyme
freshly ground black pepper

1 Cut the swede into 1 cm/½ inch dice. Put into a pan, add the stock and bring to the boil. Lower the heat, cover and simmer gently for about 15 minutes until just tender when pierced with the point of a sharp knife.

2 Meanwhile, prepare the sprouts. Wash well and cut a cross in the base of each. Bring a pan of salted water to the boil, add the sprouts, cover and cook for 10-12 minutes until just tender. Drain thoroughly.

3 Add the sprouts, margarine and thyme to the swede, then season to taste with salt and pepper. Cover the pan and cook over low heat for 3-5 minutes so that the flavours have time to blend.

4 Spoon the vegetables into a warmed serving dish and pour the pan juices over the top. Serve at once.

Cook's Notes

TIME
Preparation takes about 10 minutes; cooking about 25 minutes.

SERVING IDEAS
Serve with a winter vegetable hotpot.

WATCHPOINT
Cook the swede gently otherwise the stock may be absorbed too quickly.

● 100 calories/415 kj per portion

Celeriac in mustard sauce

PAUL WEBSTER

SERVES 4-6

750 g/1½ lb celeriac
salt
1 tablespoon French grainy mustard
150 ml/¼ pint double cream
freshly ground black pepper
finely chopped parsley, to garnish
(optional)

1 Scrub and peel the celeriac (see Preparation). Quarter each celeriac root and cut the quarters across into fairly thin slices.
2 Bring a pan of salted water to the boil and drop the celeriac slices into it. Bring back to the boil and boil for 4 minutes, until the celeriac is just tender. Drain well.
3 Rinse out the saucepan, stir the mustard into the cream and put it in the pan with the drained celeriac. Season to taste with salt and pepper.
4 Heat through gently, stirring carefully, then transfer the mixture to a warmed serving dish and garnish, if liked, with a light sprinkling of parsley. Serve at once.

Cook's Notes

 TIME
This dish takes 25 minutes preparation and cooking.

 DID YOU KNOW
Celeriac is a round root vegetable that looks like a cross between a swede and a parsnip and, as its name suggests, tastes very much like celery.

 PREPARATION
Celeriac has a very knobbly surface and requires thorough scrubbing before peeling to remove all the mud lodged between the knobbles. When buying celeriac, choose the smoothest roots that you can find, as these are the easiest ones to clean and prepare for cooking.

●190 calories/800 kj per portion

Sweet potatoes in orange sauce

SERVES 4
750 g/1½ lb sweet potatoes
25 g/1 oz margarine or butter
6 spring onions, thinly sliced
juice of 2 oranges
1 tablespoon cornflour
¼ teaspoon ground cinnamon
150 ml/¼ pint vegetable stock
15 g/½ oz sugar
finely grated zest of 1 orange
salt and freshly ground black
    pepper
orange wedges, to garnish

1 Scrub the potatoes, then put them into a large saucepan and cover with cold water. Bring to the boil, then lower the heat slightly and simmer for 20-30 minutes until just tender. Drain, leave until cool enough to handle, then peel and cut into thick even-sized slices.

2 Make the orange sauce: melt the margarine in a large saucepan, add the onions and fry gently for 5 minutes until they are soft and lightly coloured.
3 Meanwhile, put half the orange juice in a bowl and blend in the cornflour and cinnamon.
4 Stir the remaining orange juice and the stock into the onions. Bring to the boil, then stir in the cornflour and orange juice mixture, sugar and orange zest. Simmer gently, stirring, until the sauce is thick and smooth, then season to taste with salt and freshly ground pepper.
5 Mix the potato slices into the sauce, heat through, then transfer to a warmed serving dish. Garnish with orange wedges and serve.

PAUL WEBSTER

FRED MANCINI

Hot beetroot with red cabbage

SERVES 6

500 g/1 lb red cabbage, shredded (see Preparation)
250 g/9 oz cooked beetroot, sliced
salt
25 g/1 oz margarine
1 onion, sliced
300 ml/½ pint vegetable stock
2-3 tablespoons lemon juice
2 cloves
1 bay leaf
freshly ground black pepper
25 g/1 oz butter, softened
100 g/4 oz cooking apple, grated
1-2 tablespoons Demerara sugar

1 Heat the oven to 110C/225F/Gas ¼.
2 Bring a large saucepan of salted water to the boil, add the cabbage, bring back to the boil, then blanch for 2 minutes. Drain well.
3 Melt the margarine in the rinsed-out pan, add the onion and fry gently for 5 minutes until soft and lightly coloured. Stir in the cabbage, stock and 1 tablespoon lemon juice, then add the cloves, bay leaf and salt and pepper to taste.
4 Bring to the boil, then lower the heat slightly, cover and simmer gently for 1 hour. Add the cooked, sliced beetroot and cook for a further 10 minutes.
5 Drain the cabbage mixture, reserving the stock. Discard the cloves and bay leaf. Put the vegetables into a serving dish and gently mix in the butter. Taste and adjust seasoning, cover and keep hot in the oven.
6 Pour about 150 ml/¼ pint of the reserved stock into the rinsed-out pan, then add the grated apple and the remaining lemon juice. Cover and cook over moderate heat for about 10 minutes until the apple is tender, then stir in the brown sugar and salt and pepper to taste.
7 Pour the sauce over the cabbage mixture and stir in gently until thoroughly combined. Serve at once (see Serving ideas).

Cook's Notes

TIME
25 minutes preparation and about 1¼ hours cooking time.

PREPARATION
A food processor with a shredding disc makes short work of preparing the cabbage, but if slicing by hand, wear rubber gloves because the cabbage will temporarily stain the skin red.

SERVING IDEAS
Try topping the tossed dish with soured cream or yoghurt. The hot cabbage is especially good with hot main vegetable dishes, such as pies or flans. Serve also with baked potatoes. For an unusual garnish, try adding a few fried chestnuts.

● 105 calories/450 kj per portion

Hot orange beetroot

SERVES 4

500 g/1 lb uncooked beetroot,
 washed (see Buying guide and
 Watchpoint)
salt
4 cloves
1 onion, quartered
300 ml/½ pint milk
2 bay leaves
6 peppercorns
1 blade mace
1 large orange
25 g/1 oz butter
25 g/1 oz plain flour
¼ teaspoon ground cinnamon
freshly ground black pepper

1 Bring a large pan of salted water to the boil. Lower the beetroot into the pan and simmer for about 1½-2 hours until tender (see Cook's tips).

2 Meanwhile, stick a clove in each onion quarter, then put in a saucepan with the milk, bay leaves, peppercorns and mace. Remove the rind of the orange with a potato peeler. Strip the pith away and add half the peel to the milk. Bring slowly to the boil, then remove from the heat and leave, covered, for 30 minutes for the flavours to infuse.

3 Using a sharp knife, cut the rest of the orange peel into thin matchstick strips. Put in a small saucepan and cover with cold water. Bring to the boil, drain and return to the pan with fresh cold water (see Cook's tips). Bring to the boil again and simmer for 15 minutes, until the strips are tender. Drain and reserve.

4 Squeeze the juice from the peeled orange and reserve. Strain the milk.

5 Just before the beetroot are cooked, make the sauce: melt the butter in a pan, sprinkle in the flour and stir over low heat for 1-2 minutes until straw-coloured. Remove from the heat and gradually stir in the strained milk, together with the reserved orange juice, cinnamon and salt and pepper to taste. Return to the heat and simmer, stirring until thick and smooth.

6 Drain the beetroot, cut away the top and bottom, and peel off the skin. Cut into thick slices and put in a warmed serving dish.

7 Reheat the sauce, if necessary, and pour over the beetroot. Sprinkle with the reserved orange strips and serve at once.

PETER MYERS

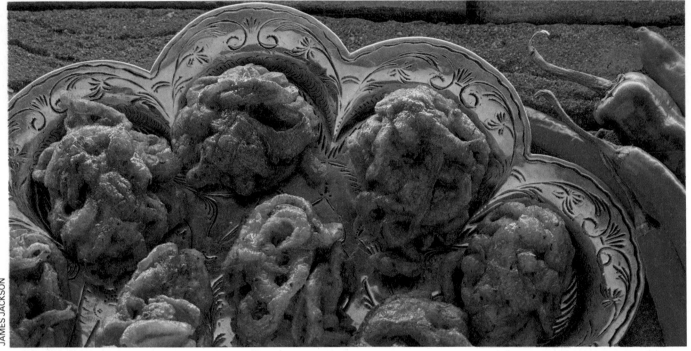

JAMES JACKSON

Indian onion fritters

SERVES 4
3 large onions, total weight about
    500 g/1 lb, thinly sliced
50 g/2 oz plain flour
¼ teaspoon dried mint
½ teaspoon dried basil
¼ teaspoon ground coriander
1 tablespoon ground turmeric
1 teaspoon garam masala
¼ teaspoon mild chilli powder
½ teaspoon salt
1 egg, beaten
2-3 tablespoons water
vegetable oil, for frying

1 Heat 3 tablespoons oil in a large
frying-pan, add the onions and cook
over the lowest possible heat,
stirring occasionally, until soft and
light golden in colour (see Cook's
tips). Remove from the heat and set
aside to cool slightly.
2 Meanwhile, sift the flour into a
large bowl, then stir in the herbs,
spices and salt until evenly mixed.
Make a well in the centre, pour the

beaten egg into the well and, using a
wire whisk, gradually draw the
flour into the egg. Gradually whisk
in water to make a thick batter.
3 Add the onions to the batter and
stir until thoroughly coated.
4 Pour a layer of oil into a large,
clean frying-pan to a depth of about
2 cm/¾ inch and heat to 180C/350F
or until a stale bread cube browns in
60 seconds.
5 Meanwhile, scoop up 1 tablespoon of the onion mixture and
place on a large flat plate. Shape
with the spoon into a round about
8 cm/3¼ inches in diameter and
about 1 cm/½ inch thick. Make 3
more rounds in this way and reserve
the rest of the mixture.
6 Carefully lift the rounds from the
plate with a fish slice and gently
slide into the hot oil with the aid of a
knife (see Cook's tips). Cook for 3-4
minutes, turning once until well
browned on both sides. Remove the
pan from the heat and lift out the
fritters with a slotted spoon, drain
on absorbent paper and keep hot.
7 Make remaining mixture into 4
more rounds, bring the oil back to
180C/350F and cook as before. Serve
at once.

ROGER PHILLIPS

Amber onions

SERVES 4
500 g/1 lb button onions, peeled
   (see Buying guide)
salt
25 g/1 oz butter
1 tablespoon clear honey
4 tablespoons tomato juice
1 teaspoon sweet paprika
freshly ground black
   pepper
margarine, for greasing

1 Heat the oven to 170C/325F/Gas 3
and grease a shallow ovenproof dish
with margarine.
2 Bring a pan of salted water to the
boil and cook the whole onions for
10-15 minutes or until just tender.

Drain well and transfer to the
prepared dish.
3 Melt the butter in a small pan,
then stir in the honey, tomato juice
and paprika. Season with salt and
pepper to taste and pour over the
cooked onions.

4 Cover with a lid or foil and bake in
the oven for 45 minutes, basting
several times with the sauce.
Uncover and bake for a further 45
minutes.
5 Remove from the oven and serve
at once, straight from the dish.

Cook's Notes

 TIME
About 20 minutes pre-
paration, including
boiling the onions, then 1½
hours cooking.

 ECONOMY
Save fuel by making full
use of the oven: cook
the onions at the same time as a
casserole and a baked custard or
other pudding needing a low
temperature.

 BUYING GUIDE
Save time and tears by
using frozen button
onions instead of raw onions.

 SERVING IDEAS
These onions combine
well with nut rissoles or
stuffed marrow – accompany
them with potatoes and peas or
beans to add colour contrast.

●90 calories/375 kj per portion

257

DON LAST

Button onions with sultanas

SERVES 4

500 g/1 lb button onions (see Buying guide and Preparation)
50 ml/2 fl oz olive oil
75 g/3 oz sultanas
300 ml/½ pint vegetable stock
50 ml/2 fl oz wine vinegar
1 clove garlic, crushed
1 tablespoon tomato purée
bouquet garni
salt and freshly ground black pepper
freshly chopped parsley, to garnish

1 Place the onions in a large pan with the oil, sultanas, stock, vinegar, garlic, tomato purée and bouquet garni. Season to taste with salt and pepper.
2 Bring the contents of the pan to the boil, then lower the heat, cover and simmer for 40-50 minutes until the onions are tender when pierced with a sharp knife.
3 Remove the bouquet garni and transfer to a serving dish. Serve hot or cold sprinkled with parsley.

Cook's Notes

 TIME
20 minutes preparation, and about 40-50 minutes cooking time.

 PREPARATION
Peeling small onions can be tedious. To make the task easier, plunge them first into boiling water, then immediately into cold water. The skins will then slide off quite easily.

 BUYING GUIDE
It is best to buy the tiny button onions, but you can use larger ones.

 SERVING IDEAS
These tiny onions are equally good hot or cold. Serve them with a rice salad, baked jacket potatoes or French bread.

● 215 calories/900 kj per portion

Onions in creamy sauce

SERVES 4-6
500 g/1 lb small pickling onions
   (see Buying guide)
40 g/1½ oz butter
25 g/1 oz plain flour
300 ml/½ pint vegetable stock
150 ml/¼ pint milk
1 tablespoon chopped fresh sage
2 tablespoons single cream
1 tablespoon chopped fresh parsley
salt and freshly ground black pepper

1 Peel the onions, trimming off the root ends (see Cook's tip).
2 Melt the butter in a large heavy-based saucepan and fry the onions over moderate heat for 4-5 minutes until lightly browned. Shake the pan constantly during this time to ensure even browning.
3 Reduce the heat and sprinkle in flour. Cook gently for 1-2 minutes, stirring all the time, then gradually stir in the stock and milk. Bring to the boil, stirring until the sauce thickens. Stir in the sage, and add salt and pepper to taste.
4 Reduce the heat until the sauce is just simmering, cover the pan and simmer for about 15 minutes until the onions are tender. Shake the pan and stir occasionally to prevent the sauce from sticking to the pan.
5 Stir in the cream and parsley, then taste and adjust the seasoning, if necessary. Heat through without boiling, then turn into a warmed serving dish and serve at once.

PETER MYERS

Two-in-one potato nests

SERVES 4
750 g/1½ lb potatoes
salt
1 large egg yolk
40 g/1½ oz butter
3 tablespoons single cream
3 tablespoons milk
freshly ground black pepper
1 small egg, beaten, to glaze
225 g/8 oz frozen mixed vegetables
    (including red pepper and
    sweetcorn)
margarine, for greasing

1 Bring a pan of salted water to the boil and cook the potatoes for about 20 minutes until tender. Drain.

2 Heat the oven to 200C/400F/Gas 6 and grease 2 baking sheets.

3 Using a wooden spoon, press the hot potatoes through a wire sieve (see Cook's tip), then beat in the egg yolk together with 25 g/1 oz butter, the cream and milk. Season to taste with salt and pepper.

4 Put the potato mixture into a piping bag fitted with a large star nozzle. Pipe 8 potato nests on to the baking sheets, spacing them well apart (see Preparation). Brush carefully but generously with the beaten egg and bake in the oven for about 25 minutes until browned.

5 Meanwhile, cook the frozen vegetables according to packet instructions. Drain, add the remaining butter and toss well to combine. Spoon the vegetables into the potato nests.

6 With a fish slice, transfer the potato nests to a warmed serving platter and serve at once.

Cook's Notes

TIME
About 40 minutes preparation and 25 minutes baking plus 5 minutes to fill.

SERVING IDEAS
These nests look most attractive when served with a vegetable pie. The combination of two vegetables in one means that at the most you will only want one more vegetable accompaniment.

COOK'S TIP
A quick way of puréeing potato is to work it through a gadget called a potato ricer. This consists of a perforated cup with a plunger.

PREPARATION
To pipe the potato nests:

Pipe a spiral base about 7.5 cm/3 inches in diameter, then pipe twice round on top to make sides, finishing with a rosette shape on one side.

●325 calories/1375 kj per portion

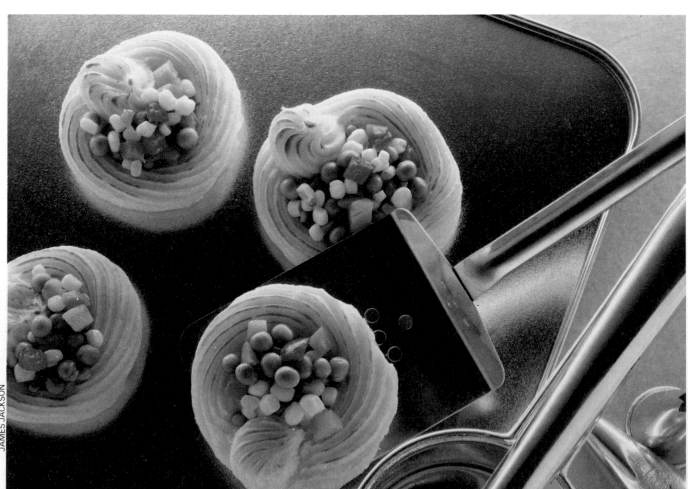

JAMES JACKSON

Chicory in cheesy sauce

SERVES 4
4 heads chicory (see Buying guide)
salt
1 teaspoon lemon juice

SAUCE
25 g/1 oz margarine or butter
25 g/1 oz plain flour
425 ml/¾ pint milk
6-8 spring onions, very finely sliced
75 g/3 oz full-fat soft cheese
¼ teaspoon made mild mustard
1½ teaspoons lemon juice
freshly ground black pepper
snipped chives, to garnish

1 Rinse the chicory under cold running water, then pat dry with absorbent paper. Using a small sharp knife, trim off any brown edges and cut a thin slice from base of each head. Cut into the chicory from the base end to a depth of about 5 cm/2 inches and twist the knife to remove the hard core.
2 Bring a pan of salted water to the boil, add the chicory with the lemon juice and bring back to the boil (see Cook's tip). Lower the heat, cover and simmer for about 20 minutes until the centre of the chicory is just tender when pierced with a fine skewer or a pointed knife.
3 Meanwhile make the sauce: melt the margarine in a saucepan, sprinkle in the flour and stir over low heat for 1-2 minutes until straw-coloured. Remove from the heat and gradually stir in the milk. Return to the heat and simmer, stirring often, until the sauce is thick and smooth.
4 Add the spring onions to the sauce and continue to cook, stirring for 3 minutes. Remove from heat and beat in the cheese, mustard and lemon juice. Season with salt and pepper to taste.
5 Drain the cooked chicory and pat dry with absorbent paper, then gently stir into the sauce. Heat through gently without boiling, then transfer to a warmed serving dish. Sprinkle the chicory with chives and serve at once.

PAUL WEBSTER

SALADS

Gone are the days when a 'salad' meant a summer dish of green, leafy vegetables, with perhaps a quartered tomato thrown in. In recent years, salads have become more and more imaginative, using a wide range of ingredients and tossed in exciting dressings. Salads may now be made of crisply cooked vegetables, pasta, rice, grains or pulses, and may include fruit, nuts, seeds and herbs of all sorts.

At one time, salads were served only as a side dish accompanying a cold main dish, such as sliced meats or quiche. With the addition of cheese, eggs or pasta, a salad quickly becomes a main dish in its own right, to be served with other side dishes or simply with bread and butter. Amongst the following recipes are several main-dish salads, such as Bean and Avocado Salad and Radish and Pasta Salad. There are others, such as Orange and Cucumber Cocktails, which would make excellent starters, particularly good served before a substantial main course.

As side dishes, salads are ideal. A simple green salad of crisp lettuce leaves, cucumber, green pepper and cress, dressed with a French dressing, will go well with a multitude of main dishes. Its fresh crunchy texture is the perfect foil to hot, spicy foods or pasta. To ring the changes, however, choose from the many side salads in this chapter. Try Alfalfa and Chicory Salad as an unusual alternative to a green salad. Side salads should be served on individual plates or in small bowls. It is best to add a dressing to a salad in a larger bowl and then transfer it to individual bowls after tossing well.

However you serve it, a good salad should be fresh, colourful and nutritious. It should combine different tastes and textures and be tossed in a carefully chosen dressing that does not overwhelm the flavours of the salad ingredients. Choose the freshest vegetables in peak condition, especially if they are to be used raw (most nutritious). Use fresh herbs rather than dried whenever possible and make use of the variety of colours available when considering a garnish.

A good salad needs a good dressing – all the salads in this chapter follow this principle. Experiment with alternative dressings, combining less familiar oils, such as walnut, sunflower and sesame, with lemon juice or wine, cider or herb vinegars. It is important not to use too much – there should be no surplus dressing lying in the bottom of the bowl! While a few salad ingredients, such as hot cooked dried beans, benefit from marinating in a dressing, in general it is better to dress a salad immediately before serving. Finally, add a decorative and colourful garnish.

Raw fruit and vegetables are an important part of a healthy diet and a salad should, ideally, be served at least once a day, either as a side dish or as the basis of a meal. They are always easy and quick to prepare, so make the most of the selection here to provide deliciously healthy salads for everyone.

Tomato and artichoke salad

SERVES 4
400 g/14 oz can artichoke hearts, drained
4 tomatoes, quartered
3 hard-boiled eggs, quartered
100 g/4 oz frozen green beans
salt
lettuce leaves, to serve
freshly ground black pepper

DRESSING
3 tablespoons olive oil
1 tablespoon white wine vinegar
2 teaspoons lemon juice
1 teaspoon caster sugar

1 Rinse the artichoke hearts under cold running water to remove any salty taste left over from the can liquid. Drain and pat dry on absorbent paper, then cut into bite-sized pieces and place in a bowl.

2 Using a metal spoon, very carefully fold in the tomatoes and eggs. Cover with cling film and refrigerate.

3 Cook the beans according to packet directions in boiling salted water until they are tender but still crisp to the bite. Drain thoroughly and refresh under cold running water. Drain the beans again and leave to cool.

4 Meanwhile, make the dressing: place all the dressing ingredients in a screw-top jar with salt and pepper to taste and shake well to mix.

5 Halve the cooled beans if they are very large, then mix them into the salad with the dressing. Turn the ingredients over gently to coat thoroughly, cover again with cling film and return to the refrigerator for a further 2 hours.

6 Line a serving dish with lettuce leaves and arrange the salad in the middle. Sprinkle a little pepper over the top and serve at once.

Cook's Notes

TIME
The salad will take about 30 minutes to prepare altogether. Allow at least 2 hours chilling before serving.

SERVING IDEAS
This tasty salad is quite filling: serve it as a fresh starter or with bread and butter as a snack or lunch dish.

● 175 calories/750 kj per portion

264

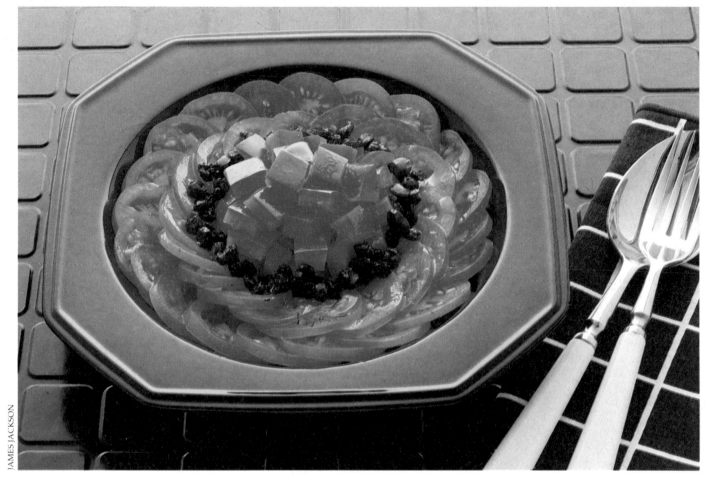

JAMES JACKSON

Tomato and red pepper salad

SERVES 4
500 g/1 lb tomatoes (see Buying guide)
1 large red pepper
50 g/2 oz currants

DRESSING
4 tablespoons olive oil (see Economy)
2 tablespoons white wine vinegar
¼ teaspoon Tabasco sauce
1 clove garlic, crushed with a pinch of salt (optional)

1 Slice the tomatoes thinly (see Preparation) and arrange them on a serving plate in overlapping circles.
2 Core, deseed and dice the pepper and pile it on top of the tomatoes, in the centre.
3 Scatter the currants in a ring round the diced peppers.
4 Beat the ingredients for the dressing together until well blended and spoon evenly over the salad. ⚠ Serve at once.

Cook's Notes

 TIME
The salad takes 20 minutes to prepare.

 WATCHPOINT
Do not dress the salad until just before serving, or the tomatoes may become soggy.

 ECONOMY
Although the flavour of olive oil is perfect for tomatoes, sunflower oil makes an acceptable substitute, and is considerably cheaper.

 SERVING IDEAS
This sweet colourful salad goes well with cheese and egg dishes.

 PREPARATION
Use a knife with a serrated edge to cut the tomatoes into thin, even slices.

 BUYING GUIDE
Choose firm, sweet, even-sized tomatoes for best results.

●70 calories/275 kj per portion

265

Egg and lettuce salad

SERVES 6

1 crisp lettuce, shredded (see Buying guide)
1 bunch spring onions, chopped
4 hard-boiled egg whites, finely chopped, to garnish

DRESSING

4 warm hard-boiled egg yolks (see Cook's tip)
150 ml/¼ pint soured cream
1 teaspoon sugar
juice of 2 lemons
salt and freshly ground black pepper

1 Make the dressing: put the warm egg yolks in a bowl with a little of the soured cream and mix to a paste with a fork. Add the sugar, lemon juice and the remaining soured cream. Whisk with the fork until the dressing is smooth and the ingredients are thoroughly combined. Season to taste with salt and pepper.

2 Place the shredded lettuce in a large salad bowl. Sprinkle the spring onions over the lettuce, then pour the dressing over the top of the salad.

3 Toss well to coat the lettuce thoroughly with the dressing, then garnish the salad with the finely chopped egg whites. Serve at once while lettuce is crisp.

MARTIN BRIGDALE

Mixed salad with hot dressing

SERVES 4-6
1 crisp lettuce (see Buying guide)
250 g/9 oz radishes
250 g/9 oz peas, unshelled weight
  (see Buying guide)

DRESSING
100 g/4 oz butter
1 tablespoon lemon juice
salt and freshly ground black pepper

1 Roughly tear up the lettuce and put into a salad bowl.
2 Slice the radishes and add them to the lettuce together with the shelled peas.
3 Make the dressing: melt butter in a small saucepan over very low heat. Stir in the lemon juice and season to taste.
4 Pour the dressing on to the salad while it is still warm. Toss the salad with dressing and serve at once. [!]

FRED MANCINI

Cook's Notes

 TIME
This summery salad only takes about 10 minutes to make.

 SERVING IDEAS
An unusual combination of a hot dressing with cold vegetables, this makes an excellent side salad. It is especially good with lentil or nut roasts.
If liked, garnish with sprinkling of bread croûtons fried in butter, oil and garlic, or with roughly chopped walnuts.

 VARIATION
Try adding 100 g/4 oz thinly sliced button mushrooms and a few sliced spring onions with the radishes and peas and serve as a salad snack, with wholemeal rolls.

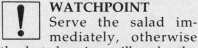 **BUYING GUIDE**
Use a crisp lettuce such as a cos, iceberg or Webb's Wonder.
This quantity of unshelled peas will produce about 100 g/4 oz peas after shelling. If fresh peas are unavailable, use 100 g/4 oz defrosted frozen peas.

[!] **WATCHPOINT**
Serve the salad immediately, otherwise the hot dressing will make the lettuce go limp very quickly.

●220 calories/925 kj per portion

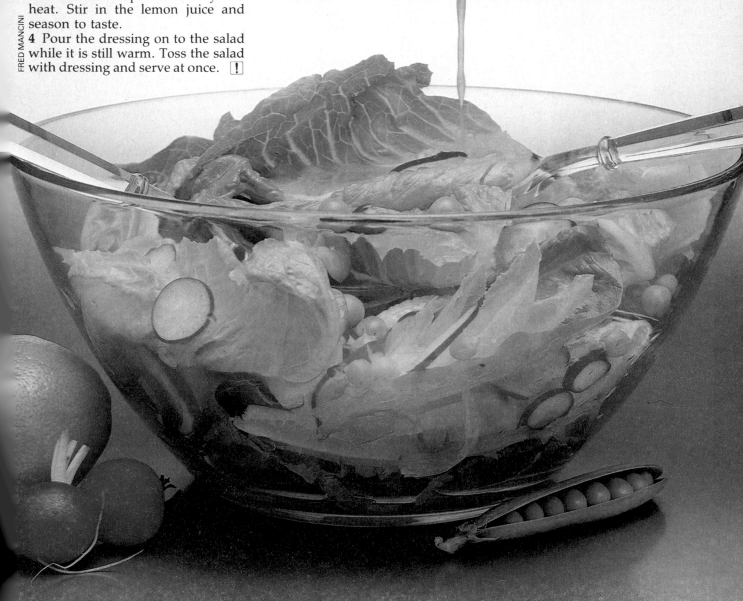

CHRIS KNAGGS

Green salad with peanut dressing

SERVES 4
1 small cos lettuce, cut crossways
   into 8 slices (see Cook's tips)
1 bunch watercress, separated
1 small cucumber, finely diced (see
   (Cook's tips)
50 g/2 oz seedless raisins
25 g/1 oz unsalted peanuts

DRESSING
1 tablespoon peanut butter
6 tablespoons vegetable oil
2 tablespoons cider or wine vinegar
pinch of caster sugar
salt and freshly ground black pepper

1 Put the sliced cos lettuce, watercress sprigs together with the finely diced cucumber in a large salad bowl.

2 To make the dressing: put the peanut butter in a bowl and then gradually beat in the oil a little at a time until the mixture is smooth and glossy. Beat in the vinegar and sugar until well blended and season to taste with salt and pepper (see Cook's tips).

3 Just before serving, add the raisins and peanuts to the salad ingredients in the bowl. Pour the dressing over the salad and, using 2 large forks or salad servers, toss until all the ingredients are well coated with dressing and glistening. Serve the salad at once, while the ingredients are still crisp.

Caesar salad

SERVES 4
1 large crisp lettuce, torn into pieces
6 tablespoons olive or sunflower oil
2 cloves garlic, crushed
6 × 1 cm/½ inch thick slices stale
   white bread, crusts removed,
   cut into squares
40 g/1½ oz grated Parmesan cheese
1 egg (see Preparation)

DRESSING
3 tablespoons olive or
   sunflower oil
1 tablespoon white wine vinegar
1 tablespoon lemon juice
pinch of mustard powder
salt and freshly ground black
   pepper

1 Put the lettuce pieces into a large wooden salad bowl and set aside.
2 Heat the oil in a heavy-based frying-pan, add the garlic and fry gently for 1-2 minutes or until soft and lightly coloured. Using a slotted spoon, remove and discard the fried garlic.
3 Add the cubes of bread and fry for 5 minutes over moderate heat, stirring to prevent sticking, until the croûtons are crisp and golden brown. Remove with a slotted spoon and leave to drain on absorbent paper.
4 Meanwhile, make the dressing: put the ingredients in a bowl, add salt and pepper to taste and beat together with a fork.
5 To serve: pour the dressing over the lettuce and toss well. Add the croûtons and Parmesan cheese and toss again. Immediately add the egg to the salad and toss thoroughly. Serve at once.

Cook's Notes

 TIME
This salad takes 15-20 minutes to prepare.

 PREPARATION
The egg can be served either raw or coddled.
   To serve the egg raw: separate the egg (reserving white for another dish) and place the yolk, in its half eggshell, in the middle of the salad. Take the salad to the table, tip in the yolk and toss before serving.
   To coddle the egg: just before serving put it (in its shell) into a bowl or cup and cover with boiling water. Leave for 1½ minutes then remove from the water: the egg will be warmed and almost set. Crack the whole egg on to the salad.

 SERVING IDEAS
Serve as a lunch or supper dish with crusty French bread, or as an unusual first course.

DID YOU KNOW
This is an American salad named after its originator Caesar Cardini. His restaurant, just south of the American border in Mexico, gained its fame during Prohibition when Americans used to cross the border to buy drink banned in their own country. They enjoyed the food too, such as this salad, and drinks such as tequila drunk with salt and lemon.

●365 calories/1525 kj per portion

ALAN DUNS

Watercress and grapefruit salad

SERVES 4

2 bunches watercress, stalks removed (see Cook's tip)
2 pink grapefruits, divided into segments (see Buying guide and Preparation)
50 g/2 oz split almonds

DRESSING

1 teaspoon finely chopped onion
½ teaspoon sugar
juice of 1 fresh lime
2 tablespoons olive oil
salt and freshly ground black pepper

1 Heat the grill to moderate and spread the almonds in the grill pan. Toast them for 8-10 minutes, turning from time to time, until they are golden brown.

2 To make the dressing: put the onion, sugar, lime juice and olive oil in a salad bowl. Whisk with a fork until the dressing is thick and all the ingredients are thoroughly combined. Season with salt and pepper.

3 Stir the grapefruit segments and any juice in the bowl into the dressing, add the watercress leaves and toss together.

4 Sprinkle the toasted almonds over the salad and serve at once.

Cook's Notes

 TIME
This salad takes 25 minutes to make, including the time for toasting the almonds.

 BUYING GUIDE
Pink grapefruits are the sweetest type of grapefruit you can buy; if not available, use ordinary yellow grapefruit and increase the quantity of sugar to 1 teaspoon.

 COOK'S TIP
Watercress will keep well for up to 1 week in the salad drawer of the refrigerator—put the trimmed and washed watercress in a plastic bag, excluding as much air as possible.

 SERVING IDEAS
Serve as a starter with Melba toast, or as an accompaniment to a nut loaf or vegetable soufflé.

 PREPARATION
Peel the grapefruit, holding it over a bowl to catch the juice. Trim away the pith with a small, sharp knife then divide into segments. Remove the pips.

●155 calories/650 kj per portion

MARTIN BRIGDALE

270

Artichoke and watercress salad

SERVES 4

400 g/14 oz can artichoke hearts, drained
2 bunches watercress, separated into sprigs
4 large tomatoes, thinly sliced
½ cucumber, thinly sliced
sweet paprika, to garnish

BLUE CHEESE DRESSING
50 g/2 oz Danish blue cheese
150 ml/¼ pint soured cream
2 tablespoons vegetable oil
1 tablespoon lemon juice
salt and freshly ground black pepper

1 First make the dressing: mash the cheese in a small bowl with a fork, then gradually blend in 2 tablespoons of the soured cream.

Beat until smooth, then beat in the remaining cream, the oil and lemon juice. Season to taste with salt and pepper.

2 Place 1 artichoke heart in the centre of 4 individual plates. Surround with a border of watercress sprigs and decorate with slices of tomato and cucumber. Cut any re-maining artichoke hearts into small pieces and place among the water-cress sprigs.

3 Pour a generous spoonful of blue cheese dressing on the edge of each salad (see Cook's tip). Sprinkle the centre of the cheese dressing with sweet paprika, to garnish, and serve the salads at once.

Cook's Notes

TIME
20 minutes preparation time in total.

VARIATION
Use Stilton cheese instead of Danish blue in the dressing, and add 1 teaspoon dry sherry together with the other seasonings.

SERVING IDEAS
Serve as a side salad or as a dinner-party starter with bread and butter. To serve as a main-meal salad, add sliced hard-boiled eggs, coleslaw and lettuce.

COOK'S TIP
Store any remaining dressing in a screw-top jar in the refrigerator. Serve with salads or vegetable dishes or as a dressing for baked potatoes.

●210 calories/875 kj per portion

DON LAST

271

Green and gold salad

SERVES 4
1 lettuce, leaves separated
2 carrots, cut into small matchstick
  pieces
¼ cucumber, thinly sliced
2 avocados (see Cook's tip)
1 tablespoon lemon juice
300 g/11 oz can mandarin orange
  segments

DRESSING
6 tablespoons thick bottled
  mayonnaise
1 teaspoon ground turmeric
2 teaspoons sweet chutney, finely
  chopped

1 Line 4 individual plates with the lettuce leaves.
2 Garnish each plate with a border of carrots and cucumber.
3 Halve, stone and peel avocados, then slice them both lengthways (see Preparation). Immediately sprinkle them with lemon juice to prevent discoloration, then arrange on the plates, on top of the cucumber slices.
4 Drain the mandarins, reserving 1 tablespoon of syrup for the dressing (see Economy). Pile a spoonful of mandarin oranges in the centre of each plate, reserving 4 segments for garnish.
5 Make the dressing: put the mayonnaise in a bowl and stir in the reserved mandarin syrup, the turmeric and chutney. Mix well.
6 Spoon a little dressing over each portion of mandarins, then garnish with a mandarin segment. Serve the green and gold salad at once, with any remaining dressing handed separately.

Cook's Notes

TIME
This attractive salad takes about 30 minutes to make, including the preparation of the vegetables.

PREPARATION
Peel the avocados as thinly as possible to keep the attractive dark green colour on the outside.

COOK'S TIP
Although the avocados are sprinkled with lemon juice, it is best to prepare them as near to serving time as possible to ensure that they do not become discoloured.

VARIATIONS
If preferred, replace the mandarins with 3 oranges, cut into segments. When peeling the oranges, catch 1 tablespoon of the juice for use in the dressing.

ECONOMY
Use remaining syrup in a fruit salad or jelly.

SERVING IDEAS
Serve as a refreshing starter, or as a colourful side salad with a pasta dish or pizza.

● 385 calories/1600 kj per portion

MARTIN BRIGDALE

Greek salads

SERVES 4
4 salad tomatoes
½ cucumber
1 small green pepper, deseeded
1 small onion
100 g/4 oz black olives, stoned
100 g/4 oz Feta cheese, cut into
  cubes (see Buying guide)

DRESSING
4 tablespoons olive oil
juice of 1 lemon
½ teaspoon dried oregano
salt and freshly ground black pepper

1 Make the dressing: put the oil in a small bowl with the lemon juice, oregano and salt and pepper to taste. Mix well with a fork.
2 Cut each tomato into 8 wedges, and cut the cucumber into thin slices. Cut the pepper and onion into thin rings.
3 Divide the tomato, cucumber, pepper and onion between 4 small salad bowls. Place a few olives and cubes of cheese on top.
4 Pour the dressing over the salads and serve at once.

CHRIS KNAGGS

Cook's Notes

TIME
These salads only take 10 minutes to prepare.

BUYING GUIDE
Feta cheese is a crumbly and very salty Greek cheese available from delicatessens or large supermarkets.

? **DID YOU KNOW**
This salad is based on the Greek salad called *horiatiki salata*, which is really an assortment of tit-bits. In Greece it is served with most meals.

●210 calories/875 kj per portion

Orange and cucumber cocktail

SERVES 4
4 large oranges
½ small cucumber
salt
a few lettuce leaves, shredded
4 orange twists and 4 cucumber twists, to garnish

DRESSING
2 tablespoons olive oil
1 tablespoon red wine vinegar
½ teaspoon Dijon mustard
2 teaspoons freshly chopped mint
freshly ground black pepper

1 Cut cucumber into small dice. Put cucumber in a large bowl and sprinkle lightly with salt (see Cook's tip). Cover the cucumber and refrigerate for about 1 hour.
2 Using a small serrated knife, peel the oranges, removing every scrap of pith. Cut the 4 oranges into segments, discarding membranes, then cut the segments into small pieces, about the same size as the cucumber dice. Put the orange pieces into a bowl, cover and refrigerate for 1 hour.
3 Make the dressing: put the oil in a screw-top jar with the vinegar, mustard, mint and salt and pepper to taste. Replace the lid firmly and shake to mix well.
4 Just before serving, thoroughly drain the cucumber and oranges, then combine in 1 bowl. Add the dressing and mix lightly together.
5 Arrange shredded lettuce in the bottom of 4 individual glasses, then divide the orange and cucumber mixture between them. Garnish each glass with twists of orange and cucumber. Serve at once, chilled.

MARTIN BRIGDALE

Cucumber and strawberry salad

SERVES 4

½ cucumber, peeled and thinly sliced

100 g/4 oz strawberries, thinly sliced lengthways (see Buying guide and Cook's tips)

sprigs of fennel leaves, to garnish

DRESSING

1 tablespoon olive oil

1 tablespoon white wine vinegar

1 teaspoon caster sugar

salt and freshly ground black pepper

1 Spread the cucumber out on a plate, sprinkle with salt and leave to stand for 30 minutes (see Cook's tips). Drain and pat dry.

2 Arrange alternate circles of cucumber and strawberries on a flat, round serving plate.

3 Make the dressing: put all the dressing ingredients in a screw-top jar with a generous seasoning of salt and pepper. Shake to mix well.

4 Spoon the dressing over the salad, garnish with fennel leaves and serve at once.

Cook's Notes

 TIME
15 minutes to prepare but allow 30 minutes for salting the cucumber.

 BUYING GUIDE
Choose medium-sized strawberries which are ripe but still firm.

! **WATCHPOINT**
This salad cannot be made in advance as the strawberries will discolour the cucumber badly.

 COOK'S TIPS
If you prefer a more decorative effect, do not hull the strawberries before you slice them.

The salt draws out excess moisture from the cucumber so finished dish is not too watery.

SERVING IDEAS
Serve this impressive and refreshing summer salad as part of a cold buffet.

● 45 calories/200 kj per portion

ALAN DUNS

Radish and pasta salad

SERVES 4-6
250 g/9 oz radishes
100 g/4 oz pasta spirals or pasta shells
salt
1 teaspoon vegetable oil
2 tablespoons snipped chives
150 ml/¼ pint soured cream
freshly ground black pepper

JAMES JACKSON

1 Bring a large pan of salted water to the boil, swirl in the oil, then add the pasta. Bring back to the boil and cook, uncovered, for 10-15 minutes until tender but firm to the bite. Drain the pasta thoroughly in a colander, then rinse well under cold running water, to remove any excess starch and to cool down the pasta. Drain again thoroughly.
2 Cut each radish into 3-4 slices.
3 Transfer the pasta to a serving dish and add the radishes, chives, soured cream and salt and pepper to taste. Toss the salad well and serve at once, while still fresh.

Sweetcorn, radish and apple salad

SERVES 4

500 g/1 lb frozen sweetcorn kernels
1 bunch radishes, thinly sliced (see Buying guide)
2 crisp green dessert apples (see Buying guide)
1 tablespoon lemon juice

DRESSING

3 tablespoons vegetable oil
1 tablespoon wine vinegar
1 teaspoon sugar
1 teaspoon mustard powder
salt and freshly ground black pepper

DON LAST

1 Cook the sweetcorn according to packet instructions. Drain and cool.
2 Core and dice the apples, then put in a bowl and sprinkle with the lemon juice. Toss to coat well.
3 Make the dressing: put the dressing ingredients into a salad bowl with salt and pepper to taste and mix together with a fork.
4 Add the sweetcorn, apples and radishes to the dressing and stir gently until mixed. Serve at once.

BRYCE ATTWELL

Beetroot and parsnip salad

SERVES 4
500 g/1 lb small whole raw beetroot, unpeeled
250 g/9 oz parsnips, cores removed, and cut into 4 cm/1½ inch chunks
6 tablespoons natural yoghurt
1 teaspoon French mustard
1 teaspoon capers, chopped
2 tablespoons chopped parsley (optional)
4 spring onions, finely chopped

1 In separate saucepans, boil the beetroot and parsnips until tender. ⚠ Whole beetroot will take 45-60 minutes to cook, depending on the size, and the parsnips 15-20 minutes. Drain thoroughly, then peel the beetroot. Cut both beetroot and parsnips into 1 cm/½ inch dice while still warm, but keep separate.
2 Mix together the yoghurt and mustard. In separate bowls, fold one-third into the parsnips and the rest into beetroot. Leave until cool.
3 Pile the dressed parsnips in the centre of a serving plate. Arrange the dressed beetroot round the edge of the plate, in a ring.
4 Scatter capers and parsley if using, over parsnips and chopped spring onions over the beetroot. Serve at room temperature as soon as possible.

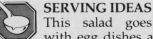
278

Beetroot and celery salad

SERVES 4

500 g/1 lb cooked beetroot (see Buying guide)
4 celery stalks
1 hard-boiled egg, quartered

DRESSING
6 tablespoons olive oil
2 tablespoons wine vinegar
½ teaspoon caster sugar
3 tablespoons French mustard
1 tablespoon chopped fresh parsley
salt and freshly ground black pepper
1 tablespoon single cream

TIME
This salad only takes 20 minutes preparation.

VARIATION
The parsley can be replaced by another herb—try tarragon or dill.

COOK'S TIP
The ingredients for this salad may be prepared in advance, but should not be combined until just before serving, otherwise the beetroot will run excessively and spoil the overall effect.

BUYING GUIDE
Ready-cooked beetroot is available from most greengrocers and supermarkets.
Alternatively, buy raw beetroot and cook it yourself: cut off the leaves 1 cm/½ inch from their base and do not trim or cut into the root. Rinse and cook in lightly salted boiling water for 1-2 hours, depending on size, or wrap in foil and bake in a 170C/325F/Gas 3 oven for 1-2 hours. Rub off skins while still warm.

● 285 calories/1200 kj per portion

1 Peel the beetroot and cut into sticks, about 4 cm/1½ inches long and 5 mm/¼ inch wide. Place in a salad bowl or on a serving plate.
2 Cut the celery stalks diagonally into 5 mm/¼ inch thick slices and reserve them separately.
3 Make the dressing: put the oil, vinegar, sugar, mustard and parsley in a screw-top jar, add salt and pepper to taste and shake well to mix. Add the single cream to the jar and stir the dressing thoroughly.
4 Add the celery to the beetroot and fold in gently. Pour over the dressing (see Cook's tip).
5 Arrange the egg in the centre of the salad and serve at once.

PAUL WEBSTER

James Jackson

Beetroot and orange salad

SERVES 4

4 cooked beetroot, skinned and
　sliced
2 oranges, peeled (see Buying guide
　and Preparation)
1 lettuce, leaves separated
2 large tomatoes, sliced
3-4 teaspoons finely chopped
　walnuts

DRESSING

1 teaspoon finely chopped onion
1 teaspoon snipped chives
good pinch of salt
½ teaspoon made English mustard
good pinch of caster sugar
freshly ground black pepper
3 tablespoons olive or
　vegetable oil
1 tablespoon wine vinegar

1 Cut the orange horizontally into
thin rings and set aside.
2 Arrange the lettuce leaves on a
salad platter.
3 Arrange the orange and beetroot
slices alternately in a ring on top of
the lettuce. Arrange overlapping
slices of tomato in the centre of the
dish and sprinkle with walnuts.
4 Make the dressing: put the
reserved orange juice from the
peeled oranges in a bowl. Add the
onion and chives to the bowl,

Cook's Notes

TIME
This unusual salad takes 20 minutes preparation.

BUYING GUIDE
Choose thin-skinned seedless oranges as these will look more attractive in the finished salad, and are much easier to cut into even slices.

PREPARATION
Peel the oranges over a bowl to catch the juices: reserve the juice. When peeling, use a fine serrated knife and a sawing action so that the rind is removed together with the pith and white membrane in a single clean cut.

COOK'S TIP
Do not prepare too soon in advance or the beetroot may discolour the oranges and spoil the overall effect.

SERVING IDEAS
Serve this colourful dish as a side salad with a cold vegetable pie, or as part of a salad buffet.

VARIATIONS
Use a herb-flavoured vinegar, such as tarragon or mint vinegar for the dressing. Use chopped hazelnuts or salted peanuts instead of the walnuts.

● 150 calories/630 kj per portion

together with the salt, mustard,
sugar and pepper to taste. Mix well
together with a fork. Add the olive
or vegetable oil and wine vinegar
and beat together until the dressing
is well blended.
5 Spoon the prepared dressing over
the salad and serve at once.

280

Chicory and orange salad

SERVES 4

3 large heads chicory (see Buying guide)
2 oranges
1 bunch watercress

DRESSING
finely grated zest of 1 orange and 2 tablespoons orange juice
6 tablespoons olive oil
½ teaspoon caster sugar
salt and freshly ground black pepper

1 Slice the chicory thinly (see Preparation) and cut into rings.
3 Peel the oranges, taking care to remove all the white pith, then slice thinly, discarding the pips. Arrange the slices in a ring around a serving plate overlapping them slightly.
3 Separate the watercress into sprigs, wash thoroughly and pat dry with absorbent paper.
4 Make the dressing: pour the orange juice into a large bowl. Add the grated zest, the oil and sugar and season with salt and pepper to taste. Beat with a fork until the dressing is well blended.
5 Toss the chicory in the dressing, then pile the salad in the centre of the oranges.
6 Arrange watercress sprigs between the oranges and the chicory and serve at once.

Cook's Notes

TIME
This salad only takes 20 minutes to prepare.

BUYING GUIDE
Choose tightly-packed heads of chicory which are milky-white and as far as possible, unblemished.

PREPARATION
To prepare and slice the chicory:

Trim off any brown edges and cut a thin slice from the base of each head. Cut into the chicory from the base end to a depth of about 5 cm/ 2 inches and twist the knife to remove the hard core, which is sometimes bitter. Slice across each head of chicory.

SERVING IDEAS
This refreshing salad makes a perfect first course served with hot crusty rolls or French bread. It is also a good accompaniment to hot or cold savoury dishes.

●230 calories/975 kj per portion

Stuffed chicory spears

SERVES 4
2 large heads chicory
8 small gherkins
250 g/9 oz carrots, grated
1 tablespoon vegetable oil
1 teaspoon wine vinegar
freshly ground black pepper

1 Cut 4 of the gherkins into fans (see Preparation) and set aside.

2 Remove 6 outer leaves from each of the heads of chicory and arrange, curved side down, in an attractive pattern on a serving plate (see Economy).

3 Chop the remaining gherkins finely and put in a bowl. Add the grated carrots, oil and vinegar and mix well. Season to taste with black pepper.

4 Spoon a little of the mixture along the length of each chicory spear, taking care not to drop any of the mixture on to the serving plate. Garnish with the gherkin fans. Serve at once.

Cook's Notes

TIME
Quick to make, this salad only takes 15 minutes to prepare (including grating the carrots).

ECONOMY
Reserve the chicory hearts for another salad, or braise them in vegetable stock together with chopped celery to make a quick and tasty supper dish.

PREPARATION
To make the gherkins into fans:

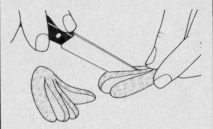

Make cuts lengthways almost to the end of each gherkin, then spread the slices open to form an attractive fan shape.

VARIATIONS
Mix about 1 tablespoon seedless raisins, or 25 g/1 oz chopped dates with the grated carrots in place of the small gherkins.

DID YOU KNOW
In many countries, chicory is known as endive. This often causes confusion—as endive is the British name for a curly headed vegetable which is known elsewhere as chicory!

SERVING IDEAS
Serve as a side salad with cheese and vege-table flans or pies, or as part of a buffet.
   Alternatively, serve as part of a light lunch accompanied by cheese, a selection of chutneys, French bread and butter, crisp-breads or Melba toast.

● 60 calories/250 kj per portion

Crisp'n' nutty salad

SERVES 4
1 crisp lettuce, shredded
4 heads chicory, separated into leaves (see Buying guide)
1 red pepper, deseeded and diced
1 green pepper, deseeded and diced

HAZELNUT DRESSING
2 tablespoons chopped roasted hazelnuts (see Buying guide)
2 teaspoons snipped chives
1 teaspoon salt
good pinch of white pepper
good pinch of paprika
½ teaspoon mustard powder
½ teaspoon caster sugar
2 tablespoons wine vinegar
6 tablespoons vegetable oil

1 Make the hazelnut dressing: place all the ingredients in a screw-top jar. Replace the lid firmly and shake well to mix.
2 Arrange the shredded lettuce on 4 individual plates, then arrange the chicory leaves on top, radiating out from the centre of the plate.
3 Mix together the red and green peppers and arrange in the centre of each plate of salad.
4 Give the dressing a last-minute shake, spoon over the peppers and serve at once.

Cook's Notes

 TIME
10-15 minutes preparation including making the dressing.

 SERVING IDEAS
Serve as a side salad or as a very nutritious starter with crusty bread.

 WATCHPOINT
Do not add the dressing until just before serving or the lettuce will go limp.

BUYING GUIDE
Look for crisp, white chicory heads with leaves firmly packed together.
Chopped roasted hazelnuts are available ready to use in packets. If they are difficult to find, use blanched hazelnuts and chop them coarsely, then lightly toast under the grill. Allow the hazelnuts to cool before using them.

●230 calories/975 kj per portion

PETER MYERS

Spring salad

SERVES 4
175 g/6 oz fresh broad beans
salt
225 g/8 oz frozen peas
2 avocados

DRESSING
6 tablespoons thick bottled
   mayonnaise
finely grated zest and juice of 1
   small fresh lime
1 teaspoon caster sugar
freshly ground black pepper

TO GARNISH
Chinese lettuce leaves
25 g/1 oz shelled walnuts, chopped

1 Bring a pan of salted water to the boil and cook the broad beans for 4 minutes, then add the peas, bring back to the boil and cook for a further 3-4 minutes until the vegetables are just tender. Drain, rinse under cold running water, then drain again (see Cook's tip). Spread the beans and peas out on absorbent paper to cool.

2 Make the dressing: put the mayonnaise into a large bowl together with the lime zest and juice, sugar and salt and pepper to taste. Mix together well.

3 Halve the avocados, remove the stones and peel off the skins. Cut the avocado flesh into cubes and gently mix into the dressing together with the beans and peas. Taste and adjust seasoning if necessary.

4 Arrange the lettuce leaves around a serving dish and spoon the mixed salad into the middle. Sprinkle with walnuts and serve at once. ⚠️

284

Bean and avocado salad

SERVES 4

225 g/8 oz shelled fresh or frozen
   broad beans (see Buying guide
   and Cook's tips)
salt
1 large avocado
4 tomatoes, thinly sliced

DRESSING

1 tablespoon wine vinegar
2 teaspoons water
1 teaspoon caster sugar
3 tablespoons vegetable oil
good pinch each of freshly ground
   black pepper and mustard powder
1 teaspoon very finely chopped
   onion
1 teaspoon very finely chopped
   mint or ½ teaspoon dried mint

1 Bring a pan of salted water to the
boil and cook the fresh broad beans,
if using, for 15-20 minutes, until
tender. If using frozen beans, cook
according to packet instructions.
Drain well and leave to cool completely (see Cook's tips).
2 Halve, stone and peel the
avocado. Cut the flesh into 1 cm/½
inch dice and put into a bowl with
the broad beans.
3 To make the dressing: place all the
ingredients in a screw-top jar and
shake thoroughly until well
blended. Pour over the avocado and
broad beans and toss to mix well.
4 Arrange the sliced tomatoes in a
border around a serving plate and
pile the prepared salad in the centre.
Serve at once. !

PAUL WEBSTER

Cook's Notes

TIME
Cooking the broad
beans takes 15-20 min-
utes. Allow 30 minutes for
cooling. Preparing the salad
then takes 10 minutes.

BUYING GUIDE
Yield from beans can
vary considerably but
1 kg/2 lb broad beans in the pod
should give you enough for this
particular recipe.

COOK'S TIPS
Wear rubber gloves
when shelling broad
beans or they may stain your
hands.
   When using larger, older
beans, remove their skins after
cooking and cooling, to leave a
bright green, tender bean.

SERVING IDEAS
Serve the salad on in-
dividual dishes as a
starter with brown bread and
butter, or serve as a side salad.
If liked, garnish the top of the
salad with chopped hard-boiled
egg.

! WATCHPOINT
Serve as soon as pos-
sible after preparation,
or the avocado may start to
discolour.

●285 calories/1200 kj per portion

French bean and almond salad

SERVES 4

500 g/1 lb frozen French beans
salt
4 tablespoons olive oil
75 g/3 oz blanched almond halves
   (see Buying guide)
juice of ½ lemon
1 tablespoon chopped fresh
   parsley
1 teaspoon chopped fresh thyme,
   or ½ teaspoon dried thyme
   (see Cook's tip)
freshly ground black pepper

1 Heat the oven to 130C/250F/Gas ½. Pour enough water into a large saucepan to come to a depth of 5 cm/2 inches. Add a pinch of salt and bring to the boil. Put in the beans, bring back to the boil and simmer gently for about 10 minutes until just tender. Drain the beans, put

them into an ovenproof serving dish and keep warm in the oven.

2 Heat the oil in a frying-pan, add the almond halves and fry over brisk heat, stirring them around until golden brown on all sides. Remove

the pan from the heat, add the lemon juice, herbs and salt and pepper to taste and stir well.

3 Pour the contents of the pan over the beans and fork through to coat thoroughly. Serve at once.

BOB KOMAR

286

PETER MYERS

Two-bean salad

SERVES 4
**100 g/4 oz dried red kidney beans,
  soaked overnight**
**100 g/4 oz dried haricot beans,
  soaked overnight**
1 small onion, chopped
1 bay leaf
2 large celery stalks, thinly sliced
1 green pepper, deseeded and diced

DRESSING
6 tablespoons olive oil
2 tablespoons wine vinegar
1 clove garlic, crushed (optional)
salt and freshly ground black pepper

1 Drain the kidney beans, transfer to a saucepan, cover with water and bring to the boil. Boil vigorously for 10 minutes, ⚠ then add the haricot beans, together with their soaking liquid. Add the onion and bay leaf and bring back to the boil. Reduce the heat slightly, half cover with a lid and simmer for about 1 hour until the beans are tender.

2 Meanwhile, make the dressing: put the ingredients in a screw-top jar, with salt and pepper to taste. Replace the lid firmly and shake well to mix.

3 Drain the beans and discard the cooking liquid and bay leaf. Transfer to a serving dish and pour over the dressing, while the beans are still warm (see Cook's tip). Mix well and leave to stand for at least 1 hour or overnight.

4 Add the celery and diced pepper to the beans, taste and adjust seasoning and mix well. Serve.

287

Mushroom and celery salad

1 Make the dressing: put the yoghurt in a bowl with the olive oil and lemon juice. Beat together with a fork, then stir in the tarragon and salt and pepper to taste.

2 Add the mushrooms and celery to the dressing and stir well to ensure the vegetables are thoroughly and evenly coated.

3 Turn the salad into a serving bowl and sprinkle with the toasted almonds. Garnish with the lemon wedges and tarragon sprigs, if using, and serve at once.

SERVES 4
250 g/9 oz button mushrooms, sliced
3 celery stalks, sliced

DRESSING
150 g/5 oz natural yoghurt
2 tablespoons olive oil
2 tablespoons lemon juice
1 teaspoon finely chopped fresh tarragon (see Buying guide)
salt and freshly ground black pepper

TO GARNISH
25 g/1 oz flaked almonds, toasted
lemon wedges (optional)
few sprigs of fresh tarragon (optional)

Cook's Notes

 TIME
This light salad takes 20-25 minutes to make.

 SERVING IDEAS
Try serving this salad as a refreshing starter or as an accompaniment.

 VARIATION
Replace the tarragon with 1-2 crushed garlic cloves—beat into the yoghurt with the olive oil and lemon juice, then taste and adjust the seasoning.

 BUYING GUIDE
It is better to use fresh rather than dried herbs, both for the flavour and the appearance. If fresh tarragon is unobtainable, substitute with either fresh parsley or chives.

●125 calories/525 kj per portion

Raw vegetable salad

SERVES 4
350 g/12 oz courgettes, cut into matchstick strips
175 g/6 oz mushrooms, quartered
4 celery stalks, cut into 1 cm/½ inch slices

DRESSING
5 tablespoons sunflower oil or corn oil
4 tablespoons wine vinegar
1 teaspoon light soy sauce (see Did you know)
1 teaspoon caster sugar
salt and freshly ground black pepper

1 Make the dressing: pour the oil into a serving bowl, then add the vinegar, soy sauce, sugar and salt and pepper to taste. Whisk together until evenly blended.

2 Stir all the prepared vegetables into the dressing, cover and leave for about 20 minutes. Serve straight from the dish.

Cook's Notes

TIME
15 minutes preparation, 20 minutes marinating.

SERVING IDEAS
Serve as a crisp and crunchy side dish with a hot or cold dried bean hotpot, or serve as part of a mixed hors d'oeuvre platter for a dinner party or buffet-style summer meal.

VARIATION
Add chopped fresh herbs to the salad and omit the soy sauce.

DID YOU KNOW
Soy sauce has a burnt sweet flavour which combines well with raw salad vegetables such as courgettes, which have a bitter taste.

● 175 calories/750 kj per portion

ALAN DUNS

Roman salad

SERVES 4
250 g/9 oz fresh young spinach (see Buying guide)
2 tomatoes, chopped
100 g/4 oz white button mushrooms, chopped

DRESSING
3 tablespoons olive oil
1 tablespoon red wine vinegar or cider vinegar
pinch of sugar
salt and freshly ground black pepper

1 Wash the spinach thoroughly, then dry in a salad drier or pat dry with a clean tea-towel or absorbent paper. Cut into 5 mm/¼ inch wide strips with a knife or kitchen scissors.
2 Make the dressing: put all the dressing ingredients into a screw-top jar with salt and pepper to taste. Replace the lid firmly and shake the jar well so that the dressing ingredients are thoroughly mixed.
3 Put the tomatoes, mushrooms and spinach into a large salad bowl.
4 Pour the dressing over the salad, turning it lightly with a wooden spoon or salad servers so that the salad is well coated with the dressing. Serve at once.

Cook's Notes

 TIME
This simple, refreshing salad only takes about 15 minutes to make.

 BUYING GUIDE
Make sure that the spinach looks bright green and crisp and only use the tender leaves.

 SERVING IDEAS
Serve as an alternative to plain green salad.

●105 calories/450 kj per portion

290

Leek and mushroom salad

PETER MYERS

SERVES 4

500 g/1 lb leeks, cut into 1 cm/
  ½ inch thick slices
  (see Preparation)
salt
100 g/4 oz button mushrooms,
  thinly sliced
25 g/1 oz butter
1 tablespoon vegetable oil
50 g/2 oz fresh white breadcrumbs

DRESSING
6 tablespoons olive oil
2 tablespoons wine vinegar
freshly ground black pepper

1 Bring a pan of salted water to the boil, add the leeks and simmer for about 5 minutes until just tender.

2 Meanwhile, make the dressing: pour the oil and vinegar into a screwtop jar. Add salt and pepper to taste, replace the lid firmly and set the dressing aside.

3 Drain the leeks and leave to cool, then put them in a bowl with the mushrooms. Shake the jar of dressing to mix and pour over the vegetables. Toss them well until thoroughly coated then cover and leave to marinate for at least 1 hour.

4 Meanwhile, prepare the fried breadcrumb topping: heat the butter and oil in a frying-pan, add the breadcrumbs and fry, stirring, until crisp and golden brown. Leave until completely cold.

5 To serve, turn the marinated leeks and mushrooms into a serving dish or divide between individual bowls. Sprinkle the fried breadcrumbs on top and serve at once.

Cook's Notes

 TIME
10 minutes preparation, 10 minutes cooking, plus marinating time.

 SERVING IDEAS
This salad makes a very easy and economical starter, which can be made in advance—serve with hot, crusty rolls. Alternatively, it makes an unusual side salad to serve with hot cheesy dishes.

 PREPARATION
Cut off and discard the roots and the ragged tops of the leeks, but do not trim away all the green parts as these are very sweet and tasty. Wash well under cold running water and drain before cooking.

 VARIATIONS
Add 1 teaspoon French mustard to the dressing for a more piquant flavour.

For a hint of garlic, add a peeled clove of garlic to the pan while frying the breadcrumbs. Discard the garlic before sprinkling crumbs over the salad.

●315 calories/1325 kj per portion

Potato and pepper salad

SERVES 4-6
500 g/1 lb small new potatoes,
scrubbed
1 green pepper
salt
2 celery stalks, diced
1 onion, finely chopped
½ cucumber, peeled and diced
celery leaves, to garnish

DRESSING
150 ml/¼ pint soured cream
1 teaspoon French mustard
pinch of cayenne

1 Cook the potatoes in boiling salted water for about 15 minutes, until just cooked. Drain and leave to cool completely.
2 Deseed the green pepper, slice off a few rings and reserve for the garnish. Dice the rest of the pepper.
3 Combine green pepper, celery, onion and cucumber in a salad bowl. Cut the potatoes in half and add them to the salad bowl of vegetables (see Cook's tip).
4 Just before serving, make dressing: put the cream in a bowl with the mustard, cayenne and 1 teaspoon salt. Mix well.
5 Pour the dressing over the salad and toss together. Garnish the salad with the reserved pepper rings and a few celery leaves and serve (see Serving ideas).

Cook's Notes

 TIME
30 minutes to make, plus cooling time.

 VARIATIONS
As a quick alternative, use drained canned new potatoes.
To give the dressing a milder flavour, use American mustard instead of French.
To serve the salad as a light supper dish, add 100 g/4 oz diced cheese at stage 3.

 SERVING IDEAS
This tasty salad is a good accompaniment to a vegetable quiche or may be served on its own with bread.

 COOK'S TIP
For convenience, all the vegetables may be prepared a few hours ahead – cover the bowl and refrigerate until required.

● 190 calories/800 kj per portion

FRED MANCINI

292

Hot potato and peanut salad

SERVES 4

750 g/1½ lb potatoes, cut into even-
   sized pieces (see Buying guide)
salt
250 g/9 oz roasted peanuts, roughly
   chopped (see Buying guide)
about 150 ml/¼ pint milk
50 g/2 oz Cheddar cheese, grated
1 small green chilli, or
   ½-1 teaspoon chilli powder
freshly ground black pepper

TO GARNISH
1 lettuce, leaves separated
2 tomatoes, sliced
1 onion, sliced into rings
watercress sprigs

1 Bring the potatoes to the boil in salted water, lower the heat and cook for 20 minutes until tender.
2 Meanwhile, reserve 25 g/1 oz peanuts and put rest with 150 ml/¼ pint milk into goblet of a blender. Purée until smooth (see Cook's tip).
3 Turn the mixture into a bowl and stir in the grated cheese.
4 Wash the chilli and remove the seeds. Rinse under cold running water, then chop finely and add to peanut mixture. Season to taste with salt and pepper.
5 Drain the potatoes thoroughly.
6 To serve: line a serving dish with lettuce leaves, pile the potatoes into the centre and pour the sauce over the top. Sprinkle with reserved peanuts. Garnish with tomato slices, onion rings and watercress sprigs.

Green cauliflower salad

SERVES 4

1 large cauliflower, broken into bite-sized florets with the inner green leaves

salt

150 ml/¼ pint thick bottled mayonnaise

1 tablespoon lemon juice

50 g/2 oz young spinach, roughly chopped

3 tablespoons chopped fresh parsley

3 tablespoons chopped watercress or snipped chives

freshly ground black pepper

snipped chives, to garnish

1 Bring a large saucepan one-third full of salted water to the boil. Add the cauliflower florets, bring back to the boil and cook for 3-5 minutes so that the florets are blanched yet still quite crisp. Drain and refresh under cold running water. Drain again, then put in a large bowl and leave to cool.

2 Put the mayonnaise in a blender together with the lemon juice, spinach, parsley and watercress. Blend until the mayonnaise has turned green, scraping down the sides of the blender if necessary (see Cook's tip). Season with salt and pepper to taste.

3 Just before serving, pour the mayonnaise over the top of the cold cauliflower and sprinkle with snipped chives.

Cook's Notes

 TIME
15 minutes preparation, 3-5 minutes for cooking the cauliflower, plus cooling time.

 SERVING IDEAS
Serve this salad as part of a mixed *hors d'oeuvre* for a starter. Or serve it as a salad accompaniment to any cold main-course dish.

 VARIATIONS
If you prefer, you can omit the spinach in the mayonnaise and add more watercress. In this case, add 1-2 tablespoons snipped chives to help reduce any bitter taste from the watercress. Alternatively, omit the watercress and increase the amount of parsley.

 STORAGE
The mayonnaise will keep for 1-2 days in a screw-top jar in the refrigerator, but it will lose its fresh green colour, and turn a little brown.

 COOK'S TIP
If the mixture seems a little runny, make it thicker: transfer to a jug then drop 1 egg yolk into the blender. Turn on the machine, then slowly pour the mayonnaise through the hole in the lid until it becomes thick again.

●265 calories/1100 kj per portion

JAMES JACKSON

Cauliflower cheese salad

SERVES 4

1 medium cauliflower, outer leaves, stalk and core removed, finely chopped
6 tablespoons mayonnaise (see Buying guide)
1 teaspoon tomato purée
salt and freshly ground black pepper
75 g/3 oz Cheshire cheese, finely grated
2 tablespoons chopped parsley

1 Place the finely chopped cauliflower in a large bowl.
2 Mix the mayonnaise with the tomato purée and season to taste with salt and pepper. Mix in 50 g/ 2 oz of the cheese.
3 Fold the dressing into the chopped cauliflower and leave the salad to stand for at least 15 minutes, for the flavours to blend (see Preparation).
4 Sprinkle the remaining cheese and the parsley over the top just before serving. Serve at room temperature.

 TIME
Preparation 35 minutes, including 15 minutes standing time.

 BUYING GUIDE
Use a good-quality mayonnaise: salad cream is not suitable because its flavour is too strong.

 PREPARATION
The salad must be left to stand for at least 15 minutes before serving. It can be prepared several hours in advance, in which case it should be covered with cling film and stored in the refrigerator. Allow to return to room temperature and toss well before serving.

 WATCHPOINT
Make sure that the cauliflower is really finely chopped otherwise the salad will have a lumpy appearance and it will also be difficult to eat.

 VARIATION
Use a mild Cheddar cheese instead of the Cheshire.

SERVING IDEAS
This salad goes well with plainly cooked cold vegetable and egg dishes. It could also be served as a light starter.

● 240 calories/1000 kj per portion

Cauliflower with peanut sauce

SERVES 4
1 large cauliflower
salt

PEANUT SAUCE
1 tablespoon chopped dry-roasted
  peanuts, to garnish
100 g/4 oz crunchy peanut butter
150 ml/¼ pint milk
300 g/10 oz can condensed cream of
  celery soup
¼ teaspoon yeast extract
freshly ground black pepper

1 Divide the cauliflower into florets, keeping the small green leaves attached.

2 Bring a pan of salted water to the boil, add the cauliflower, bring back to the boil, lower heat and cook for about 10 minutes.

3 Meanwhile, make the sauce: put peanut butter in a pan and blend in the milk, soup and yeast extract.

Bring to the boil, stirring, remove from the heat and season to taste.

4 Drain the cauliflower and transfer to a warmed serving dish. Pour the hot sauce over the cauliflower, sprinkle the top with chopped peanuts and serve at once.

Cook's Notes

 TIME
This tasty cauliflower dish takes about 20 minutes to make.

 COOK'S TIP
Peanut butter helps to thicken the sauce.

 VARIATIONS
Use a cream of mushroom soup in-stead of cream of celery. Cook finely diced carrot or swede with the cauliflower to add colour to the dish.

 SERVING IDEAS
Serve as a light supper or lunch snack accompanied by slices of wholemeal toast or warmed baps.

●280 calories/1175 kj per portion

Swede mayonnaise salad

SERVES 4-6

500 g/1 lb swede, coarsely grated
    (see Preparation)
100 g/4 oz pressed dates, chopped
    (see Buying guide)
4 tablespoons thick bottled
    mayonnaise
2 large tomatoes, thinly sliced
bunch of watercress
50 g/2 oz roasted cashew nuts,
    chopped (see Cook's tip)

1 Put the grated swede and chopped dates in a bowl, then stir in the mayonnaise and mix gently to combine the ingredients well.
2 Spoon the mixture into shallow serving dishes. Arrange the tomato slices and watercress round the edge of the dishes and sprinkle with chopped nuts just before serving.

MARTIN BRIGDALE

297

Apple coleslaw

SERVES 4
350 g/12 oz white cabbage
2 dessert apples (see Cook's tip)
3 tablespoons lemon juice
2 carrots
150 g/5 oz thick bottled mayonnaise
salt and freshly ground black pepper

1 Shred the cabbage finely with a sharp knife, discarding the central core. Put the shredded cabbage into a large bowl.

2 Coarsely grate the apples without peeling them. Sprinkle the grated apples with 2 tablespoons of the lemon juice in order to prevent the flesh from discolouring.

3 Scrape the carrots, then grate coarsely. Add the apple and carrots to the cabbage and toss well.

4 Mix the mayonnaise with the remaining lemon juice and salt and pepper to taste. Add to the cabbage mixture, toss thoroughly to combine then transfer to a dish.

White cabbage and cucumber salad

SERVES 6
500 g/1 lb white cabbage
½ cucumber
6 spring onions

DRESSING
5 tablespoons vegetable oil
2 tablespoons white wine vinegar
2 tablespoons chopped fresh mint
¼ teaspoon French mustard
salt and freshly ground black pepper
3 hard-boiled eggs, to garnish

1 Remove the coarse stalk of the cabbage. Finely shred the cabbage and put into a salad bowl.
2 Cut the cucumber into small dice about 5 mm/¼ inch square and add to the cabbage.
3 Thinly slice the spring onions and add to the salad.
4 Make the dressing: mix all the ingredients together in a screw-top jar until well combined.
5 Cut the hard-boiled eggs into thin slices. Place the egg slices around the edge of cabbage and cucumber salad. Pour over the dressing, toss until salad is well coated and serve at once (see Serving ideas).

Cook's Notes

TIME
Preparation takes about 15 minutes.

SERVING IDEAS
This crunchy salad makes a delicious lunch or supper served with chunks of French or thickly sliced wholemeal bread and butter. It goes well with cheese.

VARIATIONS
For a creamy salad, use 150 ml/¼ pint soured cream and 2 tablespoons lemon juice instead of oil and white wine vinegar.
Other fresh herbs may be used like dill or parsley instead of the mint.

●165 calories/700 kj per portion

MARTIN BRIGDALE

MARTIN BRIGDALE

German cabbage salad

SERVES 4-6
500 g/1 lb firm white cabbage,
   shredded
500 g/1 lb canned pineapple rings,
   drained and cut into small pieces
sweet paprika, to garnish

DRESSING
225 g/8 oz natural yoghurt
1 tablespoon wine vinegar
1 teaspoon caraway seeds
1 teaspoon sweet paprika
1 small onion, finely chopped
salt and freshly ground black pepper

1 Make the dressing: put the yoghurt in a bowl with the vinegar, caraway seeds and paprika. Mix well with a fork until the ingredients are thoroughly blended, then stir in the onion. Season to taste with salt and pepper.

2 Put the pineapple pieces into a large bowl. Add the cabbage and mix together. Pour the dressing over the salad, toss until well coated and sprinkle with a little paprika. Serve the salad at once, before the dressing settles.

MARTIN BRIGDALE

Crunchy orange salad

SERVES 6

2 oranges

350 g/12 oz red cabbage, finely shredded

250 g/9 oz carrots, grated

50 g/2 oz seedless raisins

150 ml/¼ pint thick bottled mayonnaise

3 tablespoons finely chopped mixed nuts

salt and freshly ground black pepper

1 Finely grate the zest from 1 orange and set aside. Peel the other orange with a sharp knife and remove all the pith from both oranges. Divide

the flesh into segments, cutting away all membranes.

2 Put the red cabbage, carrots and raisins in a large salad bowl, and gently stir in two-thirds of the orange segments.

3 Put the mayonnaise into a bowl and stir in the reserved orange zest

and chopped nuts. Add to the salad and season to taste with salt and pepper. Toss well until all the ingredients are thoroughly coated with mayonnaise.

4 Garnish the salad with the remaining orange segments and serve at once.

Autumn salad

SERVES 4
3 dessert apples (see Buying guide)
1 onion, thinly sliced and separated into rings
425 g/15 oz can butter beans, drained
50 g/2 oz walnut pieces
sprigs of mint, to garnish

DRESSING
150 g/5 oz natural yoghurt
1 tablespoon chopped mint
2 teaspoons lemon juice
salt and freshly ground black pepper

1 Make the dressing: mix yoghurt, mint and lemon juice in a large bowl and season to taste with salt and pepper.
2 Quarter, core and thinly slice the apples and then toss them in the yoghurt dressing until well coated.
3 Add the onion, butter beans and walnuts to the bowl and toss together. Turn the salad into a serving bowl, garnish with mint and serve at once.

Cook's Notes

 TIME
This refreshing salad takes only 20 minutes to prepare and dress.

 BUYING GUIDE
To give the salad some colour, choose a red-skinned apple such as Red Delicious or Worcester.

 VARIATIONS
To make a more substantial lunch dish, add 50 g/2 oz diced Edam cheese to the salad.

For a different dressing, use mayonnaise instead of yoghurt and double the lemon juice.

●190 calories/800 kj per portion

MICHAEL KAY

Cottage cheese and fruit salad

SERVES 4
1 large pear
2 bananas
juice of 1 lemon
500 g/1 lb cottage cheese
4 tablespoons thick bottled
  mayonnaise
1 small crisp lettuce (see Buying
  guide)
4 small tomatoes, quartered
½ cucumber, thinly sliced
4 carrots, grated
200 g/7 oz can sweetcorn, drained
2 peaches, sliced
25 g/1 oz raisins, to garnish

DRESSING
2 tablespoons vegetable oil
2 tablespoons red wine vinegar
good pinch of dried basil
salt and freshly ground black pepper

1 Peel, core and slice the pear, slice the bananas and then sprinkle the slices with a little lemon juice to prevent them from discolouring.
2 Mix the cottage cheese with the mayonnaise. Divide the lettuce leaves between 4 plates and pile a portion of the cottage cheese mixture in the centre of each.
3 Surround each serving of cottage

cheese with the prepared vegetables and fruit, arranging the ingredients separately, in portions. Sprinkle the raisins on to the banana slices.
4 Make the dressing: put all the ingredients in a screw-top jar and shake until thoroughly blended. Sprinkle the dressing over the tomato wedges, sliced cucumber and grated carrot. Serve at once.

Carrot and banana salad

SERVES 4
350 g/12 oz carrots
25 g/1 oz sultanas
8-12 lettuce leaves
4 bananas
sprigs of parsley, to garnish

DRESSING
5 tablespoons sunflower oil
2 tablespoons lemon juice
1 teaspoon curry powder
pinch of mustard powder
pinch of sugar
salt and freshly ground black pepper

1 Make the dressing: put all the dressing ingredients into a small bowl and beat with a fork until thoroughly combined. Season to taste with salt and pepper.

2 Finely grate the carrots, put into a bowl with the sultanas and mix well. Pour two-thirds of the dressing over the carrot mixture and toss to coat well.

3 Arrange the lettuce leaves on 4 individual salad plates. Halve the bananas lengthways and lay 2 halves on each bed of lettuce.

4 Drizzle the remaining dressing over each banana half, then divide the carrot mixture between each plate, spooning the mixture between the banana halves.

5 Garnish each serving with sprigs of parsley and serve at once.

DON LAST

304

PAUL WEBSTER

Sweet and sour salad

SERVES 4

$\frac{1}{2}$ teaspoon hot curry powder
150 g/5 oz natural yoghurt
1 tablespoon chutney (see Buying guide)
salt and freshly ground black pepper
1 small head celery, sliced (see Cook's tips)
100 g/4 oz Cheshire cheese, crumbled (see Economy)
50 g/2 oz stoned dates, sliced
2 crisp dessert apples

1 Beat the curry powder into the yoghurt, then stir in the chutney, season well with salt and pepper and set aside.
2 Toss together the celery, cheese and dates. Core and chop the apples and add to the other ingredients.
3 Pour the yoghurt dressing over the salad and fork through lightly until all the ingredients are evenly coated. Taste and adjust seasoning. Serve as soon as possible.

Cook's Notes

 TIME
The salad takes about 20 minutes to prepare.

 VARIATIONS
Half a crisp white cabbage, finely shredded, or 2 heads of chicory can replace the celery.

Use 2 small oranges, segmented with all the pith removed, instead of the apples and 50 g/2 oz sultanas or seedless raisins in place of the dates.

Substitute another white, crumbly cheese such as Lancashire or Wensleydale for the Cheshire.

Mayonnaise can be used instead of natural yoghurt.

BUYING GUIDE
Use an apple-based chutney in the dressing for this salad.

 COOK'S TIPS
Celery should be stored in a cool place, ideally in the salad compartment of the refrigerator. It is possible to crisp up celery which has become a little limp by plunging it in iced water or washing it in cold water and putting it in the coldest part of the refrigerator.

 ECONOMY
As the cheese is crumbled, this is a good recipe for using up cheese which has become crumbly in the freezer.

Use the trimmings from the celery to flavour soups or casseroles. Or infuse it in the warmed milk for making a white or cheese sauce to serve with cooked vegetables.

SERVING IDEAS
Sprinkle 2 tablespoons chopped peanuts, walnuts or almonds over the surface of the salad for a crunchy and attractive garnish.

● 190 calories/800 kj per portion

305

Bulgur wheat and parsley salad

SERVES 4
225 g/8 oz bulgur wheat (see Buying
    guide)
1.25 L/2 pints warm water
175 g/6 oz fresh parsley, chopped
4 spring onions, finely chopped
6 tablespoons olive oil (see Buying
    guide)
juice of 1 lemon
1 clove garlic, crushed (optional)
salt and freshly ground black pepper
250 g/9 oz tomatoes, cut in wedges
4 thin slices lemon, to garnish

1 Put the bulgur wheat into a large
bowl. Pour in the water and leave to
soak for 45 minutes. Drain the
wheat in a sieve and using your
hands, squeeze out as much water
as possible. Put the drained wheat
into a large bowl.
2 Mix the chopped parsley and
spring onions into the wheat.

3 Beat together the oil, lemon juice,
garlic, if using, and plenty of salt
and pepper. Fold the dressing into
the wheat and parsley mixture.
4 Pile the salad on to a flat serving
dish, building it up into a pyramid.

Cook's Notes

TIME
Allow 45 minutes for
pre-soaking. Prepara-
tion takes about 20 minutes if
you chop the parsley in a food
processor.

BUYING GUIDE
Bulgur wheat and other
more unusual grains and
pulses are available from most
health food shops. Bulgur wheat
may be stored for up to 1 year in
an airtight container in a cool,
dry place.
    Olive oil is really essential for
this recipe: other vegetable oils
will not give the right flavour or
consistency.

PREPARATION
To make a lemon twist
for garnish, make a cut
from the outside of the lemon
slice to the centre, then twist one
half of the slice backwards.

DID YOU KNOW
This recipe is a version of
a very popular Middle
Eastern salad called *tabbouleh*.

SERVING IDEAS
Serve with quiches and
cold soufflés, or as an
appetizing summer starter, in
bowls lined with lettuce.

●415 calories/1725 kj per portion

Arrange the tomato wedges around
the edge of the dish.
5 Twist the lemon slices (see
Preparation), then place on top of
the salad. Serve at room
temperature.

306

Andalusian sweet pepper salad

SERVES 6

4 peppers
1 Spanish onion, finely sliced
4 tablespoons olive oil
2 tablespoons white wine vinegar
salt

1 Heat the grill to high.

2 Wash the peppers and pat dry thoroughly with absorbent paper. Place the peppers on the grill rack and grill them, turning them often until the skins are charred black on all sides (see Variations).

3 Immediately transfer the peppers to a large bowl and cover closely with several layers of absorbent paper to seal in the heat and allow the peppers to cook through. Cover the bowl tightly with a clean cloth; leave at room temperature for at least 24 hours.

4 The next day, remove the skins: one at a time, hold the peppers under cold running water and rub off the skins with your fingers. Pull out and discard the cores and seeds, (see Preparation) then rinse peppers under cold running water.

5 Tear peppers into long strips (see Preparation) and arrange on a serving dish with the onions.

6 Put the oil in a small bowl with the vinegar and salt to taste. Mix well with a fork, then pour over the peppers. Serve as soon as possible, at room temperature.

JAMES JACKSON

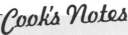 *Cook's Notes*

 TIME
About 30 minutes to prepare and grill, plus 24 hours cooling, then about 15 minutes finishing.

 VARIATIONS
Add extra flavour to the peppers by barbecuing them instead of grilling.

Use the fragrant juices that collect inside the peppers during grilling instead of some of the vinegar in the dressing.

● 100 calories/425 kj per portion

 PREPARATION
To prepare the pepper strips:

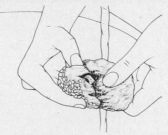

2 *Using your fingers, gently tear the pepper into long strips.*

1 *Gently squeezing the base of the pepper, pull out the core and the seeds in one piece.*

 DID YOU KNOW
This recipe originated in Spain where peppers grow in abundance.

DESSERTS

Most people, especially children, like to end a good meal with a little bit of something sweet. The desserts a vegetarian family eat will hardly differ from those enjoyed by any other family. All children (and many adults!) indulge, from time to time, in a fruit crumble with custard or a milk pudding, such as Chocolate Nutty Tapioca!

From a health point of view, a dessert can be important in making up the nutritional content of a meal, and providing extra energy for active children. Fruit is the ideal ingredient with its natural sweetness and good supply of fibre, vitamins and minerals. A milky pudding will be full of calcium, and any egg-based desserts will provide protein. So you don't need to feel guilty about eating delicious desserts – just think of all the good they are doing you!

At the end of a filling meal, fresh fruit may be all that is needed to round it off. This can be served straight from the fruit bowl or made into a refreshing fruit salad, combining familiar fruits with some of the more exotic varieties available these days. Either way, make sure you choose fruit in good condition and as fresh as possible. There are several ideas for fruit salads in this chapter. You could try Fresh Fruit Salad with Honey Cream, or Melon Fruit Salads. For an imaginative presentation, Pineapple and Grape Salad looks very impressive.

Dried fruits make a more unusual ingredient. They may be combined with fresh fruits in desserts or served in their own hot fruit salad. Dried fruits often taste sweeter than their fresh counterparts so are ideal to combine with other tart fruits, such as stewed apples or rhubarb, as they add natural sweetness.

Among the recipes in this chapter you will find some firm family favourites such as English summer pudding and two upside-down puddings. There are also many lighter and more elegant desserts that would be best served when entertaining. Lemon Granita and Apricot Nut Meringue are two good examples.

You might find custard is the most popular accompaniment for family desserts, but there are many alternatives. Natural yoghurt and soured cream are less sweet, although you could always stir in a little honey to add a touch of sweetness. Cream is, of course, the most popular accompaniment when entertaining. Single is best for pouring, while double is ideal when serving whipped cream as an accompaniment. Whipping cream can be used to incorporate in a dish or for decorating.

Make good use of soft summer fruits when they are available by choosing recipes that incorporate them. There are plenty of other recipes to choose from in the winter months. Make your desserts look attractive by decorating as suggested in the recipes, with whipped cream, glacé fruits, grated chocolate, etc., so that they really are irresistible!

Melon fruit salads

SERVES 4

2 small melons (see Buying guide)
1 mango, thickly sliced and cut into cubes
300 g/ 11 oz can mandarin orange segments, drained
1 tablespoon frozen concentrated orange juice, defrosted
250 g/9 oz raspberries, hulled
caster sugar and soured cream, to serve

1 Prepare the melons (see Preparation), reserving the trimmings. Wrap the melons in polythene bags, seal [!] and chill until required.

2 Trim the flesh from the melon trimmings and place in a bowl with the mango. Add the mandarin segments and orange juice and stir the fruits gently to mix. Cover the bowl with cling film and chill in the refrigerator for at least 1 hour.

3 To assemble: drain any juice from the melons, then place them on 4 dessert plates. Drain the other fruits well, then gently stir in the raspberries. [!] Pile the mixture into the melons. Leave to stand at room temperature for a few minutes before serving to take the chill off. Hand a bowl of caster sugar and a jug of soured cream separately.

PAUL WEBSTER

JOHN WOODCOCK

Cook's Notes

 TIME
40 minutes preparation, plus at least 1 hour chilling time.

 BUYING GUIDE
Charentais or small cantaloupe melons are the perfect size for this dessert, and their sweet, orangy-coloured flesh blends beautifully with the other fruits. If neither is available, use green-fleshed ogen melons instead.

Ripe melons feel heavy for their size and the end opposite the stalk will 'give' slightly if gently pressed. At their peak, charentais and cantaloupe melons have a strong, musky scent.

 PREPARATION
Small melons make attractive edible containers for fruit salads. (The melon flesh is eaten when the filling is finished.) To prepare: trim off the stalk, then cut the melons horizontally in half. Scrape out the seeds and membrane. Cut small 'V'-shaped wedges around the cut edges of each melon half to give a waterlily effect. Drain any juice from the cavity.

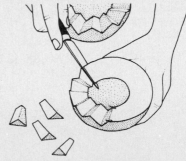

[!] **WATCHPOINTS**
Once cut, melon must be tightly wrapped or its scent will permeate other foods in the refrigerator.

Do not add the raspberries until ready to assemble the salad, or their colour will run and spoil its appearance.

●155 calories/650 kj per portion

Fresh fruit salad with honey cream

SERVES 6
2 large oranges
juice of 1 lemon
175 g/6 oz black grapes, halved and deseeded
2 large dessert pears
1 red-skinned dessert apple
½ melon
1 large banana

HONEY CREAM
75 g/3 oz full-fat cream cheese
2 tablespoons milk
2 tablespoons clear honey
grated zest of 1 lemon
150 ml/¼ pint double cream

1 Make the honey cream: soften the cheese with a wooden spoon, then gradually beat in the milk, honey and lemon zest.
2 Whip the cream until thick but not stiff, then gradually whip in the cheese mixture. Cover the bowl and refrigerate the cream while preparing the fruit.
3 Using a sharp knife, thickly peel the oranges, taking care to remove every bit of white pith. Squeeze the peel with your fingers over a large bowl to extract any juice.
4 Divide the oranges into segments by cutting between the membranes. Remove any pips. Cut the segments in half and place in the bowl with the lemon juice and grapes.
5 Peel, halve and core the pears; cut into cubes and mix with the orange segments and grapes. Halve and core, but do not peel, the apple; cut into cubes and mix with the other fruit in the bowl.
6 Scrape out the seeds and membrane from the melon; scoop out the flesh with a melon baller (see Preparation) and add to the bowl.
7 Peel and slice the banana and add to the bowl. ❗ Mix the fruit gently but thoroughly, then transfer to a serving bowl with a slotted spoon. Serve the honey cream separately.

Cook's Notes

 TIME
The honey cream takes 10 minutes to prepare; the fruit about 30 minutes.

 COOK'S TIP
Tossing the fruit in the lemon juice prevents it discolouring, and also helps bring out its flavour.

BUYING GUIDE
The fruits listed in this recipe are intended only as a guide. You can use any favourite fresh ripe fruit in season, but choose a sweet fleshy melon not a water melon which takes much more time to seed and prepare.

 PREPARATION
A melon baller is a special cutter, used for scooping out melon flesh in small neat rounds. Press the baller firmly into the melon flesh using a circular action, then lift it away and gently shake out the melon ball.
If you do not have a melon baller, scoop out the flesh with a spoon then cut it into cubes.

❗ WATCHPOINT
Do not prepare the banana until just before serving as the slices quickly turn mushy.

● 295 calories/1225 kj per portion

PAUL FORRESTER

Sliced oranges in syrup

SERVES 6

9 juicy oranges, preferably seedless
75-100 g/3-4 oz sugar
grated zest and juice of 1 lemon

1 Peel the oranges using a fine serrated knife to remove the rind, pith and thin white membrane, leaving the flesh exposed (see Preparation).
2 Cut the oranges horizontally into thin slices with a sharp knife, removing any pips.
3 Arrange the orange slices in layers in a large glass serving dish, sprinkling each layer with some of the sugar, a little of the grated lemon zest and lemon juice.
4 Cover and refrigerate for at least 4 hours. Serve well chilled.

PAUL WILLIAMS

Tea and fruit compote

SERVES 6

500 g/1 lb dried mixed fruit (see Buying guide)
1 tablespoon jasmine tea (see Variation)
1.5 L/2½ pints boiling water
75 g/3 oz walnut halves
2 tablespoons light soft brown sugar
1 tablespoon lemon juice
1 tablespoon rosewater or orange flower water

1 Put the tea into a heatproof bowl, pour over the boiling water and leave to stand for 5 minutes.

2 Put the dried fruit in a large bowl and strain the tea through a very fine sieve over the fruit. Leave to soak for 24 hours.

3 Lift out the soaked prunes from the bowl of fruit, then carefully remove the stones from the prunes. Stuff the cavity of each prune with a walnut half.

4 Put the stuffed prunes in a large pan with the rest of the fruit and tea liquid. Add the sugar and lemon juice, then cover and simmer for 20 minutes. Remove from heat and leave to stand until completely cold.

5 Stir in the rosewater and transfer to a serving dish. Cover the bowl with cling film and refrigerate for about 2 hours.

6 Serve the tea and fruit compote chilled (see Serving ideas).

ROGER PHILLIPS

Cook's Notes

TIME
About 15 minutes to prepare, plus 24 hours soaking, then about 20 minutes cooking and 2 hours chilling.

VARIATION
Replace jasmine tea with any delicately flavoured Chinese tea.

SERVING IDEAS
Served with cream, this compote makes a light, fragrant dessert. Alternatively, serve as a breakfast dish.

BUYING GUIDE
Many supermarkets and delicatessens sell packets of dried mixed fruit, usually containing about 12 prunes, plus a selection of apricots, apple rings or pears and sultanas.

Alternatively, some greengrocers and many health food shops sell loose dried fruits so that you can make up your own mixture – for this recipe include 12 prunes.

●235 calories/1000 kj per portion

ALAN DUNS

Apples Bristol

SERVES 4
4 dessert apples
pared zest and juice of 1 large
orange (see Variation)
75 g/3 oz sugar

CARAMEL CHIP TOPPING
100 g/4 oz sugar
150 ml/¼ pint water
vegetable oil, for greasing

1 Peel, core and cut the apples in to quarters. Cut each quarter in half lengthways.
2 Make up orange juice to 175 ml/6 fl oz with water. Put in a pan with sugar. Heat gently, stirring, until the sugar has dissolved, then boil gently for 1 minute. Add sliced apples, cover and simmer gently for 5 minutes until the fruit is tender. Remove from the heat and leave, covered, until cold.
3 Cut orange zest into thin shreds. Put in a small saucepan, cover with cold water and bring to the boil. Boil for 1 minute, then drain and pat dry with absorbent paper. Place on a saucer, cover and refrigerate.
4 Make the caramel chip topping: grease a baking tray with oil. Put the sugar in a small heavy-based saucepan with the water, then heat gently, stirring, until the sugar has dissolved. Using a dampened pastry brush, brush down sides of the pan, to stop crystals forming.
5 Bring the sugar syrup to the boil and boil for 5 minutes until the syrup turns deep golden. 🔲
6 Immediately remove from the heat and plunge the base of the pan into iced water to stop the syrup from cooking any more. Leave for a few minutes until sizzling stops, then remove pan from the water.
7 Pour the syrup immediately into the prepared baking tray to form a thin layer, then leave until cold.
8 Transfer the cold apples to a glass bowl with a slotted spoon, then pour the syrup left over from the apples over the fruit. Scatter the orange zest shreds over the top, then refrigerate for 1 hour.
9 To serve: crack the set caramel with a rolling pin to form fine chips, then sprinkle over the dish and serve at once, before the caramel chips begin to melt into the apples and fruit syrup.

Cook's Notes

TIME
45 minutes preparation, but allow for cooling and chilling time.

WATCHPOINT
Watch the sugar syrup constantly – remove it from heat as soon as it turns a deep golden colour.

VARIATION
The orange flesh may be used: remove the pith, then slice the orange. Add to the apples at stage 8.

SERVING IDEAS
Serve with whipped double cream.

●245 calories/1025 kj per portion

Fruit salad in a melon basket

SERVES 8

1 large melon (see Buying guide)
600 ml/1 pint water
350 g/12 oz sugar
juice of 2 lemons
1 pineapple
2 large oranges, cut into segments
    with juice reserved
1 red dessert apple
1 green dessert apple
2 large pears
250 g/9 oz dessert plums halved,
    stoned and sliced
100 g/4 oz black grapes, halved and
    deseeded
100 g/4 oz green grapes, halved and
    deseeded
3 kiwi fruit, halved and sliced
single cream, to serve

JAMES JACKSON

1 Make the melon basket (see Preparation) and reserve the melon balls in a bowl. Double wrap the melon basket in cling film. ⚠
2 Make the fruit salad: put the water and sugar into a saucepan, bring to the boil and boil, without stirring, for 2 minutes. Pour the hot syrup into a large bowl and stir in the lemon juice.
3 Twist the leaves off the pineapple, then slice off the skin, taking care to cut deeply enough to remove the black 'whiskers'. Cut lengthways into quarters and cut away the core. Cut each quarter in half again, then slice across each piece and add to the syrup with the orange segments.
4 Core and quarter the apples and pears, then thinly slice across each quarter into the bowl of fruit and sugar syrup.
5 Add the reserved melon balls to the bowl, together with the plums, grapes and kiwi fruit. Mix gently together, cover the bowl tightly and refrigerate overnight.
6 Put the wrapped melon basket in the freezer overnight.
7 To serve: put the frozen melon shell in a serving bowl and surround with ice cubes. Place this bowl in a larger, shallower bowl, then fill the melon and larger bowl with the chilled salad. Serve at once, with cream.

Cook's Notes

TIME
1 hour to make, plus overnight chilling and freezing.

⚠ **WATCHPOINT**
Be sure to wrap the melon basket and fruit salad carefully – melon tends to taint the flavour of other foods in refrigerator and freezer.

BUYING GUIDE
Use a round-shaped melon for this dish – a charentais, cantaloupe or ogen.

● 295 calories/1250 kj per portion

PREPARATION
To prepare the melon basket:

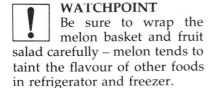

1 *Cut a thin slice off melon base so melon will stand upright, then with tip of a knife, score horizontally all round melon. Starting about 1 cm/½ inch to the right of top centre, cut down to scored line. Cut horizontally on scored line from the* right side of the melon. Remove this wedge and repeat on other side. Reserve wedges for another use.

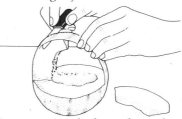

2 *Scoop out seeds from the melon then carefully cut away the melon flesh from piece remaining in middle to form the handle. Using a melon baller, cut the flesh from the remaining base to leave a neat basket shape.*

315

Pears and prunes in white wine

SERVES 8-10
350 g/12 oz large prunes
750 g/1½ lb firm dessert pears
lemon curls, to decorate (see
  Preparation)
whipped cream, to serve

WINE SYRUP
70 cl/1¼ pint medium dry white
  wine
75 g/3 oz sugar
pared zest of ½ lemon
pinch of freshly grated nutmeg

1 Cover the prunes with cold water
and soak for 1 hour.
2 Meanwhile, make the wine
syrup: put the wine into a saucepan
with the sugar, lemon zest and
nutmeg. Bring to the boil, stirring
occasionally, then lower the heat,
cover and simmer for 20 minutes.
Strain into a clean pan.
3 Peel, quarter and core the pears
over a plate to catch any juice and
cut them lengthways into slices
1 cm/½ inch thick. Bring the wine
syrup to the boil, add the pear slices

and juice, and bring back to the boil.
Simmer very gently, uncovered for 1
minute. !! Using a slotted spoon,
remove the pears and transfer them
to the plate.
4 Drain the prunes and add them to
the wine syrup. Bring to the boil and
simmer, uncovered, for 4 minutes.
Pour the prunes and syrup into a
large serving bowl, then add the
pear slices, plus any syrup and juice
on the plate, and mix gently.
5 Cool, then cover and refrigerate
for 24 hours.
6 To serve: remove from the
refrigerator 2-3 hours before serving
to take the chill off the fruit.
Decorate with a sprinkling of lemon
curls. Serve with a bowl of whipped
cream handed separately.

Cook's Notes

TIME
Preparation, including
soaking time, about 1¼
hours, plus 24 hours chilling
and 2-3 hours to bring to room
temperature.

PREPARATION
To make lemon curls,
pare the zest from ½
lemon and cut it into long, thin
sticks. Plunge into boiling water
and continue to boil for 2
minutes. Drain and cover with
cling film until required.

! WATCHPOINT
Do not cook the pears
for more than 1 minute
or they may disintegrate.

●180 calories/750 kj per portion

Mixed fruit delight

SERVES 8-10
6 satsumas or clementines, divided
  into segments
350 g/12 oz green grapes, halved
  and deseeded (see Buying guide)
2 crisp dessert apples, cored and
  sliced
425 g/15 oz can black cherries,
  drained, halved and stoned
2-3 bananas, sliced
50-75 g/2-3 oz flaked almonds (optional)
whipped cream, to serve

DRESSING
6 tablespoons clear honey
6 tablespoons orange liqueur or
  orange juice
6 tablespoons lemon juice

1 Put all the prepared fruit into 1
large or 2 smaller serving bowls.
2 Put all the dressing ingredients
into a bowl and stir until well
mixed. Pour over the fruit, turning
them gently with a large metal
spoon until thoroughly coated.
3 Cover with cling film, then
refrigerate for 2-3 hours. Before
serving, remove from the refrigerator
and allow to come to room temperature for at least 30 minutes. Serve
decorated with flaked almonds,
if wished with a bowl of whipped
cream handed separately.

Cook's Notes

TIME
Preparation time 45
minutes, plus 2-3 hours
chilling time and at least 30
minutes to bring to room
temperature.

VARIATION
Instead of satsumas, use
a 300 g/11 oz can of
thoroughly drained mandarin
segments.

BUYING GUIDE
Save time by choosing
seedless Californian or
Cypriot grapes if available.

●230 calories/975 kj per portion

ROGER PHILLIPS

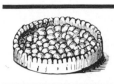

JAMES JACKSON

Rhubarb and gooseberry compote

SERVES 4
250 g/9 oz tender rhubarb, cut into
2.5 cm/1 inch lengths (see
Watchpoints)
250 g/9 oz gooseberries, topped and
tailed

SYRUP
275 g/10 oz caster sugar
300 ml/½ pint water

1 Place the rhubarb and
gooseberries in a heatproof bowl
and mix gently together, taking care
not to crush them (see Cook's tip).
2 Make the syrup: put the sugar
into a large saucepan with the
water. Heat gently, stirring, until
sugar has dissolved, then boil the
syrup rapidly for about 15 minutes
without stirring.
3 Cool the syrup for 1 minute,
then pour over the fruits. Cover and
leave to cool for 1 hour.
4 Refrigerate the compote for at
least 2 hours, or overnight, before
serving (see Serving ideas).

Pineapple and grape salads

SERVES 6

25-50 g/1-2 oz sugar
150 ml/¼ pint water
150 ml/¼ pint dry white wine
2 small pineapples
350 g/12 oz black grapes, halved,
  pips removed

1 Put the sugar and water into a saucepan and heat gently until the sugar has dissolved. Stir in the wine, pour into a bowl and cool.

2 Leave the leafy tops on the pineapples and cut them into 3 wedges. Using a sharp stainless steel knife, carefully cut away the flesh, about 1 cm/½ inch from the outer skin. Dice the flesh and stir into the syrup with the grape halves.

3 To serve: place pineapple shells on serving dishes and fill with fruit. Spoon over the syrup, cover and refrigerate for at least 1 hour.

GRAHAM YOUNG

PAUL KEMP

Stuffed peaches

SERVES 4
4 fresh peaches or 8 canned peach halves
75 g/3 oz full-fat soft cheese
3-4 tablespoons natural yoghurt
2 drops almond essence
2 teaspoons caster sugar
1 tablespoon flaked almonds

1 Skin the fresh peaches, if using (see Cook's tip), then cut the peaches in half and carefully remove the stones.

2 Blend the cheese with just enough yoghurt to give a thick, smooth mixture. Add the almond essence plus sugar to taste.

3 Spoon the mixture into the cavities of each peach half then refrigerate.

4 Toast the almonds in a moderate oven or under the grill.

5 Just before serving the peaches, sprinkle with the almonds.

Spiced pears

SERVES 6

425 ml/¾ pint dry cider
75 g/3 oz apricot jam, sieved
40 g/1½ oz soft brown sugar
¼ teaspoon ground cinnamon
2 whole cloves
6 firm pears
thin strips of orange zest
juice of ½ lemon
3 tablespoons flaked almonds,
   toasted (optional)

1 Bring the cider, jam, sugar and spices slowly to the boil in a deep saucepan.
2 Peel the pears, leaving them whole and with the stalks on. Immediately stand them upright in the saucepan, add the orange zest and lemon juice, cover tightly and simmer gently for 20-30 minutes or until just tender but not too soft (see Cook's tip).
3 Cut a thin slice from the base of each pear. Stand the pears upright in a serving dish. Boil the liquid in the uncovered saucepan for about 10 minutes to reduce by half. Strain and pour over the pears. Leave overnight to soak in the refrigerator or in a cool place. About 1 hour before serving, baste the pears well with the syrup.
4 Sprinkle the almonds over the pears just before serving.

Cook's Notes

 TIME
Preparation and cooking take 40 minutes. Allow for soaking overnight.

 COOK'S TIP
This is a good way of using hard pears. Cooking time will depend on the hardness of the fruit.

 SERVING IDEAS
Serve with whipped cream and crisp biscuits. Almond biscuits go particularly well with pears.

 PRESSURE COOKING
Cook the pears at high pressure for 1 minute.

 VARIATIONS
Use red or white wine instead of cider and substitute 50 g/2 oz sugar for the jam. To use canned pear halves instead of fresh pears, boil the other ingredients together until the mixture is reduced by half, pour over the well-drained fruit and soak.

●125 calories/525 kj per portion

English summer pudding

SERVES 4

250 g/9 oz mixed blackcurrants and redcurrants, stripped from their stalks
100 g/4 oz caster sugar
1 tablespoon orange juice or water
250 g/9 oz raspberries
5-7 thin slices day-old white bread, with crusts removed

1 Put the mixed currants into a heavy-based saucepan. Add the caster sugar and orange juice and bring slowly to the boil. Cover and cook very gently for about 5 minutes, stirring occasionally, until the currants are tender and the juices are flowing
2 Add the raspberries and cook gently for 2-3 minutes. ! Remove from the heat and leave to cool.
3 Meanwhile, use most of the bread to line the base and sides of a 600 ml/1 pint pudding basin. Cut the bread so that it fits neatly and use the trimmings to fill any gaps. !
4 Put 5 tablespoons of the fruit juices and 2 tablespoons of fruit into separate small containers, cover and reserve in the refrigerator. Spoon the remaining fruits and juices into the bread-lined basin and cover completely with the remaining bread.
5 Put a small plate or lid which fits just inside the rim of the basin on top of the pudding. Weight the plate down, then leave the pudding in the refrigerator overnight.
6 To serve: run a round-bladed knife around the top edge of the pudding to loosen it, then turn it out on to a serving plate. Spoon the reserved fruit juices over any areas of bread that are not coloured and pile the reserved fruit on top.

Continental-style cheesecake

MAKES 8 SLICES

BASE
50 g/2 oz self-raising flour
50 g/2 oz caster sugar
50 g/2 oz soft tub margarine
1 egg
margarine, for greasing

FILLING
450 g/1 lb Quark (see Buying guide)
75 g/3 oz caster sugar
grated zest of 1 lemon
1 tablespoon plain flour
3 eggs
150 ml/¼ pint soured cream
6-8 drops vanilla flavouring
40 g/1½ oz seedless raisins

1 Heat the oven to 170C/325F/Gas 3. Grease an 18 cm/7 inch loose-based cake tin.

2 Make the base: sift the flour into a bowl. Add the caster sugar, margarine and egg. Mix well with a wooden spoon, then beat for 1-2 minutes until evenly blended. Spread evenly over base of the tin.

3 Bake in the oven for 20-25 minutes, until springy to the touch. Set the base aside and leave it to cool slightly.

4 Meanwhile, make filling: whisk the Quark, caster sugar and lemon zest together with a rotary or hand-held electric whisk. Sift in the flour, then beat in the eggs, one at a time. Add the soured cream and vanilla and continue whisking until the mixture is smooth and shiny. Stir in the raisins.

5 Pour the filling into the tin and bake the cheesecake in the oven for 1-1½ hours, until set and firm. Turn off the heat and leave the cheesecake to cool in the oven, with the door ajar, for 2 hours (see Cook's tip).

6 Run a palette knife around the sides of the cheesecake to loosen it, then remove the sides of the tin. Cover the cake and refrigerate for at least 8 hours before serving (see Storage).

Cook's Notes

 TIME
25-30 minutes (including baking) for base, then 10 minutes preparation and 1-1½ hours baking time, plus 2 hours cooling and 8 hours chilling.

 BUYING GUIDE
Good supermarkets and delicatessens now stock Quark, a continental soft cheese made from skimmed milk. It is sold in tubs and it is ideal for this type of cheesecake.

If you cannot buy Quark, use curd cheese instead, which is more readily available. (The latter gives a more 'solid' filling.)

 COOK'S TIP
Cooling the cheesecake slowly in the oven reduces its tendency to shrink and crack slightly.

STORAGE
The cheesecake can be kept, covered, in the refrigerator for up to 4 days.

● 315 calories/1325 kj per slice

PAUL FORRESTER

Spiced peach compote

SERVES 4
4 large firm peaches
little lemon juice, for brushing
25 g/1 oz flaked almonds, toasted
pouring cream, to serve (optional)

SYRUP
150 ml/¼ pint water
50 g/2 oz sugar
**finely grated zest and juice of
   1 orange**
2 tablespoons redcurrant jelly
small piece cinnamon stick
3 whole cloves

1 Cut the peaches in half and re-move the stones, then brush the cut surfaces with lemon juice to prevent the flesh discolouring.

2 Make the syrup: pour the water into a large heavy-based saucepan and add the sugar, orange zest and juice, the redcurrant jelly and spices. Heat gently, stirring, until the jelly has melted and sugar has dissolved, then bring to the boil.
3 Using a slotted spoon, lower the peach halves into the syrup. Bring back to the boil, then lower the heat, cover and poach the peaches gently for 5-10 minutes, until just tender all the way through. [!] Remove the pan from the heat.
4 Using a slotted spoon, transfer the peaches to a plate. Leave for a few minutes until cool enough to handle, then peel off the skins with your fingers. Place the peaches in a heatproof serving bowl, then strain the hot syrup over them.
5 Serve the peaches warm, cold or chilled, scattering over the almonds just before serving. Hand a jug of cream separately, if liked.

Cook's Notes

TIME
40-45 minutes prepara-tion time.

WATCHPOINT
Take care not to over-cook the peaches as it is important that they retain their shape for this dish.

VARIATIONS
Stir 4 teaspoons sherry or an orange-flavoured liqueur into the syrup before straining it over the peaches.

For a peach melba compote, add 100 g/4 oz raspberries to the poached and skinned peaches at stage 4, before straining over the hot syrup.

● 165 calories/700 kj per portion

FRED MANCINI

Apple layer pudding

SERVES 4
1 kg/2 lb cooking apples, sliced
100 g/4 oz caster sugar
finely grated zest and juice of 1 large orange
150 g/5 oz fresh brown breadcrumbs
100 g/4 oz soft brown sugar
1 teaspoon ground cinnamon
butter, for greasing

TO DECORATE
thinly pared rind of 1 orange, cut into matchstick strips
150 ml/¼ pint double cream

1 Heat the oven to 200C/400F/Gas 6. Grease a baking tray.
2 Put the apples into a saucepan with the sugar and the orange juice. Cook over gentle heat for about 10 minutes until the apples are soft, then remove from the heat and beat to a smooth purée. Leave to cool.
3 Meanwhile, mix together the breadcrumbs and brown sugar and spread over the greased baking tray. Heat through in the oven, for about 15 minutes, turning every 4-5 minutes, until the sugar has caramelized and the crumbs have turned dark brown. Leave to cool.
4 Meanwhile, put the orange strips in a small pan and cover with cold water. Bring to the boil, drain, return to the pan and cover with fresh cold water. Bring to the boil once more and simmer gently for about 20 minutes. Drain and refresh under cold running water.
5 When the breadcrumbs are cold, put them in a polythene bag and crush them to small crumbs using a rolling pin. Mix the grated orange zest and cinnamon into the crumbs.
6 To assemble: divide half the apple purée into individual glass bowls, then divide half the crushed crumbs over the apple. Spoon the remaining apple on top and finish with the remaining crumbs.
7 Whip the cream until it forms soft peaks, then spoon into a piping bag fitted with a star nozzle. Pipe the cream into the centre of each bowl and decorate with the orange strips. Chill until ready to serve.

Cook's Notes

TIME
1 hour preparation and cooking, plus 10 minutes assembling.

●545 calories/2275 kj per portion

Rhubarb roulade

MAKES 6 SLICES
750 g/1½ lb rhubarb, chopped
100 g/4 oz sugar
3 tablespoons water
4 large eggs, separated
50 g/2 oz self-raising flour, sifted
50 g/2 oz caster sugar
few drops red food colouring
icing sugar, for dredging
vegetable oil, for greasing
cream or custard, to serve

FILLING
1 dessert apple
finely grated zest and juice of
　½ lemon
225 g/8 oz cottage cheese, sieved
25 g/1 oz caster sugar, or to taste

1 Put chopped rhubarb into an enamelled pan with the sugar and the water. Cover and simmer until tender, then remove from heat and cool completely.

2 Heat the oven to 190C/375F/Gas 5. Grease a 33 × 23 cm/13 × 9 inch Swiss roll tin, then line the base of the tin with non-stick vegetable parchment paper.

3 Drain the rhubarb, then put it into a large bowl with the egg yolks and mix with a fork until blended. Stir in the flour, caster sugar and red food colouring and mix well.

4 In a clean dry bowl, whisk the egg whites until standing in stiff peaks. Using a metal spoon, fold the egg whites into the rhubarb mixture. Pour the mixture into the prepared tin and immediately bake in the oven for 20-25 minutes, until springy to the touch.

5 Meanwhile, prepare the filling: core, but do not peel the apple, then coarsely grate it. Put the grated apple into the bowl and thoroughly stir in the lemon zest and juice.

6 Lay a large sheet of greaseproof paper on top of a clean, damp tea-towel. Sprinkle paper evenly with icing sugar.

7 Cool the rhubarb sponge in the tin for 10 minutes, then run a round-bladed knife around the sides to loosen it and turn out on to the sugared greaseproof paper.

8 Drain the apple and mix with the sieved cheese and caster sugar, to taste. Spread the mixture over the rhubarb sponge. Roll up the sponge, from one short end, with the aid of the paper. Press the join. Carefully transfer rhubarb roll to a serving plate, placing it seam-side down. Sift icing sugar over the top and serve at once.

Cook's Notes

 TIME
Total preparation time is about 1¼ hours.

 WATCHPOINT
The sponge will become soggy if left to stand; serve it as soon as it is ready, cutting it into neat slices with a sharp serrated knife.

 DID YOU KNOW
Roulade is the French word for roll.

● 255 calories/1075 kj per slice

ROGER PHILLIPS

Hazelnut and apple shortcake

MAKES 8 SLICES
75 g/3 oz butter, softened
50 g/2 oz light soft brown sugar
100 g/4 oz plain flour, sifted
75 g/3 oz hazelnuts, toasted, skinned and finely ground (see Preparation)

FILLING
500 g/1 lb dessert apples
1 tablespoon clear honey
50 g/2 oz sultanas
1 teaspoon ground cinnamon
150 ml/¼ pint whipping cream
icing sugar, for dusting

1 Heat the oven to 190C/375F/Gas 5.
2 Beat the butter together with the sugar until pale and fluffy. Using a large metal spoon, stir in the flour and nuts, then mix to a firm dough with your hand.
3 Turn out the dough on to a lightly floured surface, knead briefly until smooth, then cut in half. Shape each piece into a ball and place, well apart, on a large baking sheet (see Cook's tip). Roll out to 20 cm/8 inch rounds. Flute. Bake in oven for 15-20 minutes, until set and golden brown.
4 Prepare the filling while the shortcakes are baking: peel, core and slice the apples and put them with the honey into a heavy-based saucepan. Cover and cook gently, stirring occasionally, for 15 minutes, until very soft. Remove from the heat, stir in the sultanas and cinnamon; cool completely.
5 Cool the shortcakes for 5 minutes, then cut 1 round into 8 wedges with a sharp knife. Transfer the wedges and whole shortcake to a wire rack and leave to cool completely.
6 To assemble: place the whole shortcake on a serving plate and spread with the apple mixture. Whip the cream until just stiff, then pipe 8 whirls on apples. Arrange shortcake wedges on top, standing them at an angle in the cream. Sift over a little icing sugar. Serve at once, or refrigerate for up to 3 hours.

Apricot nut meringue

SERVES 4-6

4 large egg whites
250 g/9 oz caster sugar
1 teaspoon vanilla essence
½ teaspoon malt vinegar (see
   Did you know)
100 g/4 oz ground almonds
melted margarine or butter, for
   greasing

FILLING

400 g/15 oz can apricot halves in
   syrup, drained
300 ml/½ pint double cream, lightly
   whipped
icing sugar, to dust

1 Heat the oven to 190C/375F/Gas 5. Grease two 20 cm/8 inch sandwich tins with melted margarine and line the bases with non-stick baking parchment.
2 Whisk the egg whites in a clean, dry bowl until stiff, then gradually beat in the caster sugar 1 tablespoon at a time. Beat in the vanilla essence and vinegar, then fold in the ground almonds with a metal spoon. ⚠
3 Fill the prepared tins with the meringue mixture and level the surfaces with a knife. Bake in the oven for 30-40 minutes until set and lightly browned. Turn out, peel off the paper, and leave to cool on a wire rack. ⚠
4 To make the filling: reserve 2 apricot halves for decoration, then purée the remainder in a blender, or pass them through a sieve. Stir the apricot purée into half the whipped cream.
5 Spread the apricot cream over 1 meringue cake and top with the other. Sift a little icing sugar over the surface.
6 Put the remaining cream into a piping bag fitted with a star nozzle and pipe whirls of cream around the edge of the meringue.
7 To decorate: cut each reserved apricot half into 4 and arrange on top of the cream. Chill until ready to serve. (Serve within 2-3 hours, or the meringues will soften.)

Cook's Notes

TIME
Preparation time 40 minutes, baking time 40 minutes. Allow at least 1 hour for the meringues to cool.

STORAGE
The nut meringues can be made 1-2 weeks in advance and stored unfilled in an airtight container.

WATCHPOINTS
When folding in ground nuts, use a metal spoon and a cutting action.
  The meringues will crack slightly after baking so turn them out very carefully.

DID YOU KNOW
The addition of malt vinegar gives the meringues a crisp exterior and a slightly chewy texture inside.

● 785 calories/3275 kj per portion

Grape syllabub

SERVES 6-8

500 g/1 lb grapes, halved with seeds
  removed
100 g/4 oz macaroons (see
  Economy), coarsely crushed
2 large egg whites
100 g/4 oz caster sugar
125 ml/4 fl oz medium dry white
  wine (see Economy)
2 tablespoons brandy or sherry
300 ml/½ pint double cream
2 kiwi fruits, peeled and sliced, to
  decorate

1 Divide half the grapes equally
between 6-8 tall stemmed dessert
glasses, then cover with half the
crushed macaroons. Place the rest of
the grapes on top and finish with a
layer of the remaining macaroons.
2 In a clean, dry, large bowl, whisk
the egg whites until standing in stiff
peaks. Add half the sugar and whisk
until the meringue is stiff and
glossy. Using a large metal spoon,
fold in the remaining sugar. Gradually fold and stir in the wine and
brandy.
3 In a separate large bowl, whip the
cream until just thickened. Stir the
frothy meringue mixture, then
whisk into the cream, about one-
third at a time. Pour the syllabub
over the biscuits and grapes, cover
the glasses with cling film and
refrigerate for 1-2 hours, until the
biscuits are moistened and
softened. !
4 Just before serving, top each
syllabub with slices of kiwi fruit. (If
added too far in advance, the slices
will loose their freshness.) Serve
chilled.

ALAN DUNS

Cook's Notes

TIME
55 minutes preparation
(including 25 minutes
seeding the grapes), plus
chilling time.

ECONOMY
Any brittle almond or
hazelnut biscuits can be
used instead of macaroons.

If you do not want to open a
large bottle of wine specially for
this dessert, buy a small, 125 ml/
4 fl oz bottle.

DID YOU KNOW
A syllabub is a tradi-
tional English dessert,
originally made from very fresh
milk or cream, and alcohol.

WATCHPOINT
The dessert needs to be
chilled, but do not leave
it too long or liquid will collect
in bottom of the glass. This will
certainly spoil the appearance,
although not the flavour, of the
dish.

●470 calories/1970 kj per portion

Apple and loganberry Charlotte

SERVES 4

500 g/1 lb cooking apples, peeled, cored and chopped

400 g/14 oz can loganberries, drained (see Cook's tips), with syrup reserved

25 g/1 oz sugar, or to taste

175 g/6 oz fresh white breadcrumbs, lightly toasted

75 g/3 oz light soft brown sugar

50 g/2 oz butter or margarine

150 ml/¼ pint soured cream

25 g/1 oz hazelnuts (optional)

1 Place the apples in a heavy-based saucepan. Add loganberry syrup, cover and cook gently, stirring occasionally, until the apples are very tender and disintegrating.

2 Remove from the heat and crush the apples with a wooden spoon or potato masher. Turn the purée into a bowl and stir in the loganberries and sugar, leave to cool completely.

3 Meanwhile, mix the breadcrumbs with the brown sugar. Melt the butter in a frying-pan, add the crumb mixture and stir over low heat until turning golden and crisp. Turn into a bowl and cool.

4 Whip the cream until thickened (see Cook's tips). Reserve in the refrigerator until required.

5 Spread one-third of the crumbs in the base of a 1.25 L/2½ pint glass serving dish. Cover with half the apple mixture and level the surface. Sprinkle over half the remaining crumbs, then add the rest of the apple mixture, followed by a final layer of crumbs.

6 Carefully spread the cream on the top. Decorate with the nuts, if using. Serve as soon as possible. [!]

Lemon granita

SERVES 4-6
juice of 6 lemons (see Buying guide)
600 ml/1 pint water
175 g/6 oz sugar

TO DECORATE
lemon twists
frosted mint leaves (see Preparation)

1 Put the water and sugar in a saucepan. Heat gently until the sugar has dissolved, then bring to the boil and boil for about 5 minutes, without stirring, until a thick syrup is formed.

2 Remove the syrup from the heat and set aside until completely cold.

3 Add the lemon juice to the cold syrup and pour into a loaf tin or ice cube trays without the ice cube divisions. Freeze in the freezer compartment of a refrigerator or in the freezer for about 1 hour (see Cook's tip).

4 Remove from the freezer and stir well with a metal spoon until evenly blended.

5 Return to the freezer and freeze for a further 3 hours, stirring with a metal spoon once every 30 minutes during this time, to form an icy slush.

6 Spoon the granita into individual glass dishes, decorate with lemon twists and frosted mint leaves and serve at once.

Cook's Notes

TIME
5 minutes preparation, plus cooling time and 4 hours freezing.

BUYING GUIDE
Choose large juicy lemons for this ice.

WATCHPOINTS
The syrup must be absolutely cold before placing in the freezer. To help cool the syrup, place the pan in a bowl of iced water.

The granita must be eaten as soon as it is ready. If it is kept in the freezer it will become too frozen and lose its texture.

DID YOU KNOW
Easy to make, a granita is a cross between a drink and a water ice; it makes the perfect refreshing follow-up to a pasta meal.

COOK'S TIP
If you are using the freezing compartment of the refrigerator, turn it to its coldest setting at least 1 hour before making the granita, and remember to return it to its original setting when finished.

PREPARATION
To frost the leaves, first wash the leaves and pat dry. Using a soft paint brush, brush the leaves with lightly beaten egg white, then dip the leaves into caster sugar. Leave to dry on a rack for about 1 hour before using.

●200 calories/830 kj per portion

JAMES JACKSON

Melon and peach sorbets

SERVES 4-6

1 ripe ogen melon, weighing about
750 g/1½ lb
4 large ripe peaches, peeled and
stoned
225 g/8 oz sugar
300 ml/½ pint water
3 tablespoons lemon juice
2 egg whites
mint sprigs, to garnish (optional)

1 Put the sugar in a saucepan with the water and stir over low heat until the sugar has dissolved. Bring to the boil, then boil rapidly for 5 minutes, without stirring, until a thick syrup is formed.
2 Remove the syrup from the heat and set aside until completely cold.
3 Halve the melon and remove the seeds. Scoop out the flesh and purée in a blender.

4 Stir half the cold syrup and half the lemon juice into the melon purée, then transfer the mixture to a rigid container.
5 Purée the peaches in a blender, then stir in the remaining syrup and lemon juice. Transfer the purée to a rigid container.
6 Freeze both mixtures for 2 hours until firm around the edges.
7 In a clean, dry bowl, whisk the egg whites until they stand in stiff

peaks. Remove the mixtures from the freezer and break up with the whisk, then fold half the egg whites into the melon mixture and half into the peach mixture. Cover tightly and return to the freezer for at least 2 hours until firm.
8 To serve: stand in container at room temperature for about 30 minutes until the sorbet is soft enough to scoop into individual glasses. Garnish with mint sprigs, if liked.

Iced bramble pots

SERVES 6
250 g/9 oz blackberries (see
    Buying guide)
2 tablespoons water
50 g/2 oz sugar
3 eggs, separated
75 g/3 oz icing sugar, sifted
¼ teaspoon vanilla flavouring
150 ml/¼ pint double cream

TO SERVE
a few whole blackberries
blackberry leaves (optional)
single cream

1 Put the blackberries into a small pan with the water and sugar. Cover the pan and cook over low heat for about 5 minutes or until the fruit is just tender. Remove from the heat, allow to cool slightly, then pureé in blender or food processor. Work the pureé through a sieve to remove all the pips, then allow to cool completely.
2 Whisk the egg yolks with 25 g/ 1 oz of the icing sugar until creamy.
3 In a clean, dry bowl, whisk the egg whites until they stand in stiff peaks, then whisk in the remaining icing sugar, 1 teaspoon at a time. Gradually whisk in the egg yolk mixture (see Cook's tips) until the mixture is thick and creamy.
4 Pour one-third of the mixture into a bowl, then stir in the vanilla flavouring. Fold the cold blackberry pureé into the larger quantity of the mixture.
5 Lightly whip the cream until it begins to form soft peaks, then fold one-third into the vanilla mixture and two-thirds into the blackberry mixture.
6 Divide half the blackberry mixture between six 150 ml/¼ pint individual moulds (see Cook's tips and Variation), then spoon the vanilla mixture on top. Spoon the rest of the blackberry mixture on top of the vanilla mixture. Freeze for about 4 hours, until firm.
7 To serve: unmould on to 6 individual plates and decorate with a few blackberries and blackberry leaves, if liked. Serve at once with cream handed separately.

MARTIN BRIGDALE

Cook's Notes

TIME
45 minutes preparation, plus cooling time, then 4 hours freezing.

BUYING GUIDE
If fresh blackberries are unavailable, use frozen blackberries, but cook with only 1 tablespoon water.

SERVING IDEAS
Serve with small sweet biscuits or wafers.

●240 calories/1025kj per portion

COOK'S TIPS
It is best to use an electric mixer to whisk the egg yolk mixture into the egg whites, as it is difficult to create enough 'bulk' if whisking by hand.
    Small cream, yoghurt or cottage cheese cartons make ideal moulds for this dessert.

VARIATION
This dessert may also be made in one 850 ml/ 1½ pint mould – a pudding basin or a loaf tin.

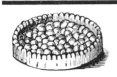

Cranberry ice cream

SERVES 4

350 g/12 oz fresh cranberries, topped and tailed, or frozen (see Cook's tips)
2 tablespoons water
175 g/6 oz icing sugar, sifted
175 ml/6 fl oz double or whipping cream

1 Put the cranberries in a saucepan with the water and simmer for 5-10 minutes until tender. Cool, then pass through a sieve, or purée in a blender, then sieve.

2 Stir the icing sugar into the cranberry purée and mix well to remove any lumps.

3 Whip the cream lightly, then fold into the cranberry purée and pour the mixture into a freezer container. Place uncovered in the freezer (see Cook's tips). When the mixture is firm around the edges and slushy in the centre (after about 2 hours), turn the sides into the centre with a fork and stir lightly to achieve a smooth texture.

4 Cover the container with a lid or foil and freeze overnight until firm, without stirring again. ✳

5 Transfer the ice cream to the main part of the refrigerator 30 minutes before serving, to soften slightly.

6 Scoop the ice cream into individual glasses to serve.

DAVID LEVIN

Cook's Notes

TIME
Preparation takes 25 minutes and the initial freezing about 2 hours. Then freeze the ice cream overnight before serving.

VARIATIONS
Other fruits can be puréed in place of cranberries. Try strawberries, blackcurrants or blackberries.

COOK'S TIPS
Cook frozen cranberries straight from the freezer, so as not to lose any of the juice.

If you do not have a freezer, you can make the ice cream in the freezing compartment of the refrigerator. Turn it to its coldest setting at least 1 hour before making the ice cream, and remember to return it to its original setting when finished.

FREEZING
Home-made ice cream can be stored in the freezer for up to 3 months.

SERVING IDEAS
The ice cream looks very pretty garnished with a few cranberries, served with wafers, preferably fan-shaped.

●355 calories/1500 kj per portion

Cheesy castles

SERVES 4

225 g/8 oz cottage cheese
150 ml/¼ pint soured cream
150 g/5 oz natural yoghurt
3-4 drops vanilla flavouring
1-2 tablespoons caster sugar
350 g/12 oz black or red cherries
  (see Serving ideas)

1 Using a skewer, punch 8 or 9 holes in the base of four 150 ml/¼ pint moulds (see Cook's tips). Line each mould with a large square of wet muslin [!] : allow the excess muslin to hang over the sides of the moulds.

2 Drain any liquid from the cheese, then press the cheese through a nylon sieve into a bowl. Slowly stir in the cream, yoghurt and vanilla flavouring. Add sugar, to taste, and mix well until evenly blended.

3 Pour mixture into prepared moulds. Fold the overhanging pieces of muslin over the cheese mixture to enclose it completely, then lightly press the top down.

4 Put the moulds on a wire rack, standing on a plate or tray, then refrigerate for at least 12 hours (and up to 24 hours) to drain away excess moisture (see Cook's tips).

5 To unmould the castles: remove one of the drained moulds from refrigerator and unwrap the top. Invert a small dessert plate on top of the mould, then carefully invert the plate and mould together. Lift off the mould, then carefully remove the muslin.

6 Unmould the remaining cheese castles in the same way (see Cook's tips). Transfer the castles to a serving plate and arrange the cherries around the base of the castles. Serve at once (see Serving ideas).

Cook's Notes

TIME
Preparation 15-20 minutes, plus at least 12 hours draining time.

COOK'S TIPS
Clean small yoghurt, cottage cheese, cream or salad cartons are ideal for this recipe. *Coeurs à la crème* moulds may also be used, with very attractive results.

The cheese mixture will shrink down in the moulds as excess moisture drains off.

Neaten the ragged edges at the base of each castle with a round-bladed knife.

WATCHPOINT
Make sure that the muslin is wet: this makes lining the moulds much easier and helps prevent the cheese mixture sticking.

SERVING IDEAS
Use fresh cherries on stalks as these look most attractive. Drained canned stoned cherries or defrosted frozen cherries can be used when fresh cherries are not available. Alternatively, use any soft fruit of your choice.

●205 calories/850 kj per castle

Kiltie creams

SERVES 4
50 g/2 oz porridge oats
150 ml/¼ pint double or whipping
    cream
150 g/5 oz natural yoghurt
3 tablespoons clear honey, or to
    taste

1 Heat the grill to moderate.
2 Spread the oats on a baking tray and toast under the grill for 4-5 minutes, stirring them frequently, until lightly browned. ⚠ Remove the oats immediately from the heat, tip into a bowl and leave for 10-15 minutes, until cold.
3 Whip the cream until standing in soft peaks. Using a large metal spoon, fold the yoghurt, honey and toasted oats into the cream. Taste and add more honey, if liked (see Cook's tip).
4 Divide the cream mixture between 4 stemmed glasses or ramekins (see Variation). Serve at once, or cover with cling film and refrigerate for up to 4 hours.

Cook's Notes

🕑 **TIME**
Preparation takes about 30 minutes.

⚠ **WATCHPOINT**
Watch the oats constantly and turn them regularly so that they brown evenly; once they start to colour they darken very easily.

 VARIATION
Top each portion with blackberries or raspberries, defrosted if frozen, and sprinkle the fruit generously with caster sugar.

COOK'S TIP
If you intend chilling the creams before serving, over-sweeten the mixture slightly as chilling mutes the flavour.

● 275 calories/1150 kj per portion

CHRIS KNAGGS

JAMES JACKSON

Prune creams

SERVES 6
225 g/8 oz prunes
300 ml/½ pint boiling water
3 tablespoons light soft brown
    sugar
pinch of ground cloves or mixed
    spice
150 ml/¼ pint unsweetened orange
    juice
2 tablespoons custard powder (see
    Cook's tip)
300 ml/½ pint milk
few drops of vanilla flavouring
150 ml/¼ pint whipping cream

1 Place the prunes in a heavy-based saucepan. Pour in the boiling water, cover and leave to soak for 2 hours.
2 Add 2 tablespoons sugar and the spice. Stir over low heat until the sugar has dissolved, then cover and simmer for about 15 minutes, until the prunes are soft and have absorbed most of the liquid.
3 Remove and discard the stones from the prunes, then puree the flesh in a blender together with any remaining cooking liquid and the orange juice. Set purée aside.
4 Blend the custard powder with the remaining sugar and 2 tablespoons milk. Bring the remaining milk almost to the boil in a small, heavy-based saucepan, then gradually stir it into the custard paste. Return the mixture to the pan, bring slowly to the boil and simmer for 2 minutes, stirring constantly.
5 Remove the custard from the heat and stir in the vanilla, then gradually blend in the prune puree. Turn the mixture into a bowl and leave to cool completely, stirring occasionally.
6 Whip the cream until just standing in stiff peaks. Using a large metal spoon, fold half the cream into the prune mixture. Divide the mixture between 6 glass dishes and level each surface. Top each portion with a swirl of the remaining cream, then refrigerate for up to 2 hours before serving.

Cook's Notes

TIME
2 hours soaking for the prunes, then 20 minutes preparation, plus cooling and chilling in refrigerator.

COOK'S TIP
To save time, fold the prune puree into 425 g/ 15 oz canned custard and omit the custard powder, milk, remaining sugar and vanilla.

●210 calories/875 kj per portion

336

Rhubarb banana whip

SERVES 4
540 g/1 lb 3 oz can rhubarb in syrup, drained (see Cook's tips)
2 small bananas, chopped
150 g/5 oz natural yoghurt
few drops of red edible food colouring
1 egg white

1 Purée the rhubarb with the bananas and yoghurt in a blender (see Cook's tips). Pour into a large bowl and stir in a few drops of food colouring to tint the mixture pink.
2 Whisk the egg white until stiff, then fold into the rhubarb mixture using a large metal spoon.
3 Divide the mixture between 4 dishes, cover and chill for at least 2 hours; top with banana if wished.

Cook's Notes

 TIME
Preparation takes about 15 minutes, but remember to allow 2 hours for chilling.

 COOK'S TIPS
When in season, use 500 g/1 lb fresh rhubarb, stewed, drained and sweetened, instead of canned fruit.

If you do not have a blender or processor, use a fork to mash the rhubarb and bananas to a pulp, then beat in the yoghurt.

Canned rhubarb varies in sweetness; taste the mixture before folding in the egg white, and, if necessary, stir in a little caster sugar.

This dessert will keep in the refrigerator for up to 4 hours.

 SERVING IDEAS
Banana slices, dipped in lemon juice to prevent discoloration, can be used to decorate the dessert. Serve with shortbread biscuits for texture contrast.

● 80 calories/325 kj per portion

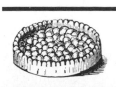

Rum and chocolate mousses

MAKES 6

250 g/9 oz plain cooking chocolate
  pieces (see Buying guide)
1 tablespoon light rum
100 g/4 oz butter, softened
100 g/4 oz caster sugar
4 eggs, separated
50 g/2 oz ground almonds

TO DECORATE
150 ml/¼ pint whipped double
  cream
1 tablespoon finely chopped
  mixed nuts

1 Put the chocolate in a heatproof
bowl with the rum. Set the bowl
over a pan half full of simmering
water and stir until the chocolate is
completely smooth. Allow the hot
chocolate to cool slightly.

2 Beat the butter and sugar
together until light and fluffy, then
beat in the egg yolks, one at a time.
Stir in the chocolate mixture and
beat for 5 minutes until creamy. Stir
in the ground almonds.

3 In a clean, dry bowl, whisk the
egg whites until they stand in soft
peaks, then fold into the chocolate
mixture with a metal spoon. Divide
between six 150 ml/¼ pint ramekin
dishes, level the surfaces and
refrigerate for 2 hours until set. ✳
4 To serve: pipe cream on to the
centre of each mousse, then sprinkle
chopped nuts on top. Serve at once.

Cook's Notes

TIME
20 minutes to prepare,
then 2 hours chilling.

FREEZING
Open freeze, then wrap
in polythene bags. Seal,
label and return to the freezer
for up to 2 months. To serve:
unwrap and defrost at room
temperature for about 4 hours.
Decorate as described.

SERVING IDEAS
Serve with Italian
amaretti biscuits or
small bite-sized macaroons.

BUYING GUIDE
Good quality cooking
chocolate, sold in blocks
or drops, is best for making
these chocolate mousses.

●630 calories/2650 kj per mousse

Coffee caramel custards

SERVES 6
2 large whole eggs
2 large egg yolks
40 g/1½ oz caster sugar
600 ml/1 pint milk
3 tablespoons instant coffee
½ teaspoon vanilla flavouring

CARAMEL
75 g/3 oz sugar
4 tablespoons water

1 Heat the oven to 170C/325F/Gas 3. Rinse out six 150 ml/¼ pint ramekins with very hot water, then stand in a roasting tin and place in the oven to keep hot.
2 Make the caramel: put the sugar into a heavy-based saucepan with the water. Heat gently, without stirring, until the sugar has dissolved, then bring to the boil and boil rapidly until the syrup turns a light golden colour. ⚠
3 Immediately remove the pan from the heat and plunge the base into cold water. ⚠ Leave

there for a few seconds until the sizzling stops, then remove the pan from the water. Take the roasting tin out of the oven and pour the caramel syrup into the ramekins.
4 Make the coffee custard: in a large bowl, mix the whole eggs and egg yolks lightly together with a wooden spoon. Stir in the caster sugar. Bring the milk almost to the boil in a small pan, then remove from the heat, add the coffee and vanilla and stir until the coffee has dissolved. Slowly stir the milky coffee into egg and sugar mixture.
5 Strain the coffee custard into a

jug, then slowly pour it into the ramekins. Pour enough hot water into the tin to come halfway up the sides of the ramekins, then bake in the oven for about 45 minutes, or until set (see Cook's tip).
6 Protecting your hands with oven gloves, lift the ramekins out of the tin and leave to cool. Remove the skin from the surface of the custards, then run a round-bladed knife around the edge of each custard to loosen it. Refrigerate for at least 2 hours (and up to 4 hours).
7 To serve: turn out on to individual dishes and serve at once.

Cook's Notes

TIME
20 minutes preparation and 45 minutes baking, plus cooling and chilling.

COOK'S TIP
To test that the custard is cooked, insert the point of a knife into the centre: it should leave a clean cut. If the custard flows together it is not set and, therefore, needs a little longer baking.

WATCHPOINTS
Remove syrup from heat as soon as it turns light golden. A dark caramel can quite easily overpower the rather delicate coffee flavour of the custards.

Do not let any water splash into the boiling hot syrup or it will spit and splutter and you could burn yourself.

●200 calories/825 kj per custard

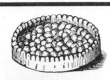

JAMES JACKSON

Chocolate nutty tapioca

SERVES 4
40 g/1½ oz flaked tapioca (see Did you know)
600 ml/1 pint milk
25 g/1 oz light soft brown sugar

TOPPING
25 g/1 oz raw peanuts, skinned and coarsely chopped
25 g/1 oz plain chocolate, coarsely grated

1 Put the tapioca into a medium heavy-based pan and pour in plenty of cold water. Bring to the boil, simmer for 5 minutes, then drain and return to pan (see Cook's tip).
2 Pour in the milk and bring slowly to simmering point. Cook, stirring frequently, for 45-60 minutes, until the tapioca is clear and the mixture is thick and creamy. Remove from the heat and stir in the sugar, to taste.
3 Heat the grill to moderate.
4 Turn the tapioca mixture into a shallow, flameproof dish. Level the surface, then sprinkle with the chopped peanuts and grated chocolate. Grill for 1-2 minutes, until the chocolate is melted and the nuts are lightly browned.
5 Serve the pudding hot or cold.

Cook's Notes

TIME
This easy-to-make pudding takes just over 1 hour to prepare and cook.

DID YOU KNOW
Tapioca comes from the root of the cassava plant, widely grown in the West Indies. It is sold in the form of medium or tiny pearls as well as flakes. Because of its high starch content it will absorb more liquid than some other grains, and is sometimes also used in savoury dishes such as soups or stews to thicken them.

COOK'S TIP
The tapioca is cooked briefly in boiling water to soften it—otherwise the milk might evaporate before it has been absorbed.

● 235 calories/975 kj per portion

TONY ROBINS

Rich rice pudding

SERVES 4
100 g/4 oz pudding rice
600 ml/1 pint milk
finely grated zest of ½ orange
75 g/3 oz caster sugar
25 g/1 oz butter
3 egg yolks, beaten
150 ml/¼ pint single cream
butter, for greasing

1 Heat the oven to 180C/350F/Gas 4. Generously butter a 1.25 L/2 pint ovenproof dish (see Cook's tip).

2 Put the rice in a saucepan with the milk and orange zest and bring slowly to the boil. Cook, stirring occasionally, for 15-20 minutes, until the rice is just tender.

3 Turn the heat off under the rice, add the caster sugar and butter and stir until melted. Allow the rice mixture to cool for 5 minutes. Thoroughly stir in the beaten egg yolks, followed by the cream.

4 Pour into the prepared dish and bake in the oven for about 40 minutes, stirring thoroughly 3 times during cooking. At the end of cooking the pudding will have a thin skin and most of the liquid will have been absorbed. Serve warm, straight from the dish.

341

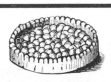

Cherry semolina

SERVES 4
350 g/12 oz black or red
 cherries, stoned
1 tablespoon sugar, to taste
softened butter or margarine,
 for greasing
pouring cream or vanilla ice cream,
 to serve (optional)

TOPPING
600 ml/1 pint milk
3-4 drops vanilla or almond
 flavouring
65 g/2½ oz semolina
50 g/2 oz caster sugar
1 egg, separated
freshly grated nutmeg, for dusting

1 Heat the oven to 180C/350F/Gas 4. Lightly butter a 1 L/2 pint shallow ovenproof serving dish. Spoon the cherries into the dish and sprinkle with sugar, to taste.
2 Make the topping: warm the milk with the vanilla in a heavy-based saucepan over low heat. Sprinkle in the semolina and stir well to mix, then stir in half the sugar. Bring slowly to boil and simmer gently, stirring constantly, for 3 minutes. Remove from the heat and cool slightly, then add the egg yolk and beat vigorously until evenly blended.
3 In a clean dry bowl, whisk the egg white until standing in stiff peaks. Whisk in the remaining sugar, 1 tablespoon at a time, and continue whisking until meringue is stiff and glossy.
4 Using a large metal spoon, fold the meringue into the semolina mixture. Spoon evenly over the cherries in the dish. Swirl the surface with the back of the spoon, then sprinkle nutmeg over the top.
5 Bake the pudding in the oven for 40-45 minutes, or until the semolina topping is puffed and browned on top. Serve at once (see Cook's tip), accompanied by pouring cream or vanilla ice cream, if liked.

ROGER TUFF

Cook's Notes

TIME
25-30 minutes preparation and 40-45 minutes baking time for the pudding.

COOK'S TIP
The pudding is best served immediately it is baked as the semolina topping sinks very quickly.

VARIATIONS
Other soft fruits can be used in place of the cherries: blackcurrants go well with the semolina and nutmeg. Dust the top with ground cinnamon, cloves or mixed spice instead of grated nutmeg.

●275 calories/1150 kj per portion

Glazed apple pancakes

MAKES 12
100 g/4 oz plain flour
pinch of salt
1 large egg, lightly beaten
25 g/1 oz butter, melted
300 ml/½ pint milk
butter, for greasing
cream or ice cream, to serve

FILLING AND GLAZE
1 kg/2 lb cooking apples
225 g/8 oz sugar
2 tablespoons water
finely grated zest of 1 lemon
1 rounded tablespoon apricot jam
25 g/1 oz shelled walnuts, chopped

1 Sift flour and salt into a bowl. Make a well in the centre. Add egg, melted butter and 2 tablespoons milk. Whisk together, then slowly whisk in remaining milk.
2 Strain batter into a jug, cover and leave for 30 minutes.

3 Meanwhile, make the filling: peel, core and slice the apples, then put into a saucepan with sugar and water. Cover and cook gently for 15-20 minutes until apples are very soft. Turn into a nylon sieve to drain off excess liquid, then return apples to pan. Stir in lemon zest, cover and keep hot.
4 Heat the oven to 180C/350F/Gas 4.
5 Melt a little butter in a heavy-based 15 cm/6 inch frying-pan over moderate to high heat. Pour off any excess.
6 Whisk the batter. Remove frying-pan from heat and pour in just enough batter to cover base thinly (see Cook's tip). Return to heat and cook pancake for about 1 minute, until underside is set. Using a palette knife, turn pancake over and cook on the other side for 20-30 seconds. Lift pancake on to greaseproof paper.
7 Continue making pancakes, interleaving each with greaseproof paper, until there are 12 altogether. Stir batter frequently and grease pan with more butter as necessary.
8 Spread about 1 tablespoon apple filling over one-half of each pancake. Fold pancakes in half, then in quarters; arrange in a buttered ovenproof dish and heat through in the oven for 10 minutes.
9 Put jam into a small pan and heat until bubbling. Brush over pancakes, then sprinkle with walnuts. Serve at once, with cream.

Cook's Notes

 TIME
Total preparation and cooking time including time for the batter to rest, is about 1 hour.

 COOK'S TIPS
As soon as the batter touches the pan, tilt the pan round using a semi-circular action to spread the batter evenly. Use the first pancakes as a 'tester' to judge the amount of batter needed and the temperature of the pan.

●200 calories/830 kj per pancake

DON LAST

Crunchy baked peaches

SERVES 6

**6 fresh peaches or nectarines,
    skinned (see Cook's tips)**
50 g/2 oz butter
100 g/4 oz muesli
**25 g/1 oz Muscovado sugar (see Did
    you know)**
2 large oranges (see Preparation)
1-2 tablespoons brandy

1 Heat the oven to 180C/350F/Gas 4.
2 Halve the peaches and discard the
stones (see Cook's tips). Place the
peach halves in an ovenproof dish,
cut side up.
3 To make the stuffing: melt the
butter in a saucepan. Remove from
the heat and stir in the muesli, sugar
and orange zest.

4 Spoon the stuffing into the
cavities of the peaches.
5 Mix the orange juice with the
brandy and pour into the dish,
around the peaches.

6 Cover the dish with a lid or foil
and bake in the oven for 20-30
minutes until tender but not too
soft. Serve hot or cold with crisp,
sesame biscuits.

Cook's Notes

TIME
Preparation 15 minutes,
cooking 20-30 minutes.

PREPARATION
Finely grate the zest
from only 1 orange and
squeeze the juice from both.

COOK'S TIPS
To halve the peaches,
cut round the centre
through to the stone, then twist
apart. For extra colour, leave the
skins on the peaches.
  To add an interesting flavour

to the stuffing crack the stones
open to extract the kernel. Chop
the kernel and add to stuffing.

VARIATIONS
The brandy could be
replaced by liqueurs
such as Grand Marnier.

DID YOU KNOW
Muscovado sugar is one
of the least refined
sugars. It is a moist, dark brown
sugar with a molasses taste.

●190 calories/800 kj per portion

Fruit fritters with raspberry sauce

SERVES 4
1 large cooking apple
1 large banana
400 g/14 oz can apricot halves, drained
1 tablespoon plain flour
1 teaspoon ground cinnamon
vegetable oil, for deep frying
caster sugar, to serve

BATTER
100 g/4 oz plain flour
pinch of salt
2 tablespoons vegetable oil
150 ml/¼ pint lukewarm water
2 large egg whites

SAUCE
225 g/8 oz raspberries, fresh or frozen
50 g/2 oz sugar

1 Make the batter: sift the flour and salt into a large bowl, make a well in centre and add the oil and water. Gradually whisk the liquid into the flour to make a batter. Cover and leave to stand for 1 hour.

2 Meanwhile, make the sauce: put raspberries and sugar in a small saucepan, cover and cook gently for 10-15 minutes until soft. Press through a nylon sieve, stir well and return to rinsed-out pan. Set aside.

3 Prepare the fruit: peel and core the apple, then cut across into 4 slices. Peel the banana, cut in half lengthways, then cut each half across. Pat the apricots dry with absorbent paper.

4 Sift the flour and cinnamon on to a plate. Dip each piece of fruit in the flour and shake off excess.

5 Heat the oven to 110C/225F/Gas ¼.

6 Heat the oil in a deep-fat frier to 190C/375F or until a cube of stale bread turns golden in 50 seconds.

7 In a clean, dry bowl, whisk the egg whites until standing in stiff peaks, then fold into the batter.

8 Drop a few pieces of the fruit into batter to coat evenly, then transfer to the pan with a fork, allowing excess batter to drain off. Fry for 3-4 minutes, turning once, until golden. Remove with a slotted spoon and drain on absorbent paper. Keep warm in the oven, while cooking remaining fruit.

9 To serve: reheat the raspberry sauce and pour into a serving jug. Arrange the fritters on a warmed serving dish, sprinkle with caster sugar and serve at once. Pour the raspberry sauce evenly over the top.

JAMES JACKSON

DON LAST

Cherry and almond slices

MAKES 4-6
215 g/7½ oz frozen puff pastry,
    defrosted
15 g/½ oz butter, melted

FILLING AND GLAZE
225 g/8 oz cottage cheese, drained
75 g/3 oz clear honey
50 g/2 oz ground almonds
2-3 drops almond flavouring
425 g/15 oz can stoned black
    cherries, drained
1 small egg, lightly beaten
1 tablespoon Demerara sugar
icing sugar, for dusting (optional)

1 Heat the oven to 200C/400F/Gas 6.
Dampen a large baking sheet with
some water.
2 Roll out the pastry on a lightly
floured surface to a 30 × 26 cm/12 ×
10½ inch rectangle. Trim all the
edges with a sharp knife. Brush the
pastry with melted butter, to within
2 cm/¾ inch of the edges.
3 Make the filling: mix together the
cheese, honey, almonds and
flavouring. Spread half this mixture
lengthways over half the pastry
rectangle, to within 2 cm/¾ inch of
the edges. Arrange the cherries over
the top in a single layer, then cover
with the remaining cheese mixture.
4 Brush the edges of the pastry
lightly with beaten egg, then fold
the plain half of the pastry over the
filling and press the edges together
to seal. Using a fish slice, carefully
transfer the pastry to the prepared
baking sheet. Knock up and flute
the edges and make 2 slits in the top.
5 Brush the top of the pastry with
beaten egg, then sprinkle with
Demerara sugar. Bake in the oven
for about 30 minutes, until the
pastry is risen, crisp and browned.

6 Carefully transfer the pastry to a
wire rack and sift icing sugar over
the top, if liked. Serve warm, cut
into 4-6 slices (see Serving ideas).

Brandied apples

SERVES 4

1 kg/2 lb dessert apples (see Watchpoints)
6 tablespoons clear honey
40 g/1½ oz caster sugar
juice of 1 lemon
4 tablespoons brandy
lightly whipped cream, to serve

1 Peel, quarter and core the apples. Cut each quarter lengthways into about 3 evenly thick slices.
2 Put the honey and caster sugar into a large heavy-based frying-pan. Heat mixture gently, stirring occasionally with a wooden spoon, until the sugar has dissolved.
3 Bring to the boil and boil gently until just beginning to smell of caramel. ⚠ Add the apple slices and turn until coated (see Cook's tip). Lower the heat and cook the apple slices gently for about 5 minutes, or until all the slices are just softened and translucent.
4 Add the lemon juice, then bring the honey mixture back to the boil. Tilt the pan slightly to one side and spoon all the juices into a warmed serving jug. Keep the juices hot until they are required for serving.
5 Pour the brandy over the apples and heat through for a few seconds, then remove from the heat and set light to it. ⚠ Let the flames die down completely, then serve the brandied apples at once, accompanied by the jug of hot juices and a bowl of lightly whipped cream.

PAUL WEBSTER

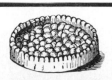

ALAN DUNS

Glacé fruit soufflé

SERVES 6
425 g/15 oz can custard
50 g/2 oz glacé pineapple, finely
chopped
25 g/1 oz angelica, finely chopped
50 g/2 oz ground almonds
3 eggs, separated
pinch of salt
50 g/2 oz caster sugar
butter, for greasing
1 tablespoon sugar, for dish

1 Heat the oven to 180C/350F/Gas 4.
2 Grease a 1.75 L/3 pint soufflé dish with butter, then coat the inside with the sugar, tipping out any excess (see Cook's tip). Refrigerate the prepared dish while making the soufflé mixture.
3 Put half the custard into a bowl with the glacé pineapple, angelica, ground almonds and egg yolks. Mix well together.
4 In a clean, dry bowl, whisk the egg whites with a pinch of salt until standing in stiff peaks. Whisk in the caster sugar, 1 tablespoon at a time, and continue whisking until the meringue is stiff and glossy.
5 Fold the egg whites into the custard mixture until well blended, then transfer to the prepared soufflé dish. Level the surface with a palette knife.
6 Bake the soufflé in the oven for 55 minutes until golden brown and firm to the touch. Serve at once, while still risen and puffy, with the rest of custard handed separately in a jug (see Variations).

Hot Melba meringue

SERVES 4
100 g/4 oz raspberries
1 teaspoon cornflour
50 g/2 oz caster sugar
4 small ripe peaches
butter or margarine, for greasing

ALMOND MERINGUE
2 egg whites
75 g/3 oz caster sugar
¼ teaspoon almond flavouring
50 g/2 oz ground almonds
2 teaspoons cornflour
flaked or slivered almonds, to
   decorate (optional)

1 Heat the oven to 180C/350F/Gas 4. Lightly butter an 850 ml/1½ pint ovenproof serving dish.
2 Put the raspberries in a bowl and crush lightly. Sprinkle over cornflour and sugar, to taste, then stir until the raspberry juices run.
3 Skin the peaches: immerse the peaches in very hot water for 1 minute. Drain, then nick the skin near the stalk and peel away the skin. Cut in half and remove the stones, then thickly slice the flesh.
4 Arrange the slices in the prepared dish, then spoon the raspberry mixture evenly on top. Cover the dish with foil and bake in the oven for 10 minutes to heat the fruit through.
5 Meanwhile, make the almond meringue: in a clean dry bowl, whisk the egg whites until standing in stiff peaks. Whisk in the sugar, 1 tablespoon at a time, and continue whisking until the meringue is firm and glossy. Whisk in the flavouring. Mix the ground almonds with the cornflour, then fold into the meringue with a large metal spoon.
6 Remove the dish from the oven. Uncover and swirl the almond meringue over the fruit. Sprinkle with flaked or slivered almonds, if using. Return to the oven for a further 20 minutes, or until the almond meringue is golden. Serve hot, straight from the dish.

FRED MANCINI

MICHAEL KAY

Prune tart

SERVES 4

375 g/13 oz packet ready-cooked
   prunes (see Buying guide)
150 ml/¼ pint red wine
75 g/3 oz ground almonds
50 g/2 oz caster or icing sugar
½ egg white (approximately)
4 tablespoons redcurrant jelly

PASTRY
100 g/4 oz plain flour
pinch of salt
2 egg yolks
50 g/2 oz caster sugar
50 g/2 oz butter, diced

ALMOND PASTRY CREAM
2 egg yolks
50 g/2 oz caster sugar
15 g/½ oz plain flour
15 g/½ oz cornflour
300 ml/½ pint milk
2-3 drops almond flavouring
75 g/3 oz ground almonds
2 tablespoons double cream

1 Simmer the prunes in the red
wine for 5 minutes, then cool.
2 Meanwhile, make the pastry: sift
the flour and salt on to a board or
work surface, make a well in the
centre and drop in the egg yolks,
sugar and diced butter. Work together with your fingertips until the
mixture resembles fine breadcrumbs, then shape into a smooth
ball of dough. Place in a polythene
bag and refrigerate for 30 minutes.
3 Heat the oven to 190C/375F/Gas 5.
4 Meanwhile, make the pastry
cream: place the egg yolks in a bowl
with the sugar and flours and mix to
a smooth cream with a little milk.
5 Bring the remaining milk to just
below boiling point, remove from
the heat and gradually stir into the
egg yolk mixture. Return to the pan
and whisk constantly over low heat
until the mixture comes just to the
boil. **!** Remove from the heat, stir in
a few drops of almond flavouring, to
taste, then fold in the ground
almonds and cream. Leave to cool.
6 Place the chilled pastry in a lightly
greased 20 cm/8 inch flan tin or flan
ring placed on a baking sheet. Carefully press it out with your fingers to
line the tin evenly. **!** Bake blind for
15-20 minutes or until biscuit
coloured. Leave to cool.
7 Meanwhile, remove the prunes
from the wine with a slotted spoon,
reserving the wine, and stone them.
Mix the ground almonds with the
caster sugar and enough egg white
to form a paste. Stuff each prune
with almond paste and reshape.
8 When the flan case is cool, carefully remove from the tin or ring and
place on a serving plate. Fill the flan
case with the pastry cream
(whisking it first if a skin has
formed) and arrange the stuffed
prunes in circles on top.
9 Boil the reserved red wine for a
few minutes, until reduced to 3-4
tablespoons. Stir in the redcurrant
jelly and melt over low heat, then
boil for 1-2 minutes until it forms a
glaze. Brush the prunes with the
glaze and leave to set. Serve at room
temperature.

Cook's Notes

TIME
Total preparation and
cooking time is 2 hours.
Add an extra 8½ hours for
soaking and cooking if not
using the ready-cooked prunes.

WATCHPOINTS
Be careful not to allow
the egg yolk mixture to
boil, or it may curdle.
   Take particular care to spread
the pastry evenly over the sides
of the tin or flan ring.

BUYING GUIDE
Ready-cooked prunes,
now widely available,
are a great time-saver as there is
no need to soak them. If you use
ordinary dried prunes, remember that they must be soaked for
at least 8 hours before cooking.

●880 calories/3700 kj per portion

Bananas in spiced orange sauce

SERVES 4

4 firm bananas
1 tablespoon sugar
¼ teaspoon ground mixed spice
finely grated zest and juice of
** 1 orange**
15 g/½ oz butter

1 Mix the sugar and spice, then add to the orange zest and juice and stir well to blend. Cut the bananas diagonally across into chunky, slanting pieces.
2 Melt the butter in a heavy-based saucepan. Add the bananas and fry briskly for 2 minutes, turning them with a fish slice and palette knife **!** until browned.
3 Stir the orange juice mixture, then pour over the bananas. Allow the mixture to bubble for a few seconds, until heated through, **!** then remove the pan from the heat.
4 Spoon the hot bananas and orange sauce into 4 bowls (see Serving ideas) and serve at once.

MICHAEL KAY

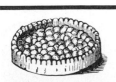

PAUL WEBSTER

Apricot soured cream flan

SERVES 6
215 g/7½ oz shortcrust pastry, defrosted if frozen
3 eggs, separated
150 g/5 oz caster sugar
150 ml/¼ pint soured cream
225 g/8 oz sultanas, chopped
finely grated zest of 1 lemon
½ teaspoon ground cinnamon
¼ teaspoon ground cloves
pinch of salt
icing sugar, for dusting

SAUCE
400 g/14 oz can apricot halves, drained
juice of 1 lemon
1 tablespoon medium sherry
1 tablespoon blanched almonds

1 Heat the oven to 220C/425F/Gas 7.
2 Roll out the pastry on a lightly floured surface and use to line a 23 cm/9 inch loose-bottomed flan tin. Place flan tin in the refrigerator while you prepare the cream filling.
3 Using a hand-held electric beater, whisk the egg yolks with the sugar until pale and thick. Beat in the soured cream, sultanas, lemon zest, cinnamon, cloves and salt.
4 In a clean, dry bowl whisk the egg whites until standing in stiff peaks. Gently fold into the soured cream mixture.
5 Spoon the mixture into the pastry case and bake in the oven for about 15 minutes. Lower the oven temperature to 180C/350F/Gas 4 and cook for 20 minutes.
6 Remove from the oven and leave to cool in the tin for 10 minutes, then remove the sides of the tin and slide the flan on to a serving plate. Leave until completely cold.
7 Meanwhile, make the sauce: reserve 6 apricot halves to decorate, then put remainder of apricots in a blender with the lemon juice, sherry and almonds. Blend until smooth, then transfer the sauce to a serving jug. Slice the apricot halves into thirds.
8 Dust the flan with icing sugar,

then decorate the top with the reserved apricot slices. Serve the flan cut into slices, with apricot sauce handed separately.

Spiced fig pie

MAKES 6 SLICES
215 g/7½ oz shortcrust pastry,
 defrosted if frozen
1 large egg white, lightly beaten

FILLING
175 g/6 oz dried figs, chopped (see
 Buying guide)
5 tablespoons clear honey
½ teaspoon ground allspice
1 large egg yolk
1 large egg
4 teaspoons plain flour
225 ml/8 fl oz single cream
1 tablespoon flaked almonds

1 Put the figs, honey and allspice for the filling into a bowl. Mix together well, then cover and leave to stand for about 30 minutes.
2 Meanwhile, heat the oven to 190C/375F/Gas 5.

Cook's Notes

TIME
45 minutes preparation (including standing time for the figs) and 40 minutes baking, plus cooling.

COOK'S TIPS
Use tip of a knife to distribute figs evenly.
Let the pie 'settle' for at least 5 minutes before serving. (The filling will sink as it cools.)

●380 calories/1600 kj per slice

FREEZING
Cool pie completely, then remove from tin and open freeze until solid. Wrap, seal and return to freezer for up to 3 months. To serve: unwrap and defrost at room temperature for 6 hours.

BUYING GUIDE
Buy whole dried figs, sold loose in packets, and carefully remove and discard any hard stalks.

3 On a lightly floured surface, roll out the pastry and use to line a loose-based 20 cm/8 inch flan tin. Brush with egg white, then prick in several places with a fork. Refrigerate while you finish preparing the spiced fig filling.
4 Add any remaining egg white to the egg yolk and whole egg in a bowl and whisk together. Whisk in the flour, then gradually whisk in the cream. Pour over the fig mixture and stir briskly until well mixed.
5 Turn the mixture into the pastry case (see Cook's tips) and sprinkle over the almonds. Bake in the oven for about 40 minutes, or until the filling is puffed, golden and set in the centre. Serve warm (see Cook's tips), or leave until cold. ✳

JAMES JACKSON

ALAN DUNS

Honey pastries

MAKES 8
400 g/13 oz frozen puff pastry,
  defrosted
20 g/¾ oz butter, melted

FILLING AND SYRUP
175 g/6 oz mixed walnuts and
  blanched almonds, coarsely
  ground or finely chopped
½ teaspoon ground cinnamon
½ teaspoon ground mixed spice
150 ml/¼ pint clear honey
juice of ½ lemon

1 Heat the oven to 200C/400F/Gas 6.
Prepare a 16 cm/6½ inch square tin
which is about 2.5 cm/1 inch deep
(see Preparation).
2 Make the filling: mix the nuts and
spices, then add 50 ml/2 fl oz honey
and mix to a stiff paste.
3 Roll out the pastry on a lightly
floured surface to a 33 cm/13 inch
square. Trim edges with a sharp
knife, then cut into 4 squares.

4 Place 1 square of pastry in the
prepared tin and brush with melted
butter. Place another square on top
and brush with butter, then using
the back of a dampened large metal
spoon, spread with the nut filling.
[!] Cover with another square and
brush with butter. Place the last
square on top. Brush with butter.
5 Using a sharp knife and cutting
through the top 2 layers of pastry
only, cut the pastry into 4 squares;
then cut each square diagonally in
half to make 8 triangles.
6 Bake in the oven for 20-25 minutes,
until risen and golden brown.
7 About 5 minutes before the pastry
is cooked, make the syrup: add the
lemon juice to the remaining honey,
then make up to 150 ml/¼ pint with
water. Mix well, then pour into a
small saucepan. Bring slowly to the
boil, stirring, then simmer for 2
minutes. Remove from the heat.
8 Slowly strain the hot syrup over
the surface of the pastry. Leave at
room temperature for about 2 hours
to allow pastry to absorb syrup.
9 To serve: cut through into
triangles and lift out of the tin with a
small palette knife.

Cook's Notes

TIME
40-50 minutes (inclu-
ding baking), plus 2
hours soaking time.

WATCHPOINT
Leave a 5 mm/¼ inch
border of pastry all
round, otherwise the edges of
the filling will burn.

DID YOU KNOW
These pastries are a
simplified, less sweet,
version of the Greek *baclava*,
which are made with papery
thin *filo* pastry.

PREPARATION
Place a 25 cm/10 inch
square of foil in the tin.
Press gently over the base and
up the sides, taking care that it
fits neatly in the corners. Turn
the edges of the foil over the rim
of the tin.

● 405 calories/1700 kj per pastry

Dutch apple tart

SERVES 8
750 g/1½ lb dessert apples
75 g/3 oz seedless raisins
1 teaspoon ground cinnamon
1 tablespoon caster sugar
little beaten egg, for glazing

PASTRY
175 g/6 oz plain flour
pinch of salt
100 g/4 oz butter, softened
75 g/3 oz caster sugar
1 egg

1 Make the pastry: sift the flour and salt into a bowl. Make a well in the centre and add the butter, sugar and egg (see Did you know).
2 Using the fingertips of one hand, gradually work the butter, sugar and egg together, then gradually incorporate the flour until the dough forms a ball. Wrap in cling film and refrigerate for 30 minutes.
3 Heat the oven to 200C/400F/Gas 6.
4 Cut off one-third of the pastry and reserve. Roll out the remaining pastry on a lightly floured surface and use to line a 20 cm/8 inch loose-bottomed flan tin. Trim the edges and reserve the trimmings.
5 Peel, core and cut the apples into 5 mm/¼ inch thick slices. Arrange the slices in the flan case: start at the centre of the flan and arrange the slices overlapping in a spiral shape. Sprinkle over the raisins, cinnamon and sugar.
6 Roll out the remaining pastry and trimmings to make a lattice decoration for the tart (see Preparation). Brush the pastry lattice with beaten egg to glaze.
7 Bake the tart for 20 minutes, then lower the oven to 190C/375F/Gas 5 and bake for a further 15 minutes. Serve hot or cold.

JAMES JACKSON

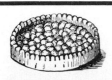

JAMES JACKSON

Rhubarb and banana pie

SERVES 4

150-175 g/6 oz shortcrust pastry, defrosted if frozen
lightly beaten egg white and caster sugar, for glazing
butter, for greasing
cream or custard, to serve

FILLING

500 g/1 lb rhubarb, cut into 4 cm/ 1½ inch lengths
75 g/3 oz Demerara sugar
1 large banana, thinly sliced and sprinkled with lemon juice
1 teaspoon ground mixed spice

1 Roll out the pastry on a lightly floured surface to 4 cm/1½ inches larger all round than the top of an 850 ml/1½ pint ovenproof pie dish. Invert the pie dish on the rolled-out pastry and cut round the edge with a sharp knife to make a lid. Then cut a strip the same width as the rim of the pie dish, from the outer edge of the pastry.

2 Use the trimmings to make decorations and refrigerate with the pastry lid and strip.

3 Heat the oven to 200C/400F/Gas 6. Lightly butter the pie dish.

4 Dampen the rim of the dish with water. Place the pastry strip on the rim and press down lightly. Spoon half the rhubarb into the dish and sprinkle with Demerara sugar. Scatter banana slices on top, then sprinkle over the spice. Pile the remaining rhubarb on top, heaping it in the centre.

5 Brush pastry strip with egg white. Place pastry lid on top of dish and press round the edge to seal. Trim any surplus pastry, then flute the edge. Brush underside of pastry decorations with egg white and stick on to pastry lid. Brush lid with egg white and sprinkle with the caster sugar, then prick in several places with a fork.

6 Bake the pie in the oven for about 30 minutes, until pastry is crisp and golden. Sprinkle with more caster sugar if liked, and serve hot, warm or cold, with cream or custard.

Cook's Notes

TIME
30 minutes preparation, plus 30 minutes baking the pie in the oven.

? DID YOU KNOW
Rhubarb originated in South-east Asia, and was esteemed for its medicinal properties. Although technically classed as a vegetable, it is usually cooked and eaten as a fruit in puddings. Rhubarb became extremely popular in Victorian England and some of the varieties grown today date from that time.

●280 calories/1175 kj per portion

Pear pie special

SERVES 4-6
215 g/7½ oz frozen puff pastry,
  defrosted

FILLING
850 g/1¾ lb firm, dessert pears,
  quartered and cored
grated zest and juice of 1 orange
25 g/1 oz caster sugar
25 g/1 oz ground almonds
½ teaspoon ground cinnamon
pinch of ground cloves (optional)
little Demerara sugar, to finish

1 Heat the oven to 220C/425F/Gas 7.
2 On a lightly floured surface, roll
out the pastry about 4 cm/1½ inches
larger all round than the top of a 700
ml/1¼ pint ovenproof pie dish.
3 Cut out a lid and a strip for the rim
of the dish from the pastry (see
Preparation). Reserve all the pastry
trimmings. Leave the pastry in a
cool place while making the filling.
4 To make the filling: place the
pears in a bowl and sprinkle with
the orange zest and juice. Mix well,
then turn into the pie dish and
arrange over the base. Mix together
the caster sugar, ground almonds,
cinnamon and cloves, if using, and
sprinkle evenly over the pears.
5 Using a pastry brush, dampen the
rim of the pie dish. Cut a small piece
from the pastry strip (so it will fit
neatly), place on the rim of the dish
and press down lightly. Brush the
strip with water.
6 Place the pastry lid on top of the
dish. With your thumb, press the lid
and strip together. Using a sharp
knife, trim the edges, then knock up
and flute them. Make a small
thimble-sized hole in the centre of
the pastry lid to allow the steam to
escape during baking.
7 Roll out the pastry trimmings and
use to make leaves or other decorations. Brush the underside of the
decorations with water and arrange
them on the pastry lid.
8 Brush the lid with water ⚠, then
sprinkle lightly with Demerara
sugar. Bake in the oven, just above
the centre, for 30-35 minutes until
the pastry is golden. Serve the pie
hot or warm.

CHRIS KNAGGS

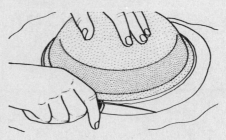

Cook's Notes

 TIME
50 minutes preparation,
30-35 minutes baking.

 WATCHPOINT
Do not let any water run
down the fluted edges
or the pastry will not rise fully.

SPECIAL OCCASION
Use a little beaten egg
instead of water to glaze
the pastry lid before baking.
Just before serving, pour 2
tablespoons double cream into
the pie through the hole.

● 365 calories/1525 kj per portion

 PREPARATION
Cut a lid for a single
crust pie as follows:

*Invert the pie dish on the rolled-
out pastry and cut round the edge
with a sharp knife to make the lid.
Then cut a strip, the same width as
rim of the dish, from outer edge.*

Rhubarb crumble

SERVES 4-6
750 g/1½ lb rhubarb, cut into
   2.5 cm/1 inch lengths (see
   Watchpoint)
grated zest and juice of 1 small
   orange
50-75 g/2-3 oz soft brown sugar
margarine or butter, for greasing

CRUMBLE TOPPING
175 g/6 oz plain flour
75 g/3 oz butter, diced
50 g/2 oz soft brown sugar
flaked almonds, to decorate
   (optional)

1 Put the rhubarb into a heavy-based enamelled or other lined saucepan (see Did you know). Add the orange zest and juice, cover and cook over low heat until the rhubarb is almost tender. Remove from the heat and stir in sugar to taste, taking care not to break up the rhubarb

Cook's Notes

 TIME
Total preparation and baking time is 1-1¼ hours.

 DID YOU KNOW
Cooked and eaten as fruit, rhubarb is actually classed as a vegetable. It is best cooked in a lined pan so that its high acidic content does not react with the metal.

 WATCHPOINT
Always cut off and discard the crinkly yellow leaves from the ends of the rhubarb stalks; they contain poisonous oxalic acid and must not be eaten.

 FREEZING
Grease a foil dish and prepare the pudding up to the end of stage 4. Wrap and freeze for up to 4 months. To serve: bake from frozen, allowing 15-20 minutes extra baking time.

 VARIATION
Thickly sliced apples make a good alternative when rhubarb is out of season.

●430 calories/1800 kj per portion

pieces. Set the rhubarb aside.
2 Heat the oven to 200C/400F/Gas 6. Grease a 1.5 L/2½ pint ovenproof dish. ✳
3 Make the topping: sift the flour into a large bowl, add the butter and rub it in until the mixture resembles fine breadcrumbs, then stir in the soft brown sugar.
4 Turn the rhubarb into the prepared dish and cover completely with the topping.
5 Scatter the almonds over the top, if using, then bake in the oven for 30 minutes. If liked, brown the topping very briefly under a hot grill.

358

Apple Grasmere

SERVES 6
1.5 kg/3 lb cooking apples, peeled,
 quartered, cored and sliced
175 g/6 oz sugar
150 ml/¼ pint water
butter or margarine, for greasing

TOPPING
175 g/6 oz plain flour
½ teaspoon bicarbonate of soda
1 teaspoon cream of tartar
2 teaspoons ground ginger
50 g/2 oz porridge oats
100 g/4 oz dark soft brown sugar
175 g/6 oz margarine

1 Put the apples into a large, heavy-based saucepan with the sugar and water. Cover and cook gently for 10-15 minutes until reduced to a soft purée. Set aside to cool for about 30 minutes.
2 Meanwhile, heat the oven to 180C/350F/Gas 4. Lightly grease a 1 L/2 pint ovenproof dish.

Cook's Notes

TIME
45-50 minutes prepara-tion, about 30 minutes baking the pudding.

DID YOU KNOW
This recipe comes from the area around Lake Grasmere in England's Lake District. The topping mixture is often baked alone, in a shallow tin, and then served cold as a biscuit, cut into sections.

SERVING IDEAS
Apple Grasmere is usually served cold: the topping becomes crisp as it cools, making a mouthwatering contrast with the soft apple purée underneath. However, the pudding is also delicious hot, when the topping is like a soft crumble – serve with a jug of whipped cream.

VARIATIONS
The ginger topping is delicious over other fruit fillings: use only 1 kg/2 lb apples (reduce the sugar by 50 g/2 oz) and fold 500 g/1 lb raspberries, blackberries or 400 g/14 oz chopped canned apricots into the cooled apple purée before spooning it into the dish at stage 4. Finish the dish as described.

●610 calories/2550 kj per portion

3 Make the topping: sift the flour with the bicarbonate of soda, cream of tartar and ginger. Stir in the oats and brown sugar. Add margarine and rub in with fingertips until mix-ture resembles fine breadcrumbs.
4 Spoon the cooled apple purée into the prepared dish, then top with the oat mixture, spreading it evenly over the apples.
5 Bake in the oven for about 30 minutes, or until topping is firm and browned. Serve hot or cold (see Serving ideas).

Eve's pudding

SERVES 4
500 g/1 lb cooking apples,
    quartered, peeled, cored and
    chopped
50 g/2 oz sugar
butter, for greasing
custard or cream, to serve

TOPPING
75 g/3 oz wholemeal flour
100 g/4 oz soft tub margarine
100 g/4 oz caster sugar
2 eggs, lightly beaten
few drops of almond flavouring
1-2 teaspoons milk
25 g/1 oz self-raising flour
1 teaspoon baking powder

1 Heat the oven to 180C/350F/Gas 4. Butter a 1 L/2 pint ovenproof pie dish.
2 Mix the apples with the sugar, then spread evenly in the prepared dish and press down well (see Cook's tips).
3 Put the wholemeal flour into a bowl. Add the margarine, sugar, eggs, almond flavouring and 1 teaspoon milk, then sift in the self-raising flour and baking powder. Beat together with a wooden spoon for 1-2 minutes, until evenly blended. Beat in the remaining milk, if necessary, to give a soft dropping consistency (see Cook's tips).
4 Spread the mixture over the apples and level the surface. Bake in the oven for 50-60 minutes, until the topping is firm to the touch and the apples are cooked (see Cook's tips).
5 Serve hot, with custard or cream.

Cook's Notes

 TIME
Preparation and baking take about 1¼ hours.

 COOK'S TIPS
Packing the apples down provides a firm base for the topping and helps it rise evenly during baking.

To test for a soft dropping consistency: spoon up some of the mixture, then hold the spoon on its side just above the bowl; the mixture should drop off within a few seconds without the spoon being moved.

Insert a warmed fine skewer through the pudding—the apples should feel tender.

 VARIATIONS
Mix 25-50 g/1-2 oz sultanas or currants with the apples. Add the finely grated zest of 1 orange or lemon to the topping mixture.

●495 calories/2075 kj per portion

MARTIN BRIGDALE

Upside-down pear pudding

SERVES 6
100 g/4 oz self-raising flour
1 teaspoon ground mixed spice
1 teaspoon ground cinnamon
pinch of ground cloves (optional)
100 g/4 oz soft tub margarine
100 g/4 oz light soft brown sugar
2 eggs, lightly beaten
soft tub margarine, for greasing
cream or yoghurt, to serve

TOPPING
400 g/14 oz can pear halves,
   drained
1½ tablespoons caster sugar
50 g/2 oz walnut halves

1 Heat the oven to 170C/325F/Gas 3. Place a baking sheet in the oven to heat. Brush an 850 ml/1½ pint round ovenproof pie dish generously with margarine.
2 Make the topping: blot the pears dry with absorbent paper and reserve. Sprinkle the sugar over the base of the dish. Press 1 walnut half, rounded side down, into the cavity of each pear. Arrange 6 pears in the dish (see Preparation). Place 6 walnut halves, flat side down, in centre of circle of pears. Chop remaining nuts and pear half and sprinkle between the pears.
3 Sift the flour and spices into a large bowl. Add the margarine, brown sugar and eggs and beat with a wooden spoon for 1-2 minutes, until evenly blended. Spread the mixture in the prepared dish, making sure the pears are covered.
4 Bake the pudding in the oven, on the baking sheet, for about 50 minutes until a warmed skewer inserted in the centre comes out clean.
5 Cool the pudding for 1 minute, then turn out on to a warmed serving dish to reveal the topping. Serve hot, with pouring cream.

Cook's Notes

TIME
25 minutes preparation and 50 minutes baking time.

WATCHPOINT
Do not press the walnuts too hard, or the pears will break. Each walnut should fit snugly inside the pear, so the pears can lie flat in the dish.
   Cover with foil after 20 minutes to prevent the Upside-down pear pudding from overbrowning.

●430 calories/1795 kj per portion

PREPARATION
Arrange the pears as below:

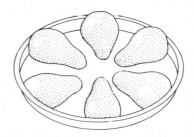

Put 6 pear halves, rounded side up, in the base of the dish with the stalk ends pointing inwards. Space the pears evenly apart and leave centre free for walnuts.

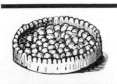

JAMES JACKSON

Crusty-topped plum pudding

SERVES 4
750 g/1½ lb red or purple plums, halved and stoned
5 tablespoons water
½ teaspoon ground cinnamon
sugar, to taste
1 teaspoon cornflour
butter, for greasing
custard or cream, to serve

TOPPING
4-5 large, thick slices white bread, crusts removed
50 g/2 oz softened butter or soft tub margarine
caster sugar, for dusting

1 Place the plums in a heavy-based saucepan. Add 4 tablespoons water and the cinnamon, then cover and cook gently for about 10 minutes, or until the fruit is very soft.
2 Cool the mixture slightly, then puree in a blender. Return the puree to the rinsed-out pan and sweeten to taste with sugar. Cook over moderate heat, stirring frequently, for about 10 minutes or until the puree is well reduced and thickened (see Cook's tip).
3 Meanwhile, heat the oven to 200C/400F/Gas 6. Grease an 850 ml/ 1½ pint ovenproof pie dish. Spread the bread with butter, then cut into neat squares and reserve.
4 When the puree is ready, blend the cornflour smoothly with the remaining tablespoon water and pour into the pan. Bring to the boil, stirring constantly, and cook for 1 minute until very thick.
5 Spoon the puree into the prepared dish, then arrange the bread squares evenly over the top, buttered side up. Bake in the oven for 30 minutes, or until topping is brown and crusty. Sprinkle with caster sugar and serve warm, with custard or pouring cream.

Fruity batter pudding

SERVES 4-6

225 g/8 oz can pineapple rings,
    drained and quartered
425 g/15 oz can apricot halves,
    drained
2 × 215 g/7½ oz cans red cherries,
    drained and stoned
50 g/2 oz seedless raisins
50 g/2 oz plain flour
½ teaspoon ground mixed spice
pinch of salt
50 g/2 oz caster sugar
3 large eggs
150 ml/¼ pint milk
150 ml/¼ pint single cream (see
    Economy)
caster sugar, for dredging
butter, for greasing

1 Heat the oven to 180C/350F/Gas 4. Butter a 1 L/2 pint ovenproof dish which is about 5 cm/2 inches deep. Mix the pineapple, apricots and cherries together, then spread in the prepared dish.

2 Put the raisins into a small saucepan and cover with cold water. Bring to the boil and boil for 1 minute, then drain and sprinkle over the fruits.

3 Sift the flour, spice and salt into a bowl. Stir in the caster sugar, then make a well in the centre and add the eggs. Gradually whisk the dry ingredients into the eggs and continue until smoothly blended. Whisk in the milk and cream a little at a time, to make a thin batter.

4 Pour the batter over the fruits. Bake in the oven for 1-1¼ hours, until the batter is firm to the touch at the centre, slightly puffed at the edges and golden brown all over.

5 Remove the pudding from the oven and cool for at least 15 minutes. Sift caster sugar evenly over the top and serve warm (see Serving ideas).

DON LAST

363

FRED MANCINI

Pear streusel

SERVES 4
4 firm, ripe pears (see Buying guide)
4 tablespoons clear honey
finely grated zest and juice of 1
    large lemon
butter, for greasing

TOPPING
50 g/2 oz butter
100 g/4 oz white breadcrumbs (see
    Cook's tips)
75 g/3 oz Demerara sugar
½ teaspoon ground mixed spice

1 Heat the oven to 190C/375F/Gas 5.
Butter a shallow, round ovenproof
dish which is just large enough to
take 8 pear halves in a single layer.
2 Peel, halve and core the pears,
then arrange cut side down in the
prepared dish. Mix the honey with
the lemon zest and juice, then spoon
or pour over the pear halves.
3 Make the topping: gently melt the
butter, then remove from the heat
and stir in the breadcrumbs, sugar
and ground spice, mixing well.

4 Sprinkle the topping evenly over
the pears. Bake in the oven for about
45 minutes, or until the topping is
golden brown and the pears are
cooked (see Cook's tips). Serve the
pears hot (see Serving ideas).

Cook's Notes

TIME
Preparation and baking
take about 1 hour.

BUYING GUIDE
Choose even-sized des-
sert pears, such as
Williams or Comice. Conference
pears do not have the right
texture for this recipe.

COOK'S TIPS
The breadcrumbs should
be dry, but soft; make
them from a day-old loaf.
The exact cooking time
depends upon the size and
ripeness of the pears. Test them
with a fine skewer: they should
feel soft all the way through.

SERVING IDEAS
Serve the pudding with
cream or custard.
If you want to 'stretch' to 8
servings, allow 1 pear half per
person and top each portion
with a scoop of ice cream.

DID YOU KNOW
Streusel is the German
word for crumble.

●320 calories/1350 kj per portion

Saucy date pudding

SERVES 6

100 g/4 oz margarine
100 g/4 oz light soft brown sugar
finely grated zest of 1 orange
2 eggs, lightly beaten
175 g/6 oz self-raising flour, sifted
100 g/4 oz sugar rolled chopped
    dates (see Buying guide)
extra margarine, for greasing

SAUCE
150 ml/¼ pint water, plus 1
    tablespoon
75 g/3 oz sugar
thinly pared rind of 1 orange
juice of 3 oranges
1 tablespoon cornflour

1 Heat the oven to 190C/375F/Gas 5. Lightly grease a deep 1.25 L/2 pint ovenproof pie dish.
2 Beat the margarine and brown sugar until pale and fluffy, then beat in the orange zest. Add the eggs a little at a time, beating thoroughly after each addition. Using a large metal spoon, fold in the flour and then the sugary chopped dates.
3 Spoon the mixture into the prepared dish and level the surface. Bake in the oven (see Cook's tip) for about 40 minutes, or until a warmed fine skewer inserted into the centre of the pudding comes out clean.
4 About 15 minutes before the pudding is ready, make the sauce: pour 150 ml/¼ pint water into a heavy-based saucepan. Add the sugar and orange rind. Stir over low heat until the sugar has dissolved, then bring the syrup slowly to the boil and simmer for 5 minutes.
5 Remove from the heat and discard the orange rind. Pour in the orange juice, then return the pan to low heat. Blend the cornflour and 1 tablespoon water to a smooth paste, then stir thoroughly into the orange syrup.
6 Bring slowly to the boil and simmer gently, stirring constantly, for 3-4 minutes, until the sauce is smooth and thick. Remove the sauce from the heat and pour into a warmed small serving jug.
7 Serve the date pudding hot, accompanied by the orange sauce.

Cook's Notes

TIME
50-60 minutes (including baking the pudding and making the orange sauce).

COOK'S TIP
Check the pudding towards the end of cooking time and cover it with greaseproof paper, if necessary, to prevent it overbrowning.

BUYING GUIDE
These dates are available in 250 g/8½ oz packets from most large supermarkets. They are ideal for this recipe, but if difficult to obtain use pressed dates (sold in blocks) and chop them yourself.

● 440 calories/1850 kj per portion

MARTIN BRIGDALE

Gooseberry puff

SERVES 4
500 g/1 lb gooseberries, topped and tailed if fresh, defrosted if frozen (see Cook's tips)
100 g/4 oz caster sugar

TOPPING
2 eggs, separated
150 ml/¼ pint soured cream
50 g/2 oz ground almonds
25 g/1 oz caster sugar
15 g/½ oz plain flour, sifted

1 Heat the oven to 180C/350F/Gas 4.
2 Place the gooseberries in a 1 L/ 2 pint soufflé or other ovenproof dish. Sprinkle in the sugar and mix well. Cover the dish and bake in the oven for about 30 minutes, or until the gooseberries are slightly soft-ened and a thin syrup has formed (see Cook's tips).
3 About 5 minutes before the end of cooking time, make the topping: beat the egg yolks together with a wooden spoon. Slowly beat in the cream, almonds, sugar and flour.
4 In a clean dry bowl, whisk the egg whites until standing in stiff peaks. Using a large metal spoon, fold the egg whites into the egg yolk and almond mixture.
5 Spoon the topping evenly over the gooseberries. Return to the oven and bake for a further 30 minutes, or until the topping is risen and golden. Serve at once, while topping is light and puffy.

366

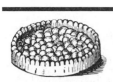

DON LAST

Candy coconut sponge

SERVES 4
100 g/4 oz self-raising flour
50 g/2 oz caster sugar
50 g/2 oz butter
1 large egg, beaten
1-2 tablespoons milk
margarine or butter, for greasing

TOPPING
25 g/1 oz margarine or butter
75 g/3 oz caster sugar
75 g/3 oz desiccated coconut
2 tablespoons evaporated milk or
single cream
½ teaspoon vanilla essence
glacé cherries, to decorate

1 Heat the oven to 180C/350F/Gas 4. Grease an 850 ml/1½ pint pie dish.

2 Sift the flour into a bowl. Stir in the sugar, then rub in the butter. Stir in the egg and milk: the mixture should have a fairly soft consistency.

3 Spread the sponge mixture in the greased dish, then bake in the oven for about 25 minutes until firm to the touch when lightly pressed in the centre.

4 Meanwhile, make the topping: melt the margarine in a saucepan; remove from the heat and stir in the sugar, coconut, evaporated milk and vanilla essence.

5 Increase the oven temperature to 200C/400F/Gas 6. Spread the coconut topping evenly over the sponge. Decorate with glacé cherries, then return the pudding to the oven and bake for 6-10 minutes until the topping is browned. Serve hot.

Cook's Notes

TIME
Total preparation and cooking time is 1 hour.

VARIATIONS
Mix 1-2 tablespoons rolled oats with the coconut for a different texture.
Use almond essence in place of vanilla, or flavour the sponge with 1 tablespoon unsweetened strong black coffee.

SERVING IDEAS
This sponge is delicious with chilled single cream or evaporated milk, or with hot custard.

●510 calories/2125 kj per portion

367

CHRIS KNAGGS

Coffee marble sponge

SERVES 6-8

175 g/6 oz margarine or butter, softened
175 g/6 oz caster sugar
3 large eggs, beaten
175 g/6 oz self-raising flour, sifted
1 teaspoon vanilla flavouring
1 teaspoon coffee and chicory essence (see Watchpoint)
margarine or butter, for greasing

1 Grease a 1.5 L/2½ pint pudding basin. Cut a circle of greaseproof paper or foil 7.5 cm/3 inches larger all round than top of basin. Grease 1 side, then make a 1 cm/½ inch pleat down the centre.

2 Beat the margarine and caster sugar together until pale and fluffy. Add the eggs, a little at a time, beating vigorously after each addition. Using a large metal spoon, fold in the flour.

3 Put half the mixture into a separate bowl and stir in the vanilla. Stir the coffee and chicory essence into the other half.

4 Place alternate spoonfuls of the 2 mixtures in the prepared basin. Swirl a skewer through the mixture, first one way, then the other. Level the surface.

5 Place the covering, greased side down, on top of the basin. Fold the edges over the rim of the basin and tie securely with fine string, making sure all the edges are caught under the string.

6 Stand the basin in a large, heavy-based saucepan and pour in enough boiling water to come halfway up the sides of the basin. Cover with a well-fitting lid and boil the pudding gently for 3 hours. Check the water level regularly during cooking and top up with more boiling water, as necessary.

7 Protecting your hands with oven gloves, lift the basin out of the pan. Leave for 5 minutes, then remove the covering. Turn the pudding out on to a warmed dish and serve.

Cook's Notes

 TIME
20 minutes preparation, plus 3 hours cooking.

WATCHPOINT
Coffee and chicory essence is essential—ordinary coffee flavouring gives taste, but not colour.

 SERVING IDEAS
Serve the pudding with Mocha sauce: melt 75 g/3 oz plain chocolate in 600 ml/1 pint milk over low heat, then stir in 50 g/2 oz seedless raisins and 1 tablespoon coffee and chicory essence. Blend 1 tablespoon cornflour with 2 tablespoons milk, then stir in the chocolate mixture. Return to pan and simmer, stirring, for 1-2 minutes. Sweeten to taste with sugar and serve hot.

●520 calories/2185 kj per portion

Raisin sponge pudding

SERVES 4

350 g/12 oz large seedless raisins
(see Watchpoints), soaked
overnight in 3 tablespoons
whisky or rum
100 g/4 oz butter, softened
100 g/4 oz caster sugar
grated zest of 1 lemon
2 large eggs
100 g/4 oz self-raising flour, sifted
extra softened butter, for greasing
cream or custard, to serve

1 Brush a 1.25 L/2 pint pudding
basin generously with butter.
Refrigerate until the butter is firm,
then butter again.

2 Line the basin with the raisins,
overlapping them slightly and
making sure there are no gaps.
(Otherwise the sponge mixture will
seep through and spoil the look of
the pudding.) ⚠ Refrigerate for 10-
15 minutes to set the raisins in place.

3 Meanwhile, cut a circle of greaseproof paper or foil 7.5 cm/3 inches
larger all round than the basin top.
Grease 1 side, then make a 1 cm/½
inch pleat down the centre.

4 Beat the butter with the sugar and
lemon zest until pale and fluffy. Add
the eggs, one at a time, beating
thoroughly between each addition.
Using a large metal spoon, fold in
the flour.

5 Spoon the mixture into the lined
basin. Place the covering, greased
side down, on top. Fold the edges
over the rim of the basin and tie
securely in place with fine string,
making sure all the edges are caught
under the string.

6 Place in a large, heavy-based
saucepan and pour in enough hot
water to come halfway up the sides
of the basin. Bring slowly to the
boil, then cover with a well-fitting
lid and steam for 2 hours. Check
during cooking and top up with
more boiling water, as necessary.

7 Protecting your hands with oven
gloves, lift the basin out of the pan.
Let the pudding stand for 5 minutes,
then remove the covering. Turn the
pudding out on to a warmed serving
dish and serve at once, with cream
or custard.

DON LAST

Cook's Notes

TIME
30 minutes preparation,
including lining the
pudding basin with raisins, and
2 hours steaming.

WATCHPOINTS
You need large seedless
raisins for lining the
basin. If they are stuck together,
separate before soaking.
Line the basin patiently and
carefully for the best result.

PRESSURE COOKING
Stand pudding on a
trivet in the cooker and
pour in 850 ml/1½ pints boiling
water. Steam without weights
for 15 minutes. Bring up to low
(L) pressure and cook for 30
minutes. Reduce pressure
slowly. Allow 5 minutes extra
cooking time if using foil
covering.

●595 calories/2475 kj per portion

BAKING

Homemade cakes, biscuits and breads always go down well with the family, either as a regular part of family meals or as occasional tea-time treats. Everybody loves the smell of bread or a cake baking in the oven, and it's impossible to resist one of those hot little biscuits left to cool in the kitchen!

There are savoury as well as sweet baked items included in this chapter. Some of the flavoursome savoury breads would make a change from French or wholemeal bread to serve as an accompaniment to any of the soups, salads or snacks earlier in the book.

The variety of recipes included means there's one for every occasion and every taste. Children will love crunchy Peanut Biscuits, Gingerbread and Muesli Munchies, any of which would make an ideal treat to drop into a school lunchbox. You could change the style of your breakfasts by serving warmed muffins or Hot Cross Buns (not necessarily at the appropriate time of year!) and you could serve some of the delicious cakes as main meal desserts. On the days when you serve a traditional English tea, you will find any number of scones, teabreads and cakes to choose from. Scones are best served warm (straight out of the oven if possible), or you could really spoil yourselves and indulge in a cream tea of scones, whipped cream and strawberry jam. Serve butter with teabreads and gingerbread, if liked. Teabreads may also be served with jam or honey or, in the traditional northern way, with cheese.

Among the cake recipes you will find some familiar traditional cakes, such as Old-Fashioned Seed Cake and a Boiled Fruit Cake, as well as more modern ones, such as the American Carrot Cake. Old favourites like Chelsea Buns (though a healthier wheatmeal variety) are also included.

If you are short of time, it might be worth your while baking cakes, biscuits or breads in large batches and storing some in the freezer so that they can be removed and thawed when required. You never know when visitors may drop in for tea and it's reassuring to think there are some scones or a cake waiting in the freezer. Otherwise, most items will keep well in an airtight container.

Baking biscuits, cakes and breads need not be as time-consuming as you might expect. The recipes given here are mostly quite simple and very easy to follow so you can be sure of success, and you'll be surprised just how quickly you can make some of them. There are no elaborately decorated cakes that need time and patience spent on them, and the ingredients used are mostly storecupboard items. Dried fruits and nuts feature quite strongly, as you might expect, but there are also recipes using fresh fruits like apple and banana, and some of the savoury recipes contain cheese and even some vegetables. The variety is enormous so you should have no trouble finding a recipe to suit your needs. Baking is a pleasure that should be matched only by your enjoyment in eating what you have produced.

FRED MANCINI

Orange yoghurt cake

MAKES 8-10 SLICES
150 g/5 oz natural yoghurt
grated zest of 1 orange
225 g/8 oz caster sugar
2 eggs, lightly beaten
225 g/8 oz self-raising flour, sifted
melted fat or vegetable oil, for
   greasing

TO DECORATE
thinly pared rind of ½ orange
100 g/4 oz icing sugar, sifted
2-3 teaspoons warm water

1 Heat the oven to 180C/350F/Gas 4. Grease a 1.25-1.5 L/2-2½ pint loaf tin. Line the base of the tin with greaseproof paper, then grease the paper.
2 Put the yoghurt into a bowl, then stir in the orange zest and caster sugar. Using a wooden spoon, beat in the eggs a little at a time, then

beat in the flour. (The mixture will be runny.)
3 Pour the mixture into the prepared tin. Bake in the oven for 45-50 minutes, until a warmed fine skewer inserted into the centre comes out clean.
4 Cool the cake for 5 minutes, then turn out of the tin and peel off the lining paper. Turn the cake the right way up, then leave on a wire rack to cool completely.
5 Meanwhile, cut the orange rind

into matchstick-sized strips. Drop the strips into boiling water and simmer for 1 minute. Drain, then rinse under cold running water and dry thoroughly on absorbent paper.
6 When the cake is cold, make the icing: blend the icing sugar with enough warm water to give a stiff coating consistency. Using a palette knife, spread the icing over the top of the cake (see Cook's tip). Leave the icing to set, ⚠ then decorate with the strips of orange rind.

Cook's Notes

 TIME
10-15 minutes preparation, plus 45-50 minutes baking. Allow 1½ hours for cooling, icing and decorating.

 STORAGE
The un-iced cake will keep for up to 1 week in an airtight container. The iced cake is best served within 48 hours, as the icing dries out.

 COOK'S TIP
Dip the knife in hot water as you work; this gives a smooth, shiny finish.

⚠ **WATCHPOINT**
Do not add the strips of orange until the icing is set, or the colour will run and spoil the look of the cake.

●295 calories/1225 kj per slice

Old-fashioned seed cake

MAKES 12 SLICES
100 g/4 oz plain flour
100 g/4 oz self-raising flour
pinch of salt
175 g/6 oz butter, softened
175 g/6 oz caster sugar
3 large eggs, lightly beaten
2 tablespoons milk
2 teaspoons caraway seeds
2 tablespoons sugar, to finish
vegetable oil, for greasing

1 Heat the oven to 170C/325F/Gas 3. Grease a 1.75 L/3 pint (1 kg/2 lb) loaf tin. Line the tin with greaseproof paper, then grease the paper.
2 Sift the flours with the salt.
3 In a separate bowl, beat the butter and sugar until very pale and fluffy. Add the eggs, a little at a time, beating the mixture thoroughly after each addition.
4 Using a large metal spoon, fold in the sifted flours, then stir in milk. Add the caraway seeds and gently fold them in, making sure they are evenly distributed. Turn the mixture into the prepared tin and level the surface, then make a shallow hollow in the centre. Sprinkle the sugar over the top.
5 Bake in the oven for 1-1¼ hours (see Cook's tip), or until firm to the touch and a warmed fine skewer inserted into the centre of the cake comes out clean.
6 Cool the cake for 10-15 minutes, then turn out of the tin and peel off the lining paper. Place the cake the right way up on a wire rack and then leave to cool completely before slicing and serving.

DON LAST

Cook's Notes

TIME
15 minutes preparation and 1¼ hours baking. Allow 2-3 hours cooling time for the cooked cake.

STORAGE
The cake (or any left-over slices) will keep for 2-3 weeks stored in an airtight container in a cool place.

COOK'S TIP
Check the cake after 1 hour's baking. Cover with greaseproof paper, if necessary, to prevent over-browning. Unlike sponges, this cake does not rise evenly, so do not worry if the top peaks and cracks slightly.

• 200 calories/850 kj per slice

DID YOU KNOW
Seed cake is an old-fashioned English recipe using a Madeira mixture with caraway seeds added.
Traditionally a round cake, this variation is made in a loaf tin so that it can be cut into slices or thick finger shapes. Serve, unbuttered, with either tea or coffee.

FRED MANCINI

Banana and Brazil cake

MAKES 10 SLICES
75 g/3 oz margarine
100 g/4 oz light soft brown sugar
1 egg, lightly beaten
2 small bananas, mashed
100 g/4 oz plain flour
1 teaspoon baking powder
vegetable oil, for greasing

ICING
1 tablespoon clear honey
75 g/3 oz icing sugar, sifted
1-2 teaspoons cold water
25 g/1 oz shelled Brazil nuts,
  coarsely chopped

1 Heat the oven to 170C/325F/Gas 3. Lightly grease an 850 ml/1½ pint (500 g/1 lb) loaf tin; line the base with greaseproof paper, then grease the paper.

2 Put the margarine, sugar, egg and mashed bananas into a large bowl. Sift in the flour and baking powder, then beat with a wooden spoon for 1-2 minutes until evenly blended.

3 Turn the mixture into the prepared tin and level the surface. Bake in the oven for 1-1¼ hours, until browned and firm to the touch (see Cook's tips).

4 Cool the cake for 10 minutes, then turn out of the tin and carefully peel off the lining paper. Place the right way up on a wire rack and leave to cool completely.

5 Make the icing: mix the honey into the icing sugar with a large metal spoon, then stir in just enough water to give a thick pouring consistency (see Cook's tips).

6 Place a plate under the wire rack. Spoon the icing over the top of the cake, allowing it to run down the sides. Leave for 10 minutes to firm slightly, then sprinkle with the nuts. Leave to set before cutting.

Cook's Notes

TIME
20 minutes preparation, plus 1-1¼ hours baking. Allow extra time for cooling, icing and setting.

COOK'S TIPS
To test that the cake is cooked, insert a warmed fine skewer into the centre: it should come out free of any sticky uncooked mixture.

Add the water a few drops at a time and mix well. If you do make the icing too thin, sift in a little extra icing sugar. The icing becomes transparent when set.

STORAGE
The uniced cake will keep for up to 6 days in an airtight container.

●190 calories/800 kj per slice

Walnut cake

MAKES 8 SLICES
225 g/8 oz walnuts, ground
6 large eggs
225 g/8 oz sugar
225 g/8 oz plain flour, sifted
1 tablespoon instant coffee
   granules (see Preparation)
few drops vanilla flavouring
butter, for greasing
walnut halves, to decorate

ICING
50 g/2 oz icing sugar
100 g/4 oz butter, softened
few drops vanilla flavouring
1 tablespoon instant coffee
   granules (see Preparation)
25 g/1 oz walnuts, ground

1 Heat the oven to 180C/350F/Gas 4. Grease a 23 cm/9 inch round cake tin. Line with greaseproof paper and grease the paper.
2 Put the eggs and sugar into a large bowl and whisk together until pale and fluffy and doubled in volume.
3 Gradually fold in the ground walnuts and flour alternately, then thoroughly stir in the dissolved coffee and vanilla flavouring.
4 Spoon the mixture into the tin and level surface. Bake in oven for 1 hour 10 minutes until a warmed, fine skewer inserted into the centre comes out clean.
5 Cool the cake for 5 minutes, then remove from the tin and peel off the lining paper. Place the right way up on a wire rack. Leave the cake to cool completely.
6 Meanwhile, make the icing: sift the icing sugar into a bowl, then add the butter. Beat until smooth and creamy. Beat in the vanilla flavouring and dissolved coffee and ground walnuts.
7 Place the cake on a serving plate and swirl the icing over the top. Decorate with walnut halves.

JAMES JACKSON

Raspberry layer cake

MAKES 6-8 SLICES
225 g/8 oz plain flour
4 teaspoons baking powder
¼ teaspoon salt
75 g/ 3 oz butter, diced
75 g/3 oz caster sugar
1 egg, beaten
3 tablespoons milk
extra butter, for greasing

TO FINISH
500 g/1 lb raspberries
75 g/3 oz caster sugar
150 ml/¼ pint whipping cream

1 Heat the oven to 190C/375F/Gas 5. Grease a loose-based, deep 20 cm/ 8 inch round cake tin.
2 Make the cake: sift the flour, baking powder and salt into a bowl. Add the butter and rub it in with your fingertips until the mixture resembles breadcrumbs. Stir in the sugar, then make a well in the centre. Add the egg and 2 table-spoons milk and mix with a fork to a soft scone-like dough, adding re-maining milk if necessary.
3 Turn the dough out on to a lightly floured surface and knead briefly, then pat out to a round. Place in the prepared tin and press gently to fit the base. Bake above centre of oven for 25 minutes, or until well risen and golden brown.
4 Cool the cake for 5 minutes, then remove from the tin and place on a wire rack. Using a serrated knife, cut the cake horizontally in half. Separate the halves and leave to cool completely.
5 Meanwhile, reserve 6-8 whole raspberries to decorate the cake. Place the remaining berries in a bowl and crush lightly. Sprinkle over the sugar and mix gently. Cover and reserve until required.
6 To serve: stir the crushed raspber-ries, then spoon half over each of the cold layers of the cake. Transfer the bottom layer to a serving plate. Place the remaining layer, raspberry side up, on top. Whip the cream until standing in soft peaks, then pipe or spoon around top edge of cake. Decorate with the reserved raspberries and serve as soon as possible (see Cook's tip).

THEO BERGSTROM

MICHAEL KAY

Carrot and almond cake

MAKES 6-8 SLICES
3 large eggs, separated
2 drops almond flavouring
grated zest of 1 orange
100 g/4 oz caster sugar
1 tablespoon orange-flavoured
   liqueur or orange juice
175 g/6 oz carrots, cooked, drained
   and puréed
100 g/4 oz ground almonds
50 g/2 oz ground rice
15 g/½ oz flaked almonds
icing sugar, for dusting
sweetened whipped cream or
   natural yoghurt, to serve
margarine or butter, for greasing

1 Heat the oven to 170C/325F/Gas 3. Generously grease a loose-based, deep 18 cm/7 inch round tin.
2 Put the egg yolks, almond flavouring and orange zest in a large bowl and whisk together with a hand-held electric whisk (see Cook's tips). Add the caster sugar, a little at a time, and continue whisking for a further 3-5 minutes, until the mixture is pale and mousse-like.
3 Whisk in the liqueur and carrot purée, then stir in the ground almonds and ground rice.
4 In a clean, dry bowl and using clean beaters, whisk the egg whites until standing in stiff peaks. Using a large metal spoon, stir one-third of the egg whites into the carrot and almond mixture, then fold in the remainder.
5 Turn the mixture into the prepared tin, level the surface and sprinkle the flaked almonds around the edge. Bake in the oven just above the centre, for 55-60 minutes, until a warmed fine skewer inserted in the centre comes out clean.
6 Cool the cake for 15 minutes, then remove from the tin (see Cook's tips) and leave on a wire rack to cool completely.
7 Sift a little icing sugar over the top of the cake and serve with a bowl of sweetened cream handed round separately.

Cook's Notes

 TIME
25 minutes preparation, plus 1 hour baking. Cooling takes about 2 hours.

 COOK'S TIPS
You can use a rotary whisk instead, but allow extra time for beating.
   Use a palette knife to loosen the cake from the tin.

STORAGE
This soft, moist cake will keep for several days in an airtight container.

 DID YOU KNOW
When sugar was a luxury, carrots were often used to give sweetness. Cakes made with carrots are still popular today, especially in Switzerland and the United States.

●265 calories/1125 kj per slice

377

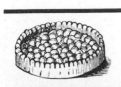

MARTIN BRIGDALE

Cider cake

MAKES 6-8 SLICES
300 g/10 oz self-raising flour
2 teaspoons ground cinnamon
175 g/6 oz light soft brown sugar
175 g/6 oz seedless raisins
125 ml/4 fl oz vegetable oil
2 eggs, lightly beaten
175 ml/6 fl oz cider
vegetable oil, for greasing

TOPPING
1-2 cooking apples, peeled, cored, halved and sliced
lemon curd, to glaze

1 Heat the oven to 180C/350F/Gas 4. Lightly grease a deep, loose-based 20 cm/8 inch round cake tin. Line the sides and base with greaseproof paper, then lightly grease the paper with vegetable oil.

2 Sift the flour and cinnamon into a large bowl. Add the sugar, raisins, oil, eggs and cider and beat together with a wooden spoon until evenly blended.
3 Pour the mixture into the prepared tin. Arrange the apple slices over the top. Bake in the oven for about 1½ hours, until a fine, warmed skewer inserted into the centre comes out clean. Cover with greaseproof paper during baking if the apples show signs of overbrowning.
4 Cool the cake for 5 minutes, then remove from the tin and peel off the lining paper. Place the right way up on a wire rack. ✳ Brush the apples with lemon curd, then leave the cake to cool completely.

Pineapple boiled fruit cake

MAKES 8-12 SLICES

425 g/15¼ oz can pineapple slices,
   cubes or rings
225 g/8 oz sugar
500 g/1 lb dried mixed fruit
1 teaspoon ground ginger
1 tablespoon lemon juice
100 g/4 oz margarine or butter,
   diced
2 eggs, lightly beaten
1 tablespoon finely chopped
   drained stem ginger
225 g/8 oz self-raising flour
225 g/8 oz plain flour
½ teaspoon bicarbonate of soda
1 tablespoon boiling water
vegetable oil, for greasing

1 Heat the oven to 180C/350F/Gas 4.
2 Purée the pineapple and its liquid in a blender, then pour into a large, heavy-based saucepan. Add the sugar, dried fruit, ground ginger and lemon juice, then bring to the boil and boil for 3 minutes. Remove from the heat, stir in the margarine and leave to cool for 10 minutes.
3 Meanwhile, grease a deep 22 cm/ 8½ inch round cake tin, line the base and sides with greaseproof paper, then lightly grease the paper.
4 Add the eggs and chopped ginger to the boiled pineapple mixture, then sift in the flours. Dissolve the bicarbonate of soda in the boiling water and add to the mixture. Stir vigorously until evenly blended.
5 Turn the mixture into the prepared tin and level the surface. Bake in the oven for about 1½ hours, or until a warmed fine skewer inserted into the centre of the cake comes out clean.
6 Cool the cake for 5 minutes, then turn out of the tin and carefully peel off the lining paper. Put the cake, the right way up, on a wire rack and leave to cool (see Cook's tip).

CHRIS KNAGGS

Chunky apple cake

MAKES 6-8 SLICES

225 g/8 oz plain flour
2 teaspoons baking powder
½ teaspoon ground allspice
¼ teaspoon freshly grated nutmeg (optional)
100 g/4 oz margarine or butter, softened
175 g/6 oz light soft brown sugar
2 eggs, beaten
50 g/2 oz sultanas
350 g/12 oz cooking apples, diced (see Preparation)
25 g/1 oz Demerara sugar
vegetable oil, for greasing

1 Heat the oven to 180C/350F/Gas 4. Grease a deep 20 cm/8 inch round cake tin with a loose base. Line the sides and base with greaseproof paper, then grease the paper.

2 Sift the flour into a bowl. Sift in the baking powder, allspice and nutmeg, if using, then stir to mix thoroughly.

3 Using a wooden spoon or hand-held electric whisk, beat the margarine and soft brown sugar together until pale and fluffy. Add the eggs, a little at a time, beating thoroughly after each addition. If the mixture begins to curdle add 1 tablespoon flour mixture with the next addition of egg.

4 Using a large metal spoon, fold in the flour mixture, followed by the sultanas and two-thirds of the diced apples. Turn into the prepared tin and level the surface.

5 Scatter the remaining apples evenly over the surface, then sprinkle over the Demerara sugar. Bake the cake in the oven for about 1½ hours, until the top is firm at the centre. Cover with greaseproof paper after 1 hour to prevent scorching.

6 Let the cake cool for 10 minutes, then remove from the tin and peel off the lining paper. Leave on a wire rack to cool completely.

Cook's Notes

TIME
1 hour preparation, then 1½ hours baking, plus cooling time.

PREPARATION
To cut the apples into small dice:

Peel, quarter and core the apples, then cut into 5 mm/¼ inch thick slices. Stack 2 or 3 slices and cut lengthways into thick strips. Give a half turn and make several parallel cuts across the strips.

● 455 calories/1900 kj per slice

Spiced marble cake

MAKES 8 SLICES
175 g/6 oz self-raising flour
175 g/6 oz margarine
175 g/6 oz caster sugar
3 eggs, beaten
½ teaspoon ground mixed spice
½ teaspoon ground cinnamon
¼ teaspoon freshly grated nutmeg
2 teaspoons black treacle (see Cook's tips)
2 teaspoons custard powder
melted margarine or vegetable oil, for greasing

FUDGE ICING
50 g/2 oz margarine or butter
50 g/2 oz dark soft brown sugar
2 tablespoons milk
75 g/3 oz icing sugar
½ teaspoon vanilla flavouring

GRAHAM YOUNG

1 Heat the oven to 170C/325F/Gas 3. Grease a deep 15 cm/6 inch round cake tin. Line the sides and base of the tin with a double thickness of greaseproof paper, then grease the paper.
2 Sift the flour into a large bowl. Add the margarine, caster sugar and eggs. Mix well with a wooden spoon, then beat for 2-3 minutes until well blended. (Or, use a hand-held electric whisk and beat for 1 minute only.)
3 Spoon one-third of the mixture into a separate bowl and thoroughly beat in the spices, treacle and custard powder.
4 Place a large spoonful of the treacle mixture in the prepared tin, followed by a large spoonful of the plain mixture. Continue in this way until both mixtures are used up. Level the surface, then make a slight hollow in the centre. Draw the blade of a knife once through the mixture, in a clockwise direction.
5 Bake the cake in the oven for 1-1¼ hours, until a warmed fine skewer inserted in the centre comes out clean. Cool for 5 minutes, then turn out of the tin on to a wire rack. Leave to cool completely (see Cook's tips).
6 Meanwhile, make the icing: put the margarine, brown sugar and milk in a heavy-based saucepan. Stir over low heat until the

margarine has melted and the sugar has dissolved, then bring slowly to the boil. Remove from the heat.
7 Sift the icing sugar into a bowl, then gradually stir in the melted mixture. Mix well, then stir in the vanilla flavouring. Leave to cool,

stirring occasionally, for about 20 minutes.
8 When the cake is cold, remove the lining paper then place the right way up on a serving plate. Beat the icing, spread it on top and mark decoratively (see Preparation).

Cook's Notes

 TIME
20-25 minutes, then 1-1¼ hours baking, plus cooling time for the cake. Allow 10 minutes, plus cooling time for the icing.

 PREPARATION
Use a round-bladed knife to spread the icing over the top of the cake. You can mark the icing in a diamond pattern as shown in the photograph or swirl it by moving the flat side of the blade in a circular direction.

 STORAGE
You can store this cake, iced or not, in an airtight container for several days. It will

stay deliciously soft and moist for all this time.

 COOK'S TIPS
Warm the treacle by standing the tin in a bowl of hot water for a few minutes. This will make it easier to measure and incorporate into the cake mixture.
Because the cake is very spongy, it is best not to remove the lining paper until the cake is cold.

! **WATCHPOINT**
Resist the temptation to overswirl the mixture, or the marbled effect will be lost.

●470 calories/1975 kj per slice

Saffron honey cake

MAKES 8 SLICES
6 saffron strands (see Buying guide)
4 tablespoons milk
175 g/6 oz plain flour
1 tablespoon baking powder
100 g/4 oz butter, softened
50 g/2 oz caster sugar
2 tablespoons clear honey
2 eggs, lightly beaten
50 g/2 oz cut mixed peel
75 g/3 oz sultanas
vegetable oil, for greasing

ICING
10 saffron strands
1 tablespoon boiling water
200 g/7 oz icing sugar
1-2 tablespoons lemon juice

1 Heat the oven to 180C/350F/Gas 4. Grease a deep 18 cm/7 inch round cake tin, line sides and base with greaseproof paper; grease paper.

2 Crush the 6 saffron strands for the cake between your fingers and put into a small, heavy-based saucepan with the milk. Bring just to the boil, then remove from heat and leave to stand for 20 minutes.
3 Sift the flour with the baking powder and reserve.
4 Beat the butter, sugar and honey until pale and fluffy. Beat in the eggs, a little at a time, adding 1 tablespoon sifted flour if mixture shows signs of curdling. Fold in the sifted flour.
5 Strain the saffron milk, then stir into cake mixture, 1 tablespoon at a time. Fold in the peel and sultanas. Turn mixture into the prepared tin and level surface.
6 Bake in oven for 65 minutes, or until a warmed fine skewer inserted into the centre comes out clean.
7 Meanwhile, put the 10 saffron strands for the icing into a small bowl with the boiling water and leave to stand until required.
8 Cool the cake for 5 minutes, then turn out of the tin and peel off the lining paper. Turn cake right way up and leave it on a wire rack to cool completely.

9 Sift the icing sugar into a large bowl and stir in 1 tablespoon lemon juice. Strain the saffron water, then stir into the icing until evenly coloured. Stir in remaining lemon juice if necessary, to give a thick pouring consistency.
10 Place a large plate under the rack. Pour icing over cake, smooth with a palette knife and leave to set before serving (see Storage).

Cook's Notes

 TIME
35 minutes preparation, 65 minutes baking, plus cooling and icing.

 BUYING GUIDE
Saffron strands are available from most delicatessens, supermarkets and Indian food shops.

 STORAGE
Store in airtight container for up to 3 days.

●380 calories/1575 kj per slice

JAMES JACKSON

Nutty chocolate triangles

MAKES 8
75 g/3 oz plain flour
25 g/1 oz cocoa powder
½ teaspoon baking powder
pinch of salt
75 g/3 oz margarine
75 g/3 oz light soft brown sugar
75 ml/3 fl oz golden syrup (see
    Cook's tips)
¼ teaspoon vanilla flavouring
2 eggs
vegetable oil, for greasing

TO FINISH
3 tablespoons hazelnut chocolate
    spread
chopped roasted hazelnuts

1 Heat the oven to 180C/350F/Gas 4. Grease an 18 cm/7 inch square tin, about 2.5 cm/1 inch deep. Line the base with greaseproof paper, then lightly grease the paper.

Cook's Notes

 TIME
15 minutes preparation and 30-35 minutes baking plus cooling and finishing.

 STORAGE
The cold (unfinished) cake can be wrapped in cling film and stored in an airtight container for 4 days.

 COOK'S TIPS
Stand the container in a bowl of hot water for 5 minutes. This makes the syrup easier to measure.
Lay a clean tea-towel over the wire rack to prevent the mesh marking the soft cake.

● 240 calories/1000 kj per triangle

2 Sift flour, cocoa, baking powder and salt into a bowl and reserve.
3 Beat the margarine, sugar and syrup until pale and fluffy, then beat in the vanilla. Beat in the eggs, one at a time, adding 1 tablespoon flour mixture with each egg. Stir in remaining flour mixture with a wooden spoon, then beat briefly until smooth and evenly blended.
4 Pour mixture into prepared tin, level the surface, then make a hollow in the centre. Bake in the oven for 30-35 minutes, or until springy to the touch. (Cover with greaseproof paper towards end of baking to avoid overbrowning.)
5 Cool the cake for 5 minutes, then run a palette knife around the sides, turn out on to a wire rack (see Cook's tips) and peel off lining paper. Turn the cake right way up and leave it to cool completely.
6 To finish: trim off crusty edges, then cover top of cake with hazelnut spread. Cut the cake into 4 squares then cut each square in half diagonally to make 8 triangles. Decorate the tops of the chocolate triangles with chopped roasted hazelnuts.

MICHAEL KAY

Spiced honey bars

MAKES 16 BARS
100 g/4 oz self-raising flour
1 teaspoon ground cinnamon
1 teaspoon ground mixed spice
1 teaspoon ground ginger (optional, see Cook's tip)
1 teaspoon bicarbonate of soda
100 g/4 oz wholemeal flour
225 g/8 oz clear honey
grated zest and juice of 1 small orange
125 ml/4 fl oz vegetable oil
75 g/3 oz soft brown sugar
2 eggs, well beaten
25 g/1 oz flaked almonds
melted margarine or vegetable oil, for greasing

1 Heat the oven to 180C/350F/Gas 4. Grease a 22 cm/8½ inch square cake tin, which is about 5 cm/2 inches deep. Line the base with grease-proof paper and then grease the paper.

2 Sift the self-raising flour with the ground spices and bicarbonate of soda into a large bowl. Stir in the wholemeal flour, then set aside.

3 Pour the honey into a large bowl. Measure the orange juice and make up to 150 ml/¼ pint with boiling water then add to the honey and stir with a wooden spoon until blended. Stir in the oil, brown sugar, eggs and orange zest.

4 Pour the honey mixture on to the flour mixture and mix thoroughly to make a smooth batter. Pour the batter into the prepared tin and sprinkle the almonds over the top. Bake the cake in the oven [!] for 50-55 minutes, until well risen and springy to the touch in the centre.

5 Cool the baked cake in the tin for 5 minutes, then run a palette knife around the edge, turn out on to a wire rack and peel off the lining paper. [!] Turn the cake the right way up. Leave to cool completely, then cut into 16 bars.

Gingerbread

MAKES 16 SQUARES
175 g/6 oz margarine
200 g/7 oz golden syrup
150 g/5 oz black treacle
225 g/8 oz dark soft brown sugar
450 g/1 lb plain flour
1 tablespoon ground ginger
1 tablespoon baking powder
1 teaspoon bicarbonate of soda
1 teaspoon salt
1 egg, lightly beaten
300 ml/½ pint milk
melted margarine, for greasing

1 Heat the oven to 180C/350F/Gas 4. Grease a deep 23 cm/9 inch square cake tin with a loose base. Line the sides and base of the tin with greaseproof paper, then grease the paper.

2 Put the margarine, syrup, treacle and sugar into a heavy-based saucepan and heat gently, stirring, until the margarine has just melted. **!** Allow to cool slightly. **!**

3 Meanwhile, sift the flour, ginger, baking powder, bicarbonate of soda and salt into a large bowl, then make a well in the centre.

4 Add the egg, milk and melted mixture to the dry ingredients and mix with a wooden spoon until smoothly blended. Pour into the prepared tin and bake in the oven for about 1½ hours, until just firm to the touch.

5 Cool for 20 minutes, then remove from the tin and peel off the lining paper. Leave on a wire rack to cool completely. Wrap in foil and store in an airtight tin for 1 week before cutting (see Cook's tip).

TONY ROBINS

Cook's Notes

TIME
10-15 minutes preparation, 1½ hours baking, plus cooling and storing time.

! WATCHPOINTS
Keep the heat low and do not allow the mixture to boil or it will turn into toffee.

The melted mixture must be cooled a little, or it will cook the other ingredients slightly and toughen the cake.

COOK'S TIP
During storage the cake develops its characteristic moist and sticky texture, the flavour mellows and the crust softens. Gingerbread keeps well for 2-3 weeks. To serve: cut into 16 squares.

VARIATION
Store the cake for 1 week, then decorate the top with glacé icing made by blending 100 g/4 oz sifted icing sugar with 2-3 teaspoons water. Top with crystallized or drained stem ginger. Allow to set before cutting.

●315 calories/1325 kj per square

385

FRED MANCINI

Banana teabread

MAKES 12 SLICES
225 g/8 oz self-raising flour
½ teaspoon ground mixed spice
100 g/4 oz margarine
100 g/4 oz light soft brown sugar
2 eggs
500 g/1 lb bananas, mashed (see Economy)
1 tablespoon Demerara sugar
vegetable oil, for greasing

1 Heat the oven to 180C/350F/Gas 4. Grease a 1.75 L/3 pint (1 kg/2 lb) loaf tin, line the base with greaseproof paper, then grease the paper.
2 Sift flour and spice into a bowl.
3 Beat the margarine and sugar until pale and fluffy, then beat in 1 egg. Add the remaining egg and 1 tablespoon of the flour mixture and beat vigorously until evenly blended (see Cook's tip). Beat in bananas.

4 Using a large metal spoon, fold in the remaining flour mixture. Spoon the mixture into the prepared tin and level the surface, then sprinkle over the Demerara sugar.
5 Bake in the oven for 1-1¼ hours, or until firm to the touch.

6 Cool the teabread for 1 minute, then run a palette knife around the sides to loosen it, turn out of tin and peel off lining paper. Turn right way up and leave on a wire rack to cool completely before slicing (see Serving ideas).

Cook's Notes

TIME
20 minutes preparation and 1-1¼ hours baking, plus cooling time.

STORAGE
The teabread will keep fresh for 3-4 days if wrapped in foil and stored in an airtight container.

FREEZING
 Wrap in a polythene bag, seal, label and freeze for up to 6 months. To serve: defrost in wrapping at room temperature for 3 hours.

COOK'S TIP
 A little flour prevents the mixture curdling when the second egg is added.

SERVING IDEAS
 This teabread is moist enough to serve plain, but can be buttered. It is ideal for picnics.

ECONOMY
 This tasty teabread is a good way to use up over-soft bananas.

● 195 calories/825 kj per slice

Syrup tea bread

MAKES 12-14 SLICES
350 g/12 oz plain flour
1 tablespoon baking powder
½ teaspoon bicarbonate of soda
50 g/2 oz stoned dates, chopped
50 g/2 oz seedless raisins
100 g/4 oz golden syrup
50 g/2 oz light soft brown sugar
300 ml/½ pint milk
50 g/2 oz margarine
vegetable oil, for greasing
butter, to serve

1 Heat the oven to 180C/350F/Gas 4. Grease a 1.75 L/3 pint (1 kg/2 lb) loaf tin, line the base with greaseproof paper, then grease the paper.
2 Sift the flour, baking powder and soda into a bowl, then stir in the chopped dates and raisins.
3 Put the syrup, sugar, milk and margarine into a heavy-based saucepan. Heat gently, stirring frequently with a wooden spoon, until the sugar has dissolved and the margarine has melted. Remove from the heat and pour on to the flour mixture, then beat with the spoon until the ingredients are evenly and thoroughly blended.
4 Spoon the mixture into the prepared tin and level the surface. Bake in oven for 1-1¼ hours, or until the bread is risen, well browned and firm to the touch.
5 Cool the bread for 5 minutes, then run a palette knife around the sides to loosen it and turn out of the tin. Peel off the lining paper. Leave on a wire rack to cool completely (see Cook's tip). Serve sliced, with plenty of butter.

Cook's Notes

TIME
20 minutes preparation, then 1-1¼ hours baking. Cooling takes about 1 hour.

COOK'S TIP
The bread is ready for cutting as soon as it is cold. It is best served within 3 days of making.

WATCHPOINTS
Do not let the syrup mixture become too hot or it will toughen the flour.
Check during baking and cover the bread with greaseproof paper, if necessary, to prevent the top overbrowning.

●215 calories/900 kj per slice

387

Cheese and walnut teabread

MAKES 1 SMALL LOAF

225 g/8 oz wholemeal flour
2 teaspoons baking powder
1 teaspoon celery salt
½ teaspoon mustard powder
50 g/2 oz margarine or butter, diced
100 g/4 oz Cheddar cheese, grated
25 g/1 oz shelled walnuts, chopped
150 ml/¼ pint milk
1 egg, beaten
melted fat or vegetable oil, for
   greasing

1 Heat the oven to 180C/350F/Gas 4. Grease a 500 g/1 lb loaf tin, line the base with greaseproof paper then grease the paper.
2 Mix together the flour, baking powder, celery salt and mustard powder. Add the margarine and rub it in until the mixture resembles fine breadcrumbs. Stir in the cheese and walnuts, then mix in the milk and egg to make a soft dough.
3 Turn the dough into the prepared tin, level the surface and make a slight hollow in the centre. Bake for 40-45 minutes until the top of the loaf is golden brown and a warmed skewer inserted in the centre comes out clean.
4 Leave the loaf in the tin for a few minutes before turning it out on to a wire rack. Peel off the paper and leave, right way up, to cool.

Cook's Notes

TIME
Preparation 15 minutes, baking 40-45 minutes. Cooling time is about 1 hour.

STORAGE
This loaf is best eaten while it is still warm, but it is also delicious served cold. It will keep for several days wrapped tightly in foil and is excellent toasted.

FREEZING
Wrap the cold loaf in cling film or foil and freeze for 3-4 months. To serve: loosen the wrapping and defrost at room temperature for 1½-2 hours. If necessary, warm through in a 190C/375F/Gas 5 oven for 15 minutes before serving to improve the texture.

SERVING IDEAS
Serve this bread, thickly sliced and buttered, with a soup or salad for a supper meal, or as part of a packed lunch or picnic.

● 1875 calories/7850 kj per loaf

MARTIN BRIGDALE

Sticky figgy loaf

MAKES 8-10 SLICES
100 g/4 oz dried figs (see
  Watchpoints), coarsely chopped
50 g/2 oz Demerara sugar
100 g/4 oz wheat bran breakfast
  cereal (see Buying guide)
1 tablespoon clear honey
300 ml/½ pint milk
100 g/4 oz self-raising flour
vegetable oil, for greasing

1 Put the figs, sugar, cereal and honey into a bowl. Pour over the milk and stir to mix. Cover and leave to stand in a cool place for 1 hour, stirring occasionally.
2 About 20 minutes before the end of standing time, heat the oven to 180C/350F/Gas 4. Thoroughly oil an 850 ml/1½ pint (500 g/1 lb) loaf tin, line the tin with greaseproof paper,
and then oil the greaseproof paper.
3 Uncover the figgy mixture. Sift in the flour and mix thoroughly with a wooden spoon. ⓘ
4 Turn the mixture into the prepared tin and bake in the oven for 1-1¼ hours, until risen, browned and just firm to the touch. Cover with greaseproof paper halfway through baking to avoid the figgy
loaf overbrowning on the top.
5 Cool the loaf for 5 minutes, then run a palette knife around the sides to loosen it and turn out of the tin. Peel off the lining paper. Leave the loaf, right way up, on a wire rack to cool completely. Wrap in foil or cling film and store for 24 hours before cutting into chunky slices (see Cook's tip).

Cook's Notes

TIME
25 minutes preparation, plus 1 hour standing and 1-1¼ hours baking. Allow time for cooling and storing.

WATCHPOINTS
Discard any hard stalks from the figs as these are unpleasant to eat.
The ingredients must be well mixed or streaks of flour will spoil the look of the loaf.

BUYING GUIDE
Look for an all-bran cereal – any high-fibre wheat bran cereal will do.

COOK'S TIP
The loaf becomes moist and sticky when stored. It will keep for up to 1 week in an airtight container. Serve with butter or cheese.

●160 calories/650 kj per slice

389

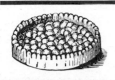

Iced walnut tea ring

MAKES 8-10 SLICES
280 g/10 oz packet brown bread mix
185 ml/6½ fl oz hand-hot water
25 g/1 oz butter, melted
50 g/2 oz shelled walnuts, finely
  chopped
25 g/1 oz caster sugar
100 g/4 oz icing sugar, sifted
about 5 teaspoons orange juice
vegetable oil, for greasing

TO DECORATE
8 walnut halves
grated zest of 1 orange

1 Brush a baking sheet with oil. Place the bread mix in a bowl, add the water and mix to a dough. Turn out on to a floured surface and knead for 5 minutes. **!**
2 Roll out the dough to a rectangle about 35 cm × 20 cm/14 × 8 inches. Brush with the melted butter, then sprinkle with the chopped nuts and caster sugar. Starting from one long side, neatly roll up the dough. Dampen the ends and join them together firmly to make a ring.
3 Place the ring on the oiled baking sheet. Using scissors, snip the ring at 2.5 cm/1 inch intervals to within 2 cm/¾ inch of the centre, without cutting right through, so that the filling shows.
4 Cover with oiled polythene and leave to rise in a warm place for about 1 hour, or until almost double in size. Meanwhile, heat the oven to 220C/425F/Gas 7.
5 Uncover the ring and bake in the oven for 15 minutes; reduce the oven temperature to 180C/350F/Gas 4 and bake for a further 15 minutes, or until golden brown. Leave on wire rack to cool completely. ✳
6 Blend the icing sugar with enough orange juice to give a coating consistency. Spoon over the ring, then arrange the walnut halves on top and sprinkle over the orange zest. Leave to set.

FRED MANCINI

Cook's Notes

TIME
The tea ring takes 2 hours to make, then 5-10 minutes for icing.

✳ FREEZING
Wrap the cold, undecorated ring in a polythene bag, seal, label and freeze for up to 6 weeks. Defrost (unwrapped) at room temperature, then ice and decorate.

! WATCHPOINT
Keep the dough warm at all times.

●260 calories/1075 kj per slice

Apricot and raisin teabread

MAKES 8 SLICES

280 g/10 oz packet white bread mix
25 g/1 oz caster sugar
½ teaspoon ground ginger
185 ml/6½ fl oz hand-hot water (see Preparation)
50 g/2 oz dried apricots, finely chopped
50 g/2 oz seedless raisins
2 teaspoons clear honey, to glaze
vegetable oil, for greasing

1 Brush the base and sides of an 850 ml/1½ pint (500 g/1 lb) loaf tin with oil; leave in a warm place.
2 Put the bread mix into a bowl and stir in the sugar and ginger. Add the water and mix to a dough.
3 Turn the dough out on to a floured work surface and knead for 5 minutes. Work in apricots and raisins, then place in the prepared tin and press gently to fit the shape.

Cook's Notes

 TIME
15 minutes preparation, 1¼ hours rising, then 40 minutes baking plus cooling before serving.

PREPARATION
To create hand-hot water, mix half boiling and half cold water.

FREEZING
Cool completely, then wrap, unglazed, in a polythene bag. Seal, label and freeze for up to 4 weeks. To serve: unwrap and defrost for 2-3 hours. Brush with honey before serving.

 VARIATION
Add ½ teaspoon ground cinnamon instead of ginger to dry bread mix. Try substituting 50 g/2 oz chopped dried (not pressed) dates and 50 g/2 oz chopped walnuts for the dried apricots and seedless raisins.

WATCHPOINT
Keep the dough warm throughout the mixing, kneading and rising processes to ensure the yeast expands the dough fully: this gives a springy texture to the baked loaf.

●165 calories/700 kj per slice

Cover the tin with oiled polythene and leave in a warm place for about 1¼ hours, or until the dough is risen and doubled in bulk.
4 Heat the oven to 200C/400F/Gas 6.
5 Uncover the loaf and bake for about 40 minutes, or until golden.
6 Leave the loaf in the tin for about 2 minutes, then turn out. Place the right way up on a wire rack. ✳ Brush the honey over the crust to glaze, then leave to cool completely.

ALAN DUNS

391

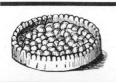

ROGER PHILLIPS

Irish soda bread

MAKES 24 SLICES
450 g/1 lb plain flour
1 teaspoon bicarbonate of soda
1 teaspoon salt
40 g/1½ oz butter, diced
300-350 ml/10-12 fl oz plain
  buttermilk (see Cook's tip)
plain flour, for dusting

1 Heat the oven to 200C/400F/Gas 6.
Sift a thin dusting of flour over a
baking sheet.
2 Sift the flour, bicarbonate of soda
and salt into a bowl, then rub in the
butter. Make a well in the centre and
pour in 300 ml/½ pint buttermilk.
Mix quickly to a soft dough with a
fork, adding more buttermilk if
necessary.
3 With floured hands, gather the
dough together, turn out on to a
floured surface and knead lightly
and briefly until smooth. Shape the
dough into a round, about 18 cm/7
inches in diameter, then place on
the prepared baking sheet.

Cook's Notes

 TIME
45 minutes preparation
plus cooling time.

 COOK'S TIP
If buttermilk is not
available, use 300 ml/½
pint fresh milk and stir in 1
teaspoon cream of tartar. Add
extra fresh milk, if necessary,
when mixing the dough to give
the right consistency.

 FREEZING
Wrap cold bread in
polythene bag and
freeze for up to 6 months. To
serve: remove from bag, wrap in
foil and reheat in a 200C/400F/
Gas 6 oven. Allow 25 minutes
for whole loaf; 15 minutes for a
quarter section.

●85 calories/350 kj per slice

 SERVING IDEAS
Eat the bread warm, or
as soon as it is cold. To
serve, break apart (do not cut)
into wedges, then slice thickly.
Any left over can be frozen, or
toasted.

 PREPARATION
To score the dough into
quarters:

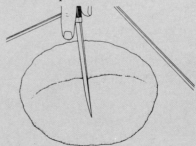

*Cut a deep cross in the dough with
a sharp, floured knife, to within 1
cm/½ inch of edges.*

4 Score round into quarters (see
Preparation). Bake the bread in the
top of the oven for about 30 minutes,
until golden brown and the underside sounds hollow when rapped.
5 Transfer the bread to a wire rack,
cover with a clean tea-towel and
leave to cool (see Serving ideas).

392

Wholemeal cheese baps

MAKES 8

450 g/1 lb wholemeal flour
1 teaspoon salt
2 teaspoons bicarbonate of soda
1 tablespoon sweet paprika
100 g/4 oz solid vegetable oil
200 g/7 oz Cheddar cheese, finely
   grated
300 ml/½ pint milk, soured with 2
   teaspoons lemon juice

1 Heat the oven to 200C/400F/Gas 6.
Prepare a large baking sheet by
sprinkling it with flour.
2 Sift the flour into a bowl with the
salt, bicarbonate of soda and
paprika, tipping in any bran left in
the sieve.
3 Cut the oil into 5 mm/¼ inch
cubes. Add to the flour and rub it in
until the mixture is crumbly. Toss in
two-thirds of the cheese and mix
everything to a dough with the
soured milk.
4 Divide the dough into 8 pieces.
On a lightly floured surface, shape
each one into a large, round, flat bap
about 2 cm/¾ inch thick. Place them
on the floured baking sheet.
5 Bake in the oven for 20
minutes. ✳ Take them out of the
oven and put a portion of the
remaining cheese on top of each.
Return to the oven for 5 minutes.
6 Serve the baps while still warm,
or let them cool on a wire rack.

Cook's Notes

TIME
Preparation 20 minutes.
Cooking 25 minutes.

FREEZING
To freeze:-cook the baps
for the full 25 minutes
without the cheese topping.
Cool, seal, label and freeze.
Store for up to 6 months. To
serve: cook from frozen in an
oven preheated to 200C/400F/
Gas 6 for 10 minutes. Add the
cheese topping and cook for
another 5 minutes.

● 360 calories/1500 kj per bap

PAUL WILLIAMS

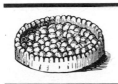

PETER HOWARD-SMITH

Apricot scone round

MAKES 6 WEDGES
50 g/2 oz dried apricots, chopped
225 g/8 oz plain flour
1 tablespoon baking powder
½ teaspoon salt
½ teaspoon ground cinnamon
50 g/2 oz light soft brown sugar
50 g/2 oz margarine or butter, diced
about 150 ml/¼ pint milk
milk, for glazing
margarine or butter, for greasing

1 Heat the oven to 220C/425F/Gas 7. Grease a baking sheet.
2 Sift the flour, baking powder, salt and cinnamon into a bowl. Stir in the sugar. Add the margarine and rub it in until the mixture resembles fine breadcrumbs. Stir in the apricots. Make a well in centre.
3 Add most of the milk and mix it in with a round-bladed knife, adding the remaining milk if necessary to give a soft, but not sticky dough. Gather the dough together with your fingers, turn out on to a lightly floured surface and knead briefly until smooth. Shape into a ball, then gently press out to a round, about 1 cm/½ inch thick. !
4 Place the scone round on the baking sheet and brush the top with milk. Using the point of a floured knife, mark into 6 equal wedges. Bake in the oven for 20-25 minutes until well risen and browned.
5 Cool, then pull the wedges apart and serve warm.

PAUL BUSSELL

Date and oatmeal muffins

MAKES 16 SMALL MUFFINS
100 g/4 oz self-raising flour, sifted
1 teaspoon baking powder
pinch of salt
75 g/3 oz medium oatmeal
50 g/2 oz caster sugar
**50 g/2 oz stoned dates, finely
    chopped**
1 tablespoon golden syrup
15 g/½ oz margarine or butter
150 ml/¼ pint milk

1 Heat the oven to 200C/400F/Gas 6.
Grease sixteen 6.5 cm/2½ inch patty
or muffin moulds (see Cook's tip).
2 Put the dry ingredients into a
bowl with the dates and stir well to
mix. Make a well in the centre.
3 Stir the syrup, margarine and
milk together in a saucepan over low
heat until the fat has melted, then
pour into the dry ingredients and
beat until smoothly blended.
4 Divide the mixture equally
between the prepared moulds, then
bake in the oven for 15-20 minutes
until well-risen and springy.
5 Serve split and buttered while still
warm (see Serving ideas).

PAUL WEBSTER

Apricot and walnut tea buns

MAKES 12
225 g/8 oz self-raising flour
1 teaspoon ground cinnamon
100 g/4 oz butter, diced
100 g/4 oz light soft brown sugar
50 g/2 oz dried apricots, finely chopped
25 g/1 oz shelled walnuts, finely chopped
1 large egg, lightly beaten
vegetable oil, for greasing

1 Heat the oven to 200C/400F/Gas 6. Brush 12 bun moulds with oil.
2 Sift the flour and cinnamon into a large bowl. Add the butter and rub it in until the mixture resembles fine crumbs. Using a fork, stir in the brown sugar, chopped apricots and chopped walnuts. Stir in the egg.
3 Divide the mixture equally between the prepared moulds, then lightly rough up each surface with back of a fork. Bake for about 20 min-utes, or until risen, and browned.
4 Cool the buns for 5 minutes, then remove from the moulds. Leave on a wire rack to cool completely before serving (see Cook's tip).

Cook's Notes

 TIME
15 minutes preparation, 20 minutes baking, plus about 1 hour to cool.

FREEZING
Pack the buns in a rigid container with waxed paper between layers; seal tightly and freeze for up to 3 months. To serve: defrost the buns at room temperature for about 2 hours, then unpack and place on a serving plate.

●185 calories/775 kj per bun

 COOK'S TIP
The buns are nicest eaten on the day of making. Any left over can be stored in an airtight container for up to 2 days; alternatively, they can be frozen (see left).

 VARIATION
Sift 5 tablespoons icing sugar into a bowl, then stir in enough strained lemon juice to give a smooth coating consistency. Trickle the icing over the buns. Leave for 15-20 minutes to set before serving.

396

Spicy drop scones

MAKES 15-18
50 g/2 oz plain flour
pinch of salt
1 teaspoon baking powder
1 teaspoon ground mixed spice
50 g/2 oz plain wholemeal flour
25 g/1 oz caster sugar
1 egg, lightly beaten
175 ml/6 fl oz milk
25 g/1 oz butter, melted
lard, for frying

1 Sift the plain flour, salt, baking powder and spice into a bowl. Stir in the wholemeal flour and sugar, then make a well in the centre.
2 Add the egg, milk and melted butter and whisk together to make a smooth, fairly thick batter.
3 Lightly grease a large heavy-based frying-pan or girdle with lard and place over moderate heat (see Cook's tips).

4 Using a large metal spoon, drop 3-4 spoonfuls of the batter on to the hot pan taking care not to overcook it (see Cook's tips). Cook for 1-2 minutes, until the bubbles rise and burst on the surface, then turn each scone over with a palette knife and cook on the other side for 30-60 seconds until a deep golden brown (see Cook's tips).

5 Remove the cooked scones from the pan, wrap in a clean tea-towel and place on a wire rack. Continue making scones until all the batter is used. Stir the batter frequently and grease the pan lightly with more lard as necessary.
6 Serve the scones as soon as they are all cooked and while still warm (see Serving ideas).

Cook's Notes

TIME
Preparation and cooking take 30 minutes.

SERVING IDEAS
These spicy drop scones are delicious with butter and jam or honey; for an extravagant treat, top them with a swirl of whipped cream.

COOK'S TIPS
To test the temperature, drop a teaspoon of batter on to the pan: it should begin to bubble within 1 minute. If not, heat the pan a little longer.

For round scones, drop the batter from the tip of the spoon; for an oval shape, let it run off the side. Space each spoonful well apart or the batter will run together.

Press the scones gently with the flat side of the knife: if they are cooked, no batter will run out of the sides.

●55 calories/225 kj per scone

JAMES JACKSON

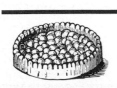

PAUL WINDSOR

Soured cream girdle scones

MAKES 12
225 g/8 oz plain flour
1 teaspoon bicarbonate of soda
1 teaspoon cream of tartar
1 teaspoon salt
15 g/½ oz butter
15 g/½ oz caster sugar
300 ml/½ pint soured cream
solid vegetable oil, for greasing
butter, to serve

1 Sift the flour, bicarbonate of soda, cream of tartar and salt into a large bowl. Add the butter and rub it in with your fingertips then stir in the caster sugar.

2 Using a fork, add enough soured cream to make a soft dough. Divide the dough in half, flour your hands lightly, then knead the dough lightly on a well-floured surface until smooth. [!]

3 Carefully shape the dough into 2 rounds, each about 1 cm/½ inch thick. Cut each round into 6 equal wedges.

4 Lightly grease a heavy frying-pan or girdle with oil and heat over moderate heat. [!] Pour away any excess oil, then cook the scones in batches for about 4-5 minutes on each side until golden and cooked through. Regrease the girdle with oil as necessary.

5 Cool the scones on a wire rack, for 20 minutes. Serve on the day of making, and spread each one generously with butter.

398

Singin'hinny

SERVES 8
225 g/8 oz self-raising flour
¼ teaspoon salt
½ teaspoon baking powder
75 g/3 oz solid vegetable oil, diced
25 g/1 oz caster sugar
50 g/2 oz currants
5-6 tablespoons milk
15-25 g/½-1 oz margarine
butter, for serving

1 Sift the flour, salt and baking powder together. Add diced oil and rub it into the flour with your fingertips until the mixture resembles fine breadcrumbs.

2 Mix in the sugar, currants and enough milk to make a fairly soft but manageable dough (see Cook's tips).

3 Roll out the dough on a lightly floured surface to a round about 20 cm/8 inches in diameter. Using a sharp knife, cut the round of dough in half, if liked (see Cook's tips).

4 Heat 15 g/½ oz margarine in a large, heavy frying-pan. Put dough in pan and cook over low heat for 10-15 minutes until the dough has risen. It should be cooked more than halfway through and be well browned underneath.

5 Lift the dough with a fish slice and add more margarine to pan, allowing it to melt and coat the pan base. Turn the hinny over, then gently lower it back into the pan. Continue cooking the hinny very gently for about 10 minutes or until brown on the underside. Check during cooking and lower the heat more, if necessary, to prevent the hinny over-browning and burning.

6 Using a fish slice, remove the hinny to a work surface or board. Split it in half horizontally while it is hot and spread with butter. Sandwich together again and cut into wedges. Serve at once, while still hot and buttery.

MARTIN BRIGDALE

Cook's Notes

TIME
The hinny takes about 35 minutes to prepare and cook.

COOK'S TIPS
The hinny is best cooked as soon as the dough is made.
Cutting the dough will make it easier to turn in the pan.

DID YOU KNOW
This recipe is traditional to Northumberland and Durham where hinny is a term of endearment. The hinny was traditionally made on a girdle and would sizzle or 'sing' as it cooked.

VARIATION
Some traditional recipes include 50 g/2 oz ground rice in place of that amount of flour.

SERVING IDEAS
The hot hinny is particularly tasty when spread with cinnamon butter. To make the butter: mix 100 g/4 oz butter with 40 g/1½ oz caster sugar and 1 pinch cinnammon.

● 250 calories/1055 kj per portion

Honey cinnamon pinwheels

MAKES 8
225 g/8 oz self-raising flour
40 g/1½ oz butter, diced
1½ tablespoons caster sugar
150 ml/¼ pint milk
1 tablespoon clear honey, to decorate
vegetable oil, for greasing

FILLING
15 g/½ oz margarine
2 tablespoons clear honey
1 teaspoon ground cinnamon
  (see Did you know)

1 Heat the oven to 200C/400F/Gas 6. Brush the bottom and sides of an 18 cm/7 inch sandwich tin with oil, then line the base with greaseproof paper and brush with oil.
2 Make the filling: in a small bowl, beat the margarine with the honey and the cinnamon until blended.
3 Sift the flour into a bowl, add the butter and rub it in until the mixture begins to resemble fine breadcrumbs. Stir in the sugar and make a well in the centre.
4 Pour the milk into the well, then gradually draw the flour into the liquid to form a soft dough. Turn the dough on to a floured surface and roll out to a 20 cm/8 inch square.
5 Spread the honey mixture over the dough to cover completely then roll up like a Swiss roll. Cut the roll into 8 even-sized slices.
6 Put one slice in centre of the prepared tin, cut-side down, then arrange the remaining slices around it (see Preparation).
7 Bake in the oven for 30 minutes or until well risen and golden brown. Remove from the oven and turn out on to a wire rack with a plate placed underneath. To decorate: trickle the honey over the top, allowing excess to fall on to the plate.
8 Transfer to a serving plate, cut the pinwheels apart and serve warm or leave until completely cold.

Cook's Notes

 TIME
20 minutes preparation, 30 minutes baking.

? DID YOU KNOW
Cinnamon is the bark of a small evergreen tree which is a member of the laurel family. The bark is peeled from the branches and dried in the sun to form curled-up rolls. Cinnamon is difficult to grind and is usually bought ready ground for use in sweet dishes and cakes. It quickly becomes stale so should be bought in small quantities and not stored for a long time.

 PREPARATION
To make the pinwheel shape in the cake tin:

Put one slice of dough in centre of the lined tin. Arrange remainder in a wheel around it.

●190 calories/800 kj per portion

Wheatmeal Chelsea buns

MAKES 8
125 ml/4 fl oz milk
1 egg, beaten
225 g/8 oz brown or wheatmeal
    flour
½ teaspoon salt
25 g/1 oz butter, diced
25 g/1 oz light soft brown sugar
½ teaspoon ground mixed spice
    (optional)
7 g/¼ oz sachet easy-blend dried
    yeast
75 g/3 oz icing sugar
vegetable oil, for greasing

FILLING
75 g/3 oz currants
25 g/1 oz cut mixed peel
50 g/2 oz light soft brown sugar
½ teaspoon ground mixed spice
50 g/2 oz butter, melted

1 Heat the milk in a pan until warm, then beat in the egg and set aside until required. Grease a 20 cm/ 8 inch sandwich cake tin.
2 Sift the flour and salt into a large bowl. Add the butter and rub in until the mixture resembles fine breadcrumbs. Stir in the sugar, spice and yeast, make a well in the centre and pour in the milk mixture. Using a fork, mix to a soft dough.
3 Turn the dough out on to a lightly floured surface and knead for about 10 minutes, until smooth. !
4 Shape the dough into a ball and place in a large oiled bowl. Cover with oiled polythene and leave to rise in a warm place for 1-1½ hours or until doubled in size.
5 Meanwhile, make the filling: mix the currants with the peel, sugar and spice, then pour over the melted butter and stir well.
6 Uncover the risen dough and turn out on to a floured surface. Knead gently until the dough is back to original size, then roll into a 30 × 23 cm/12 × 9 inch rectangle. Pour the filling over the rectangle and spread it out to cover dough.
7 Starting at a short edge, roll up like a Swiss roll, to enclose the filling. Brush the end with water and press firmly to seal, then slice across into 8 pieces.
8 Place 1 piece, cut-side up, in the centre of the prepared tin. Arrange the remaining pieces around it so that they are just touching. Cover with oiled polythene and leave in a warm place for 45 minutes or until the buns have risen.
9 Heat the oven to 200C/400F/Gas 6.
10 Bake the buns in the oven for about 30 minutes until risen and golden brown. Transfer to a wire rack and leave to cool completely.
11 Make the icing: sift the icing sugar into a bowl, then stir in enough water to give a smooth coating consistency. Drizzle the icing over the top of the cooled buns before serving.

Cook's Notes

TIME
30 minutes preparation, 1¾-2¼ hours rising and about 30 minutes baking, plus cooling time.

WATCHPOINT
The dough will be very sticky: do not add any extra flour to it; just continue kneading until dough becomes soft, pliable and elastic.

● 290 calories/1225 kj per bun

JAMES JACKSON

MARTIN BRIGDALE

Mustard knots

MAKES 8
280 g/10 oz packet brown bread mix
1 teaspoon mustard powder
freshly ground black pepper
65 g/2½ oz Leicester cheese, grated
200 ml/7 fl oz hand-hot water
milk, for glazing
vegetable oil, for greasing
butter, to serve
slices of cheese (optional)

1 Place the bread mix in a bowl and stir in the mustard, a grinding of black pepper and 50 g/2 oz cheese. Pour in the water and mix to a dough. Turn out the dough on to a floured surface and knead it for 5 minutes.

2 Oil a large baking sheet.

3 Divide the dough into 8 equal pieces. Using your fingertips, roll each piece back and forth on the work surface to make a 'rope', about 30 cm/12 inches long. Shape each 'rope' of dough into a knot (see Preparation). Place the knots well apart on the prepared baking sheet. Cover with oiled polythene and leave to rise in a warm place for about 40 minutes, until they have doubled in size.

4 About 20 minutes before the dough is ready, heat the oven to 220C/425F/Gas 7.

5 Uncover the knots and brush each with milk, then sprinkle lightly with the remaining cheese. Bake in the oven for 25-30 minutes, until risen and golden. Transfer to a wire rack to cool. Serve the knots warm or cold, split in half and generously buttered, or filled with slices of cheese, if liked. Serve alone or with a soup or salad.

Cook's Notes

TIME
1½ hours (including rising and baking), plus cooling time.

PREPARATION
Shape the dough into knots as follows:

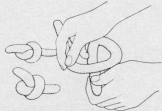

Make a loop (see above), 5 cm/2 inches from one end, then gently pull the longer end through the loop to make a knot.

●160 calories/650 kj per knot

402

Hot cross buns

MAKES 12
150 ml/¼ pint milk
4 tablespoons water
1 large egg
500 g/1 lb strong white flour
1 teaspoon salt
50 g/2 oz butter, diced
50 g/2 oz caster sugar
1 teaspoon ground mixed spice
½ teaspoon ground cinnamon
½ teaspoon freshly grated nutmeg
175 g/6 oz currants
50 g/2 oz cut mixed peel
2 × 7 g/¼ oz sachets easy-blend
   dried yeast
vegetable oil, for greasing
50 g/2 oz sugar and 4 tablespoons
   water, to glaze

PASTRY CROSSES
50 g/2 oz plain flour
about 2 tablespoons water

1 Heat the milk and water in a pan until warm, then pour into a jug. Beat in the egg and set aside. Grease 2 large baking sheets.
2 Sift the flour and salt into a warmed, large bowl. Add the butter and rub it in with your fingertips. Stir in the sugar, spices, currants and peel, then stir in the yeast. Pour in the milk mixture and then mix to a soft dough.
3 Turn the dough out on to a lightly floured surface and knead for about 10 minutes, or until it is elastic. [!]
4 Shape into a ball and place in an oiled large bowl. Cover with oiled polythene and leave to rise in a warm place for 1½-2 hours or until the dough has doubled in size.
5 Uncover the risen dough and turn out on to a floured surface. Punch down the dough with your knuckles, then knead for 2 minutes. Divide into 12 pieces and shape each into a round.
6 Place the rounds, well apart, on the baking sheets. Cover with oiled polythene and leave to rise in a warm place for 30-40 minutes or until almost doubled in size.
7 About 20 minutes before the rounds are risen, heat the oven to 220C/425F/Gas 7. Then make the crosses: sift the flour into a bowl and stir in just enough water to make a firm dough. Knead gently on a floured surface until smooth, then roll out and cut into 24 strips, each 7.5 cm × 5 mm/3 × ¼ inch.
8 Uncover the buns. Brush underside of pastry strips with water and place 2 strips on top of each bun to form a cross. Bake in the oven for 15-20 minutes, until risen and golden brown. Transfer to a wire rack, placed over a tray.
9 Make the glaze: heat the sugar and water in a saucepan, stirring until the sugar has dissolved. Brush over the warm buns. Leave the buns to cool completely.

PETER MYERS

Apple and sultana tartlets

MAKES 15
RICH SHORTCRUST PASTRY
200 g/7 oz plain flour
pinch of salt
2 tablespoons icing sugar
1 egg, separated
100 g/4 oz butter, softened

FILLING
1 cooking apple, about 175 g/6 oz
75 g/3 oz sultanas
1 teaspoon ground cinnamon
2 tablespoons soft brown sugar

1 Heat the oven to 200C/400F/Gas 6.
2 To make the pastry: sift the flour and salt on to a work top and sift on the icing sugar. Make a well in the centre and put in the egg yolk and butter. With your fingertips, gradually work in flour from the edges until a smooth ball of dough is formed. Cover it with a clean tea-towel and leave it to relax while you prepare the filling.
3 Peel, core and very finely chop the apple and mix it in a bowl with the sultanas, cinnamon and sugar.
4 Roll out the pastry and stamp out equal numbers of 6.5 cm/2½ inch and 5 cm/2 inch rounds. Using an apple corer or a very small pastry cutter stamp out a small round in the centre of each 5 cm/2 inch circle. Use the trimmings to make more circles in the same way.
5 Line small, floured tartlet tins with the large circles. Put a pile of apple mixture into each, moisten the edges with water and cover with a small holed circle. Gently press down the edges, making slightly raised volcano shapes.
6 Brush the tartlets with the egg white and bake them for 15-20 minutes or until golden brown.
7 Serve hot for dessert with cream, or leave to cool on wire racks.

PETER MYERS

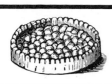

ALAN DUNS

Date rolls

MAKES 18
250 g/9 oz self-raising flour
175 g/6 oz butter, diced
25 g/1 oz caster sugar
1 egg, beaten
melted fat or vegetable oil, for
 greasing

FILLING AND GLAZE
250 g/9 oz stoned dates (see Buying
 guide), chopped
finely grated zest and juice of 1
 large orange
2 trifle sponge cakes, crumbled
1 tablespoon milk
2 tablespoons caster sugar

1 Sift the flour into a bowl. Rub in the butter, then stir in the sugar. Add 2 tablespoons of the beaten egg and mix to a stiff dough.

2 Turn the dough out on to a lightly floured surface and knead briefly until smooth. Wrap in cling film and refrigerate.

3 To make the filling: mix the dates, orange zest and juice together in a saucepan. Cover and cook over very low heat for about 10 minutes, until the dates are soft. Remove from the heat and stir in the crumbled sponges. Set aside to cool completely.

4 Heat the oven to 190C/375F/Gas 5. Grease a large baking sheet.

5 Cut the dough into 3 equal pieces. On a lightly floured surface, roll out each piece to a 30 × 10 cm/12 × 4 inch rectangle. Trim the edges.

6 Divide the date mixture into 3. With your hands, shape each into a roll, 30 cm/12 inches long. Place a date roll lengthways on each rectangle of dough, close to the edge, then roll up from a long edge, to enclose the date filling.

7 Beat the milk with the remaining egg and brush over the rolls, then sprinkle with caster sugar. Cut each roll across into 6 pieces and transfer to the prepared baking sheet.

8 Bake in the oven for 20-25 minutes until golden. Loosen the rolls with a palette knife; cool on a wire rack.

Cook's Notes

TIME
1½ hours preparation, 20-25 minutes baking, plus cooling time.

BUYING GUIDE
Ready-stoned dates are sold either pressed into blocks, or loose in bags. Do not use the sugar-coated kind; they are too sweet for this recipe.

●205 calories/850 kj per roll

405

Crunchy date layer

SERVES 6-8
225 g/8 oz pressed dates, roughly chopped
4 tablespoons water
3-4 teaspoons ground cinnamon
175 g/6 oz butter
50 g/2 oz Demerara sugar
100 g/4 oz porridge oats
100 g/4 oz wholemeal flour
margarine, for greasing

1 Heat the oven to 180C/350F/Gas 4 and thoroughly grease a 20 cm/8 inch sandwich tin.

2 Put the chopped dates in a saucepan with the water and cinnamon. Cook gently for about 5 minutes, or until the dates are soft and will spread. Remove from heat. ☐

3 Put the butter and sugar into a clean pan and heat gently until the butter has melted. Remove from the heat, sprinkle in the oats and flour and stir to mix in thoroughly.

4 Spread half the oat mixture over the base of the prepared tin, then cover with the dates, spreading them evenly. Spread the remaining oat mixture over the top. Bake in the oven for 30 minutes.

5 Remove from the oven and allow to cool for 10 minutes, then mark into wedges. Leave until completely cold in the tin (see Cook's tip).

PAUL WEBSTER

406

Muesli munchies

MAKES 12

350 g/12 oz muesli
  (see Cook's tips)
6 tablespoons sunflower or
  vegetable oil
4 tablespoons clear honey
4 tablespoons golden syrup
½ teaspoon vanilla flavouring
extra oil, for greasing

1 Heat the oven to 180C/350F/Gas 4. Thoroughly grease two 16 cm/6½ inch round sandwich tins, then line the base of each tin with a round of non-stick vegetable parchment paper.

2 Place the muesli in a large bowl. Add the oil, honey, syrup and vanilla and stir until well mixed. Spoon half the mixture into each tin, press evenly over the base, then Level each surface with the back of a large metal spoon. (Dip spoon into hot water to prevent sticking.)

3 Bake in the oven for about 15 minutes, or until golden brown (see Cook's tips). Cool the rounds for 5 minutes, then cut each round into 6 wedges with a small, sharp knife. [!]

4 Using a round-bladed knife, loosen the wedges from the sides of the tin. Leave to cool completely, then remove from the tins (see Serving ideas and Storage).

Cook's Notes

 TIME
10 minutes preparation, plus about 15 minutes baking and 1 hour to cool.

 WATCHPOINT
Be sure to cut right through the mixture, or the wedges will stick together.

COOK'S TIPS
Use any brand of muesli cereal available, but if it contains large pieces of fruit or nuts chop them before using or the rounds will be difficult to cut.

The mixture is very soft when the tins are removed from the oven; it firms up as it cools.

 SERVING IDEAS
These wedges make a wholesome and nutritious addition to packed lunches and picnic hampers.

STORAGE
The wedges will stay fresh and chewy for 2-3 weeks in an airtight container.

● 205 calories/875 kj per wedge.

DON LAST

ALAN DUNS

Brown sugar cinnamon cookies

MAKES 16
175 g/6 oz dark soft brown sugar
¾ teaspoon ground cinnamon
100 g/4 oz margarine
1 teaspoon vanilla flavouring
150 g/5 oz plain flour
¼ teaspoon salt
vegetable oil, for greasing

1 Heat the oven to 190C/375F/Gas 5. Grease 2 baking sheets.
2 Grind the sugar, in batches, to a fine powder in an electric grinder or use a food processor. Mix 50 g/2 oz sugar with ¼ teaspoon cinnamon, then spread over a flat plate and reserve for the coating.
3 Put the remaining sugar into a large bowl with the margarine and beat together until pale and fluffy.

Then beat in the vanilla flavouring.
4 Sift the flour with the salt and remaining cinnamon, then add to the margarine and sugar mixture. Beat with a wooden spoon until the mixture begins to cling together, then work to a soft, slightly sticky dough with your hands.
5 Divide the dough into 16 equal pieces. Roll each piece into a ball between the palms of your hands and place on the prepared baking sheets, spacing them well apart to

allow for spreading of the dough.
6 Bake the biscuits in the oven for about 20 minutes, or until set and just beginning to brown. !
7 Using a palette knife, lift 1 biscuit off a baking sheet and place in the reserved sugar mixture on the plate. Turn the biscuit over, so that both sides are coated, then transfer to a wire rack. Coat the rest of the biscuits in sugar mixture in the same way and leave to cool completely before serving (see Storage).

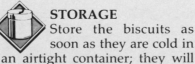

Cook's Notes

TIME
15 minutes preparation and 20 minutes baking.

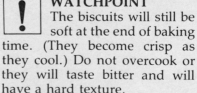

STORAGE
Store the biscuits as soon as they are cold in an airtight container; they will keep fresh for up to 1 week.

! WATCHPOINT
The biscuits will still be soft at the end of baking time. (They become crisp as they cool.) Do not overcook or they will taste bitter and will have a hard texture.

●120 calories/500 kj per biscuit

Easter biscuits

MAKES 15

225 g/8 oz plain flour
½ teaspoon ground mixed spice
100 g/4 oz margarine or butter,
   softened
100 g/4 oz caster sugar
grated zest of 1 lemon
1 large egg, beaten
50 g/2 oz currants
1 teaspoon milk
melted margarine or butter, for
   greasing

TO GLAZE
lightly beaten egg white
25 g/1 oz caster sugar

1 Heat the oven to 180C/350F/Gas 4. Brush 2 large baking sheets with melted margarine.
2 Sift the flour with the mixed spice and set aside.
3 Beat the margarine with the caster sugar and lemon zest until light and fluffy. Beat in the egg, a little at a time. Work in the sifted flour, currants and milk, then mix to a stiff dough using a fork.

TIME
Preparation 30 minutes, baking 20 minutes, plus cooling time.

WATCHPOINTS
Take care not to over-bake the biscuits, or they will be unpleasantly hard.

The biscuits are still soft when removed from the oven, so let them 'firm up' on the baking sheets—if lifted on to the wire rack immediately they may break or become misshapen.

STORAGE
Easter biscuits will keep fresh and crisp for 3-4 days if stored in an airtight container.

FREEZING
Open freeze the un-cooked biscuits on the baking sheets; remove with a palette knife, pack in a rigid container with waxed paper between each layer and return to the freezer. Store for up to 6 months. Glaze, then bake from frozen for 25 minutes.

Alternatively, pack the baked biscuits in a rigid container, interleaving them with waxed paper, and freeze for up to 6 months. Defrost at room temperature for about 1 hour. If the biscuits are soft, refresh them in a 180C/350F/Gas 4 oven for a few minutes.

● 145 calories/600 kj per biscuit

4 Turn out the dough on to a lightly floured surface and, with a lightly floured rolling pin, roll it out until about 5 mm/¼ inch thick. Cut the dough into rounds with a lightly floured 7.5 cm/3 inch fluted pastry cutter.
5 Transfer the rounds to the prepared baking sheets with a palette knife, then prick each in several places with a fork. ✳ Brush the tops lightly with egg white and sprinkle with caster sugar.
6 Bake the biscuits in the oven for 20 minutes ! or until golden. Let the baked biscuits 'settle' on the baking sheets for 1-2 minutes ! then transfer them to a wire rack. Leave the biscuits to cool completely before serving.

CHRIS KNAGGS

Crunchy ginger biscuits

MAKES ABOUT 30
225 g/8 oz wholemeal flour (see Buying guide)
1½ teaspoons ground ginger
1 teaspoon bicarbonate of soda
100 g/4 oz margarine
100 g/4 oz Demerara sugar
1 egg, lightly beaten
1 tablespoon clear honey
25 g/1 oz desiccated coconut
25 g/1 oz fine oatmeal
margarine, for greasing

1 Heat the oven to 180C/350F/Gas 4. Lightly grease 2 baking sheets.
2 Sift the flour with the ginger and bicarbonate of soda and reserve.
3 In a large bowl, beat margarine and the sugar together until light and fluffy. Add the egg, a little at a time, beating vigorously after each addition. ⚠ Beat in the honey. With a large metal spoon, gradually fold in the flour, followed by the coconut and oatmeal.
4 Divide the mixture into 30 equal pieces and shape each into a round between the palms of your hands. Place rounds on prepared baking sheets and space them well apart.
5 Mark each biscuit with the prongs of a fork, then bake in the oven for 10-15 minutes, until golden brown.
6 Allow the biscuits to 'settle' for about 1 minute. ⚠ Transfer to a wire rack and leave to cool completely (see Storage).

Cook's Notes

TIME
20-30 minutes preparation (including baking), plus 50-60 minutes to cool.

STORAGE
Store the biscuits in an airtight container as soon as they are cold. They will keep for up to 2 weeks.

BUYING GUIDE
Good supermarkets and health food stores stock the plain wholemeal flour needed for this recipe. Do not use strong wholemeal flour (for bread-making) as this will produce tough biscuits.

●75 calories/325 kj per biscuit

WATCHPOINTS
Add the egg slowly to avoid the margarine and sugar mixture curdling.
The biscuits need to firm slightly: if removed from the sheets while still very hot and soft they could lose their attractive round shape.

PETER MYERS

Peanut biscuits

MAKES ABOUT 40-50
1½ cups plain flour
½ teaspoon bicarbonate of soda
½ cup peanuts, unsalted
90 g/3 oz butter, softened
1 cup moist brown sugar
1 egg, beaten
additional ⅓ cup peanuts,
  halved, to decorate

1 Heat the oven to 190C/375F. Prepare the baking sheets (see Cook's tips).
2 Sift the flour with the bicarbonate of soda.
3 Grind ½ cup peanuts in a blender or clean coffee grinder.
4 Beat the butter to a cream. Add the sugar and beat until fluffy.

5 Beat in the egg.
6 Stir in the flour and ground peanuts.
7 Form mixture into teaspoon-sized balls and then place on to the prepared baking sheets, 5 cm/2 inches apart. Flatten them slightly with a wet fork and put a half peanut in the

centre of each of the flattened shapes.
8 Bake the biscuits for 8-10 minutes. Keep a careful eye on them because they burn easily.
9 Cool them for 5 minutes on the baking sheets, then lift them with a palette knife or fish slice on to wire racks to cool completely.

Cook's Notes

 TIME
Preparation will take about 20 minutes. If you have to cook the biscuits in batches, each batch will take 15 minutes to cook and cool.

 COOK'S TIPS
Non-stick baking sheets need only be floured; others should be buttered and then floured.

If you are baking in advance

for a party, or have some biscuits left over, store them in an airtight tin when cool.

 VARIATIONS
To keep brown sugar moist, store a dried apple ring in the same canister. If you use salted (but not dry roasted) peanuts the biscuits will taste less sweet.

● 60 calories/250 kj per portion

Crispy lemon slices

MAKES 16 SLICES
75 g/3 oz margarine or butter
100 g/4 oz caster sugar
grated zest of 1 lemon (see Cook's tip)
2 eggs, separated
100 g/4 oz self-raising flour, sifted
150 g/5 oz natural yoghurt
40 g/1½ oz cut mixed peel
margarine, for greasing

TOPPING
100 g/4 oz caster sugar
juice of 1 small lemon

1 Heat the oven to 180C/350F/Gas 4. Grease a 28 × 18 cm/11 × 7 inch Swiss roll tin with margarine.
2 Beat the margarine, sugar and lemon zest together until pale and fluffy. Add the egg yolks, 1 at a time, beating thoroughly after each addition.
3 Using a large metal spoon, fold in the sifted flour alternately with the natural yoghurt. Fold in the cut mixed peel.
4 Stiffly whisk the egg whites and fold them into the cake mixture, using a large, clean metal spoon to cut through the mixture.
5 Turn the mixture into the greased tin and spread it evenly. Bake in the oven for 30 minutes until the cake is a light golden colour and just firm to the touch.
6 Meanwhile, make the topping: mix together the caster sugar and lemon juice in a bowl to make a thin paste.
7 Let the baked cake stand in the tin for a few seconds, then carefully turn it out on to a wire rack and immediately spread the lemon paste over the surface. (The paste sinks in to make a crispy top.)
8 Leave the cake until quite cold before cutting into 16 rectangles. !
For a special treat, you can easily turn these slices into the 'mimosa cakes' shown in the picture (see Variation).

ALAN DUNS

Cook's Notes

TIME
The cake takes about 25 minutes to prepare, 30 minutes to bake and 30 minutes to cool.

COOK'S TIP
A citrus zester removes the aromatic lemon zest quickly and easily. If you do not have one, use the small holes of a grater and take care to grate the thin outer yellow layer of the lemon only—not the bitter white pith just beneath. Brush the zest which collects on the grater on to the rest of the grated zest with a stiff pastry brush so that none is wasted.

WATCHPOINT
Serve the slices the day they are made as they soften if stored.

VARIATION
Make up only half the amount of lemon paste. Cut the baked cake in half lengthways and spread one half with lemon paste. When the cakes are cold, spread the plain half with lemon curd and place the other half on top. Cut into 8 pieces. Decorate each slice with crystallized mimosa balls and 'diamonds' of angelica.

●130 calories/550 kj per slice

INDEX